Steven Paas

Johannes Rebmann

A Servant of God in Africa
Before the Rise of Western Colonialism

Missiologica Evangelica

Volume 14

edition missiotop – mission academics

Volume 32

Steven Paas

Johannes Rebmann
A Servant of God in Africa
Before the Rise of Western Colonialism

Second Edition

(revised, enlarged)

WIPF & STOCK · Eugene, Oregon

Wipf and Stock Publishers
199 W 8th Ave, Suite 3
Eugene, OR 97401

Johannes Rebmann
A Servant of God in Africa Before the Rise of Western Colonialism
By Paas, Steven
Copyright©2018 Verlag für Kultur und Wissenschaft
ISBN 13: 978-1-5326-5762-7
Publication date 5/14/2018
Previously published by Verlag für Kultur und Wissenschaft, 2018

Contents

Preface		9
	Motivation	9
	Acknowledgments	10
Abbreviations		13
1.	**Introduction**	15
	German sources	15
	English manuscripts	17
	Lost material	18
	Biography	21
2.	**Spiritual roots**	25
	Reformation and Pietism	25
	Revivals and awakenings	27
	Pregizer and Hahn	28
	Pietism in Gerlingen and Korntal	32
3.	**From Gerlingen to Islington (1820-1846)**	41
	Early years in Gerlingen (1820-1839)	41
	At the Basler Mission Seminary (1839-1844)	44
	At the CMS Seminary, Islington (1844-1846)	47
4.	**With Johann Ludwig Krapf (1846-1855)**	55
	Rebmann's arrival	55
	Krapf in Ethiopia	56
	From Mombasa to Rabai/Kisuludini	58
	Chain of mission stations	59
	Erhardt and Rebmann	65
	Conflicting visions	68
	Krapf's last attempts	72
	Mission impossible	76
	Josenhans' comment	83
5.	**From Cairo to Zanzibar (1851-1859)**	93
	Marriage	93
	Emma's observations	96

	Consolidation	99
	Helpers and visitors	102
	Exile	104
6.	**Fruits and loss**	113
	Hopeful new start	113
	Widening missionary interest	118
	Shifting CMS positions	122
	The Bombayers	125
	Emma's death	132
7.	**Lonely and enduring (1866-1875)**	139
	Rebmann in CMS policy	139
	Accused of stagnation	144
	Against vacating Mombasa	146
	Bartle Frere's observation and advice	150
	The establishment of Frere Town	155
	Last years in Africa	159
8.	**The last passages (1875-1876)**	167
	Back to Europe	167
	Dependent on Krapf	168
	The mission bride	171
	The manuscripts	175
	Rebmann's death	178
9.	**Language Worker**	183
	Two tragic aspects	183
	Krapf on Rebmann's work	184
	Rebmann on Krapf's work	192
	Rebmann defended	196
	The Kinika Dictionary	198
	The Kiniassa Dictionary	199
10.	**The context of Muslim Slavery**	209
	Nofa and Salimini as types	209
	Britain and the slave-trade	209
	Long-distance slave routes	211
	Domination by the Swahili-Arabs	216
	Salimini and the Rebmanns	219
	Salimini as a person	224

11.	**Missionary**	227
	Character	227
	Calling	230
	Methods	231
	Message	241
	Theology	248
	Rebmann and Krapf	253
12.	**Herald**	259
	Ploughmen and sowers	259
	The scramble for Africa	260
	Missions before 1885	261
	Missions after 1885	265
	To the memory of Rebmann	267

Bibliography 277
   Original sources 277
   Rebmann's Contemporaries 280
   Secondary Sources 281
   Contemporary Mission Magazines 288

Appendix I: Salimini's Chichewa 291
   Salimini's Home 291
   The Name of the Language 295
   The Spelling 295
   Grammatical Features 298
   Vocabulary 301
   Cultural Information 302

Appendix II: A history of Chichewa lexicography 309
   Two names, one language 309
   Lingua franca 313
   Crisis of communication 314
   CE Dictionaries 315
   EC Dictionaries 319
   New Dictionaries 322

Index 327

Preface

Motivation

There are good reasons for studying the life and work of Johannes Rebmann and for writing his biography. Therefore I am glad that the publication of the results of my research in 2011[1] is followed now by an updated version. Some disturbing writing errors have been corrected. Moreover, this new edition has been slightly revised and enlarged. I am also grateful that in the meantime a German translation has seen the light.[2]

Rebmann was a 19th-century German Christian, who was trained in Switzerland to be a missionary, and joined an English Missionary Society, which sent him to Muslim-ruled East Africa, present-day Kenya; there he lived and worked for 29 years, before returning home, blind and sick, soon to die. This sounds interesting, but frankly speaking these details alone would not have motivated me to write a biography of Rebmann.

I first stumbled on Rebmann when I lived and worked in Africa. It was in Malawi, more than 2000 kilometres from the place where Rebmann lived. In the city of Zomba I taught future pastors. Although English is the official language in Malawi, most communication is in the local language, Chichewa, also named Chinyanja. When learning that language, I noticed that no comprehensive dictionary was available. Lexicographical work in the past had produced several collections of vocabulary into and from English. However, somehow all attempts to create a permanent dictionary at the required scholarly and practical levels had failed. That undesirable situation belongs to the past now. In a process of research from 1997, together with a team of some students and other contributors, we managed to produce various editions of a Chichewa/Chinyanja Dictionary.[3]

It took some time before I discovered that this lexicographical activity had closely connected me to Johannes Rebmann. He and his informant Salimini belong to the earliest fathers of Chichewa lexicography, alt-

---

[1] Steven Paas, *Johannes Rebmann: A Servant of God in Africa Before the Rise of Colonialism*, Nuremberg/ Bonn: Verlag für Theologie und Religionswissenschaft/ Verlag für Kultur und Wissenschaft, 2011; ISBN 978-3-941750-48-7/ 978-3-86269-029-9.

[2] Idem, *Johannes Rebmann: Ein Diener Gottes in Afrika vor dem Aufkommen des westlichen Kolonialismus,*

[3] Idem, *Oxford Chichewa Dictionary,* fifth edition, Cape Town: Oxford University Press – ORBIS, 2016.

hough they called the language Kiniassa. Probably they are preceded only by the Portuguese army officer Gamitto, who wrote a few pages of Chichewa vocabulary in 1831-1832.[4] Rebmann was not aware of Gamitto's notes. Independently he reduced Chichewa to writing. His collection is the first Chichewa (Kiniassa) Dictionary that was published.[5] In chapter 9 the story of its origin is told.

The history of Chichewa lexicography stirred my interest in Rebmann, but there was more than linguistics that attracted me to him. In his correspondence, in his journal, and in biographical notes by contemporaries I recognised situations that are familiar to the situations of present-day transcultural workers in Africa and elsewhere. Like Rebmann, today's missionary expatriates are challenged by the relationship or the failing communication with the sending agency at home, with relatives and friends far away, with foreign colleagues, with local fraternal workers or colleagues, with people of other churches and religions, with the poor and destitute at one's doorstep. Like Rebmann, they experience estrangement, solitude, threats to the safety and health of themselves and of their spouses and children, and difficulties in bridging the gap between cultures and languages. Like Rebmann, today's Christians feel called to be instruments in furthering God's Church. Like him, today's messengers of the Gospel are crippled by their own weaknesses, failures, and sins, and by the deep-seated animosity of worldly powers and Satan. Finally, like him, in faith they are victorious through the power of Christ on whom they are depending.

Acknowledgments

I am happy to cite the institutions and individuals that have assisted in my research, and in the preparations for this book. First I acknowledge the *Johannes Rebmann Foundation* in Gerlingen for their moral and financial support.[6] The *City Archive* of Gerlingen provided access to their collec-

---

[4] Cf. Appendix II, 'A History of Chichewa/Chinyanja Lexicography'.
[5] Cf. Appendix I where Andrew Goodson reviews Rebmann's Kiniassa Dictionary, deals with some linguistic characteristics of Salimini's language, and considers the place where Salimini came from.
[6] At present the Foundation is represented by the following members of its Board: Mr. Christian Haag, Mrs Martina Koch-Haßdenteufel, Mr. Jürgen Schilbach; and also by Mr.Tobias Schölkopf, who serves as the office manager. Other important names are mentioned in the footnotes, especially in chapter 12. http://www.johannes-rebmann-stiftung.de/cms/missionare-aus-gerlingen/johannes-rebmann/rebmann-johannes-dokumente/.

tion of original and secondary Rebmann material in German.[7] Some other material was made available by the Archive of the *Evangelische Brüdergemeinde* in Korntal.[8] An important place for finding original and secondary Rebmann documents in German is *Mission 21* in Basel, which keeps the Archive of the *Basler Mission*. I am grateful to its staff[9] who made my stay at the Archive a pleasure. The main treasury of original and secondary Rebmann material is the University of Birmingham, Cadbury Research Library, located in the Muir Tower, which keeps the Archive of the *Church Missionary Society*. I am thankful to the members of the Special Collections team,[10] who faithfully assisted me during my stay in the Library.

In addition I thank Mr. Rob Kool, who acquainted me with the history of German Pietism in general and in particular with the movement of *Württemberg Pietism*, in which Rebmann was rooted, the late Pfarrer Rolf Scheffbuch and his wife Sigrid, who hospitably received us, organised board and lodging, provided us with indispensable details on Pietist church life, and with much needed introductions to persons and agencies, Dr. Jochen Eber, who sent me details on Rebmann collected during the research for his valuable Krapf study, Mr. Andrew Goodson of Kamuzu Academy, who –apart from adding an appendix – did a lot of proofreading of the text (NB, remaining mistakes are mine, not his.), and my brother Wim Paas, who designed the lay-out of the book. My wife Rita was especially helpful in searching for Rebmann details on the internet, and by asking critical questions when I reported results of my research to her.

I am especially grateful to God, who blessed me with health and perseverance to finalise this research.

Veenendaal, 2018

Steven Paas

---

[7] Dr. Klaus Herrmann (Archivleiter) and Mrs Beate Wagner were very helpful.
[8] I am grateful for the help of Mr. Werner Bichler and Mr. Erich Hieber.
[9] Dr. Guy Thomas (Head of the Archive), Claudia Wirthlin, Barbara Frey Näf, Anna Sommer, and former Head Dr. Paul Jenkins.
[10] Philippa Bassett (Senior Archivist), Jenny Childs (Archivist), Anne Clarke (Information Assistant), Mark Eccleston (Information Assistant), Helen Fisher (Archivist), Ivana Farlan (Project Archivist), Ian Killeen (Library Support Assistant), John Lanchbury (Library Support Assistant), Fred Nicholls (Library Support Assistant).

Abbreviations

ADB	Allgemeine Deutsche Biographie.
AIM	Africa Inland Mission.
AMZ	Allgemeine Missions Zeitschrift.
ATR	African Traditional Religion.
BBKL	Biographisch-Bibliographisches Kirchenlexikon.
BDCM	Biographical Dictionary of Christian Missions.
BFBS	British and Foreign Bible Society.
BM-B	Basler Missionsarchiv – in Basel.
BM-DZ	Basler Mission – Deutscher Zweig.
BMM	Basler Missionsmagazin.
Briefe	Letters in German by Rebmann to his closest relatives
BV	Brüderverzeichnis (preceding the numbers of the files inthe Basler Mission Archive)
CCAP	Church of Central Africa Presbyterian.
CE	Chichewa/Chinyanja – English.
CLAIM	Christian Literature Action in Malawi.
CLS	Centre for Language Studies (in Zomba, Malawi)
CMS	Church Missionary Society
CSM	Church of Scotland Mission.
EC	English – Chichewa/Chinyanja.
EH	Evangelischer Heidenbote.
G.H.	Gerlinger Heimatblätter
JRSG	Johannes Rebmann Stiftung Gerlingen.
LEM	Leipziger evangelisch-lutherische Mission.
LIM	Livingstone Inland Mission.
LMS	London Missionary Society.
MCP	Malawi Congress Party.
MWC	Mtanthauziramawu wa Chinyanja.

SEM	Swedish Evangelical Mission.
SPCK	Society for Promoting Christian Knowledge.
Tagebuch	Rebmann's Diary in German, 1848-1849
UMCA	Universities' Mission to Central Africa.
UMFC	United Methodist Free Church.
YMCA	Young Men's Christian Association (CVJM).
ZTC	Zomba Theological College.

1. Introduction

German sources

Johannes Rebmann was one of the very first missionaries in 19th-century East Africa. This study is a comprehensive biography, describing and assessing his life and work, especially his impact as a missionary and as a language worker. Its scope is limited by the availability of original literature, i.e. material that directly originates from Rebmann himself, from his first wife and his second wife, and from contemporaries that were associated with him. The main corpus of primary Rebmann material is found in three countries: Germany, Switzerland and England.

In Germany, his relatives, including his second wife, were the keepers of his personal letters (*Briefe*) and his Journals (*Tagebücher*). In 1976 Rebmann descendants transferred the letters to the City Archive (*Stadtarchiv*) of Gerlingen, where they were transcribed and published.[11] In the same year the City Archive received Rebmann's Journal of 1848-1849. It was transcribed and published in 1997.[12] Apparently a lot of effort to assemble and save these original Rebmann documents was made by Rebmann's grandnephew Oskar Rebmann. The City Archive is in possession of a manuscript, written by Oskar about 1935, which is an almost literal representation of Rebmann's *Briefe* and *Tagebuch*. Unfortunately Oskar was killed in the Second World War, and his manuscript has remained un-

---

[11] Schenkungs-Urkunde of '22 Originalbriefe Johannes Rebmanns' by Bertha Rebmann, widow of Gerhard Rebmann, of 19 November 1976 to the City Archive of Gerlingen. According to City Archivist Otto Schöpfer in the *Gerlingen Anzeiger*, 25/1958, it was Lydia Rebmann from Stuttgart-Plieningen who transferred 21 Original-Briefe to the Gerlinger City Archive.

[12] Rebmann's 'Tagebuch des Missionars vom 14. Februar 1848-16. Februar 1849' was possessed by Walter Ringwald until 1976. In a *Schenkungs-Urkunde* of 6 November 1976 Ringwald handed over the Tagebuch to the Mayor of Gerlingen to be kept by the Stadtarchiv. In the *Urkunde* Ringwald said that the document was inherited by him from missionary Gerhard, who received it from Gerlinger missionary Rudolf Höhn (1874-1897), who worked in India. Höhn had received it from Rebmann's colleague Thomas Sparshott. The *Tagebuch* was transcribed by Edelgard Frank, and edited by missionary Klaus-Peter Kiesel in Moshi, Tanzania, who also added explanatory notes, cf. his correspondence with Gerlinger Archivist Agnes Maisch; It was published by the City Archive in 1997. cf. *Gerlinger Stadt Anzeiger*, 12-11-76.

published.¹³ In addition, the Archive keeps an interesting file of mainly secondary material.¹⁴

Since 2002 there has been a *Johannes Rebmann Foundation*, based in his birthplace Gerlingen. Its bilingual website and the memorial room in the Rebmann House at the Kirchstrasse (Church Street) 18, offer interesting details on Rebmann's life and work.¹⁵

Switzerland is the base of the Basler Mission (*BM-B*) and most of the material of the German missionaries who studied in Basel is supposed to be there. However, since the beginning of Nazi rule in the 1930s there has also been a German branch, called Basler Mission Deutscher Zweig (*BM-DZ*). Hitler did not want German money to go to Switzerland or Germans to study there. This situation may have waylaid some of the archive material.¹⁶ Anyway BM-B used to keep Rebmann's initial biographical material accompanying his application for the BM Seminary, and the letters they received from him throughout the years of his stay in England and

---

¹³ Oskar Rebmann, 'Missionar Johannes Rebmann' ['Manuskript eines Grossneffen des Missionars Johannes Rebmann': unpublished document, n.d., about 1935, transcript of 154 pages is kept by City Archive Gerlingen, KAT 5/17.1/23a No 876]. An addendum of 10 July 1958, signed by Maria Müller says: 'Die Unterlagen für vorstehende Arbeit sind von einem Großneffen des Missionars Johannes Rebmann, Oskar Rebmann (gefallen im letzten Weltkrieg in Lemberg), der sie in mühevoller Arbeit zusammengetragen hat. Die Schwester Elisabeth Rebmann (meine Base) hat sie mir in liebenswürdigster Weise zur Verfügung gestellt'. Besides, the Rebmann Foundation possesses an inpubished manuscript of appr. 360 pages by Oskar Rebmann, consisting of e.g. a journal of Rebmann's travels, which is also included in Krapf's *Travels, Researches and Missionary Labours*, and of extracts from Rebmann's letters.

¹⁴ Stadtarchiv Gerlingen: Missionar Johannes Rebmann, KAT 10/17.1/1 and KAT 5/17.1/19-25.

¹⁵ Cf.: <www.johannes-rebmann-stiftung.de/en/start.html>; see especially publications by: Imanuel Stutzmann, 'Johannes Rebmann: Leben und Werk des Missionars', address in the city hall of Gerlingen, 11-5-2003; Idem, 'Johannes Rebmann im Spiegel seiner Briefe: Auszüge aus den Briefen von Johannes Rebmann', in: *Gerlinger Anzeiger*, Februar-Mai, 1998; Idem, 'Vor 150 Jahren sieht Missionar Rebmann den schneebedeckten Kilimandscharo', in: *Schwäbische Heimat*, S. 53-55, Januar-März, 1998.

¹⁶ Apart from the Basler Mission, other missions must keep information in German on Rebmann, for example the Hermannsburg Mission started by Ludwig Harms; also the Leipziger Mission missionary Bruno Gutmann collected details about Rebmann and his wife (see: bibliography).

1. Introduction

in East Africa. They also keep the relevant mission magazines, which contain articles by Rebmann himself and by contemporaries.[17]

His fellow Basel brother and colleague Johann Ludwig Krapf, with whom he cooperated in Africa for seven years from 1846 to 1853 wrote an account in two volumes of his journeys in East Africa, in which he refers to Rebmann on several pages.[18] Other fellow-workers and important informants are Jakob Johannes Erhardt, who worked with Rebmann in East Africa from 1849 to 1855, and Johann Gottfried Deimler, who was with him from 1856 to 1858. In addition, Rebmann is mentioned in the journals and reports of Von den Decken and other explorers who visited him when searching for the sources of the Nile. Comments on Rebmann's account of spotting Mount Kilimanjaro became a special source of information. His report of the event made him a target first of criticism and later of praise by European geographers. References to his life and work are found in several encyclopaedic works.[19]

English manuscripts

Almost all English Rebmann material was received or sent by his employer the Church Missionary Society in London. It mainly consists of manuscripts for publication, annual or biennial reports and especially letters. There is also information in the CMS *Proceedings*, the *Records*, and the magazines *Intelligencer* and *Gleaner*.[20] For the CMS Rebmann translated part of his German journal in English. It is included in the *Intelligencer*, and in Krapf's *Travels and Researches*.[21] All these documents are kept in the Special Collection's Department of the Archive of the University of Bir-

---

[17] Of special importance may be the large number of hand-written original letters from Rebmann's second wife, Luise, née Däuble (Finckh), which I have been unable to study.
[18] Johann Ludwig Krapf, *Travels and Researches*, 1860; cf. Jochen Eber, *Johann Ludwig Krapf: Ein schwäbischer Pionier in Ost Afrika*, Riehen/Basel: arte Media Johannis, 2006; Karl Friedrich Ledderhose, 'Johann Ludwig Krapf', in: *Allgemeine Deutsche Biographie* 17 (1883), S. 49-55.
[19] E.g. E.K.A.H. Dammann, 'Johannes Rebmann', in: Bautz, *Kirchenlexikon*, vol. 7 (1994) col. 1457-1458 <http://www.kirchenlexikon.de/r/rebmann_j.shtml>; Dammann, 'Rebmann Johannes', in: *Die Religion in Geschichte und Gegenwart - Handwörterbuch für Theologie und Religionswissenschaft*, 3rd ed. vol. 5. Tübingen 1961, S. 815.
[20] I scrutinised the 1844-1875 issues of these minutes and magazines.
[21] Johann Ludwig Krapf, *Travels and Researches*, part II, p. 56-73; cf. Rebmann, *Tagebuch*, 15-4-1848, 13-10-1848.

mingham.[22] Not all the English Rebmann material is in Birmingham. BM-B has a typed extract of an account of the years after 1852, written from her memory by Rebmann's first wife Emma Kent, known under the name of her first husband Tyler. It bears a hand-written note saying that the unabridged original is with the City Archive of Stuttgart.[23] Probably these original Kent papers were destroyed by the end of the Second World War.[24] Rebmann sometimes features in books and reports by contemporary explorers and geographers like Burton, Speke, Cooley, and in manuscripts held by other missionary organizations, like the Universities' Mission and the United Free Methodist Mission, but we have not targetted this material as it probably would not have added much to the available original sources.

Lost material

With regard to the primary Rebmann literature there is a serious problem. The file at BM-B indicates that a lot of material got lost. The missing German papers concern two categories. First, his biography and application (*Meldungspapiere*) sent to the BM, and personal letters, e.g. to the Inspektor of the BM, and to Johann Ludwig Krapf.[25] It appears that in 1887 the BM sent a packet (*Faszikel*) of manuscripts including Rebmann's biography and correspondence to an interested pastor in Baden, Karl Frie-

---

[22] <http://www.calmview.bham.ac.uk/Overview.aspx?src=QuickSearch.Catalog>; An excellent listing and guide to any Rebmann study is: CMS Archive, Section IV: Africa Missions, Parts 16-19, London: Adam Matthew Publications, 2004. The majority of relevant Rebmann documents are in Part 16, Kenya Mission 1841-1888. They are available on microfilm: Reel 316.

[23] Emma Rebmann/Tyler (née Kent), 'Journal 1852-1857', Basler Mission Archive. A. Jehle in a letter to BM-B (secretary Leuschner) of 21-1-35, states: 'at the Stadt Archive of Stuttgart there is a Journal in English by Mrs Rebmann, it consists of 119 small pages.'

[24] Letter from Christina Wewer of Stadtarchiv Stuttgart of 14 April 2011 to Tobias Schölkopf of the Rebmann Foundation, Gerlingen: 'In den Beständen des Stadtarchivs Stuttgart konnten leider keine Hinweise auf das von Ihnen gesuchte Tagebuch von Emma Rebmann ermittelt werden. Das Stadtarchiv Stuttgart verlor 1945 durch Kriegseinwirkungen sein historisches Archiv sowie etwa die Hälfte der zentralen Aktenbestände des 19. und frühen 20. Jahrhunderts. Möglicherweise befand sich das gesuchte Tagebuch darunter'. Emma's Diary was possessed for a time by Bruno Gutmann (1876-1966), a German missionary of the *Leipziger Mission* in German East Africa (now Tanzania), who translated portions of it into German (see: Bibliography).

[25] Cf. Rebmann, *Briefe*, 27-4-1864, where he refers to correspondence with Krapf.

1. Introduction

drich Ledderhose.[26] The papers were not returned, and after Ledderhose's death in 1890 they are said to have been burnt by his heirs.[27] A note in the Gerlinger City Archive, possibly derived from the BM-B Archive, says that Ledderhose's son-in-law Karl Hesselbach confirmed this unfortunate event.[28] Friedrich Schaffer, City Archivist of Gerlingen thinks it is possible that not all papers were burnt and that they may turn up sooner or later.[29] However, this hope has not been fulfilled until now. Ledderhose's article on Rebmann in the *Allgemeine Deutsche Biographie*, based on the lost documents, is probably the only existing reflection of that original material.[30] The second category of missing papers pertains to the Rebmann letters that were received by his relatives in Germany. Unfortunately that file is far from complete. Apart from his journal (*Tagebuch*) of 1848/1849, there seem to have been journals of other years which have disappeared.[31] Imanuel Stutzmann, who published extracts of the remaining letters in 1998, assumes several are permanently lost.[32] BM-B blames

---

[26] Karl Friedrich Ledderhose (1806-1890), Dekan Pfarrer in Baden-Baden, a church historian, who wrote in the *Allgemeine Deutsche Biographie* more than 40 contributions on German missionaries in the service of the Basel Mission, including one on Rebmannn and one on Krapf.

[27] BM-B archive, file BV.246, see a letter from Karl Biegel, 1907; letter of 21-10-1927 by BM-B to Ledderhose's successor, asking him to search for 'these very valuable papers', and a letter of 22-2-1940 by BM-B to one Paul Schwär of Machame Mission in Moshi, Tanganyika, BM-B admitting that the 'Originalakten von Rebmann' got lost, and a letter of 1948 by BM-B informing Oelschner that after Ledderhose's death in 1890 these papers were burnt by L.'s heirs.

[28] Note by U. Bächtold of 8 May 1959.

[29] Letter from Friedrich Schaffert, 28-8-1976, to the Schiller Nationalmuseum in Marbach: 'Anfrage bei Erben erfolglos. Es ist ja nicht auszuschließen, daß die Sachen irgendwo abgegeben worden sind'.

[30] Ledderhose, 'Rebmann', in: *Allgemeine Deutsche Biographie*, vol. 27 (1888), S. 485-489. The article refers to Rebmann's autobiography of his childhood and youth sent to BM-B, to his diaries, and also to letters sent to BM-B's executive head Hoffmann: 'Wir besitzen eine Reihe von Briefen von ihm an den damaligen Inspector Hoffmann ... in welchen er seine Erlebnisse in Islington schildert'.

[31] E.g. a holiday report (*Praktikumsbericht*), 'Tagebüchlein in der Vacanz des Jahres 1840', mentioned by Eber.

[32] Imanuel Stutzmann, 'Johannes Rebmann im Spiegel seiner Briefe: Auszüge aus den Briefen von Johannes Rebmann', in: *Gerlinger Anzeiger*, Februar-Mai, 1998. In Teil III Stutzmann says '... besitzen wir aus den Jahren 1847 bis 1854 keine Briefe von Rebmann. Vermutlich gingen sie verloren'. In Teil IX, referring to the years 1864-1868, he says: '... scheint mancher Brief verloren gegangen zu sein'.

Rebmann's relatives for this loss.[33] According to my count the Rebmann Foundation and the BM-B together possess 32 personal letters (*Briefe*) sent by Rebmann from his departure for London in 1844 until his return to Gerlingen in 1875.[34] The hand-written originals and a typed transcript of 23 letters are with the City Archive of Gerlingen.[35] All letters were sent to his closest relatives, except for one to Hermann Gundert, and one to Christian Gottlob Barth. Rebmann is likely to have written more letters to friends and relatives, which are now missing.[36] Of the period 1864-1868 no letters at all to relatives were found in the files of the Rebmann Foundation, of the Gerlinger City Archive, or of the BM-B.

The problem of loss also pertains to the English Rebmann material. There are at least three leakages. First, of the manuscripts Rebmann sent to the CMS in London, ahead of his return to Europe, some could not be traced, e.g. the fair copy of his Nika Dictionary. Secondly, on Rebmann's return to Gerlingen in 1875 he carried with him a chest full ('eine Kiste voll') of diaries and letters. They may have included the correspondence of his wife Emma Kent (Tyler), and letters received from friends of the CMS, which cannot be found now. Probably the chest also contained German material that is missing, e.g. his correspondence with German friends like BM Inspektor Hoffmann, and letters received from his relatives. Thirdly, in March 1876, after Rebmann had moved to Korntal, he received from the CMS in London a bookcase containing manuscripts that he and Krapf had to work on. A lot of it seems to have disappeared.

---

[33] A letter of 24-5-29 to one R.F. Merkel, from BM states that from BM correspondence can be concluded that on Rebmann's return in 1875 extensive diary material was at hand: 'eine Kiste voll ... Leider sind auch diese Tagebücher bei den Verwandten verloren gegangen'. The lost material is likely to include letters he received from e.g. his relatives, friends, e.g. Krapf, Stange, and his BM director Hoffmann.

[34] Eber suggests that the typed letters at BM-B are transcripts taken there by Rebmann's grandnephew Oskar Rebmann.

[35] Johannes Rebmann, *Seine Briefe*; Idem, *Tagebuch des Missionars vom 14. Februar 1848-16. Februar 1849*, City Archive Gerlingen, 1997.

[36] In a letter of 22-10-1940 to Machame Mission, Moshi, Tanganyika, BM-B gives a list of 23 letters from Rebmann, 14 of them are similar to the list of Stadt Archive Gerlingen. In 2011, I found only 9 in the BM-B Archive. The other 5 seem to be missing, perhaps one of them is the letter of 16 November 1866, which is referred to in BMM 1867, S. 429, 430. One letter possessed by BM-B in typed transcript was missed by City Gerlingen, i.e. 1 October 1853 [BM-B Archive: 1-10.21; Auszug für Oelschner, IV 1948]. Another letter from Rebmann in Cairo to Barth in Calw, of 4-12-1851 I traced on the internet, http://www.zvab.com/display BookDetails.do?itemId=156026619&b=1

Biography

Previous studies on Rebmann were articles or compositions mainly based on German material.[37] The present study is different in two aspects. First, it is meant as a scholarly presentation of the known facts of Rebmann's life and work. As such it is a monograph and a biography. Secondly, this study taps not only the limited number of German literary sources, but also the more numerous Rebmann documents in English.

We trust the following chapters will throw more light on the life and work of the missionary, and of his place in the pattern of 19th century relationships between Europe and Africa. *Chapter 2* pictures the setting of German Pietism that fed Rebmann. *Chapters 3-8* describe the course of his life. *Chapters 9 and 10* deal with his work as a linguist, particularly as a lexicographer. The two *Appendices* to the book are especially related to these chapters. *Chapter 11* reviews the various aspects of his work as a missionary. *Chapter 12* is an evaluation of Rebmann's significance for developments after him.

I am aware that my survey of Rebmann's life on two continents still leaves a lot of blank spots and hazy clouds. Sources, as far as noticed, have been relatively or completely silent on his early 19 years in Gerlingen, his 5 and 2 years as a student in respectively Basel and London, the 2 years of exile of the Rebmann family in Zanzibar, and the final 18 months of his life in London, Gerlingen and Korntal. His close relatives, his first wife Emma Kent, and his second wife Luise Däuble could have revealed details about themselves and about him. However, they have remained in relative obscurity. May this study set the trend, and encourage others to discover more.

---

[37] Cf. Ledderhose 1883/1888, Oskar Rebmann approximately 1935, Jehle 1935, Weishaupt 1926, Lehmann 1955, Dammann 1961, Ringwald 1977, Staiger 1988, Kustermann 1992/1997, Stutzmann 1998/2003, Rösler 2007, Scheffbuch 2010.

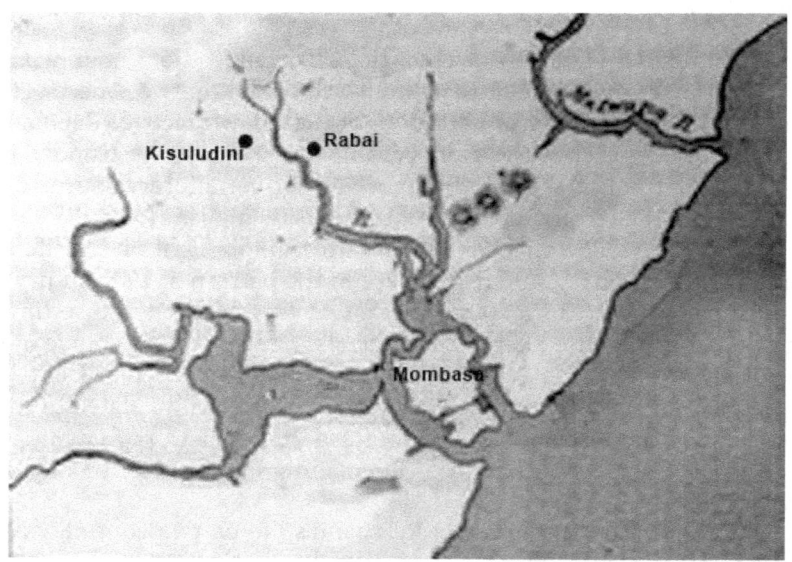

*Rebmann's mission field in Mombasa, Rabai and Kisuludini
(CMS Annual Report 1877).*

*Fort Jesus on the Mombasa coast,
built by the Portuguese, in 1593
(Wikimedia, CC BY-SA 3.0, by Zeljko).*

*A slave dhow in the harbour of
Mombasa (through Eber, p. 82).*

1. Introduction

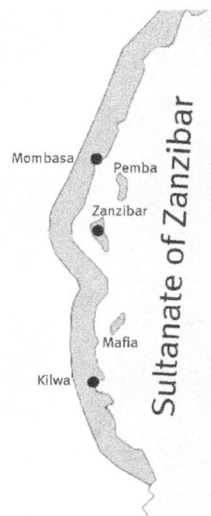

The Sultanate of Zanzibar in Rebmann's time
(Wikimedia, CC BY-SA 3.0, by Algovia and HCB).

Johannes Rebmann, bust in the
Town Hall of Gerlingen
(Stadtarchiv Gerlingen).

2. Spiritual roots

Reformation and Pietism

Rebmann's spiritual roots are in the 16th-century Protestant Reformation, which in its Lutheran form deeply influenced many people in the German state of Württemberg where he was born. Though drawing different conclusions, his colleague Krapf also underwent the influence of the Reformation climate. In the 17th century the Lutheran Reformation had lost a lot of its original fervour and enthusiasm. This affected its Biblical message of the three sola's, salvation only by grace, only by faith, only by the Scriptures, taken together in one powerful adage: through Jesus Christ alone! Decay had crept into the Lutheran Church. In the wake of the Renaissance and the Humanism that once paralleled and sometimes helped the Reformation, now a one-sided concentration on man's autonomy developed in the movement of the *Enlightenment*. Its rationalism and later its emotionalism sought its origin and foundation in man himself, and drastically decreased room for God, revelation and faith. This philosophy was strengthened by an enormous outburst of human capabilities through science and technology. This phenomenon was not limited to Germany. It had great consequences in the whole of Europe, and later in America, and ultimately in the rest of the world.

In view of decayed churches and weakened Christianity, movements sprang up that aimed for revival, reform or restoration. Examples are the *Puritanism* in the Anglo-Saxon world, the *Further Reformation* in The Netherlands, and the *Pietismus* (Pietism) in Germany. These movements influenced one another and interacted. In their protest against the *Enlightenment* and its godlessness, they also underwent the influence of its methods. This explains why the awakening movements took rationalist and emotionalist forms, sometimes to an extreme extent. In Germany Pietism started with Philip Jacob Spener, August Hermann Francke, and Nikolaus Ludwig von Zinzendorf.[38] In line with Luther, Calvin and other Reformers, they stressed the necessity of forgiveness, rebirth, and a Christian life. Except for Von Zinzendorf they emphasised the importance of a continuation of the *Bußkampf* after justification, i.e. of a

---

[38] Philip Jacob Spener (1635-1705), August Hermann Francke (1663-1727), and Nikolaus Ludwig von Zinzendorf (1700-1760); cf: Steven Paas, *Christianity in Eurafrica: A History of the Church in Europe and Africa*, CLF: Wellington (SA), 2016; NAP: Washington DC (USA), 2017, p. 235-237, 251-252.

continued struggle of faith in which believers repent their sins consciously with tears and prayers, and ask for forgiveness. Their followers gathered for Bible study and prayer in special meetings, called *conventicles*, which sometimes led to separation from the official Lutheran state churches. Because their meetings lasted an hour (*eine Stunde*) or so, they were called *Stundenleute*.

A special branch of German Pietism flourished in the state of Württemberg. It widened Luther's centrality of personal salvation, faith and love to an extra emphasis on the importance of Christian hope and the approaching fulfilment of the Kingdom of God.[39] Württemberg Pietism was first promoted by Johann Albrecht Bengel, called by Murray the most eminent disciple of Spener and Francke.[40] Duke Christoph of Württemberg had closed the monasteries and opened Latin schools, some of which later turned into theological seminaries for the training of pastors and teachers. The Duke was very reluctant to allow separate Pietist groups. For this reason teachers and pastors were instructed to keep Pietism within the state church. In one of these seminaries, at Denkendorf, Bengel taught for 30 years. As a Bible scholar he defended the unity and authority of the New Testament against *Enlightenment* liberalism. At the same time he deviated from Lutheran orthodoxy in expounding Scripture on the basis of a symbolism of prophetic numbers in the *Revelation* to John, which he claimed to have discovered in a vision (*Schlüsselerlebnis*) in 1724. His millennium speculations were misunderstood in communities that expected Christ's *Second Coming* in the year 1836.[41]

Unlike Pietist conventicles elsewhere, the followers of Württemberg Pietism remained in general inside the Lutheran state church. Reasons were the anti-separatist sentiment of Bengel, and the policy of the political rulers of Württemberg. In 1743 Carl Friedrich, Duke of Württemberg, in a law called *Pietisten-Reskript*, allowed the Pietists to have their own separate meetings (*Stunden*, or *Konventikel*), provided that the local pastor of the state church attended, and that the Pietists attended the Sunday-morning service of the local congregation.

---

[39] Richard Haug, *Reich Gottes im Schwabenland*, Metzingen: Ernst Franz Verlag, 1981, S. 152, 153.

[40] Johann Albrecht Bengel (1687-1752); Ian Murray, *The Puritan Hope*, London: The Banner of Truth Trust, 1971, p. 132.

[41] W. Hehl, *Johann Albrecht Bengel: Leben und Werk*, Stuttgart: Quellverlag, 1987, S. 96, 97; cf. Imanuel Stutzmann, 'Johannes Rebmann: Leben und Werk des Missionars', Vortrag 11-5-2003 in Gerlingen, S. 2.

Revivals and awakenings

In the 18th and 19th centuries the movements for more and deeper spiritual life were followed by newer expressions. In England the Puritan ideals were rephrased by the Methodist revival. The work of John and Charles Wesley, influenced by Von Zinzendorf, would eventually cause many to leave the Anglican state church and establish a new Methodist denomination. The influence of Calvin-oriented George Whitefield led to a revival inside the Anglican Church, which shaped the Evangelical branch of Anglicanism. In Lutheran Germany the original or *Alt-Pietismus* was rejuvenated from different angles, with influences from Calvinist awakenings in Holland, Scotland, and Switzerland, and from Evangelical Anglicanism. A wide variety of Pietist centres emerged. In Niedersachsen *on the Lüneburger Heide* Ludwig and Theodor Harms from Hermannsburg shaped a movement of 'Old-Lutherans' (*Altlutheraner*), first inside and then also outside the Lutheran state church. To the North-East, in Mecklenburg, Pietism reconciled and joined nobility and farmers. In Wittgenstein, enthusiastic (*schwärmerisches*) Pietism of a Reformed type developed, recalling radical Anabaptism in the 16th century. It was centred mainly in Berleburg, and to a lesser extent in Reformed Nassau-Siegen.

Other centres of Pietist revival were Berlin, with Gustav Knak and Baron von Kottwitz; Central Germany, especially Wernigerode and Bad Blankenburg in the Harz Mountains; and Niederrhein and Wuppertal, where the Krummachers, Kohlbrugge and Geyser were active. Another centre of Old Lutherans was Neuendettelsau with Wilhem Löhe; there was also Minden-Ravensberg with Volkening[42] and Rahlenbeck,[43] and Bentheim on the Dutch border, influenced by the movement of *Further Reformation*. Down south, just north of Württemberg, a Pietist awakening also took place in Baden. It started among ordinary Lutheran and Reformed church members. It touched Roman Catholic circles; many were impressed by the evangelical witness of the Bavarian priest Martin Boos.[44] Another priest, Aloys Henhöfer,[45] left the Roman Catholic Church,

---

[42] Julius Rössle, *Zeugen und Zeugnisse: Die Väter des rheinisch-westfälischen Pietismus*, Konstanz: Christliche Verlagsanstalt, 1968, Johann Heinrich Volkening, (1796-1877) 'der Pietistengeneral', S. 197, 199, 202, 209, 212.

[43] Rössle, *Zeugen und Zeugnisse*, Theodor Heinrich Rahlenbeck (1784-1864), 'der Fienenpastor von Herdecke', S. 214, 215, 218.

[44] Martin Boos (1762-1825); J. Gossner (Herausgeber), Martin Boos der Prediger der Gerechtigkeit die vor Gott gilt: seine Selbstbiogr., Leipzig: Tauchnitz, 1826; J. Gossner (ed.), *The Life and Persecutions of Martin Boos, an evangelical preacher of the Romish Church*, chiefly written by himself, London: Seeley and Burnside, 1836;

desiring freedom for his message of free grace and justification by faith in Christ alone.

The Pietism in Württemberg, Rebmann and Krapf's home area, continued to have a different tinge in its newer expressions. There were various groups, the mainstream or the classical Pietists (*Altpietisten*), the Herrnhuters, and the followers of Pregizer and Hahn. An important representative of the classical original Pietist mainstream was Ludwig Hofacker. In his short life he was extremely influential, through his powerful preaching on sin and grace, on the need for penance and conversion, and on the centrality of justification through Christ and the cross.[46] Influenced by Von Zinzendorf, he preached justification by faith in such a way that the objective basis for it is Christ's suffering according to God's will. He was a pietist of the conviction that justification and sanctification are both found in Christ. They are to be experienced in the heart, and shown in daily life. Hofacker's message recalls Henhöfer's witness in Baden.

Pregizer and Hahn

Pregizer[47] and Hahn[48] deviated from the classical orthodox mainstream of Pietism. The views of both were expressions of a heterodox aspect of 'old' Württemberg Pietism, but they took opposite sides, of respectively *antinomianism* and *legalism*. Antinomianism[49] is a one-sided explanation of the teaching of justification by faith in Christ alone, suggesting that God's law did not apply anymore to those who were saved, thus neglecting the code of conduct for a Christian life. In Calvin's terms they did not distinguish

---

Steven Paas, 'Priester Martin Boos: Prediker der Gerechtigheid', in: *Protestants Nederland*, April 1986 no.4.

[45] Wilhelm Heinsius, *Aloys Henhöfer und seine Zeit*, neu herausgegeben von Gustav Benrath, Neuhausen-Stuttgart/Karlsuhe: Hänssler-Verlag/Verlag Evangelischer Presseverband für Baden, 1987.

[46] <http://www.bibelbund.de/htm/98-4-299.htm> F.W. Bautz, 'Ludwig Hofacker, der bedeutendste Prediger der württembergischen Erweckungsbewegung', Biographisch-bibliographisches Kirchenlexikon, vol. 2 (1990) col. 941-942; Ludwig Hofacker (1798-1828); cf. Markus Seeb, 'Ludwig Hofacker – Leben und Wirken: Zum 200. Geburtstag des württembergischen Erweckungspredigers'; Rolf Scheffbuch, *Ludwig Hofacker: Vor allem: Jesus!*, Neuhausen – Stuttgart: Hänssler, 1998.

[47] Christian Gottlob Pregizer (1751-1824).

[48] (Johann) Michael Hahn (1758-1819).

[49] Greek: ἀντί = against; νόμος = law.

2. Spiritual roots

'the third use of the law'.⁵⁰ The Pregizers, called after the Lutheran pastor Christian Gottlieb Pregizer, tended to that idea. Although Pregizer in his own life had experienced a period of *Bußkampf* being stricken by guilt and despair, his followers rejected this aspect of the order of salvation and claimed that the law had no significance in the life of a believer.⁵¹

The Hahners, on the other hand, one-sidedly stressed the law,⁵² i.e. the necessity of following religious instructions, and doing good works, thus decreasing the sufficiency of Christ's saving act for believers. This was the idea of the butcher and farmer Michael Hahn.⁵³ The Pregizers wanted a joyful Christianity, and were therefore sometimes called *Juhe-Christen*, or jubilant Christians. The Hahn followers were called *Seufzer* (sighers), for their lives were characterized by sighing because of realizing their sins and imperfections.⁵⁴

Pregizer and Hahn were both deeply influenced by the thought of Friedrich Christoph Oetinger, who in his turn had derived his ideas from the mystic Jakob Böhme. Oetinger believed in a continuation of sacred revelation after the Biblical period. Reminding somehow of Bengel's speculations with Biblical numbers, he claimed that any word of Christ contained an 'unlimited all'.⁵⁵ Oetinger said that the Church was mistaken

---

50 John Calvin, *Institutes of the Christian Religion*, Grand Rapids: Eerdmans, 1998 (first 1989) [translated by Henry Beveridge of Calvin's original manuscript in 1559], p. 304-309. Calvin distinguishes three uses of the law, the first to admonish unconverted sinners to repent and flee to Christ, the second to be obeyed by citizens in political life. The third use pertains to believers and instructs them how to act in the struggle of faith and be grateful for their salvation.
51 L.Tiesmeyer, *Die Erweckungsbewegung in Deutschland während des XIX. Jahrhunderts*, issue 7 (vol. 2, issue 3) Württemberg, Kassel: Ernst Röttger, 1906, S. 39: 'Das Kapitel von der Busse ist bei den Anhaengern Pregizers abgetan. Die ganze Bekehrung und Wiedergeburt kann sich in sehr kurzer Zeit vollziehen. Busslieder werden in ihren Versammlungen nicht gesungen und die fuenfte Bitte im Vaterunser betet man nicht'.
52 Latin: lex = Law (plural: leges)
53 Cf. Joachim Trautwein, *Die Theosophie Michael Hahns und ihre Quellen*, Stuttgart: Calwer Verlag, 1969.
54 Cf. Gerhard Staiger, 'Gerlingen und die Mission', in: *Gerlinger Heimatblätter: Gerlinger Missionare*, Gerlingen: Verein für Heimatpflege, n.d., S. 4 [further: G.H.: Gerlinger Missionare].
55 Cf. backside cover of F.C. Oetinger, in: 'Die Weisheit auf der Gasse', vol. 2, Metzingen: Fransverlag, 1962: 'Jedes Wort der Sohn ... ist ein unendliches Wort, weil aus jedem Wort die ganze Wahrheit und ein unendliches All herausblickt'; cf. Hahn, in: *Ausgewählte Betrachtungen aus Joh. Michael Hahns Schriften*, vol. 2, Stuttgart: Hahnsche Gemeinschaft, 1959, 1. Betrachtung, S. 3: 'Der Mensch ist quintessen-

in teaching God's eternal punishment of the unconverted after their death.[56] Pregizer and Hahn continued along this unorthodox line of thinking.[57]

Hahn claimed that he had received a vision (*Zentralschau*) of the 'restoration of all things' (*Wiederbringung aller Dinge*).[58] He said that this vision had enabled him to look into 'the full plan of God', which revealed that finally the whole of creation would be 'brought back to its original harmony and completion'. Although the Hahner do not like the term *Allversöhnung* this view explicitly suggests that eventually in eternity all unbelievers will be saved, though it may happen after many *aeons*[59] of being lost and condemned. Hahn concluded that the imputation of Christ's saving work on the cross keeps its power even after the death of an unconverted sinner. He would prefer not to have been born if the teaching of eternal condemnation were true. Eventual salvation for all made him happy for his unbelieving fellow men. They are kept in detention ('*nachsitzen*') until Satan has to give up keeping them in his grasp. These are intriguing statements, especially because Hahn stressed that he did

---

tialisch, extraktisch aus allem dem, worin sich Gott geoffenbart hatte, zum Bilde Gottes geschaffen worden'.

[56] J. Roessle, *Von Bengel bis Blumhardt*, Metzingen: Fransverlag, 1966, S. 137, 138: 'Alle und jede die ins Gericht fallen ... werden für ihre Strafen Gott danken und Recht geben ... die Strafen sind nicht ohne Ende'. Cf. Tiesmeyer., *Die Erweckungsbewegung*, S. 22-24.

[57] G. Müller, *Christian Gottlob Pregizer (1751-1824): Sein Leben und seine Schriften*, Stuttgart 1961, S. 313-317, 52 questions 'von der ewigen Liebe Gottes in Wiederbringung aller Dinge', implicitly teaching salvation for all, 'Die Liebe führt das Regiment, Die Hölle wird durch sie verbrennt', and 'Was Deine Macht gesetzt ins Wesen, Muss Deinen Preis zu seiner Stund Mit ewigem Jubel machen kund, Wenn alles, alles ist genesen'; Tiesmeyer, *Die Erweckungsbewegung*, S. 38, 39: 'M. Hahn vermeinte eine tiefere Erkenntniss zu besitzen als die Kirche, die ueber die Anfangslehren des Christentums nicht hinaus komme'. [Die Pregizer] 'sind, wie die Micheliander [= Hahner], Anhänger der Wiederbringungslehre'.

[58] In Greek: apokatastasis panton = ἀποκατάστασις πάντων; Gerhard Schäfer (ed.), *Michael Hahn: Gotteserkenntnis und Heiligung* [Aus seinen Betrachtungen, Briefen und Liedern], Metzingen: Ernst Franz Verlag, 1994, S. 11, 12, quotes Hahn as follows: 'Ich konnte vom Geheimnis des Kreuzes aus als der Zentralkenntnis in den ganzen Plan Gottes hineinsehen, und ... wurden mir alle mögliche Fragen ... auf eimal beantwortet'. Schäfer adds that in Hahn's thought 'wie alles, was ist, aus Gott kommt und nach aller Entzweiung durch Gott wieder in die ursprüngliche Harmonie und Ganzheit zurückgebracht wird', and also that Hahn 'sich nicht denken kann, daß auch nur einer ewig verloren sein würde'.

[59] aeon, Latin term derived from Greek αἰών, now used for a very long period of time.

2. Spiritual roots

not want to depend on them for himself!⁶⁰ Hahn emphasised strongly the need for an ethic of abstention or ascesis in a life of purity and obedience.⁶¹ Tiesmeyer says that in Hahn's theology justification was absorbed by sanctification. For his visions Hahn recruited business-men, teachers, and lawyers country-wide, and organised them in communities of the *Hahn'sche Gemeinschaft*. The original Pietists, of the Bengel line and of classical Lutheran Hofacker-orientation, were mostly farmers, wine-growers, and craftsmen, and they did not follow Hahn's ideas.

Although not liberal in the sense of modern 19th/20th-century Modernism, the thinking of Pregizer and Hahn was influenced by human centred philosophy of Enlightenment Rationalism.⁶² Their unorthodox teaching of 'the restoration of all things' has been rejected as speculation, not only by basic Lutheran and Calvinist teaching, but also by original Pietism, Puritanism and Further Reformation. Hahn has been resisted as well by the late 19th and early 20th-century movements of revival and holiness, Brethren, Pentecostals, Charismatics, and Evangelicals. In order to avoid censure by the Lutheran Church, Hahn formulated his teaching in such a way that it would not formally contradict the formulation of Article 17 of the *Augsburg Confession*.⁶³ One could argue that Hahn's belief in a restoration of everything diminishes the urgency for mission to those who do not know Christ to lead them to faith in Him as the only way of salvation. Because in Hahn's thought, in the end even those who consciously rejected Jesus will be saved, though after a very long time. When Hahn died, in 1819, Immanuel Gottlieb Kolb,⁶⁴ a teacher in Dagersheim, took over as leader of the Hahner communities.

The 18th and 19th-century movements of revival and awakening in Europe and America renewed the Church in answer to the challenges of

---

⁶⁰ Schäfer (ed.), *Michael Hahn: Gotteserkenntnis und Heiligung*, S. 89, 'Ich für meinen Teil wünschte lieber nicht geboren zu sein, als keine Wiederbringung aus der Heiligen Schrift glauben zu können, ob ich schon für meine Person mich nicht darauf verlasse. Es freut mich aber für meine ungläubigen Mitmenschen, seien sie, wer und wo sie wollen'; Roessle, *Von Bengel bis Blumhardt*, S. 247ff, 276, 277.
⁶¹ Trautwein, *Die Theosophie Michael Hahns*, S. 39, 40.
⁶² Cf. Hahn's variation of Descartes' adage 'I think, therefore I am': 'Wenn du wirklich nur ein Traum wärest, dann könntest du doch unmöglich träumen; träumst du, dann bist du auch' (Anonymous, *Die Anfänge der M. Hahn'schen Gemeinschaft*, Böblingen: M. Hahn'sche Gemeinschaft, 2001, S. 16).
⁶³ Article 17 of the Lutheran *Augsburg Confession* or *Book of Concords* teaches that at the end of time Christ will come back to give eternal life to the godly and elect and to judge the ungodly men and the devils, who will be condemned to eternal torment; there will be no end to their punishments.
⁶⁴ Immanuel Gottlieb Kolb (1784-1859); Roessle, *Von Bengel bis Blumhardt*, S. 292ff.

emerging secular *Modernism*. They gave birth to intensive evangelisation of the people at home who had become strangers to church and faith, and to a worldwide activity of mission. They also made Christians conscious of the need for social reform, for example to help the poor and liberate slaves.

Pietism in Gerlingen and Korntal[65]

Rebmann grew up under the aegis of Lutheranism of the type of mainline orthodox Württemberg Pietism, mixed with influences of Calvinist and Evangelical revivals elsewhere in Europe. He was a reader of Karl Heinrich von Bogatzky, pupil of Spener and Franke, who would summarise salvation theology as follows:

> 'There is but one way to be justified, and to obtain and preserve the blessing of a good conscience, which is by humbling ourselves, confessing that we are guilty, and looking only for forgiveness and righteousness in Christ'.[66]

That was the spiritual climate of his Pietist Evangelical Lutheran home congregation in Gerlingen. Although they had a privileged position in the Württemberg state church, many Pietists did not feel at home in it. Some desired to organise themselves in separate colonies. The official state policy ran against this ideal. For this reason Pietists began to leave the country and settle in countries that allowed them full freedom, for example in Russia, where they were called *Stundisten*. The Württemberg state hated to see the best of its citizens go. Therefore a compromise was introduced in two instances, allowing a colony of Pietists, or a 'Brüdergemeinde' to exist. One of these is Wilhelmsdorf, near Friedrichshafen, in the far south of Württemberg, on Lake Constance or the *Bodensee*.[67] It is the daughter-congregation of the other one, which was established in Korntal, not far from Gerlingen. With special consent from King William of Württemberg, whose father Friedrich I had been elevated to kingship by Napoleon, and who in accordance with Lutheran church order acted as bishop, in 1819 a

---

[65] The name used to be spelled: Kornthal.
[66] Karl Heinrich von Bogatzky (1690-1774). From a translation of Bogatzky's 'Schatzkästlein', *Golden Treasury for the children of God*, London/Edinburgh/New York: Nelson, 1881, Daily observations April 23, p. 114.
[67] Johannes Ziegler, *Wilhelmsdorf, ein Königskind: Die Geschichte der Brüdergemeinde Wilhelmsdorf erzählt für meine Söhne*, 1929.

2. Spiritual roots

semi-separatist[68] Pietist colony of convinced Christians was formed. Until 1918 the Korntal community and the Korntal Brüdergemeinde were the same. It was and until today it has remained a special congregation within the Lutheran Württemberg Church. In accordance with Pietist tradition there has always been a congregational service in the morning and conventicle meetings in the afternoon. The founder of Korntal was the lawyer Gottlieb Wilhelm Hoffmann. He did not believe in the perfection of Christians, but knew and experienced from day to day that even convinced Christians are sinners. However, those people who wanted to be members of the congregation should take things seriously. They should not only intend to follow Jesus Christ, but they should really do so. Hoffmann wanted to realise Martin Luther's vision of a congregation of people, who really and earnestly wished to be followers of Christ. He himself did not belong to a specific stream, but followed Bengel in the conviction that the Korntal congregation should have two worship services every Sunday. The Korntaler group is called a congregation of brethren (*Brüdergemeinde*). Their church-building, is 'the large hall' (*der Große Saal*), and is almost similar to the Moravian Convocation Hall. Although Bengel disagreed with Von Zinzendorf there are traces of Moravian influence in Korntal.

From the angle of mainstream orthodox Protestant teaching the Korntal congregation has a problem with theological unity. Rolf Scheffbuch published on the early history of the congregation.[69] He prefers the term 'tensions' when he explains that Korntal has been prayed for and financed until today by two different groups, the original 'old' Pietists (*Altpietisten*) of the classical orthodox Lutheran type, and the 'old' Pietists that belong to the Hahner group. Although the latter group were pious and faithful church members, they one-sidedly stress sanctification, be-

---

[68] Rolf Scheffbuch, *Große Entdecker und schwäbische Apostel: Von Korntal bis ans Ende der Welt*, Holzgerlingen: SCM Hänssler, 2010, S. 76, 'Korntal war auch trotz der ihm als königliches Privileg zugesagten Selbständigkeit nie so extrem separatistisch geprägt, dass es den lebendigen Kontakt mit der Landeskirche verloren hätte'.

[69] Rolf Scheffbuch [retired minister and Prälat (assistant bishop) in the Württemberg Evangelical Lutheran Church, is now a member of the Korntal congregation], *Aus den Anfängen Korntals*, vol. 1, 'Das Gute behaltet'; vol. 2, 'Nicht aus eigener Kraft', Korntal: Ludwig-Hofacker-Vereinigung/Evangelische Brüdergemeinde, 2001 and 2003. In 'Das Gute behaltet', S. 77, he describes Hoffmann's qualification of the congregation of Korntal: 'Korntal war und blieb für ihn vorbildlich mit seiner pietistischen Jesusfrömmigkeit, die Frömmigkeits- und Bekenntnisstandpunkte zweitrangig sein liess'.

lieve in eventual salvation for all, and have therefore a problem with Scripture and orthodox Christian teaching. They attend the ordinary worship services in the Brüdergemeinde, but also have separate meetings. Hahn-people are mostly interested in holiness, preparing for the expected millennium, the 'first resurrection', and the final victory of God's love. In the Korntal congregation from the beginning they and their teaching have been given a legal position. Michael Hahn himself was meant to be the first leader of the Korntaler Brüdergemeinde, and he designed a plan for it.[70] However, he died before the congregation was started. The classical 'old' Pietists (Altpietisten) are convinced of human sinfulness, the immediate need for justification by Christ's sacrifice, and daily conversion, i.e. in the new life the continuation of the struggle of faith against Satan, world and one's own nature. However, the Korntal congregation tolerate those like the Hahner, who 'for Biblical reasons have different convictions'. In Korntal there seems to operate an underlying tradition of tolerating the idea of Allversöhnung. The influential 'catechism', originally published by the Korntaler Latin School Director J.G. Pfleiderer in 1874, was re-edited by the Hahner in 1937. It emphatically claims that all men, including unbelievers finally will be saved.[71] Scheffbuch notes that newer expressions of Pietism in the congregation have

---

[70] *Johann Michael Hahns Schriften*, vol. 12, 2nd ed., Stuttgart 1960, S. 953-966, 'Verfassungskonzept einer wahren Gemeine nach Herzensverfassung mit Erläuterungen von J.M.Hahn, aufgesetzt im Jahre 1817'. In 64 points Hahn described his thoughts about the organisation of the congregation.

[71] J.G. Pfleiderer, *Evangelische Glaubens- und Sittenlehre*, 1874. The title is now '*Glaube und Leben: ein Katechismus*'. It has been re-edited and re-published by the Hahn'sche Gemeinschaft several times, first in 1974 and latest in 2004. Question/answer 86 (p. 72) says: 'Frage: Gilt die Erlösung allen Menschen? Antwort: Ja, allen Menschen. Wer von Herzen an Jesus Christus glaubt, der wird selig: alle Ungläubigen aber bleiben so lange unter der Herrschaft Satans, bis auch sie durch den Glauben an Jesus Christus die Erlösung erfahren'; Question/answer 119 (p. 175) says: 'Frage: Sind nun die Menschen, die in ihrem irdischen Leben nicht berufen worden sind oder die Berufung gleichgültig übergangen oder ihr bewusst widerstanden haben, für immer verloren? Antwort: Nein. Die Ersteren werden in der anderen Welt einen Ruf und eine Möglichkeit zur Entscheidung bekommen, denn Jesus war das wahre Licht, das alle Menschen erleuchtet, die in diese Welt kommen (Joh.1:9) Die Letzteren aber werden Gerichte der Ewigkeit auszustehen haben, bis sie ihre Knie beugen und Gott recht geben werden. ... Die Stufen der Wiederbringung (1.Kor.15: 22-24) sind auch in den Gesetzen über die jüdischen Feste erkennbar.An sieben aufeinander folgenden Tage wird je ein Farre weniger geschlachtet als am Vortag. Das bedeutet unseres Erachtens, das die Gerichtsorte nach und nach leerer werden'. Cf. Scheffbuch, *Aus den Anfängen Korntals*, vol. 2, 'Nicht aus eigener Kraft', S. 965ff.

2. Spiritual roots

been critical towards this idea, demanding that *Allversöhnung* should not be taught. These 'new' Pietists are strong in evangelisation and mission; they challenge the 'old' Pietists who have sometimes neglected their basic missionary task.

Amazingly Rebmann's colleague Ludwig Krapf was a strong advocate of Hahn, thus of the idea that everyone would be saved in the end, irrespective of people's conversion to Christ before their death.[72] In Krapf's thought Hahn belonged to the very best expounders of the 'whole truth of Scripture'.[73] At first, during a brief period in Basel, he had come under the influence of the mystic enthusiasm (*Schwärmerei*) of Madame de Guyon[74] and Jakob Böhme[75] and the idea that a real believer had climbed up to perfection. Consequently at the Basel Missionary Seminary he experienced a spiritual crisis. He lost his conviction of being called as a missionary, and left Basel. Then, influenced by reading Oetinger and Hahn, he shifted from mysticism to rationalism, although some consequences of mysticism remained.[76] The shift to a rational approach motivated him for the study of theology, which he did at the University of Tübingen, 1829-1834.

After some years as a vicar and a home teacher the ideal of becoming a missionary re-emerged. Peter Fjellstedt, a Swedish CMS missionary in Smyrna, was instrumental in this.[77] In the autumn of 1836 Krapf re-entered Basel Mission Seminary. After finishing the course, he was transferred to the CMS, who sent him to Ethiopia. Unlike most other Basler Brothers in CMS service he was not ordained as an Anglican priest, because he was already a minister in the Lutheran Church.[78] Throughout

---

[72] Cf. Scheffbuch, *Große Entdecker*, S. 77.
[73] Eber, *Krapf*, S. 186, 187 quotes Krapf as follows: 'Ich habe die Schriften aller Jahrhunderte durchforscht, aber keine Schriftsteller gefunden, die wie Bengel, Oetinger, Pfarrer Hahn und Michael Hahn die ganze Schriftwahrheit so umfassend dargelegt, Grund und Aufbau so klar entwickelt, Geist und Buchstaben der Schrift so innig verbunden und so erfahrungsmäßig dargestellt hatten'.
[74] Cf. Eber, *Krapf*, S. 21, 22. Madam Guyon (Jeanne-Marie Bouvier de la Motte-Guyon), 1648-1717, a French mystic and advocate of the movement of Quietism. http://www.ccel.org/g/guyon;
[75] Jakob Böhme (1575-1624), a German mystic, who derived from the Kabbala, alchemy etc. and believing that God reveals Himself from within creation when the individual submits his will to the will of God. http://mythosandlogos.com/boehme.html
[76] Cf. Eber, *Krapf*, S. 27, 29.
[77] Eber, *Krapf*, S. 33, 34.
[78] Roland Oliver, *The Missionary Factor in East Africa*, London: Longmans, 1965 (first 1952), p. 5.

Krapf continued to belong to the *Hahnsche Gemeinschaft*. He even influenced Martin Flad,[79] a fellow missionary to Ethiopia, to join. They were probably the only Basler alumni, although Wilhelm Dürr, the first Basler brother, had a relationship with Kolb, a teacher from Dagersheim, who was the successor of Hahn. Krapf was on friendly terms with Kolb during his time in Africa. When on furlough in Germany he would visit him.[80] What would have motivated these renowned missionaries? Could they have been persuaded by the 'tremendous' support they received from the Hahner communities? However, this is not likely to be the final reason.

Rebmann never joined the Hahner community. Although in the last period of his life he was in Korntal with Krapf, he was connected to Gerlingen all his life. At that time practically all Gerlinger citizens were Protestants. There was only one church, a typical Evangelical Lutheran Württemberg congregation with Pietist characteristics. Its minister, Karl Friedrich Stange,[81] was one of a succession of orthodox Pietist pastors, serving all members of the village. He ardently supported the pietistic coventicle (*Stunde*) in the congregation, and as a pastor, shaped by the Württemberg Pietism, he propagated and supported the work of mission. Today a small remnant of classical 'Pietismus' still exists in Gerlingen, i.e. an 'old' Pietist (*altpietistische*) community, and a YMCA group that is conscious of its roots in original Pietism.

---

[79] Johann Martin Flad (1831-1915); Cf. Scheffbuch, *Große Entdecker*, S. 73, 75, 109-126.

[80] Cf. Letter from Krapf, while staying in Dagersheim, to the CMS (Venn?), 14 October 1850 [G/AC 16/57].

[81] Karl Friedrich Stange (1792-1865), cf. *Gerlinger Heimatblätter/Gerlinger Missionare*, S. 4-8; http://de.wikisource.org/wiki/ADB:Stange,_Karl_Friedrich; for his family tree, see: Die Geschichte von Friedrich Ludwig Carl Christian Stange, S. 22, http://rootseekers.com/ Friedrich_Stange.pdf; In 1822 Stange married Magdalena Jäger, who died in 1876, http://www.buchfreund.de/productListing.php?used =1&productId=33710326.

2. Spiritual roots

Johann Albrecht Bengel
(1687-1752), prominent initiator
of Pietism in Württemberg
(Wikimedia, public domain).

August Hermann Francke
(1663-1727), representative
of German Pietism
(Wikimedia, public domain).

Philip Jacob Spener
(1635-1705),
most important initiator
of German Pietism
(Wikimedia, public domain).

Church of the Evangelische Brüdergemeinde in Korntal in 1870 (Archive EBK).

(Johann) Michael Hahn
(1758-1819)
(S. Paas).

Ludwig Hofacker
(1798-1828)
(Wikimedia, public domain).

2. Spiritual roots

Worship Hall of the Evangelische Brüdergemeinde Korntal, 'Der große Saal'
(S. Paas).

3. From Gerlingen to Islington (1820-1846)

Early years in Gerlingen (1820-1839)

On 16th January 1820 Johannes was born in the winegrower's farmhouse of Johann Rebmann and Anna Maria Rebmann-Maisch at the Kirchstraße (*Church Street*) in Gerlingen,[82] a small village[83] near Stuttgart in South German Württemberg. Johannes was fourth of their eight children; two had already died before his birth, and only three survived Johannes.[84] Undoubtedly his father Johann and mother Anna had no idea that God had destined their little Johannes to spend more than half of his life as a missionary in faraway Africa. Yet being shaped by the 19th-century awakening movement in the line of German Pietism and the Reformation they believed that God had a plan for him. Like any Christian their son was called to be a witness of Jesus Christ.

It seems that already at an early age Rebmann was captured by the thought of being a servant in God's Kingdom. The pietistic climate of Gerlingen was conducive to the development of a spirit of mission-mindedness. The Christian community of Gerlingen sent 14 missionaries overseas during the 19th century.[85] Two of them bear the name of Rebmann's mother, Maisch, although they may not have been close relatives. He was influenced by godly people, among them one Gottfried and one

---

[82] Geburtsurkunde, 16. Januar 1820, Familien Register 339. The entry in the baptism register says that he was baptised by 'Pfarrvicar M. Ruoff', and that the witnesses were: 'Johann Georg Knoblauch, Krämer und dessen Ehweib Margaretha Catharina Dorothea, geb. Maisch'. Cf. Peter Kustermann, *Johannes Rebmann, Missionar und Entdecker*, in: *1200 Jahre Gerlingen 797-1997*. At the end of his article, based on details by Markus Rösler, he briefly describes the ancestry of the Rebmann family from the 15th century.

[83] Officially since 1958 Gerlingen has been a city. Cf. Stadt Gerlingen, 'Festschrift zur Stadterhebung 1958'.

[84] Markus Rösler has compiled a family tree, which shows that the following members of the family were alive at the time of Rebmann's departure for the Basler Mission Seminary in 1839: his parents Johann Rebmann († 1854) and Anna Maria née Maisch († 1846), his brother Johann Georg († 1885/1886), his sister Anna Margaretha († 1842), his brother Gottlob († 1894), his sister Katharina Margarethe († 1904). Consequently, at Rebmann's death in 1876 two brothers and one sister were alive (see: http://www.johannes-rebmann-stiftung.de/de/missionare/rebmann/Rebmann-Verwandte-18-11-2008.pdf).

[85] Cf: http://www.johannes-rebmann-stiftung.de/en/missionaries/gerlingen_missionaries.html

Jakob. Decades later he remembered them as spiritual guides who took his hand.[86]

Gerlingen was deeply influenced by the movement of Pietism and revival. Like in most Evangelical Lutheran churches in Württemberg, in the Lutheran congregation conventicles (*Stunden*) took place, private gatherings of pietistically oriented people, apart from the ordinary services of worship. Such meetings had been taking place in Gerlingen since 1775. Later the participants were called 'old' Pietists. In Rebmann's time about 100 of the 1000 to 1500[87] citizens of Gerlingen belonged to the group. Without following the fixed Lutheran liturgy, the conventicle members met for free prayers, Bible reading, singing and meditation.

They found a faithful friend in the local Lutheran pastor, Karl Friedrich Stange. He served in the Petruskirche of Gerlingen from 1835 until his death in 1865 as a prophet of Christ-centred Pietism against the man-centred *Enlightenment* that one-sidedly relied on human wisdom, and against rigid Lutheranism that had lost its Evangelical zeal. Stange resolutely rejected the liberal theology of fellow Württemberg theologian David Friedrich Strauß, who had declared the Gospels to be legends that do not represent the historical Jesus. He was an outspoken opponent of the revolutionary spirit that raged in Europe in 1848, in the wake of the *French Revolution*.[88] In his call for mission and evangelism he was warmly supported by the Pietists. Like Von Zinzendorf and Ludwig Hofacker, Stange was deeply moved by what Christ had done for him in suffering on the cross for the atonement of his sin, making him righteous before God, so that he had become a new creature. This wonderful act of justification by God, could only be followed by thankfulness. Stange called for finding a new life of thankfulness in Christ, and expressing it in tender love to God and one's neighbour, especially in reaching out the Gospel of Christ's riches to those who do not know Him, either in the work of external mission to other continents, or in inward mission to compatriots estranged from the Church.[89] Influenced by Anglo-Saxon revivalism, mis-

---

[86] Rebmann, *Briefe*, 2-5-1861; cf. Stutzmann, 'Johannes Rebmann: Leben und Werk des Missionars', Vortrag, S. 5.

[87] Estimations vary: from appr. 1000 to 1400 to 1500.

[88] David Friedrich Strauß (1808-1874), *A new Life of Jesus* (1879). He claimed that the Jesus of the Bible was not the real Jesus of history but a person transformed by the religious consciousness of Christians. Cf. Stutzmann, 'Johannes Rebmann: Leben und Werk des Missionars', Vortrag, S. 3.

[89] Stange, 'Predigt am Feiertag Johannis', Text, Luc. 9: 51-56, in: *Predigte über freie Texte, Evangelische Zeugnisse süddeutscher Prediger*, herausg. Von Stadtpfarrer Stan-

3. From Gerlingen to Islington (1820-1846)

sion to the Jews drew his special attention.[90] He composed several hymns, including a well-known mission hymn.[91] Of the unusually large number of missionaries who have come from Gerlingen since the beginning of the 19th century, at least six went on their way personally encouraged by Stange's powerful missionary incentive. Information published by the City of Gerlingen includes Stange's grateful observation that he had never before experienced a congregation with 'such a desire for the pure evangelical, apostolic word' of Jesus who calls His people to go out into the world.[92] With his strong and warm personality Pastor Stange influenced the Gerlinger community for 30 years, not only through his sermons, but also through the so-called *Kirchenkonvent*, a disciplinary body that censured public sinners. Moreover, he was head of the public registry and supervisor of the local school.[93]

From 1826 Johannes attended this school, the *Volksschule*, in Gerlingen. The school, built in 1818, is now the City Archive. There some 250 pupils were taught by a teacher and an assistant-teacher (*Provisor*).[94] His teacher, Mr. Braun, was a friend of Pastor Stange. Johannes was a gifted pupil, and he quickly learnt how to read and write. The Bible became his most beloved reading book. Fellow pupils sometimes ridiculed him and said he might become a pastor. Once Braun in public called him the best-behaved pupil. At the time this exposure was not well received by Johannes. He said that exactly the teacher's words drove him to frivolity. After school he worked with his father on the farm. At that time his parents probably had not yet joined the Pietists. Apparently his father converted later. When he died in 1853, in a letter to his brother and sister Johannes rejoiced because of his passing away in peace with God.[95]

---

denmener, Jahrgang 1851, Stuttgart: Verlags-Expedition der Zeit-Predigten, 1851. S. 533-540.

[90] Michael Kannenberg, *Verschleierte Uhrtafeln: Endzeiterwartungen im Württembergische Pietismus*, 2007, S. 295, footnote 125, refers to Stange's address on the issue to the Stuttgarter Missionsfest of 1846.

[91] Albert Knapp, *Evangelischer Liederschatz für Kirche, Schule und Haus: eine Sammlung geistlicher Lieder aus allen christlichen Jahrhunderten*, Nr. 1214, 1377, : 'Wir gehn auf ernsten Gang hinaus' (to the melody of 'A mighty fortress is our God'/Ein' feste Burg ist unser Gott); Koch, *Geschichte des Kirchenlieds*, 3rd ed., vol. 7, S. 301f.; Wetzstein, *Die religiöse Lyrik der Deutschen im 19. Jahrh.*, Neustrelitz, 1891, S. 250.

[92] http://www.gerlingen.de/servlet/PB/menu/1190950_l1/index.html

[93] Staiger, 'Gerlingen und die Mission', in G.H.: *Gerlinger Missionare*, S. 5, 6.

[94] Staiger, 'Gerlingen und die Mission', in: G.H.: *Gerlinger Missionare*, S. 4.

[95] Stutzmann, 'Johannes Rebmann: Leben und Werk des Missionars', Vortrag, S. 4, 5; Rebmann, *Briefe*, 19-9-1854.

A vicar of the state church prepared him for confirmation, but failed to unfold the essentials of the Gospel and of Biblical teaching. This gap was filled by the Biblical teaching of Pastor Stange and others, in the Sunday morning services in the Petruskirche and in the afternoon conventicle. The very first time he took part in a conventicle meeting of the Gerlinger Pietists there was a sermon on Matthew 28:16-20, Jesus' *Great Commission* to spread the glad tidings to all the nations of the world. The message challenged him, and from then on he faithfully attended the meetings of the *Stundenleute*. However, this was not generally appreciated. In his autobiography, which was sent to the Basel Mission together with an application, he said that he experienced mockery by the world. He movingly described how a struggle started in him of the flesh against the spirit. The thought of becoming a missionary continued to be in his mind. When he was 19, he formally applied. Pastor Stange knew Johannes well, and he recommended him as follows: 'In spirit and heart, in natural talents and physical constitution, especially, however, in his life, which comes from God, Rebmann is suited for serving in the work of mission.'[96]

At the Basler Mission Seminary (1839-1844)

In 1815 in nearby Basel a mission organisation was started, the Basler Mission (*BM*). It was consciously meant to challenge ordinary Lutheran church members to take a position as witnesses of Christ, or realise that they were opponents of mission.[97] In a wide area of Switzerland and South Germany, especially Swabia (*Schwaben*) overlapping Württemberg, the Pietist movement began to support the new Mission, through a special society (*Hilfsverein für Basel*) established in 1816. Although that year there was hunger in Gerlingen, the local congregation was first to join the society, and sent money.[98] Other villages also raised money.

In subsequent years dozens of young men were recruited for the Mission. The first one was Wilhelm Dürr, and the first Gerlinger was Jakob

---

[96] Ledderhose, Rebmann, in: *ADB*, S. 485; cf. Scheffbuch, *Große Entdecker*, 85.
[97] Cf. BM's later Inspektor, Wilhelm Hoffmann, *Elf Jahre in der Mission: Ein Abschiedswort an den Kreis der Evangelischen Missionsgesellschafft zu Basel*, Stuttgart: Steinkopf Verlag, 1853, S. 112: 'Unsere Absicht war nur, durfte nur sein, die Masse der Evangelischen Kirche, so viel an uns lag, in zwei Lager zu scheiden, das der Freunde und das der Feinde der Mission, und die dazwischen liegende große Schaar der aus Unwissenheit Gleichgültigen wegzuräumen'.
[98] Scheffbuch, *Große Entdecker*, S. 85.

3. From Gerlingen to Islington (1820-1846) 45

Maisch.[99] Johannes Rebmann became a student there at the age of 19 in 1839. He was certainly not the last student to come from South Germany. Some people called the new Basler missionary institution a 'barracks of Swabians' (*Schwabenkaserne*).[100] Christian Friedrich Spittler[101] was the most important man when the BM was founded. The impulse came from his friend, pastor Karl Steinkopf,[102] in those days active in London, especially in the British and Foreign Bible Society, and also in the Church Missionary Society. Steinkopf built bridges between Basel and London, so that BM students were sent out by the CMS. Instrumental in this liaison was BM's executive head (*Inspektor*) Christian Gottlieb Blumhardt, from 1816 to his death in 1839. Through Blumhardt's journalistic qualities German Pietists were informed about missionary initiatives in the Anglo-Saxon world. He helped to create the mission's organisational structure and defined the nature and curriculum of the mission's seminary.[103] It included Biblical subjects, the original Biblical languages, and English,[104] as well as instruction in practical work. When Wilhelm Hoffmann,[105] son of the founder of the Korntal congregation, succeeded Blumhardt as executive head of the BM, he continued along the same lines and emphasised that first-class missionaries had to be trained, just as CMS required. They should have a thorough exegetical-theological training, including the classical languages, similar to the training of pastors in the Lutheran and Reformed home churches.[106] The solid academic character of the training by the BM invalidates Colin Reed's argument that 'not many' of the early

---

[99] G. Arthur Jehle, *Der Entdecker des Kilimandscharo: Aus dem Leben des Missionars Johannes Rebmann*, Stuttgart/Basel: Evang. Missionsverlag, n.d., S. 3.
[100] Cf. Stutzmann, 'Johannes Rebmann: Leben und Werk des Missionars', Vortrag, S. 5.
[101] Christian Friedrich Spittler [Internet] See Klaus-Gunther Wesseling, in: *BBKL*, vol. 10, Herzberg (1995), col. 1031-1035.
[102] Karl Friedrich Adolf Steinkopf [1773-1859], *Letters relative to a tour on the continent, undertaken at the request of the Committee of the British and Foreign Bible Society in the year 1812*, London: Hatchard/Seeley, 1813 [German translation, Ulrich Fick (ed.), Karl Friedrich Steinkopf: *Reisebriefe Europa 1812*, Stuttgart: Deutsche Bibelgesellschaft/Hänssler, 1987]; cf. Karl Rennstich, in: *BBKL*, vol. 10 (1995), col. 1306-1309).
[103] Christian Gottlieb Blumhardt (1779-1839), see: F.W. Bautz, in: *BBKL*, vol. 1 (1990), col. 630-631; Paul Jenkins, in: G.H. Anderson, Biographical Dictionary of Christian Missions; Blumhardt started the Basler Missions Magazin (1816), and the Evangelische Heidenbote (1828), and he set up the first BM mission fields, in southern Russia, Ghana and southern India.
[104] Cf. Scheffbuch, *Große Entdecker*, S. 100.
[105] Ludwig Friedrich Wilhelm Hoffmann (1803-1873); Paul Jenkins, in: G.H. Anderson, Biographical Dictionary of Christian Missions; cf. Scheffbuch, *Große Entdecker*, S. 71, 170.

missionaries in East Africa were well educated, or of great intellectual and spiritual stature.[107] Many 19th-century Western missionaries in Africa were Germans. Many studied in Basel, some at other institutions as well, and one was later awarded an honorary doctorate from the University of Tübingen. In general BM alumni were pious people of good intellectual capacity.

When Hoffmann left Basel, his friend Joseph Josenhans became head of the Basler Mission. Both Hoffmann and Josenhans hoped and prayed for an interdenominational, or even supra-denominational Christianity, in the spirit of the founders of the YMCA and the Evangelical Alliance.

The emphasis on academic theology and classical Pietism deviated from Spittler's original concept. Spittler had shifted to newer approaches, and had adopted the ideal of tentmaker-missionaries (*Handwerker-Missionare, Pilger-Missionare*). Therefore he founded at St. Chrischona, near Basel, the Pilgrims' Mission. It was a kind of Bible school, which taught practical subjects as well. It had a tremendous influence on Protestant presence in the Near East, especially in Jerusalem, and also played a role in Africa in the time of Rebmann and Krapf.

Johannes Rebmann started his training at the Basler Mission Seminary on 1 August 1839, the same year its first head Blumhardt died. His teachers were of the opinion that he was fit to be a missionary because of his natural constitution and mental stability, his faith in Christ, and his humility.[108] After five years of study Rebmann was ready for a final course with the CMS in London, and then the mission field. Rebmann kept contact with Basel. Ledderhose notes that he and the Seminary's head, Wilhelm Hoffmann, had a special 'father and son' relationship and continued exchanging letters for some years.[109]

---

[106] Bengt Sundkler and Christopher Steed, *A History of the Church in Africa*, Cambridge University Press, 2001 (first 2000), p. 112, 113. The training of the Basel Mission Seminary 'was thorough extending to five years and including daily studies in Latin, Greek, Hebrew and English on a level comparable to any university instruction at the time'.

[107] Colin Reed, *Pastors, Partners Paternalists: African Church Leaders & Western Missionaries in the Anglican Church in Kenya*, 1850-1900, Leiden/New York/Köln: Brill, 1997, p. 3.

[108] BM *Protokollen* XIV, S. 168: Sitzung vom 8.Juli 1839, Präparandenaufnahmen; cf. BM Protokollen, XIV, 211; Scheffbuch, *Große Entdecker*, S. 85, 86; Stutzmann, 'Johannes Rebmann: Leben und Werk des Missionars', Vortrag, S. 5.

[109] Ledderhose, Rebmann, in *ADB*, vol. 27, S. 485, says he is in the possession of letters from Rebmann to Hoffmann. Probably they belonged to the material that was burnt by Ledderhose's heirs after 1890; cf. Scheffbuch, *Große Entdecker*, 87.

3. From Gerlingen to Islington (1820-1846)

At the CMS Seminary, Islington (1844-1846)

As the Basler Mission did not yet need many people for its work in Ghana and India, many of its students joined the like-minded English Church Missionary Society (CMS) connected to the Evangelical branch of the Anglican Church, and a product of the Methodist revival of the 18th century. During the first decades after its establishment in 1799, the CMS failed to find enough British workers for its expanding activities in Asia and Africa. In the course of time 88 Basel-trained men were sent out as Anglican missionaries through CMS after an additional training at the Society's seminary in Islington, London. Apparently their Lutheran origin was not a problem for the Evangelical Anglicans. This lasted until the 1850s when the recruitment from Basel 'came to an end and the CMS could recruit its own men and women from the British Isles'.[110]

After a letter of recommendation by Inspektor Hoffmann,[111] Rebmann was welcomed at the Seminary of the CMS in Islington, London, where he finished his training.[112] The journey to London started on 13 June 1844, and was minutely reported to his family in Gerlingen. His remarks on the places in Germany and The Netherlands that he passed show consciousness of history. Worms reminded him of the Diet of 1521, where Martin Luther heroically witnessed his faith. In Elberfeld and nearby Barmen he saw mission-minded brethren, and in Rotterdam he met with a Christian tradesman B. Ledeboer, Secretary of the first Dutch Missionary Society (*Nederlandsch Zendeling Genootschap*).[113] After some seasickness they arrived in London on 11 July 1844. The training at the CMS Seminary of Islington included the observation of teaching in English schools in order to stimulate thoughts on the didactical methods that would be required

---

[110] Sundkler and Steed, *A History of the Church in Africa*, p. 113. Paul Richter, 'Geschichte und Arbeitsfelder der Englischen Kirchenmissionsgesellschaft', in: AMZ, 1897, S. 497-528. From 1802 the Berliner Mission also sent candidates, 22 in number, and from 1807 also a few English candidates started to join the CMS.

[111] Letter from Inspektor Hoffmann in Basel to D. Coates of CMS, 16-4-1844. 'On your request we shall be ready to send you this year too two students of our institution, who we humbly hope will become very able missionaries after due preparation in Islington. Both of them are very talented young men, both of Württemberg'. One name is illegible but probably is Friedrich Schnurr, the other is Rebmann. Hoffmann suggests that after completion of their studies they will be ordained and sent as missionaries to Bengal, India [G/AC 14 A/180].

[112] In *EH*, 1844, July, no 7, S. 65, BM-B mentions Rebmann's departure to Islington.

[113] Rebmann, *Briefe*, 27-7-1844; *BMM*, 1844, III, S. 190, IV, S. 201; cf. *BMM* 1816; The Society was founded in 1797 at the initiative of Theodorus van der Kemp; Jehle, *Entdecker*, S. 4.

in the African mission field. He studied in a group, mainly consisting of candidates for the CMS mission fields in India.[114] After 18 months at Islington a written examination of three days took place. It was followed by two ordination ceremonies by the Bishop of London. The one, of 6 June 1845, was for inclusion in the deacon's orders,[115] and in the other, of 26 October 1845, he was ordained for priestly orders.[116] Rebmann had become an Anglican clergyman, according to the ordination certificate, 'for the cure of souls in Her Majesty's foreign possessions'.[117]

Where would he be sent to? When he was still at the Basler Mission House, a visiting alumnus and Calcutta-based CMS missionary Johann Jakob Weitbrecht in a letter to the CMS had begged for Rebmann to be sent with him to India.[118] However, after some hesitation the CMS destined Rebmann for the Mombasa region in East Africa. The Basler Mission agreed to this decision.[119] Two years earlier, on behalf of the CMS, a fellow-brother of the Basler Mission Johannes Ludwig Krapf had started to work there. In February 1846 Rebmann boarded ship and began his voyage to Mombasa. He left behind his brethren in Basel and London, and also his dear parents, and his two brothers, Johann Georg and Gottlob, and one sister Katharina Margarethe in Gerlingen. He left them in the hands of God. The City Museum of Gerlingen has a book that he gave to his father and mother at his departure. It is a collection of meditations by the influential Pietist writer Von Bogatzky.[120] His parents he would never

---

[114] A farewell album belonging Alexander Acheson (in Benares, India 1847-1852), presented to him when he left Islington in 1845, bears the signatures of fellow-students, including Rebmann's [CMS/ACC329 F1].

[115] Letter from CMS Secretary Henry Venn to the Bishop of London presenting 5 candidate missionaries for being ordained for Deacon's orders, one of them John Rebmann [G/AC/4/1, 1846, p. 372].

[116] Letter from CMS Secretary Henry Venn to the Bishop of London presenting two already ordained for Deacon's orders, to be ordained now for priestly orders, one of them John Rebmann' [G/AC/5, 1846, p. 30]; Rebmann, *Briefe*, 3-7-1848 and 8-10-1845.

[117] Ordination Certificate of Johannes Rebmann, 18 May 1845, effective July 1845, signed and sealed by the Bishop of London [copy in City Archive Gerlingen 10/17.1/026, original in Württ. Landesbibliothek Stuttgart].

[118] Johann Jakob Weitbrecht (1802-1852) in a letter to D. Coates of the CMS. Weitbrecht was another Württemberg CMS missionary, from 1831 in India; like Rebmann he was influenced by the Pietism of Ludwig Hofacker [CI1/O 306/20].

[119] BM *Protokollen*, 25. June 1845.

[120] Karl Heinrich von Bogatzky, *Die geistlichen Friedensstörer: nebst einem Anhang von den untrüglichen Kennzeichen der Kindschaft Gottes*, Bern, 1842 (first edition, Waysenhaus: Halle, 1759).

see again. Half a year after his arrival in East Africa his mother Anna died. She may have read the letter her son wrote on his way to Africa, noting her birthday when the ship passed the imaginary line of the tropics, and reminding her to look through 'the little kitchen window' ('durchs Küchenlädchen'), the right direction, and imagine her son is 'at a distance of 2500 hours'.[121]

---

[121] Rebmann, *Briefe*, 17-4-1846 (added to a letter of 13-4-1846).

*Johannes Rebmann
when he studied at the
Basler Mission Seminary
(G.H. p. 13).*

*The Petruskirche of Gerlingen
in 1892 (G.H. p. 9).*

*The house where Rebmann was born,
Kirchstraße 18, Gerlingen
(Stadtarchiv Gerlingen).*

3. From Gerlingen to Islington (1820-1846)

Christian Friedrich Spittler (1782-1867), who founded the Basler Mission in 1815 and the St. Chrischona Pilgrim Mission in 1840 (Basler Mission Archive: QS-30.022.0027)

Basler Mission House, founded 1815 (G.H. p. 7).

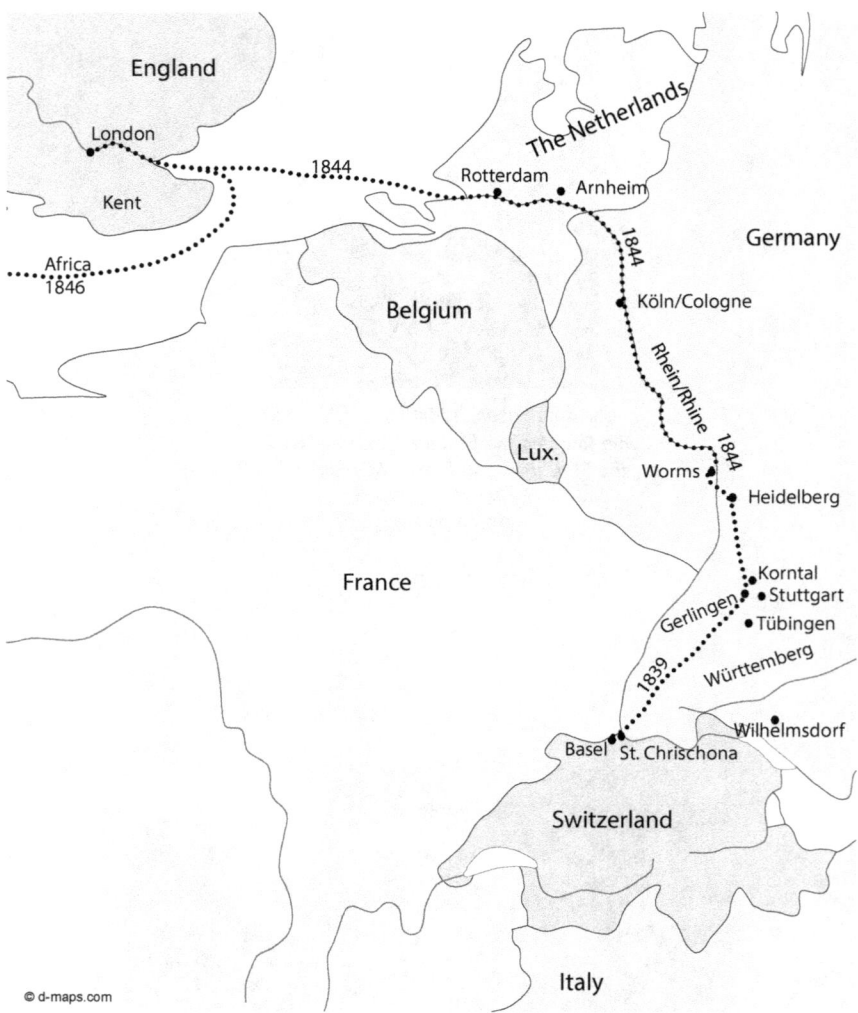

*Rebmann's youth in Gerlingen, Basel and London
(S. Paas and VKW; based on a map of d-maps.com).*

3. From Gerlingen to Islington (1820-1846)

*Wilhelm Hoffmann, Basler Mission Inspektor
(Basler Mission Archive: QS-30.016.0022).*

*St. Chrischona Pilgrim Mission in 1845
(Painting of J.F. Wensel, through Eber, p. 167).*

CMS Seminary at Islington in London (E.H. 1860-8, p. 60).

4. With Johann Ludwig Krapf (1846-1855)

Rebmann's arrival

In the eyes of the outside world Rebmann has always been considered the junior partner of Krapf. His life was overlapped by that of Krapf, who was born 10 years before him and who died 5 years after him. Krapf travelled and published more than Rebmann did, and had a more extended network among the opinion-makers of his time. This is one reason why for a long time Rebmann's independent identity as a missionary and as a linguist has been hidden. Generally Rebmann showed respect for Krapf. Even before they met in Mombasa, he agreed to Krapf's words in a magazine that mission is a task for 'body and soul' and that a missionary himself should be 'converted and ever more converted' before he can understand this.[122]

The voyage via the Cape of Good Hope on a ship called *Arrow* took 4 months before he arrived at Zanzibar.[123] From there an Arab boat took him to Mombasa. On 10 June 1846 he met there with Krapf, who was suffering from ill-health at that time.[124] Krapf had prepared for the coming of Rebmann. He had sent Swahili language material to London, which Rebmann took aboard with him, and diligently learnt.[125] On top of his

---

[122] Rebmann, *Briefe*, 3-6-1845, quoting from *Der Heidenbote*.
[123] Until the opening of the Suez Canal in November 1869, there was no direct connection between the Mediterranean Sea and the Red Sea, ships to East Africa had to navigate around Africa.
[124] BMM, 1846, II, S. 126, IV, S. 9; In his letter of 10 April 1846 (Fischer, 'Extracts', BM-B Archive 14.IX 48; vgl F2.Abtg III, no 7) Krapf looks forward to Rebmann's arrival and complains he is very sick without hope of full recovery ('von schwerer Krankheit geplagt, ohne Aussicht auf gänzliche Erholung'); *EH*, 1847, July, no 7, S. 55, 56, 60, publishes Krapf's letter of 26 June 1846, in which he reports Rebmann's arrival. Krapf welcomes him to the mission in East Africa, now that 'Islam is weak', and says that both of them are hindered by bodily weaknesses; *EH*, 1847, September, no 9, S. 73-75 quotes from Rebmann's letter of 31 June 1846 about his voyage and arrival at Zanzibar, on 27 May 1846.
[125] Johann Ludwig Krapf, *A Dictionary of Suahili language*, containing an Outline of a Suahili Grammar, Edinburg: Ballantyne & Hanson/London: Trübner, 1882, Preface, p. vii-xii: 'The first of these who arrived was the Rev. J. Rebmann, who reached Mombas in June, 1846. While yet in England he made a copy of my manuscripts, and, during the long voyage of 140 days from London to Zanzibar, committed the whole of their contents to memory. This gave him a great advantage in mastering the language after his arrival in Mombas.'

house in Mombasa Krapf had built a cool room for his newly arrived colleague.[126] For seven years they would be almost uninterruptedly together in the CMS mission in East Africa. Although each worked in his own way, the histories of their lives and work would remain intertwined.

Krapf in Ethiopia

Johann Ludwig Krapf had been in Africa since 1837. He started his missionary career in Ethiopia (Abyssinia). The first Protestant missionaries in that country were CMS missionaries Samuel Gobat[127] and Christian Kugler, who had arrived in 1829. Kugler soon died and was replaced by Karl Wilhem Isenberg[128] in 1830. Karl Heinrich Blumhardt[129] and Krapf came in 1837. When Gobat left Ethiopia a year later, Isenberg, Blumhardt and Krapf continued together. As they were independent minds, cooperation did not always go smoothly.[130] Yet they agreed in their vision of reforming the Ethiopian Orthodox Church and equipping it for the missionary task of counteracting the penetration of Islam into Africa. However, this plan ran against the ideas of the Ethiopian elite, and met with envy from representatives of the Roman Catholic Church. Consequently, in 1838 the missionaries were expelled from Tigre Province by Prince Ubie.[131]

When Krapf failed to find support he changed direction and wanted to go south to the heathen Galla, to instil among them the Christian faith before they would surrender to Islam. To reach Galla land one had to pass Shoa. In 1839 and 1842 Krapf and Isenberg made new attempts, now in Shoa Province, protected by King Sahila Selassie. At first the King was very welcoming. Krapf and Isenberg worked in the capital Ankober for almost three years, were facilitated to be in contact with the Oromo or Galla-tribe during the King's expedition against them, and collected a lot of valuable Amharic manuscripts.[132] However, at last the King, under the influence of Orthodox priests, turned against them, and they had to give

---

[126] Krapf, *Reisen* I, S. 281.
[127] Samuel Gobat, 1799-1879; see: F.W. Bautz in *BBKL*, vol. 2 (1990) col. 258.
[128] Karl Wilhelm Isenberg (1806-1864). H.Gundert, *Biography of the Rev. Charles Isenberg, Missionary of the CMS to Abyssinia and Western India from 1832 to 1864*, London: CMS 1885 [translated into English by C. and M. Isenberg]. Cf. Scheffbuch, *Große Entdecker*, S. 94-107.
[129] Karl Heinrich Blumhardt, 1807-1883, was a nephew of the first BM Inspektor, C. G. Blumhardt.
[130] Cf. Eber, *Krapf*, S. 50.
[131] Cf. Eber, *Krapf*, S. 49.
[132] Eber, *Krapf*, S. 53-58.

4. With Johann Ludwig Krapf (1846-1855)

up.¹³³ Blumhardt and Isenberg left the country respectively in 1839 and 1843. Both went for the CMS to India.

Krapf decided to try and reach the Galla from the south through the African east coast. Soon he realised that from this angle too there were many problems. In his connections with mission friends at home in England and Germany he was more successful. In September 1842 in Alexandria he married Rosine Dietrich from Basel.¹³⁴ In the same year the philosophical faculty of the university of Tübingen gave him a PhD, honoris causa, thus rewarding him for uncovering and collecting the above mentioned ancient Amharic manuscripts.¹³⁵ Krapf's star in the intellectual world would rise even more in later years. He produced many manuscripts that attracted the attention of philologists and geographers. In his personal life and as a missionary, however, he experienced serious setbacks.

In May 1843, after having returned from Shoa to the coast, Rosine Krapf delivered a daughter Eneba (*tears*), who died after two hours.¹³⁶ In January 1844, after being robbed in a first attempt, their ship arrived from Aden in Zanzibar. Soon after arriving in Mombasa in July 1844, Rosine delivered another daughter. However, within two weeks both died, which was a terrible blow.¹³⁷ Yet like David Livingstone who some years earlier had started his African journeys, Krapf was able to persevere in the midst of troubles and disappointments. In 1845 and 1846 he made journeys to Takongo, Emberria and Malindi to find a way to the Galla. Soon he fell sick again and had to withdraw to Zanzibar. When he realised that the way to reach the Galla was long and difficult, he started concentrating on the Swahili culture of the African east coast. From Zanzibar he was able to send to the CMS in London an outline of a Swahili grammar and translations of at least the Gospel of John, and vocabularies in Swahili, Nika, Pokomo and Galla.¹³⁸ That was the material Rebmann gratefully used during the months of his voyage to Mombasa, in preparation

---

[133] Eber, *Krapf*, S. 74.
[134] Eber, *Krapf*, S. 65, 73.
[135] Eber, *Krapf*, S. 61, 78, 79, 61, 78, 79, who derived from Krapf's *Reisen*, I, S. 50, 65, 100, 181, 483. Krapf acquired by buying, exchanging or copying about 80 Amharic Manuscripts, which he sent to the CMS, to European universities (25 to the University of Tübingen).
[136] Eber, *Krapf*, S. 74 (Krapf, *Reisen* I, S. 470, 471).
[137] Cf. CMS, *Proceedings*, 1842-1843, p. 48; 1843-1844, p. 49-51; Eber, *Krapf*, S. 90, 91 (Krapf, *Reisen*, I, S. 211, 212). Rosine and her daughter were buried on the mainland opposite Mombasa, the US consul at Zanzibar paid for a stone memorial.
[138] CMS, *Proceedings*, London 1847, p. 49-51.

for his task. The German mission media were also informed about Krapf's language exploits in Swahili and Nika.[139]

From Mombasa to Rabai/Kisuludini

Soon after joining hands Krapf and Rebmann made an important decision. The Swahili-Muslim environment and the unhealthy heat of the Isle of Mombasa limited their activities. In 1837 after a brief British interregnum, and a lot of infighting between members of the ruling Muslim dynasty, Mombasa was nominally annexed by the Sultan of Oman and Zanzibar. Sultan Sayyid Said shifted his residence from Oman's capital Muscat to Zanzibar in 1840.

The Sultan was friendly to foreigners, especially those who were linked to Britain, because of his pact with London, which protected his political position and economy. Nevertheless Krapf and Rebmann thought it wiser to move beyond the narrow channel between Mombasa and the mainland, and live at a higher place among the heathen Nika people. They decided to settle in Rabai Mpia, at a distance of about 25 km from Mombasa.[140] During a preparatory visit the chiefs and elders of Rabai promised them welcome and accommodation. On 22 August 1846 they left Mombasa with their luggage, first by boat to a landing place at the foot of Rabai hill, then the rest of the distance by foot. By that time both had become unwell because of fever, and they spent two nights before they could climb up to Rabai. The last stretch of the journey, on 25 August, they described as a *via dolorosa*. Being so much struck by fever that they could not walk anymore, they at last used a donkey, and arrived with great suffering.[141] In particular Krapf was very weak. As the hut that had been promised to them was not ready, they first moved in with the local chief, and then to a hut that was not more than a ruin covered by tree leaves. A new dwelling had to be built. The work on the primitive loghouse was mainly done by Rebmann, as Krapf was too sick and exhausted by malaria to contribute a lot. By the end of August 1846 they occupied their new home.[142]

However, the missionaries soon discovered that this was not the best place for their missionary headquarters. They therefore moved on a few

---

[139] An article in *BMM*, 1847, IV, S. 16-18 lauds Krapf's language activity.
[140] mpia = new.
[141] Krapf, *Reisen*, S. 489-493; *BMM*, 1847, II, S. 184; cf. Scheffbuch, *Große Entdecker*, 88; Eber, *Krapf*, S. 95.
[142] Cf. Krapf, *Reisen* I, S. 493-497.

kilometres, and settled in Kisuludini (Kizurini or Kisulutini in today's usual spelling), on the border between the Nika and Kamba peoples. On 16 October 1846 the new house was occupied, a hut of about 7 by 6 metres, with walls of poles and earth and a roof thatched with bananaleaves. Krapf saw it as the first step of his plan for a chain of mission stations across Africa. Later, a kitchen, a store room and an oven were added. Again later, separate from the house, a chapel was built.[143]

From Mombasa there were two routes to get to Rabai/Kisuludini. One could walk up the 25 kilometres of the gradually sloping hill until the top at Rabai, and then go down to Kisuludini. The other route started by rowing about 17 kilometres up the Rabai branch of the Mombasa creek, until one arrived at the foot of Rabai hill. After climbing to the top, there was first a steep slope downwards and then a gentle slope of some 8 kilometres down to the Kisuludini mission house.[144]

In the midst of the Nika cattle-breeders and their chiefs, Rebmann and Krapf immediately started work. Krapf saw the Nika as 'a people enslaved in misery, sorcery and abominations ... not the wise and mighty'. Rebmann described how they went from hut to hut to talk to the people and to attract them to teaching and catechism classes. He was hospitably received, but at the same time noticed a hardness of heart towards the Gospel. Only Mringe, a vulnerable man with mutilated legs, seemed to open his heart. Also Rebmann saw the evil of local slavery among Africans themselves.[145] In addition to evangelism they started language work. Lexicographical collections of Kinika, the language of the Nika, and Kikamba, the language of a neighbouring group, reached some completion, apart from the continuing activity of collecting Swahili vocabulary.

Chain of mission stations

At the same time the missionaries did not forget their wider vision of preparing the outreach of the Gospel to the people of Africa's interior. To Krapf the arrival of Rebmann meant a new chance for realising his dream, or at least part of it, of a chain of mission stations across equatorial Africa, from Mombasa to Cameroon. He first mentioned this idea in his journal of 1844.[146] The idea came from Christian Friedrich Spittler, the

---

[143] Eber, *Krapf*, S. 96, 97; cf. Jehle, Der *Entdecker*, S. 5.
[144] Description by John Hanning Speke, *Journal*, 17 January 1857, who together with fellow-explorer Richard Burton visited Johannes and Emma Rebmann.
[145] *BMM*, 1847, IV, S. 16-18; *BMM*, 1848, IV, S. 17; *Proceedings of CMS*, London, 1850, S. xcv.
[146] Krapf, *Reisen* I, S. 213.

first Inspektor of the Basler Mission, and in 1840 the founder of the St. Chrischona Pilgrim Mission. Spiritual streets, each materialised by a series of stations, were to open mission fields, especially in southern Europe and the Middle East. Later the concept was amended, to an apostles' street (*Apostelstraße*), i.e. a route for present-day apostles of Christ beginning in Jerusalem along the Nile to the Galla of Ethiopia, which would open Africa for the Gospel. Krapf extended the idea of an apostles' street along the Nile with a chain of nine or ten mission stations from Mombasa along the equator to Gabon north of the Congo delta on the Atlantic Ocean.[147] In Krapf's enthusiastic view first the Galla or Oromo people of Kenya and southern Ethiopia would play a key role in Christianising the whole of Africa.[148] He paralleled their supposed strategic significance with the position of pre-Christian Germanic tribes in Europe.[149] Hence his continual attempts to reach and evangelise the Galla.[150] Now that approaching them through Ethiopia had failed, the way to the Galla and others in Africa's interior led via the Swahili-speaking peoples on Africa's east coast. Especially the Kamba people of Ukambani were to play the role he first had assigned to the Galla. Krapf saw his efforts for Kamba and Swahili lexicography as an important step in the realisation of his vision. He never abandoned this ideal. Many years later, in 1881, in the introduction to his Swahili Dictionary, he wished that 'under the Divine blessing this volume may be of material aid in the spread of Christianity and Christian civilization in Central and Southern Africa'. He added: 'May [the dictionary] also help in forming a great chain of mission stations which shall unite East and West Africa. This has been an object of the author's most earnest desire since 1844.'[151]

The vision of a chain of missions from Jerusalem along the Nile and then across Africa became an infectuous concept with many thinkers in

---

[147] Martin Weishaupt, *Rebmanns Reisen im Dschaggaland - Mit 7 Abbildungen*, Leipzig: Verlag der Evangelisch-Lutherischen Mission, 1926, S. 4. Krapf estimated the distance at 900 hours, and he planned a mission station at every 100 hours, with 4 missionaries for each station. In his thought the execution of the plan would take 4 or 5 years.

[148] Cf. Eber, *Krapf*, S. 57.

[149] Eber, *Krapf*, S. 86 (Krapf, *Reisen* I, 189) calls this 'patriotisch angehauchtes Schwärmen'.

[150] Scheffbuch, *Große Entdecker*, S. 72 summarised Krapf's vision in five points: 1.conquering Africa for Christianity from its East coast, 2.a key role for the Galla (or Oromo) people, 3.a chain of mission stations, 4.a Christian colony of liberated slaves in Mombasa, 5.as soon as possible the ordination of Africans as pastors and bishops.

[151] Krapf, *Dictionary of the Suahili Language*, Introduction, p. xi.

4. With Johann Ludwig Krapf (1846-1855)

terms of transcontinental strategies.[152] At first Rebmann was interested too, but with regard to the feasibility of this far-reaching plan, he was more down-to-earth and practical than his friend, and also more patient. He was prepared to make some efforts to penetrate into the interior, but he also realised that time had not come for the full realisation of such a pretentious plan. His journeys taught him that for the time being consolidation on the Mombasa coast was the thing to do. That was what he did after his forays into Teita and Jagga-land, for the rest of his 29 years in Africa. By faithful perseverence at Rabai and Kisuludini he established a bridgehead from which later missionaries would be able to extend the Christian message north and south along the coast and west to the great lakes.

In March 1847 Rebmann and Krapf stayed in Zanzibar to recover for a few weeks. In May 1847 they travelled North-West to the Teita and Kamba peoples and the Kadiaro Mountain.[153] In November 1848 they tried to make a voyage along the coast to the mouth of the Juba river in present-day Somalia. The trips miscarried due to contrary winds.[154] They sailed half-way to the island of Patta, attempting to find a passage to the land of the Galla, a main objective in Krapf's missionary vision.[155] These exercises served as a preparation for longer journeys, made by the two missionaries separately.

During his first few years in Africa Rebmann thought it was possible for him to eventually reach the land of the great interior lake, which in the imagination of explorers was known as *Unyamwezi*.[156] However, in between there were the Jagga[157] and the Kikuyu peoples. Rebmann made three journeys to Jagga-land, but never reached the Kikuyu.[158] One of the reasons was that the Jagga-leaders did not allow their important white guest to pass before he had parted with all his gifts and valuables. In oth-

---

[152] Sundkler and Steed, *A History of the Church in Africa*, p. 154, 510.
[153] EH, 1848, June, no 6, S. 42-48 quotes from Rebmann's reports on the period April-October 1847, e.g. about sorcery, the name Mulungu referring to both God and heaven, the transfer to Rabai Mpia, and an attack by ants.
[154] BMM, 1848, IV, S. 17; EH, 1848, October, no 10, S. 76-78; cf. Eber, *Krapf*, S. 125 (Krapf, *Reisen* I, S. 366f).
[155] EH, 1849, September, no 9, S. 72.
[156] Often spelled: *Uniamesi*.
[157] Also spelled Chagga.
[158] Ledderhose, 'Rebmann', in: ADB, vol. 27, S. 486, summarised his diary notes on the three journeys into Jagga land, including the Kilimanjaro event. Cf. Krapf, *Reisen*, II, S. 58, 72, 86; see also: http://www.johannes-rebmann-stiftung.de/en/missionaries/rebmann/diary.html and NTZ, http://www.ntz.info/gen/n00518.html

er words, Rebmann was robbed on his second attempt by Masaki, chief of the Kilema, one of the Jagga clans, and on his third journey even more by Jagga paramount Chief or King Mamkinga of Majame. This was a humiliating experience. He painfully noted that they and the Teita were not interested in the 'Book of God showing the way to heaven', nor in the missionary himself as soon as no further material gain was to be expected from him.[159]

His first and shortest journey to Jagga-land has contributed most to Rebmann's fame among explorers and geographers and their institutions and media in Europe and America. On 11 May 1848 he saw a very high mountain, with two peaks. He was told that the highest was called Kibo and the other Mawenzi. They were covered with a white substance, called 'beredi' (*cold*), which the Africans regarded with suspicion, thinking of magic.[160] Rebmann with his Swiss experience of mountains, immediately knew it was snow. The magnificent view and beauty of the mountain made him look for a quiet place for prayer and the reading of *Psalm* 111, 'He has shown his people the power of his works' (:6). Rebmann was the first European to observe Kilimanjaro Mountain.[161] When he reported this event to Europe,[162] experts in England and Germany at first doubted his observation and some mocked him. The geographer William D. Cooley even wrote a book against him.[163] The famous German naturalist and explorer Von Humboldt[164] also doubted at first. How could there be snow on the Equator? However, the geographers of the French Academy of Sciences (*Societé Géographique – Institut de France*) realised that Rebmann had not been mistaken, and in 1852 they awarded him the Volney medal for being the first European to see the Kilimanjaro.[165] Krapf also got a medal

---

[159] Cf. Krapf, *Reisen*, II, S. 34-37.
[160] The snow was thought to be silver. According to Jagga tribal legend a great treasure existed on the mountain, protected by powerful spirits ready to punish anyone who dared to climb it. The legend is related to stories on the supposed presence of King Solomon's mines on Kilimanjaro, even his grave.
[161] Cf. Krapf, *Reisen*, II, S. 30-31.
[162] Rebmann, account of his first journey to Jagga land, in: *The Church Missionary Intelligencer*, vol. 1, No. 1, May 1849.
[163] William Desborough Cooley, *Inner Africa Laid Open: In An Attempt To Trace The Chief Lines Of Communication Across That Continent South Of The Equator* (1852). Cooley had never travelled in Africa, but he thought that the snow was a lightly-coloured quartz that existed on equatorial mountains.
[164] Friedrich Wilhelm Heinrich Alexander von Humboldt (1769-1859), specialist botanical geography and founder of biogeography.
[165] Weishaupt, *Rebmanns Reisen im Dschaggaland – Mit 7 Abbildungen*, Leipzig: Verlag der Evangelisch-Lutherischen Mission, 1926 [40 pages], S. 13, 14, refers to the

4. With Johann Ludwig Krapf (1846-1855)

from them, because in 1849 he had seen Mount Kenya. In a letter to his relatives Rebmann stressed that this honour was of no significance in comparison to his task of making known salvation in Jesus Christ to the peoples that are in darkness.[166] It took many more years before all criticism from European intellectuals was silenced, until 1863, when the German explorer Baron Karl Klaus von der Decken and the British geologist Richard Thornton, climbed the mountain to a height where they experienced snowfall, thus confirming the existence of snow in the heart of tropical Africa. Climbing Kilimanjaro was resisted by Africans who expected evil from such an attempt. In 1870 Charles New and his African guide climbed up as far as the snowline.[167] In 1884 the naturalist Henry Hamilton Johnston made an intensive study of the flora and fauna of Kilimanjaro. The first to climb all the 5895 metres to the top of Kilimanjaro were Hans Meyer and Ludwig Purtscheller, in 1889.[168]

The one journey to the Teita and Kamba peoples and the three journeys to Jagga-land belong to the best documented periods of Rebmann's life. He himself described them in his only existing German journal of 14 February 1848 to 16 February 1849.[169] The accounts are included in Krapf's *Travels, Researches* (*Reisen*),[170] and in summaries by Richards,[171] and

---

Spaniard Fernandez de Encisco, who visited Mombasa, ruled by the Portuguese since 1507, and who in 1519 in his 'Summa de Geographia' was first to mention the mountain that became known as Kilimanjaro. It is doubtful whether he saw the mountain himself.

[166] Rebmann, *Briefe*: letter dated 1-10-1853 in Kisuludini, to his father, brothers and sister: '... I need to say also, that I got a nice silver medal from the Geographic Society in Paris, for my discovery of the snow mountain Kilimanjaro. Dr. Krapf got the same (for his discovery of the Kenya). You must not think that this made me very happy. I learned to see that all as vanity ..., also I didn't come here to make geographical discoveries, but to uncover the release and the salvation in Jesus Christ for the people who sit in darkness and the shadow of death' (Cf. *Luke* 1: 79; *Psalm* 107: 10).

[167] Cf. Charles New, *Wanderings and Labours in Eastern Africa*, London: Hodder and Stoughton, 1873; cf. Ledderhose, 'Rebmann', in: *ADB*, vol. 27, S. 487.

[168] Ludwig Purtscheller, in: *Erschliessung der Berge*, vol. 2, München: Deutsch-Österreichischer Alpenverein, 1926. S. 44-72.

[169] Johannes Rebmann, *Tagebuch des Missionars vom 14. Februar 1948-16.Februar 1849*, Veröffentlichung des Archivs der Stadt Gerlingen, vol. 3, Herausgegeben vom Stadtarchiv Gerlingen, 1967; cf. Jehle, *Der Entdecker*, S. 5-9.

[170] Cf. Eber, *Krapf*, S. 12-129, 134-137; Johann Ludwig Krapf, *Reisen in Ostafrika 1837-1855*, 2 Teile, Korntal 1858 (reprint 1964), I, 22,f, 113, 355, 363, 385; II, 3f, 18, 30-39, 58-72, 86.

by Weishaupt.[172] German letters from Rebmann of the period 1847 to 1853 seem to be missing; perhaps they are permanently lost. The same is true for other diaries or journals by Rebmann himself. They are not available in the archives or with the Rebmann family. In order to get a picture of the periods that are not covered by journals or letters from Rebmann himself, we depend on details in the accounts by his contemporaries, e.g. his wife Emma,[173] Johann Ludwig Krapf,[174] and Johann Jakob Erhardt.[175]

Of the three, Krapf especially was a prolific writer, but it should be kept in mind that his publications often contain the work of others, in addition to a lot of stories on his own travels and researches. In 1848 and 1849, during the absence of Rebmann in Jagga-land, Krapf made some exploratory journeys, one to the Usambara people to the south-west along the coast between Mombasa and Zanzibar, and another to the Kamba people of Ukambani north-west of Mombasa. He returned to Kisuludini exhausted, but in time to receive two new Basler brothers, Jakob Erhardt and Johannes Wagner, sent by the CMS. Both were seriously ill. They had arrived in Zanzibar in May, sailed to Mombasa, and with great difficulty had reached Rabai. There Wagner died on 1 August 1849. For the first time the surrounding Nika people saw a Christian funeral.[176]

A few days earlier Rebmann had returned from his third Jagga journey, which was an unsuccessful attempt to find access to peoples and lakes in the interior of Africa.

---

[171] C.G. Richards, *Ludwig Krapf: Missionary and Explorer*, Nairobi: East African Literature Bureau, n.d. [Summary of 88 pages A5 of Krapf's *Travels, Researches* (1860); chapters 6, 7, 8, 10 are on Rebmann's 4 journeys in 1848/1849].

[172] Martin Weishaupt, *Rebmanns Reisen im Dschaggaland - Mit 7 Abbildungen*, Leipzig: Verlag der Evangelisch-Lutherischen Mission, 1926 [40 pages].

[173] Emma Rebmann/Tyler (née Kent), 'Journal 1852-1856' [A typed manuscript, consisting of 22 pages (A4) of summarised reports]. Cf. Otto Gutmann's translation of portions of Emma's Diary into German, 'Fragmente eines Tagebuches der Frau des Missionars Johannes Rebmann 1952-1957', with a hand-written correction: '1852-1857'. See: Bibliography.

[174] Krapf, *Reisen*, Teil I: S. 195-465, 484, 485, 501; Teil II: S. 1-135, 499-521.

[175] E.g. Letter from Erhardt in Secundra Orphanage at Agra, to CMS, 8 March 1877 [CI/O 103/8].

[176] Cf. Letter from Krapf 16 Sept. 1849; Mayer, 'Erhardt', in *Zeitschrift des Zabergäuvereins*, 1960, no 3, S. 36, 47; Eber, *Krapf*, S. 141.

Erhardt and Rebmann

The surviving newcomer, Johann Jakob Erhardt, was from Bönnigheim in Württemberg, where he was born on 17 April 1823.[177] He was a BM-B alumnus with 'some medical training'.[178] Erhardt was to stay in East Africa for six years. After his return in June, Rebmann immediately started to extend their house with a 'dwelling place' for his new colleague.[179] Erhardt had arrived just in time to have an experience of cooperation with Krapf, who was to end his permanent presence in Africa, and leave the service of CMS. Before Krapf's departure for Europe, in 1850, he took Erhardt with him on a voyage to the south as far as Cabo Delgado. They started on 4 February. At Niali there was a problem with the boat, Krapf almost drowned. They passed Kilwa with its market where thousands of slaves were sold who had been captured in the Lake Nyasa region. On their way back they visited Zanzibar, and returned to Rabai/Kisuludini on 23 March.[180]

Erhardt and Rebmann thought about and discussed the geography of the interior of Africa, which was not accurately known at that time. Together they tried to make a map of Central Africa. Rebmann's version was published in Germany in the *Calwer Missionsblatt* in 1855. It showed the southern half of the African continent. Its centre consisted of a region called Unyamwezi and a vast lake. Rebmann referred to a more detailed map, made by himself and Erhardt, of only the interior of Africa with its supposed lake. Together with an explanatory text it was published in England by the CMS *Intelligencer* in 1855 and in Germany in the *Calwer Missionsblatt*,[181] and by Petermann in 1856.[182] Petermann defended Erhardt

---

[177] The only substantial survey of his life, which I found, is based on German secondary sources: Ernst Mayer, 'Missionar Johann Jakob Erhardt aus Bönnigheim 1825-1901: Einem vergessenen Afrika-Pionier zum Gedächtnis', in: *Zeitschrift des Zabergäuvereins*, Güglingen, 1960, no 3, S. 33-48.
[178] Sundkler and Steed, *A History of the Church in Africa*, p. 517.
[179] In a note of September 1849 Rebmann says that the building kept him busy from his return on 27 June until September.
[180] Krapf, *Reisen* II, S. 171-194; cf. Eber, *Krapf*, S. 142-144.
[181] Mayer, 'Erhardt', in *Zeitschrift des Zabergäuvereins*, 1960, no 3, S. 42-46; BMM, 1861, S. 32.
[182] August Petermann, *Mittheilungen über wichtige Forschungen auf dem Gesamtgebiete der Geographie*, Gotha: Justus Perthes, 1856. Petermann included: I. J.Erhardt, Mémoire zur Erläuterung der von ihm und J. Rebmann zusammengestellten Karte von Ost- und Central-Afrika; II.W.Desborough Cooley's 'Bemerkungen' i.e. his rejection of the findings of Erhardt and Rebmann; III.Petermann's own

and Krapf against onesided criticism by geographers Cooley and Schirren. He valued the contribution they had made to geographical science of the interior of Africa.[183] In his German Journal of 1858 (and its English version of 1860) Krapf included news about the maps. In their attempt to clarify the geographical characteristics of Central Africa the missionaries inspired explorers and geographers in their scholarly research of Africa's interior. Soon it would be discovered that the supposed interior lake in reality was a chain of lakes from Lake Victoria Nyanza through Lake Tanganyika to the Malawian lakes.

The missionaries knew about the Nyasa region and its lake, and the people living west of it. At that time the Jumbes of Nkhotakota had extended the slave-trade into the interior of present-day Malawi, and the Yao, notorious for their intermediary role in the slave-trade, had started to convert to Islam, and to migrate into the south of Malawi. At first Erhardt and Rebmann's maps were considered disdainfully by the geography experts at home. Cooley, who had criticised Rebmann because of his observation of snow on Kilimanjaro, now ridiculed the maps by Erhardt and Rebmann.[184] Yet the descriptions by the missionaries attracted a lot of positive attention. Some explorers like Burton and Speke were sent by the British *Royal Geographic Society* to East Africa, and met with Rebmann in person. When they had had 'a peep at the snowy Kilimanjaro Mountain' and had done some checking of the missionaries' map in the interior, they were able to correct 'our usually sedate though speculative carpet-geographers' at home.[185]

Erhardt collected vocabulary of the languages spoken by the tribes in their map of the interior. The political confusion in Usambara, where he stayed after Krapf had failed to establish a mission station there, largely limited him to linguistic research in preparation for later missionary effort. His informants were slaves, traded by the Swahili-Arabs. They explained the routes to Unyamwezi and Lake Nyasa. Apart from wordlists in Kimakua, the language of the Makua people to the south-east of Lake Nyasa, in Kisamba and in Kinyamwezi, Erhardt compiled a vocabulary of the language of the Loikop people. This was a language between Semitic and Hamitic, spoken by a pastoralist society who dominated the plains of the

---

Bemerkungen, generally in defence of the missionaries on scholarly grounds; IV.Petermann's notes in answer to critical comments by C. Schirren.

[183] On Rebmann's death in 1877, Petermann said: 'Wir beklagen in Rebmann einen um die Geographie Ost-Afrikas hochverdienten Mann', in: August Petermann, *Mittheilungen über wichtige Forschungen auf dem Gesamtgebiete der Geographie*, Gotha: Justus Perthes, vol. 23, 1877, S. 170.

[184] Cf. Mayer, 'Erhardt', in *Zeitschrift des Zabergäuvereins*, 1960, 'No. 3, S. 44-45.

[185] John Hanning Speke, *Journal*, January 1857.

4. With Johann Ludwig Krapf (1846-1855)

Rift Valley. These people were also known as Wakuafi (or Wakwavi). One of their sub-tribes, the Masai, became most powerful.[186] Krapf had started a collection of their vocabulary.[187] Erhardt made his own collection, with the help of his Masai informant Arnsha Kuba.[188] The nomadic Masai often threatened the peoples on the coast and the CMS mission station. Not only Krapf and Erhardt but also Rebmann collected useful information on the Masai, during his journeys inland in 1848 and 1849. In the next chapter we will see that the Rebmanns temporarily had to leave Rabai/Kisuludini when the Masai attacked Mombasa and its hinterland in 1855 and 1857.

Before he left Africa in 1853 Krapf had persuaded Erhardt to continue his work in Usambara and try to realise the chain of mission stations. In 1853/1854 Erhardt was in Usambara. He was forced by the Sultan to withdraw to Tanga, on the coast, opposite the island of Pemba. He was troubled by health problems, and by the experience of the hostility of people, backed by proud Muslim authorities, who preferred his gifts to hearing the Word of salvation. For a time he worked on collecting vocabulary, mainly of Kisamba. Ill-health and the political situation compelled him to go back to Kisuludini. He and Rebmann felt strongly that the time for the interior had not yet come; they wanted to concentrate on the coast.[189] In 1855 Erhardt was withdrawn by CMS, first to Germany, where he married Marie Dürr, daughter of the first Württemberg alumnus of the Basler Mission. Subsequently, in 1856 the CMS posted him to India. Erhardt compiled hymnaries in Hindustani and worked in the orphanage Secundra and various other places until 1891. He died in Stuttgart on 14 August 1901.[190]

---

[186] Christian Jennings, 'Beyond Eponymy: The Evidence for Loikop as an Ethnonym in Nineteenth Century East Africa', in: *History in Africa* 32, 2005, p. 199-220.

[187] J.L. Krapf, 'Vocabulary of the Engutuk Ekoilob or the Wakuafi-Nation in the Interior of Equatorial Africa', Tübingen, 1854; J.L.Krapf, 'Kurze Beschreibung der Masai- und Wakuafi-Stämme im Südöstlichen Afrika' Ausland 30, 1857, S. 437-442, 461-466; Jennings, 'Beyond Eponymy', p. 199, Krapf used Lemasegnot, a Loikop slave who had been sold to Mombasa, and much later Justin Lemenye as informants.

[188] Johann Erhardt, 'Vocabulary of the Enguduk Illoigob as Spoken by the Masai-Tribes in East Africa', Ludwigsburg 1857 [CMS CA5/O16]; CMS, *Intelligencer*, April 1855, p. 96: Report by Erhardt after he had left Tanga (Usambara) in October 1854. Many slaves in the slave markets 'from Mosambique to Mombasa were from the tribes of Lake Nyasa, the 'Wamakua, Waniasa, Wahio, Wamgindo'; cf. Mayer, 'Erhardt', in *Zeitschrift des Zabergäuvereins*, 1960, No. 3, S. 42.

[189] CMS, *Proceedings 1853-1854*, p. 52-54, *1854-1855*, p. 57-59; Eber, *Krapf*, S. 161 (Krapf, *Reisen* I, 452f).

[190] Mayer, 'Erhardt', in *Zeitschrift des Zabergäuvereins*, 1960, No. 3, S. 45; CMS, *Proceedings 1858-1859*, S. 56, 57.

Conflicting visions

Differences in missionary approach and character had led to disagreements between Krapf and Rebmann. Erhardt sided with Rebmann. He agreed with Rebmann that a congregation of Christians had to be established in the coastal region first. He also thought that poverty and slavery were important hindrances to the spreading of the Gospel and that their eradication had to be prioritised.[191]

Eber thinks that the missionaries did yet not openly clash at this time.[192] Yet together with health problems the looming conflict formed part of the background of Krapf's departure in 1850. He wanted to seek support in Europe. He desired to convince the home front of the feasibility of his vision of a chain of mission stations across Africa. This ideal he pursued in relentless efforts of publishing and travelling. In June he arrived in Europe. Visiting his contacts in England, Germany and Switzerland he commuted between those countries. In Switzerland he saw Josenhans, the new Inspektor of the Basler Mission. In Germany he met his friends of the Hahn community, and was in the house of their leader Kolb for three weeks. He also went to Tübingen, where his Swahili grammar and a vocabulary of six African languages went to press, and to Berlin, where the Prussian King Friedrich Wilhelm IV together with other celebrities, e.g. geographer Alexander von Humboldt and egyptologist Richard Lepsius, received him at a banquet and honoured him because of his discoveries. In England he stayed in the house of CMS secretary Venn for two weeks, and he was received by the British elite, including Queen Victoria's husband Albert von Sachsen-Coburg-Gotha, Prime Minister Palmerston and Archbishop of Canterbury Sumner.

Krapf's meeting with the CMS Committee for East Africa in Islington, in January 1851, resulted in seemingly contradictory consequences. First, it led to his 'valedictory dismissal'. We do not know the exact reason, and whether the initiative to this important decision came from the CMS Committee or from Krapf. Remarkably Krapf's biographer Jochen Eber is silent on the dismissal, although he reports the meeting with the CMS Committee.[193] In the *Proceedings* it says that Krapf 'disconnected himself from the Missions of the Society by his family circumstances'.[194] Practically it was a kind of retirement, which gave him time for convalescence.

---

[191] Mayer, 'Erhardt', in *Zeitschrift des Zabergäuvereins*, 1960, No. 3, S. 37, 38.
[192] Eber, *Krapf*, S. 136, 137.
[193] Eber, *Krapf*, S. 147.
[194] CMS, *Proceedings 1860-1861*, p. 55-59.

4. With Johann Ludwig Krapf (1846-1855) 69

Besides it allowed him more freedom for his missionary approach, without the CMS being directly responsible.[195] In general the CMS sympathised with Krapf's missiological drive and erudition, but apparently his approach and the policy of the CMS, devised by its new secretary Henry Venn, did not fully agree with one another. However, the CMS continued to give him assignments and to support him. Finally, in 1856 Krapf asked for complete retirement from active CMS service.[196]

Immediately after his 'valedictory dismissal' Krapf went to Basel and the St. Chrischona Piligrim Mission in Switzerland in order to recruit new helpers. In 1851 he left for East Africa again, accompanied by two Basler brothers, C. Pfefferle and C. Diehlmann (Dihlmann), ordained by the Bishop of London. On their way they were joined by three other Germans, craftsmen from St. Chrischona, a carpenter Hagenmann, a farmer Kaiser, and a blacksmith Peter Martin Metzler.[197] They were to open mission stations in Usambara, Teita and Ukambani.[198] The journey had an unhappy ending. Shortly after their arrival in Mombasa on 3 April 1851 Pfefferle died of fever, and Kaiser and Metzler experienced a period of serious illness before returning home. Only Krapf's favourite Hagenmann stayed some time longer. Before their arrival in Mombasa, Diehlmann had left the party and returned to Germany. BM-Principal Josenhans explained to the CMS the reasons of Diehlmann's separation from the CMS. His decision was not only inspired by the thoughts of the *Altlutherans*, whom he joined at home, a group that had separated from the Lutheran Church:

> Also 'I believe that my dear Dr Krapf has a share in the cause. He is as I perceive from his letter [Diehlmann's or Krapf's?] somewhat prejudiced against brethren educated in missionary seminaries and may have given them to feel rather too much his own superiority.[199]

Soon after Krapf's return to Africa from his first visit to Europe the missionaries openly clashed. Rebmann and Erhardt had bought more than 30 acres, and had built two spacious houses for married couples at Kisuludini, which would be the new centre for the mission work. They had also started the practice of agriculture. Krapf criticised them for these activi-

---

[195] AMZ, 1882, S. 296, refers to the farewell ceremony at Islington on 2 January 1851.
[196] Letter from Krapf to the CMS, 22 May 1856 [CMS C A5/O16/121]; cf. Eber, *Krapf*, S. 180, 181.
[197] EH, 1851, September, No. 9, S. 75, 76, quotes from Krapf's account of his journey to Aden and then to Rabai; cf. Eber, *Krapf*, S. 147; Krapf, *Reisen* I, S. 448-449.
[198] CMS, *Proceedings 1850-1851*, p. xcvii-cxxvi; CMS, *Proceedings 1851-1852*, p. 59-64.
[199] Letter from Josenhans to the CMS Committee, 9 August 1851 [G/AC 16/69].

ties. He thought the houses fixed the missionaries at Kisuludini in a luxurious position and it endangered the execution of his idea of a chain of mission stations. Krapf complained that Rebmann and Erhardt had settled in their new houses, whereas he himself remained in his old hut, being involved in daily evangelising to the people, thus implying that his colleagues were not faithful to their calling whereas he was.[200] He said that missionaries, when they had begun to live in good houses, were not ready to be mobile anymore. Then they were tempted 'just to sit in their nice little room, to sit and to smoke, they establish a school, write books, in brief the missionary spirit is apt to cool down'. Krapf not only criticised the building of good houses, but he also condemned any outward improvement or alteration that could direct the missionary to secondary matters and distract him from direct missionary work, i.e. from visiting people in their huts and proclaiming the Word of God to them. In his view concentration on schoolwork, language work, and industrial activities could weaken or stop the missionary's 'direct attack against heathenism by spurring people through the Word of the cross'.[201]

Krapf's reproaches do not seem fully honest if one considers he departed from East Africa in 1853 and permanently withdrew from practical mission work in 1855. The last 26 years of his life he mainly devoted to the linguistic and literary activities that he condemned in Rebmann and Erhardt in 1851. Eber notes that after 1855 Krapf for at least a period suffered from spiritual fatigue, and lost his desire for mission.[202] After 1855 it was Rebmann, not his critic Krapf, who remained at his remote mission post in East Africa for another 20 years.

In some letters Krapf informed the CMS about his serious dissatisfaction. He said that Rebmann and Erhardt did not want to obey his advice, because they were 'too young and unexperienced', and were hindered by a 'German spirit of independence and wilfulness'. They should first travel into the interior, and not first build houses and marry on the coast. Krapf said he was filled with 'holy anger' by their worldliness and disobedience.[203] Especially Erhardt was the target of Krapf's criticism. He had influenced Rebmann to an easy life of 'reading books and papers and smoking cigars'.[204] Mockingly he called him 'our missionary architect', who

---

[200] Eber, *Krapf*, S. 161.
[201] Krapf, *Reisen*, I, S. 448-450.
[202] Eber, *Krapf*, S. 123; Krapf, Reisen, I S. 270.
[203] Letter from Krapf in Rabai to CMS secretary Venn, 10 April 1851 [CMS CA5/O16/88].
[204] Letter from Krapf to the CMS, 22 April 1852 [CMS CA5/O16/91].

4. With Johann Ludwig Krapf (1846-1855)

wanted to build a chapel at Rabai but first should make a chapel in the hearts of the people by preaching the Gospel to them.[205] Krapf informed the CMS that Erhardt had dragged Rebmann from the right track and proposed that he be transferred to Bombay.[206] Rebmann should not listen to Erhardt, and he should pray more and be more diligent in his missionary work.[207] Even after settling in Korntal in 1855, Krapf continued to pressurize his colleagues through letters to the CMS. He wrote that Erhardt's plans for settling in good houses and evangelising from a fixed position had changed Rebmann's mind in the wrong direction. Krapf claimed that Rebmann was persuaded by Erhardt to propose the termination of the mission field in East Africa.[208] In the German and English versions of his *Travels, Researches* of respectively 1858 and 1860 he publicly attacked Rebmann by suggesting that the real work of the CMS mission had been endangered in 1850/1851 when Rebmann had refused to travel inland but spent most of the time building a permanent house.[209] After 1860, when a small church had emerged, Krapf had to admit that God had worked though 'the faith, patience and perseverance' of his humble servant Rebmann. At the same time, however, he found that Rebmann still lacked a 'burning missionary spirit'.[210] Of course these words in his letters to London were highly suggestive. Krapf pictured his colleagues as lukewarm or disobedient Christians, thus damaging their image before the CMS. He accused his fellow-missionaries of not having evangelised the Nika-people, and of prioritising the Christian cultural mandate to the detriment of the message of reconciliation. He said that they waited for the natives to start thirsting after the Gospel by trying to rouse their interest by teaching them agriculture.[211] His main reproach was that Rebmann withheld the mission from penetrating into the interior.

Rebmann was not captivated by Krapf's grand design.[212] He was convinced that the time for going into the interior of Africa had not yet

---

[205] Letter from Krapf to the CMS, 11 September 1852 [CMS CA5/O16/92].
[206] Letter from Krapf to the CMS, March 1853 [CMS CA5/O16/93].
[207] Letter from Krapf in Cairo to the CMS, 15 January 1855 [CMS CA5/O16/112].
[208] Letter from Krapf in Korntal to the CMS, 6 August 1855 [CMS CA5/O16/115].
[209] Krapf, *Reisen* I, S. 449-450; Krapf, *Travels, Researches*, p. 508; cf. R.C. Bridges, 'A Manuscript Kinika Vocabulary and a letter of J.L. Krapf', in: Bulletin of the Society for African Church History, vol. 2, No. 4, 1968, p. 295.
[210] Letter from Krapf in Mombasa, 17 April 1862 [CMS CA5/O16/133].
[211] Letter from Krapf to the CMS, 25 September 1855 [CMS CA5/O16/155]. Cf. Eber, *Krapf*, S. 180.
[212] Krapf, *Reisen* II, S. 87-89; cf. Sundkler and Steed, *A History of the Church in Africa*, p. 518.

come. He wanted to consolidate on the coast. In the opinion of Rebmann and Erhardt, Krapf's three handworkers who had come with him from Europe, two whom had fallen ill in the mean time, were useless because they were strangers to the African culture and language, and their work could be done by Africans.[213] Probably it took a long time before Rebmann read the offending passages in Krapf's *Travels, Researches*, and perhaps never became fully aware of Krapf's letters to the CMS that blackened him. Only at a later stage did he start to defend himself in more detail.

Krapf's last attempts

Krapf held to his idea of a chain of mission stations. Eber says that he threatened to cut connections with the CMS if they would not support his strategy.[214] This sounds a bit strange because since his dismissal he had formally ceased to be a CMS employee. Krapf tried to deploy his next mission station from Kisuludini. It was to be at Yata, '110 hours' from Kisuludini, with the Kamba people in Ukambani, North-West of Mombasa. He had visited the Kamba people before, together with Rebmann in 1848, and alone in November 1849. This had left favourable impressions. From a distance he saw Mount Kilimanjaro, and he was the first European to see Mount Kenya. His meeting with Chief Kivoi at Kitui had been promising. In Krapf's mind the Kamba people had replaced the Galla as a key-people for access to the interior of Africa, 'who seemed particularly endowed to take the Gospel to both neighbouring and distant peoples'.[215] He 'saw the mobile and enterprising Kamba as the potential missionary agents of Kenya'.[216] However, the new expedition to Ukambani, which started on 11 July 1851, miscarried utterly. The Kamba people had become hostile, and his guide and helper Chief Kivoi was killed. His Nika helpers fled, the subjects of Kivoi blamed him for the death of their chief, he was robbed of all his luggage, and barely escaped with his life. In September 1851 he was back in Rabai Mpia. Eber says that it began to dawn upon Krapf that the whole of his strategy had failed.[217]

Now that access into the interior through Ukambani was blocked, Krapf made other attempts, through Usambara south-west of Mombasa. He had been there initially together with Rebmann in 1848, and had met

---

[213] cf. Eber, *Krapf*, S. 149-151 (Krapf, *Reisen* I, S. 448, 449).
[214] Eber, *Krapf*, S. 151.
[215] Eber, *Krapf*, S. 137-141 (Krapf, *Reisen* II, S. 136-169); Sundkler and Steed, *A History of the Church in Africa*, p. 456.
[216] Sundkler and Steed, *A History of the Church in Africa*, p. 517.
[217] Eber, *Krapf*, S. 151-157 (Krapf, *Reisen* II, S. 195-254).

4. With Johann Ludwig Krapf (1846-1855)

with King Kmeri in his capitals Fuga and Salla. In 1852 we see Krapf again in Usambara, attempting to establish in Fuga, the beginning of his chain of mission stations into the interior. He was accompanied by Hagenmann, one of the St. Chrischona handworkers who he had brought with him from Europe, who he considered his 'spiritual brother',[218] and by catechumen Abe Gunja. The enterprise miscarried. There was strong Muslim opposition, and King Kmeri refused to have a mission station on his territory. However, Krapf did not accept reality; in his view Usambara could be accessed by the mission. In 1853 he tried to introduce Erhardt to the Usambara, and charged him to continue the work. In October 1853 Krapf himself had to give up, plagued again by weak health. He also felt offended by the treatment he had received from some chiefs and from the Sultan's Governor, who demanded ever more money for allowing him to travel into the interior.[219] Consequently on 25 September 1853 Krapf left and undertook his second journey to Europe. By Christmas he was back in Germany, and he settled in Korntal, from where he continued to propagate his missionary approach to his friends in England, Germany and Switzerland.

The CMS Committee in London had not ceased to have confidence in Krapf. Though 'perplexed' by the miscarriage of his recent attempts, they were 'not in despair'. Their hopes of a chain of missions across the continent of Africa were 'for a time cast down, but not destroyed'. Although Krapf was not a CMS employee anymore, they waited 'for a personal interview' with him before deciding 'upon the measures which may be adopted for the revival of the East Africa Mission'.[220] In April 1854 Krapf appeared before the Committee with his report. In the subsequent vote some members voted for discontinuation of the East African mission field, but the majority decided in favour of continuation, and even of the sending of additional personnel, i.e. Gottfried Deimler from Bavaria.[221]

Although formally the CMS Committee had not given up their East African mission, it took a long time before a new vision of missionary policy was born. From 1855 to 1860 the *Proceedings* of the CMS were almost completely silent on Rebmann and the mission station at Kisuludini, apart

---

[218] Eber, *Krapf*, S. 157; Krapf, *Reisen* I, S. 451, says on 0078 'Sein demütiger, offener, tätiger, zum Dienen und Helfen bereitwilliger Charakter gereichte mir zu besonderer Freude und Stärkung in Rabai Mpya'. Hagenmann returned to Germany in 1852.

[219] Eber, *Krapf*, 157-162 (Krapf, *Reisen* II, S. 278-320); Rebmann/Tyler (née Kent), *Journal*, p. 2 (1853).

[220] CMS, *Proceedings 1853-1854*, p. 54; cf. CMS, *Record*, January 1853, p. 1-4.

[221] Eber, *Krapf*, S. 164 (Krapf, *Reisen* I, S. 461f).

from the information that it was 'suspended', because of the 'unsettled state of the country' and that the missionaries had been removed to 'a place of safety'.²²²

This was not yet the end of Krapf's activities in Africa or even in the Mombasa area. He continued, concentrating on writing in his travel journals and on editing the Swahili and Nika dictionaries, which had been continually expanded by the collection work of Rebmann. In a final attempt to reach the Galla, and from there connect to Mombasa as a station in the chain of missions, Krapf shifted his attention to his first love, Ethiopia. Blessed by the CMS Board and by the Anglican bishop of Jerusalem, Samuel Gobat, together with his friend Johann Martin Flad and some students of the St. Chrischona Institute near Basel, in November 1854 he travelled via Cairo to Abyssinia, where he was hospitably received by King Tewodros. However, the king's war with Shoa frustrated Krapf's attempt in 1855 to go down to the Galla and Somali.²²³ In September 1855 he was back again in Württemberg, affected in bodily health, but mentally unbroken.²²⁴

Krapf's connection with the Swiss St. Chrischona Pilgrim Mission interacted with his missionary vision and method. The St. Chrischona institute was indirectly related to the Basler Mission, as both were started by the same person, Christian Friedrich Spittler, respectively in 1815 and 1840. Both were faith missions, not organisationally linked to one denomination. Yet they were different, because the Basler Mission prepared missionaries through theological training to be preachers of the Word, whereas St. Chrischona included craftsmen and Christian families to serve in the mission field through example, as pilgrims. For a long time Krapf expected that through this institute he could realise his 'chain' concept. In 1857 he became their Inspektor or Secretary. He moved the old idea of Spittler of an apostles' street (*Apostelstraße*), by planning and directing a 'pilgrim mission' from Jerusalem and then creating a chain of stations from Alexandria up the Nile to Gondar, then through Ethiopia to Mombasa, from where in an earlier stage he had planned a chain of mission stations across Sub-Saharan Africa to the Atlantic. Krapf was charged with the realisation of the idea of the Apostelstraße, and he

---

[222] Cf. *Proceedings 1854-1855*, p. 57-59, *1855-1856*, p. 53-54, *1856-1857*, p. 50-51, *1857-1858*, p. 65, *1858-1859*, p. 56-57, *1859-1860*, p. 60.

[223] BMM, 1856, IV, S. 76-110: Albert Ostertag, 'Die Reise des Missionars Dr. Krapf nach Abessinien im Jahre 1855'; IV, S. 111-183: extracts from Krapf's diary of his journey of 1854/1855. CMS, *Proceedings 1855-1856*, p. 53-54.

[224] Cf. Eber, *Krapf*, S. 167-179.

4. With Johann Ludwig Krapf (1846-1855)

wrote a Programme for it, printed 1863. It contained plans for the establishment of the stations St Matthew in Alexandria, St. Mark at Cairo, St. Paul at Metemma (Sudan), St. Thomas at Khartum (Sudan), St. Peter at Aswan, and others.[225] The programme was partly realised in the period 1860-1866. According to Sundkler, of the twelve stations along the Nile only the first two became a reality, St Matthew in Alexandria and St Mark in Cairo.[226] They existed for some time. Krapf's journey to Ethiopia was meant to organise connecting stations. However, the whole plan miscarried, and the stations had to be abandoned, because when the main donor withdrew, St. Chrischona's pilgrim mission was unable to keep up the finances. Moreover, Krapf's mission to Ethiopia had become a failure.

Krapf did not give up. Once again he found an ally, the United Methodist Free Churches. This denomination had planned to start mission work among the Galla, starting from East Africa. Krapf offered assistance and in autumn 1861 he was on his way to Zanzibar with two Methodist missionaries and two St. Chrischona craftsmen. They received permission from the new Sultan Sayyid Majid. By that time Krapf's group, through defection and disease, had decreased to one missionary, Thomas Wakefield. Apparently Krapf saw no problem in establishing the new Methodist station only 25 km north of Mombasa, at Ribe, very close to Rebmann's Kisuludini![227]

Krapf returned to Ethiopia only once more, for a few months, as an interpreter for the British army that under General Robert Napier in the tragic battle of Magdala beat the Ethiopian army of King Tewodros in April 1868.[228] The expedition was meant to liberate a number of missionaries, e.g. the Flad family, whom the king had imprisoned and misused for forced labour, e.g. as gunmakers.[229] This military adventure in a colonial war concluded his presence in Africa and was more or less an anti-climax of his career as a missionary. The same year his wife Charlotte Pelargus died.

---

[225] Eber, *Krapf*, S. 7, 199, 200. Cf. Andreas Baumann, *Die Apostelstraße Eine aussergewöhnliche Vision und ihre Verwirklichung*, Biblische Archäologie und Zeitgeschichte, 8, Gießen: Brunnen, 1999.

[226] Sundkler, *A History of the Church in Africa*, p. 519; cf. 154, 303, 510.

[227] AMZ, 1887, 185-191.

[228] Bengt Sundkler and Christoffer Steed, *A History of the Church in Africa*, p. 61, 62; Steven Paas, *Christianity in Eurafrica*, Wellington: CLF, 2016/ Washington: NAP, 2017, p. 316-318.

[229] Cf. Eber, *Krapf*, S. 206-217. Krapf was employed as a guide and a translator, for 600 pounds.

For the rest of his life until 1881, we see him, cared for by his new wife Nanette Schmid (since 1869), in Korntal[230] with a colony of Pietists, being active with translation work for the British and Foreign Bible Society,[231] with fundraising for the St. Chrischona Institute,[232] and with his literary corpus, writing about journeys, geography, languages, and dreams of the 'apostles' street' or the 'chain of missions'.

Mission impossible

Experiences during his journeys into Jagga-land and disagreements with Krapf had contributed to Rebmann's conviction that the East African mission field first of all needed consolidation in the Mombasa area, and patient in-depth evangelism for many years. There was not to be a penetration of mission into the interior of Africa without a solid base on the coast. Moreover, he became convinced that Christian mission could not succeed without removing the reality of Muslim rule, which facilitated slavery and the slave-trade. In his view Krapf's vision lacked understanding of the real situation and of the fundamental requirements for mission in East Africa.

In 1854, after Krapf's departure, in a report to the CMS, Rebmann looked back at the events of recent years. Explaining the consequences of Krapf's approach, he told about Erhardt's painful experiences in Usambara, where he had been sent by Krapf. Erhardt's story was an 'unbroken tale of miseries'. In Tanga he 'more than Krapf and I suffered in East Africa ... A missionary suffers more than a soldier or a sailor, a missionary remains in the field, whereas a soldier can leave after the battle'. He quoted Moffat's words on missionaries who have to stay for a long time, that 'these sufferings do not vanish by the light of Gospel Day.' He also quoted a visiting physician from England, 'How could you have remained so long in such a wretched country?' Erhardt's health had not been good. That is why Rebmann had urged him to return to the mission station at Kisuludini.[233]

In his explanation of the reason for Erhardt's return from Usambara, Rebmann wanted to defend himself against Krapf's accusation that he

---

[230] In Korntal Krapf lived at Görlitzstrasse 13; cf. F.Grünzweig, 'Johannes Rebmann', S. 2.
[231] Eber, *Krapf*, S. 219-229.
[232] Eber, *Krapf*, S. 184-199.
[233] Half-year account from Rebmann in Kisuludini, 19 (?) September 1854 [CMS/B/OMS/C A5 O24/16A].

4. With Johann Ludwig Krapf (1846-1855)

protected Erhardt on ill gounds,[234] and that Erhardt and Rebmann by deviating from Krapf's plan had opposed CMS instructions. Krapf had blackened Erhardt's reputation in various letters to the CMS. He had also caused BM-Principal Josenhans to write to the CMS in this vein. Josenhans blamed Erhardt for being behind this supposed act of insurrection: 'Of this I am sure Erhardt is alone the cause, who seems to be wanting of the real missionary spirit'.[235] Rebmann rejected this accusation. He backed Erhardt, and commented on Krapf and his vision as follows (in summary):

> 'Dr Krapf never stayed in Usambara any longer than he required for delivering up his ... presents', without 'getting acquainted to the wretched state of things in that country. ... A few speeches to the king and his councillors are not enough. Africans do not believe us at face value, think we are liars just as they themselves. Years, years are required before even a shadow of a conviction is forming in their dark minds, that we unlike them really mean what we say. A missionary therefore, who does not mean to stay himself [in] a country [that] he has thus opened by presents, had far better have left it altogether. If he travels, let him do so, without engaging himself or others ... except [for the things] that can be done at once, for if only one year should elapse, some presents must be given again'. The goal must be a mission station. Distinguish between what can be done at once and what takes time. For now, 'have a sober view', there are too many difficulties for stations in the Interior. There would be no possibility for good communication with them from Rabai, e.g. for sending letters (carriers is unsafe and requires a lot of money, presents, and letters often are not delivered), or for employing servants (they do not want to look like slaves). Life is at risk in the hands of savage chiefs, who 'turn into all powerful beggars'. 'I wonder now how we could ever talk of a chain of missions to be established through the whole breadth of the Continent in a way as if we had all the advantages, securities and facilities of British power and influence at our command.'[236]

Apart from his doubt whether missionary activity depending on the favour of Muslim rulers in East Africa was feasible, Rebmann believed that God in his own proper time would give fruit to the work they did in East Africa. God does not depend on our plans and activity, however well-meant and powerful they are. Krapf on the other hand wanted to see

---

[234] Cf. Letter from Krapf, March 1853 [CMS CA5/O16/93].
[235] Letter from Josenhans to CMS secretary Venn, 9 August 1851 [G/AC O16/69].
[236] Half-year account from Rebmann in Kisuludini, 19 (?) September 1854 [CMS/B/OMS/C A5 O24/16A].

fruits in direct and immediate relationship to his efforts. Rebmann gave an example:

> 'In 1851, when he went to establish a mission in Ukambani, Krapf told me he would consider it as his own fault if there should be no converts within the very first year of his labours. I said I did not think so, people here were too thoroughly ignorant. What was the result? There were not only no converts, but the missionary himself returned after a few months, simply because he had found no house to live in, and would take no time to build one.'[237]

Rebmann was convinced that 'a missionary who is not able or willing to give himself first to the work of building [for] himself a proper dwelling house, will not be the right one for this part of the world'.[238] His uncompromising criticism did not please the CMS Committee. Although they had not fully backed Krapf's missionary methods, and had formally dismissed him, they thought a lot of his expertise, and wanted to uphold a good relationship.

The CMS Committee frowned even more at Rebmann's critical remarks on the very existence of the mission field in the Mombasa area itself. He tried to explain to the CMS secretaries in London that for the missionaries life was unsafe in Muslim-ruled East Africa. Rebmann, Krapf, and Erhardt had experienced that they lacked protection, and that their credibility was undermined. Because of this Rebmann suggested the temporary interruption of some sensitive activities in the mission field until the termination of the power of the Sultanate and the slave-trade by European countries.

> 'It becomes more and more my conviction that no missionary work can be carried on in East Africa to any great extent before the sons of Japhet have taken it under their rule and government'. Until then do the missionaries have to leave or to stay? I think that 'unsuspicious staying is possible'. The time could be used for 'reducing the languages to writing of all those slaves in the Mombasa area that represent 'almost every nation and tribe in the Interior'. I expect that there is 'abundant work for at least ten years'.[239]

---

[237] Letter from Rebmann in Mombasa to the CMS Commitee, 2 May 1868 [CMS/B/OMS/C A5 O24/42].

[238] Letter from Rebmann in Mombasa to the CMS Committee, 13 April 1860 [CMS/B/OMS/C A5 O 24/36].

[239] Letter from Rebmann in Kisuludini to CMS secretary Henry Venn, 27 January 1852 [O24/15A].

4. With Johann Ludwig Krapf (1846-1855)

Rebmann pointed to Krapf's and Erhardt's experiences in Usambara and Kadiaro, which showed that mission now to the heathen Samba, Kamba and Nika tribes is very difficult.

> 'We are weak and exposed. Therefore send no new missionaries. For now better send 'all your missionaries to such nations as by Providence have already been taught to cry with the Macedonian: Come over and help us.'[240]

The idea of a moratorium of the sending of missionaries was not well accepted by many Western Christians in the 20th century.[241] It must have sounded offensive in the ears of 19th century mission directors who were inspired by a powerful missionary consciousness. At least they did not like such a proposal coming from their employees in the mission field.

In a statement of November 1854 Rebmann and Erhardt tried to explain to the CMS Committee their difficult position with regard to the Muslims and the adherents of African Traditional Religions. Their credibility was at stake and with it the possibility for mission.

> As the situation is now the heathen people of East Africa find believing a missionary 'a moral impossibility. Why? Because they do not know Christians, but more than that they cannot understand how Europeans who they consider as superior to Arabs and to themselves, at the same time are represented by missionaries who depend on permission by the Muslim rulers in reaching out to heathen tribes who themselves practically are independent from the Muslim Government. This feeling of strangeness is increased by the presents the missionaries give. Consequently 'they suspect the missionaries of being the Portuguese Wasungu of old who want to reoccupy their territories. ... Muslim power is in between the missionaries and the heathen. The heathen see how the missionaries stoop to that power. Consequently they consider the missionaries as fugitives or spies, or people who do not know what to do with themselves and their riches. Therefore they are not believed.'[242]

To what extent the CMS Committee understood the reasoning of their missionaries in East Africa? Apparently they found it difficult to appreciate the situation. Anyway, they were shocked by the conclusion the missionaries drew. It seemed their German employees on Africa's east coast had lost control of their minds, when they said:

---

[240] Idem.
[241] Cf. Paas, *Christianity in Eurafrica*, p. 437, 438.
[242] Rebmann and Erhardt in an evaluation of 'ten years of labour', summarised by the CMS secretaries, point 9, November 1854.

'How will the heathen appropriate our intentions among them 'as long as a Muhamadan power stands between them and us? To them we are with the Muslims who in their eyes are the strongest party. Experience has forced the conviction upon me that the heathen of East Africa need first as much 'being broken with a rod of iron and being dashed in pieces like a potter's vessel' as their brothers in Europe did 'before they will prove fit material for missionary labour'. The heathen consider us as liars, with contempt, 'this all by no means for the sake of the Gospel. Therefore, had not East Africa 'for the present better be left until providential changes in its political and social aspects, perhaps similar to those in the West and the South will have taken place?'

Rebmann tried to bring home to his employers that the missionaries were in between two dangerous fires. Basically the slave-trade hampered their work. On the one hand, 'the Muhamedan government finds us dangerous', because by our opposition to its trade we decrease 'the resource from which it has to drag out its existence'. On the other hand the Africans despised the missionaries because of their apparent dependence on the Muslim rulers, which in their eyes boiled down to an alliance between the 'Wasungu' (Europeans) and the Arab slave-traffickers. 'They find it a disgrace to be servants of a Msungu. Erhardt told that even those who are very poor and wanted to be fed by him, refused to feed grass to his donkey, although it would have given them enough food for 2 or 3 days'. Rebmann urged the CMS Committee to answer quickly to his urgent question 'in order to be relieved from the painful uncertainty about our position'. He also suggested the Committee to pay a visit to the mission field.[243]

CMS secretary Venn wrote in the margin of Rebmann's letter: 'What does he mean?' At a distance in London he could not fathom the frustration of a Christian missionary who was held by the Africans for an ally of the Muslim slave-holders and slave-traders by whom they were dominated or ruled. The *Moresby Treaty* of 1822 and the *Hamerton Treaty* of 1845, which the British government had concluded with the Sultan of Zanzibar, was intended to limit the slave-trade, but in practice these pacts legalised internal slavery and the growing slave-trafficking in the coastal dominions and islands of the Sultanate. This created a humiliating situation for the missionaries. Sayyid Said had ruled over the Oman Sultanate since 1804, and in 1840 he shifted his capital from Muscat to Zanzibar. In 1837 Mombasa was added to the Sultanate. The practice of slave-trading met with a lot of criticism from Western diplomats and missionaries, but the

---

[243] Letter from Rebmann in Kisuludini to the CMS Committee, 27 November 1854.

4. With Johann Ludwig Krapf (1846-1855)

Sultan was able to hide behind the treaties with Britain. He cleverly avoided collisions with countries like England, France and America, and acted carefully with their citizens. Others were treated less respectfully.

In May/June 1854 in Mombasa the Rebmanns witnessed an event that showed the political reality in the region. A group of German 'colonizers' consisting of missionaries and farmers of the Hanoverian Hermannsburg Mission, on board of their ship the *Candace*, called a 'floating temple',[244] were refused permission to disembark, although they were sick and lacked food.[245] The group, sent by Ludwig Harms, had passed through their mission station at Port Natal. They wanted to reach the Galla people, starting from Mombasa. However, their status as German citizens did not impress the Muslim rulers of the Sultanate. After some days in Mombasa harbour the suffering Germans sailed back to South Africa. Rebmann, who had helped his fellow Germans as an interpreter, in an account to the CMS used this story as an example to show that Muslim-ruled East Africa does not convert at the desire of some helpless strangers.[246] Rebmann's wife Emma Kent expressed her anger because of the despotic behaviour of the Sultan's governor who forbade his people to assist the unfortunate strangers.[247]

Protest by the missionaries was not backed by Atkin Hamerton, the British consul in Zanzibar, who had to supervise the working of the treaty. Rebmann said that Hamerton did not sympathise with the missionaries, and was 'unconverted'.[248] 'We depend on the English consul, but only if he is interested are we protected'. Lack of support and protection by the consul aggravated their weakness and vulnerability before the Sultan. Apart from having a difficult life in the Mombasa area, access to the interior of Africa was practically denied to the missionaries by the Sultan, and the consul did not provide effective help. Our 'present situation is very unnatural and very unpleasant'.[249] Rebmann wondered 'whether it was ever right to begin a mission under the auspices of a Muhamadan

---

[244] Cf. Gustav Arthur Jehle, in: *Hermannsburger Missionsblatt*, 5 May 1935; cf. Sundkler and Reed, *A History of the Church in Africa*, p. 114.

[245] Rebmann, *Briefe*, 19 September 1854. The Hermannsburg Mission from the (then) Kingdom of Hanover was established by Ludwig Harms in 1849; Eber, *Krapf*, S. 163.

[246] Half-year account by Rebmann to CMS, 19(?) September 1854 [O24/16A].

[247] Rebmann/Tyler (née Kent), *Journal*, p. 4 (1854).

[248] Letter from Rebmann in Kisuludini to CMS secretary Henry Venn, 27 January 1854 [O24/15A].

[249] Letter from Rebmann in Kisuludini to CMS secretary Henry Venn, 25 September 1854.

Prince whose very religion is destructive of all missionary efforts (See 1 John 2, 23)'. On the treaty between London and the Sultan with regard to the slave-trade, he commented, it 'is nothing more, but to throw sand into the eyes of the Christian public, for the slave-trade goes on almost undisturbed'. Rebmann emphatically asked CMS secretary Venn to react: 'This important question I should like to have answered in your next'.[250]

However, it took some time for the CMS to realise how serious the situation was. Only gradually did the Committee come to understand the negative effects of the treaties. In 1869 the secretaries demanded from the British government 'an entire abandonment of all the protective treaties' with the Sultan, and force him to terminate all 'remaining' slave-traffic. The real situation was worse than the CMS even then had begun to realise. It had dawned upon the CMS that the 'treaty of 1845 protects domestic slavery, and the transport of slaves from the African mainland to the islands' of the Sultanate, and that 'consequently until now inland slave-trade has continued on a very large scale'.[251] In addition, there was the reality of an enormous growth of slave-trade from the interior, and the increase of illegal export of slaves by the Sultanate overland to the Somali ports north of it,[252] from where slaves were shipped to clientèle on the Arab and Indian coasts. The CMS memorandum to the Secretary of State for India of February 1869 reflected more precisely the current situation.

> 'The dealers instead of purchasing at Zanzibar, which was an open slave market licensed by the Sultan, procured their cargoes from various parts of the mainland, shipping them for Arabia as opportunity offered to evade the few cruisers on the coast'. Consequently 'the measures instead of checking the trade, aggravated the miseries of the slave, and increased the very cruelties under which the trade is carried on, 'far into the interior'.[253]

---

[250] Letter from Rebmann in Mombasa to CMS secretary Henry Venn, 27 September 1854.

[251] CMS, *Intelligencer*, April 1869, quoting from a pamphlet by CMS secretary Hutchinson: 'The slave-trade of East Africa, is it to continue or to be surpressed?'.

[252] According to CMS, *Intelligencer*, December 1872, the over land transports ran from Lamu, the most northern position of the Sultanate, to the Somali ports. To this end slaves were 'legally' taken from Zanzibar to Lamu, 2804 were counted from 1 May to 12 June 1871.

[253] Memorandum of CMS to the Secretary of State for India, 16 Febr 1869, signed by CMS president Chichester president, and by CMS secretaries Henry Venn, C.C. Fenn, J.Mee, E.Hutchinson, in: CMS, *Intelligencer*, February 1869.

4. With Johann Ludwig Krapf (1846-1855)

By being identified with Muslim-Zanzibar power on the coast the missionaries had lost credibility, and were unable to bring the power of the Gospel and of the Christian culture home to the Africans captured in the darkness of superstitions and witchcraft. Rebmann and Erhardt were convinced that relying on the protection by the Sultanate disabled mission work. Krapf took a different position. With less feeling for building sensitive relationships and in-depth evangelism, and having focused on his 'grand design' of a chain of mission stations, he would even use Muslim power if it were convenient. One of the reasons why his chain should start in Ukambani was that they were 'living in the neighbourhood, and in case of misdemeanour on the part of the people they could be brought to justice by the Governor of Mombas'.[254] In a summary of ten years of missionary labour, Rebmann and Erhardt stressed that only God himself could make East Africa accessible to Christian mission.

> Not the missionary societies, not the most wicked Boers, not the most cruel slave-dealers, but He prepares the field. Like in the South and in the West of this Continent the heathen 'will first be crushed and laid low by His Almighty arm, only then it will present a field for missionary labour'.[255]

Rebmann not only revealed his doubts on the feasibility of the East African mission field to the CMS secretaries in London, he also informed the 'home front' in Germany, by publishing an article in the 'Calwer Missionsblatt' an influential mission magazine. The people at home were entitled to know why practically no converts had yet been made, and why all plans to penetrate into the interior had failed. People should also understand why, for the time being, for the mission at Kisuludini/Rabai it was more important to concentrate on language work, i.e. translating the Scriptures into the local languages and collecting vocabulary, than making futile efforts to reach people who could not yet be reached. Practically 'only literary work is left to them', until the conditions change.

Josenhans' comment

Rebmann's article in the *Calwer Missionsblatt* was a letter that accompanied the map, made by Erhardt and him, which he wanted to publish. Editor Christian Gottlob Barth[256] had added the letter to the map as an im-

---

[254] Letter from Krapf in Korntal, in German, to CMS Committee, 18 March 1876 [G/4/A5/1/2].
[255] Idem.
[256] C.G. Barth (1828-1918).

portant explanation of the situation. The reason why the publication roused a hornet's nest was not so much Rebmann's article, but a rejoinder of it addressed to the German and Swiss Christian public by Krapf. This reaction made the disagreements between Krapf and Rebmann public knowledge. Principal Joseph Friedrich Josenhans[257] of the Basler Mission, worried about the relationship with the CMS, sent a letter to London together with a translation of Rebmann's article, which he disavowed. He said that Rebmann's argument concerning lacking results of the mission field was not right, and that he had exceeded his competence. Others had worked longer before seeing results, e.g. among the peoples of West Africa or among the Maori in New Zealand. The decision of continuing the mission or not was not Rebmann's business but the CMS Committee's.

> 'He is certainly wrong to assert that the East African Mission has no ground of existence, because those tribes are unable to acknowledge the missionary as a messenger of Christ, that the African tribes are under the judgments of God, through which they must pass before they can experience the efficiency of the Gospel, that the country must first be subjected to some Christian government.' ... Even if 'the only conclusion to be drawn is that for a long time no result of the work is to be hoped for, so that the mission to be abandoned forever, ... it is not befitting a missionary to express in public papers his opinion concerning the measures to be adopted in a mission before his Committee has taken a decision about it. ... Mr. Rebmann's letter gave us the impression that he felt it necessary to apologize before the German public for his retirement from the East African Mission'.[258]

Together with 'more judicious men among us' Josenhans was convinced that 'by far not every possible effort has been made to make the Gospel known in East Africa ... It cannot be said that the East African mission must have miscarried because it was premature. On the contrary, more recent events show rather that the time for gracious visitation of Africa is at hand'.

Apparently Josenhans missed Rebmann's point. The issue at stake, according to Rebmann, was not at all to give up the spreading of the Gospel in East Africa, but to shape the conditions that were necessary for it, i.e. the removing of Muslim rule and effective measures to abolish slavery

---

[257] J.F. Josenhans (1812-1884).
[258] Letter from Principal Josenhans in Basel to Henry Venn, 28 Dec. 1855 [G/AC 16/101].

4. With Johann Ludwig Krapf (1846-1855)

and the slave-trade. Josenhans failed to understand the main reason of Rebmann's frustration and his amendments for the mission plan. He suggested that 'the disunion which prevailed among the East African brethren' was 'the deeper cause' of the poor results of the mission field and of 'all its vacillations', at which 'many Christians had taken offence'. At this deeper level his main criticism was directed at Krapf.

> Dr. Krapf instead of continuing his labours at his station and securing a firm footing on the coast, from which he might gradually and step by step have advanced into the interior, formed the plan to penetrate through the centre of Africa as far as the Western coast, an idea which, though it is of great geographical and historical value, has no connection whatever with the viability of the East African Mission. From this emanated the project of establishing a series of missionary stations towards Western Africa, another grand scheme, the execution of which in the form presented by Dr. Krapf we from the first considered as an absolute impossibility. We told him this plainly more than once, but he has had no ear for our remonstrances. We are, however, convinced that it was chiefly owing to these plans that the brethren became disunited. But his health was prematurely injured, and that to all probability he unfitted himself for the prosecution of the mission work'.[259]

Josenhans dissuaded the CMS Committee from giving Krapf another chance in East Africa. If Krapf could make up his mind to remain on the spot and do the work that was needed, he would 'decidedly be the best one for it.'. However, Josenhans realised that Krapf was not likely to do so, 'his thoughts are too wide, he is not stable enough', 'he has no sitting leather'.

> 'He has enough of courage, ... but has he also enough bodily strength and calmness? It does not appear so.' His ideas 'tend too much towards the grand and universal, but in East Africa the work must be commenced on a small scale and extended gradually. The people must not only be instructed in the Word of God, but at the same time civilised. They must also build schools and teach the people to cultivate the ground and trades.'[260]

Barth who was responsible for including Rebmann's article and Krapf's rejoinder, added: 'Krapf 'has a self-denying spirit, but is too unsteady in his mind and cannot stay where he is. He has worn himself out by travelling'.

Showing that he was unbiased, Josenhans did not spare Rebmann and Erhardt his criticism. In his view they too had committed faults.

---

[259] Idem.
[260] Idem.

> 'Instead of being satisfied with a plain dwelling they built a larger house, the construction of which absorbed all their time and strength. Instead of settling in the midst of the people they located themselves at some considerable distance from the village, and then complained that the people did not call on them. The religious meetings begun by Dr. Krapf and enjoying the blessing of the Lord, were discontinued by them, instead of proceeding and progressing on the same foundation. The artists brought over by Dr. Krapf, instead of receiving them with affection, attending to them when ill, and employing them as colonists after their recovery were treated by them almost injuriously and sent away again'.[261]

These allegations are almost literal quotations from Krapf. They were one-sided and ill-founded as Rebmann could easily prove. In Josenhans' evaluation of the conflict Erhardt became the scapegoat. He had criticised Krapf's policy, of which he had experienced the painful consequences in Usambara. As a young colleague he had collided with the man in authority. Krapf himself must have been the source of this verdict:

> 'Erhardt especially seems to have been wanting even in Christian spirit, and more so in missionary spirit. He seems to have been the originator of all the disagreements on that mission field. ... Erhardt ... ought not to be sent there again.'[262]

Eventually Krapf seems to have learnt a lesson from the failure of his 'grand and universal' designs. In 1876 in Korntal, where Rebmann and he had met again, he admitted to the CMS that accessing the interior of Africa was unwise before making solid preparations on the coast. He referred to the dangers of the Ukambani route, and to the unpleasant experience of Bishop Steere who due to lack of preparation on his late travel to Lake Nyasa 'lost all his European companions', because they 'had not been seasoned previously at Zanzibar'. He warned travellers to be careful:

> 'A further point to which Mr. Rebman and myself [sic!] do attach great importance will be the acclimatisation of the missionaries on the coast before they proceed to the Interior. Let no European start for inland before he has been seasoned on the coast, and got African blood as it were. If the fever breaks out on the road the traveller will be in a perilous position as he cannot take care of himself as in the case on the coast.[263]

---

[261] Idem; Statement by Barth attached to Josenhans' letter, in answer to Venn.
[262] Idem.
[263] Letter from Krapf in Korntal to CMS Secretary Wright, 2 March 1876.

4. With Johann Ludwig Krapf (1846-1855)

If Krapf had realised this in the early 1850s he and Rebmann probably would have clashed less seriously with regard to missionary method. Rebmann was not against going into the interior and the establishment of more mission stations. He only rejected Krapf's lack of patience and his desire to jump to the interior without having secured a solid base on the coast. Rebmann and Krapf agreed that mission in Muslim-ruled East Africa would be seriously undermined as long as it depended on protection by the slave-trading Zanzibar Sultanate. BM-B Inspektor Josenhans overlooked this aspect, and it took some time before the CMS grasped it.

*Johann Ludwig Krapf in 1837
(Basler Mission Archive:
QS-30.001.0132.01).*

*Johannes Jakob Erhardt in 1846
(Basler Mission Archive:
QS-30.001.0208.01).*

*Kilimanjaro Mountain. Picture by Hans Meyer, who on 6 October 1889,
together with Ludwig Purtscheller and Yohani Kinyala Lauwo,
was first to reach summit Kibo (Stadtarchiv Gerlingen).*

4. With Johann Ludwig Krapf (1846-1855)

The French medal Rebmann received
for being the first European to see
Kilimanjaro Mountain.
Rebmann Foundation
(S. Paas).

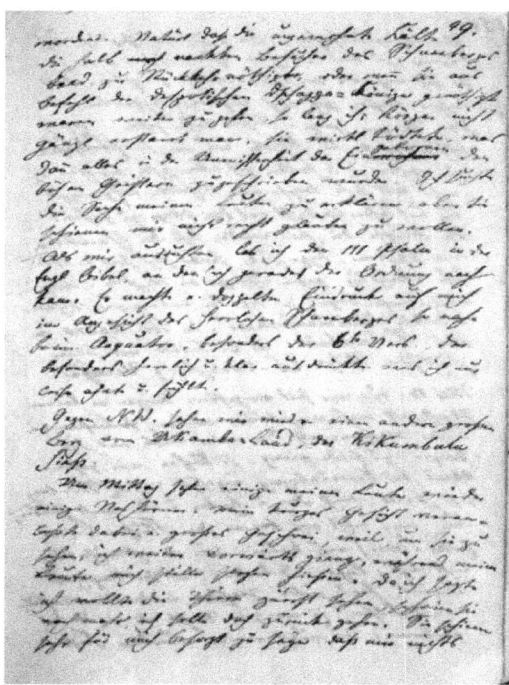

Passage of Rebmann's diary of 11 May 1848,
the day when he first saw the top of the
Kilimanjaro Mountain.

Rebmann's later house in Rabai (Stadtarchiv Gerlingen).

Jagga huts in 1889 (picture by Hans Meyer).

4. With Johann Ludwig Krapf (1846-1855)

*Rebmann's mission station in Kisuludini
(Stadtarchiv Gerlingen).*

Johannes Rebmann assisted when crossing a river (through G.H. p. 15).

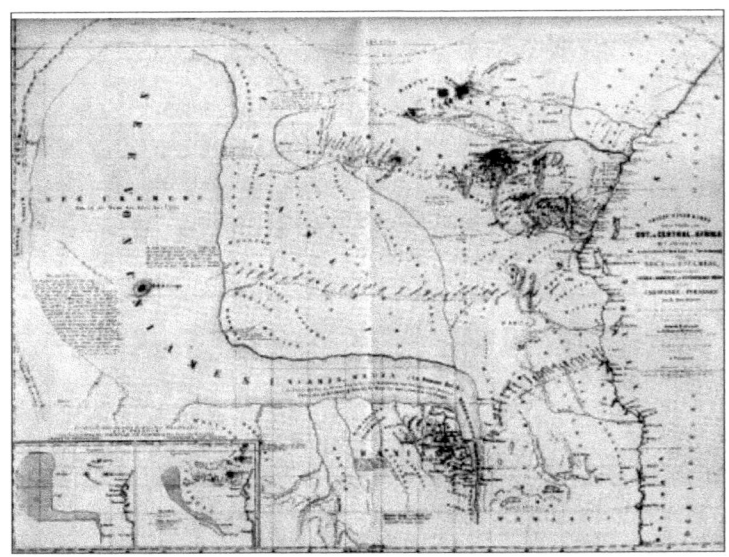

Map of Africa's Interior in the understanding of Erhardt and Rebmann (published by Petermann 1856).

5. From Cairo to Zanzibar (1851-1859)

Marriage

Gerlinger City Archivist Agnes Maisch was right when she demanded recognition for the wives of missionaries. They made an 'essential contribution to the work of mission', and they were 'self-sacrificing companions of their husbands'.[264] That is certainly true for Emma Kent. In October 1851 Johannes Rebmann departed for Cairo to marry her. He was accompanied by Kaiser and Metzler, the St. Chrischona handworkers brought by Krapf, who had failed to acculturate at Kisuludini, and now went home.[265] Krapf saw Rebmann's marriage plan as a consequence of a colonisation scheme which he had rejected.[266] However, Rebmann was not impressed by his colleague's opinion.

Emma Kent was an English lady, born in 1810, probably in the county of Yorkshire. She was the widow of a Mr. Tyler, whose name she used even after her husband's death. Perhaps they were cousins, because Emma's maternal uncle was a Tyler too,[267] hence her mother must have born that name. Through a letter by Rebmann we know that Emma had three sisters, one of whom has remained completely unknown; one was married to a Mr. Tozer in Tottenham and had a daughter, Elisa. The third sister we know by name, Miriam Kent. She was a few years older that Emma, born in c.1806. Miriam belonged to the early British settlers in South Africa, who arrived from 1824. She married Thomas Gleadow Fearne, who became Archdeacon in the Anglican Church at Richmond, Natal.[268] Miri-

---

[264] Agnes Maisch, 'Die Geschichte der Gerlinger Missionare: Auch eine Geschichte Gerlinger Familien', in: *Gerlinger Heimatblätter: Gerlinger Missionare*, Gerlingen: Verein für Heimatpflege, n.d., S. 9.
[265] *Briefe*, 4-12-1851 (to Christian Gottlob Barth in Calw); Eber, *Krapf*, S. 157.
[266] Cf. Krapf, *Reisen* I, S. 449, 451.
[267] Rebmann, in a PS to his letter to the CMS, 16 Nov. 1866 [CMS/B/OMS/C A5 O24/47], on Emma's passing away, asked to pass the message on to her relatives, e.g. the maternal uncle William F. Tyler [born 1808 in Boston, Lincs, married to Mary-Ann Hamsell]., Rebmann says: 'I believe the same who printed Hambleton's Sermons and Lectures on the Holy Scriptures, is their uncle on the mother's side'; cf. Tyler and Reed, Printers, Bolt-Court, Fleet Street, London. Sir Charles Reed 'In 1842, in conjunction with Mr. Tyler, he founded at Bolt Court, Fleet Street, London, the firm of Tyler & Reed, printers. In 1849 he left Tyler ...'.
[268] Rebmann, letter of 16 Nov. 1866 to the CMS [CMS/B/OMS/C A5 O24/47], Rebmann gave instructions to inform Emma's sisters on her death: 'I am very sorry

am was a teacher and together with her husband she founded the first Diocesan College for Girls at Richmond.[269]

Emma was a teacher too, at least in Cairo she functioned as a teacher of the CMS Girls' School. She came to Cairo in August 1846, at the time when Rebmann and Krapf moved to Rabai.[270] Was she together with her husband at that time? Probably not, because in the CMS registers there is no mention of a CMS missionary Tyler in Cairo. Also the name Emma Kent does not appear in the indexes and catalogues of the CMS.[271] Perhaps Tyler had already died before Emma left for Africa. Emma was to be part of the attempts of the CMS to win over Coptic Christians to a Protestant-Evangelical persuasion. The school where she taught was supervised by the German CMS missionary Johann Lieder and his English wife Alice, née Holliday.[272] The school applied a comparatively modern method of peer tutoring, or learning by teaching, bearing the name of

---

for being obliged to trouble you with the letter inclosed – not knowing the full address. 'Mrs Tozer, is a sister of my departed wife, a widow with one daughter, called Elisa, and I just remember that in her 'address the name of Tottenham occurs twice'... 'If I was writing from Mombas where Mrs Rebmann kept her writing case I might from thence have found out her sister's address'. Another sister is 'the wife of Archdeacon Fearne in Richmond, Port Natal'.

[269] Shelagh O'Byrne Spencer, *British Settlers: A Biographical Register in Natal 1824-1857*, Volume 6, p. 84 [under the heading Thomas Gleadow Fearne] . Miriam Kent, born in Yorkshire c.1806, died on 31 August 1885 at South Hills, near Springvale Anglican Mission Station, in today's Ixopo area. They had two children, Miriam Jane (1840-1925), who married Alexander Daniel Gilson, and Herbert Kent Fearne, who disappeared. Miriam Fearne and her daughter are mentioned in: Eliza Whigham Feilden, *My African home: Bush Life In Natal When A Young Colony* , Honton Sampson Low, Marston, Searle, & Rivington Crown Buildings,188, Fleet Street, 1887 [1852-7]. Cf. http://www.archive.org/stream/myafricanhomeorb00feil/myafricanhomeorb00feil_djvu.txt. Cf. http://natalia.org.za/Files/5/Natalia%20v05%20article%20p39-41%20C.pdf.

[270] Cf. Rebmann/Tyler (née Kent), *Journal*, p. 11 (1856).

[271] Confirmed in an e-mail by Birmingham University Special Collections Archivist Helen Fisher of 2 June 2011.

[272] CMS, *Proceedings1830*, p. 308, *Proceedings 1843*, in Missionary Register, p. 330. In Cairo the CMS opened a girls'school in 1830, which later became part of a CMS Seminary. Ledderhose, when referring to Emma Rebmann/Tyler's (b. Kent) years as a teacher there, called it the 'Lieder'sche Schule' (see his 'Rebmann', in: *ADB*, vol. 27, S. 487), after its supervisors Johann Rudolf Gottlieb/Theophilus Lieder (1798-1865), and his wife Alice (née Holliday); cf. Scheffbuch, *Große Entdecker*, 89. For Lieder in Egypt, see: E. Stock, *The History of the Church Missionary Society: Its Environment, its Men, its Work*, London, 1899, p. 351, and *Proceedings 1851-1852*, p. 73; *1855-1856*, p. 64; *1856-1857*, p. 59; *1860-1861*, p. 59.

5. From Cairo to Zanzibar (1851-1859)

educationalist Lancaster.[273] The student who learns the material was to pass on the information to the next pupil, and so forth.[274] For five years Emma was one of those who monitored this system. After her marriage to Rebmann and consequently her departure from Cairo a friendly relationship with Alice Lieder continued, maintained by correspondence and by a visit to Cairo in 1855.[275]

The BM-B Archive and the CMS registers of missionaries only mention her very briefly, as respectively 'Witwe Emma Tyler, geb. Kent', and 'Mrs Tyler, born Kent', in reference to her marriage with Rebmann. The *Proceedings* of 1852, referring to the *Record* and the *Intelligencer*, only inform on Rebmann's 'marriage to a lady engaged in female education in the Cairo Mission'.[276] Probably she had come to Cairo on the personal invitation of her friend Alice Lieder, and as such was not officially registered as a CMS employee. Apparently she was not included in the group of 87 women that the CMS accepted apart from 902 men, between 1804 and 1880.[277] Practically nothing is known about Emma's life before her marriage with Johannes Rebmann. He referred to her correspondence, which was 'kept in her writing case',[278] and which probably would have revealed more on her credentials. However, the case and the letters I have been unable to trace.

Had Rebmann met with Emma in England before his departure for Africa in 1846? It is possible, but we do not know. The marriage plans had been made through correspondence, previous to Rebmann's journey to Cairo to meet his bride. In March/April 1852 he brought her to Rabai, and

---

[273] Joseph Lancaster (1778-1838), an English Quaker who established schools of the 'Monitorial system' called after him, Lancasterian or Lancastrian.

[274] Paul, D. Sedra, *From Mission to Modernity: Evangelical Reformers and Education in nineteenth-century Egypt*, London: Tauris, 2011, p. 34-64 on John Lieder, Alice Holliday.

[275] Rebmann/Tyler (née Kent), *Journal*, p. 11, 13 (1856); Rebmann, *Briefe*, 21-4-1854, where Alice is mentioned as one of the godparents of Samuel, son of the Rebmanns, who was born in 1854 and lived for only six days.

[276] BV-Auszug: Verh. mit Witwe Emma Tyler geb. Kent 1851 von der Cairo Female School, gest. Kisulutini 8.11.1866; CMS, *Register of Missionaries* (Clerical, Lay and Female) and Native Clergy, from 1804 to 1904, in two parts, p. 66 Rebmann 'married Mrs Tyler of the Cairo Female school'; CMS, *Missionary Register*, vol. 40, p. 107, says Rebmann arrived in Cairo end November 1851 for marrying 'Mrs Tyler, who has been assisting Mrs Lieder for several years in the care of the Girls' School at Cairo'; CMS, *Proceedings 1851-1852*, p. 64.

[277] Isichei, *A History of Christianity in Africa: From Antiquity to the Present*, London: SPCK, 1995, p. 80, quoting from Stock, *The History of the Church Missionary Society*, I, p. 75.

[278] Rebmann, letter of 16 Nov. 1866 to the CMS [CMS/B/OMS/C A5 O24/47].

then to Kisuludini. Krapf and Erhardt were there to welcome them, and they remained with the couple until respectively autumn 1853 and 1855. Emma was ten years older than her husband, which made her an agemate of Krapf, who in 1851 had terminated his official CMS employment, to be free for new attempts to realise his vision. We noted that after his departure in 1853 Krapf would appear at Kisuludini a few times more. It seems Krapf reconciled himself to the idea of Rebmann being married. He considered Emma 'a true missionary's wife', who would be 'a blessing to her husband and this land'.[279] Emma liked his friendliness towards her, recognised him as a 'dear Christian', but at the same time noticed his petulance when disappointed, and thought that 'his feelings perhaps sometimes mislead him'.[280]

Emma's observations

Emma's first two years in Kisuludini were very difficult, bodily and spiritually. She suffered because of the unhealthy climate, and felt burdened and lost by her sinful nature. However, gradually she got used to the climate and the attacks of fever grew less. Helped by an environment of balanced Biblical spirituality, her problem was solved when she came to understand the significance of Christ's work on the cross. Her husband's spiritual guidance assisted her, e.g. in the reading of Scripture and of Reformation-related literature. He must have pointed her to Ludwig Hofacker's impressive witness of the Gospel of free grace for repentant sinners. She was a reader of Hofacker-influenced Johann Jakob Weitbrecht, another Basler Mission brother, who had worked for the CMS in India.[281] She also had at hand John Bunyan's *Pilgrim's Progress*.[282] The comfort of being forgiven overwhelmed her and made her live in gratitude to God.[283]

Emma Kent was a complicated character. On the one hand she was, like her husband, a humble down-to-earth practical person, a strong personality, able to maintain herself in loneliness. Moreover, she was fearless even in very dangerous situations. When they were caught in the midst of a tribal war between the Rabai and Kamba peoples, or threatened by invading Masai robbers, or molested by Mombasa's raging Mus-

---

[279] Letter from Krapf to the CMS, 22 April 1852 [CMS CA5/O16/91].
[280] Rebmann/Tyler (née Kent), *Journal*, p. 2 (1853).
[281] Johann Jakob Weitbrecht (1802-1851), memoir by his widow Martha (née Edward) in 1854; cf. Rebmann/Tyler (née Kent), *Journal*, p. 11 (1856).
[282] Rebmann/Tyler (née Kent), *Journal*, p. 18 (1856).
[283] Rebmann/Tyler (née Kent), *Journal*, p. 1 (1852).

5. From Cairo to Zanzibar (1851-1859)

lim Governor, or in the vicinity of roving lions or leopards, Emma felt protected, 'with a God above and a husband by the side'.[284] On the other hand she never felt really at ease with the local people. Apparently she was not a talker, and not an easy-going type good at building relations. Communication with the Africans continued to be a problem, not in the least because it took her a long time before she could effectively speak the local language. After a year in Kisuludini she was desperate. 'I tried to make the women as friendly with me as I could, but what can I say with my stammering tongue and in a foreign language'.[285] It is true that later her communication in Kinika improved, but she kept complaining that the African women remained at a distance.

In January 1857 the Rebmanns had to leave their home for a period because of the dangers of tribal attacks and wars between Muslim leaders. At that moment of evaluation Emma concluded bitterly: 'I can truly say that in the five years I have been here I never received one kind act from women, although I am not aware of ever refusing the sick or old or very poor any of their simple wants when they applied.'[286] Lack of positive response made her feel useless at times. She had rather a low self-esteem and her view of the impact of her presence and work was sometimes too negative and pessimistic. At times she felt guilty because she 'had done nothing for Jesus and her husband'. Her relatively old age in comparison to her husband's played a role: 'he is young and strong though I am not'.[287] In general she felt happy, except for 'the only drawback ... that I do not feel in the least useful to my fellow creatures. There are times when I feel it agonisingly, that I have not yet been instrumentally the means of bringing one precious soul to Jesus.'[288] Yet she persevered in reaching out to women, and in that way prepared for the harvest to be reaped after her life.

Emma did her best to make guests feel at home.[289] Sometimes this was noticed and appreciated. On their first visit to Kisuludini in January 1857 the explorers Speke and Burton 'found Mr. Rebmann with his amiable English wife, living in their peaceful retreat. They gave us a free and cordial welcome, and supplied us with all the delicacies of a dry Wanika season.'[290] However, Emma did not always manage to be very welcoming to

---

[284] Rebmann/Tyler (née Kent), *Journal*, p. 4, 6 (1855); cf. p. 2 (1853), p. 18, 19 (1856).
[285] Rebmann/Tyler (née Kent), *Journal*, p. 2 (1853).
[286] Rebmann/Tyler (née Kent), *Journal*, p. 21 (1857).
[287] Rebmann/Tyler (née Kent), *Journal*, p. 11 (1856).
[288] Rebmann/Tyler (née Kent), *Journal*, p. 3 (1854).
[289] Rebmann/Tyler (née Kent), *Journal*, p. 21 (1857); cf. p. 11, 13, 15 (1856).
[290] Speke, *Journal*, January 1857.

the European visitors who came to the station. She mistrusted visiting explorers and strangers. They are 'friendly indeed at present, but of whose constancy we have very little trust. May our covenant keeping God guard and guide us.'[291] When some visitors, for reasons of safety, had dressed in Muslim frocks, she wrote: 'I suppose they will travel with a tissue of lies in their train. May wisdom from above be given to my dear husband in connection with these men.'[292] Her mistrust was not completely unjustified, as would become clear later.

What she most preferred was being on her own at home together with her husband. Emma was very critical about Africans and whites who in her view behaved dishonestly or ungratefully. She could not bear that the missionary activities of her husband in word and deed remained without much visible fruit. In her view this was because of 'the perfect apathy and indifference shown by the people to the missionaries'.[293] In her view the situation in the East African mission field was more or less hopeless, and she expressed the hope that she and her husband would be sent to India or West Africa, where in her vision people were more receptive to Christianity. Yet Emma felt well at her husband's side. She faithfully supported him wherever she could, in the house and elsewhere. She was proud of his strength and health, and commended him for his patience, his ability to teach the Word of God, to study the languages and to do all kinds of practical jobs. Emma and Johannes felt most at home together with no interference from lodging visitors or helpers. They would have much valued the presence of a few Christian families in the East Africa mission field. However, the continuous company of strangers or even missionary helpers in their house they did not appreciate. This kind of society distracted them from their main objective, and interfered with their family basis. When visitors had left, Emma commented: 'What a perfect relief we find it to be alone'.[294] She realised that she did not long for company as she did before in her life. 'We felt glad when a friend was to be with us, though we often make the remark that we are happiest alone.'[295] They were a happy couple, targeting their missionary goal.

---

[291] Rebmann/Tyler (née Kent), *Journal*, p. 9 (1856).
[292] Rebmann/Tyler (née Kent), *Journal*, p. 22, 23 (1857).
[293] Rebmann/Tyler (née Kent), *Journal*, p. 13 (1856).
[294] Rebmann/Tyler (née Kent), *Journal*, p. 14 (1856).
[295] Rebmann/Tyler (née Kent), *Journal*, p. 11 (1856).

5. From Cairo to Zanzibar (1851-1859)

Consolidation

In the meantime Rebmann had quietly continued his activities to attract surrounding Nika people to Christ and his Word. The mission was consolidating. Despite meeting with a lot of indifference, a few years later the patient preparations by the Rebmanns would lead to the baptism of the first converts to the Christian faith. Besides, he continued his linguistic work, e.g. collection for the Swahili and Nika lexicons. Emma noted that her husband had started to work on another dictionary as well, of a faraway language spoken by the Nyasa people West of a lake of that name. Rebmann reported on finding an informant for that work.

> 'Just at present we have a man in our service who is a native from a country bordering on Lake Niassa, who having been captured as an adult still fully remembers his native language, a vocabulary of which I am about to gather'.[296]

Salimini was the name of the slave who assisted Rebmann. Especially during the years 1854-1855, and at times during the years thereafter Rebmann was joyfully absorbed in the Kiniassa dictionary, helped by Salimini.

There were also sad events. On 22 April 1854 the Rebmann couple was blessed with the birth of a son. Two days later the baby was baptised by his father and given the name Samuel.[297] However, on 28 April the boy died, leaving the parents in distress. Their friend and catechumen Abe Gunja carried the child to his grave. Mother Emma was too weak to attend. She was sure that she 'could never cease to think of sweet little Samuel', but entrusting him to Jesus, she could say no more than: 'It was love that gave him, and love that took him'.[298]

The same year through messages from his brother Gottlob and the schoolteacher of Gerlingen, Rebmann was informed of the death of his father, Johann Rebmann, in 1853.[299] The death of father Rebmann ex-

---

[296] Letter from Rebmann in Kisuludini, to CMS secretary Henry Venn, 27 January 1854.
[297] Rebmann, *Briefe*, 21-4-1854. Godparents were Krapf, Erhardt, and Emma's friend Alice Lieder in Cairo.
[298] Rebmann/Tyler (née Kent), *Journal*, p. 3 (1854).
[299] Rebmann, *Briefe*. In his letter of 19-9-1854 to his brothers and sister, Rebmann refers to letters received by him, i.e. from Gottlob (of 18-9-1853), from the teacher (of 20-1-1854) and from Krapf (of 7-3-1854). Possibly the letters he received throughout the years in Africa were with him on his return in Gerlingen in 1875,

plains why in August 1855 Johannes started to address the correspondence for his closest relatives to his brother Gottlob, who apparently had come to act as the new head of the family. In his letters Rebmann always showed an interest in the situation at home, for example on the occasion of the birth of Gottlob's son Samuel, apparently named after his own late son, and in the economic problems of the family, and on the marriage of his sister Katharina. Not only the next of kin received attention, but also others, for example the local schoolteacher Braun, pastor Stange, and the pastor's wife and daughters Pauline and Sophie, and neighbour Georg Kappus, whose conversion to Christ was gratefully noticed.[300] Ecclesiastical events and developments in Pietist Württemberg did not remain unnoticed by him, for example secessions from the regional state-church (*Landeskirche*), radical Judaistic end-time visions,[301] and extreme expectations of faith healing on prayer.[302]

At times Johannes and Emma Rebmann interrupted their work in Kisuludini. Sometimes they briefly withdrew to Rabai or Mombasa. There were also longer absences at greater distances. In 1855 the couple travelled to Cairo and stayed there for a while, to overcome the death of their son, and to be away from the exhausting situation of primitive conditions in a difficult climate and much demanding people. The original plan was to withdraw to Aden and perhaps to Cairo, because of rumours about an invasion by Masai warriors. At some days' distance in the Duduma country they were said to have 'set fire to the cottages, killed the men, taken women and children prisoners, and carried off large herds of cattle'. Erhardt did not wait for further developments and left for England. The Rebmanns announced their departure locally and sent word to London. In a letter to CMS secretary Venn he said: 'I need scarcely say that I do not consider it our duty to brave danger in which the great question is only about cattle'.[303] In the meantime the rumours subsided, and by autumn 'all fear of the Masai had died away'.[304]

---

and got lost after his death; cf. Stutzmann, 'Johannes Rebmann: Leben und Werk des Missionars', Vortrag, S. 9.

[300] Rebmann, *Briefe*, 2-10-1862.
[301] Rebmann, *Briefe*, 18-9-1858; cf. Stutzmann, 'Johannes Rebmann: Leben und Werk des Missionars', Vortrag, S. 3.
[302] Rebmann, *Briefe*, 9-9-1854; cf. James 5:14, 15 and Mark 16:15-20. Not all believing patients will be healed on prayer, e.g. sick Trophimus who was left behind by Paul in Miletus, 2 Timothy 4:20.
[303] Letter from Rebmann to CMS secretary Henry Venn, 18 April 1855 [CMS CA5/O24].
[304] Rebmann/Tyler (née Kent), *Journal*, p. 5 (1855).

5. From Cairo to Zanzibar (1851-1859)

However, they kept to the original plan of going to Cairo. The main reason had become an urgent need for good communication with the CMS headquarters in London. The CMS Committee for East Africa considered moving Rebmann's mission station to Teita-land at Mount Kadiaro, at a greater distance from the coast. When the threat by the Masai frustrated this plan, the CMS changed their policy, and even wanted to withdraw Rebmann and close down the station at Rabai/Kisuludini. The Rebmanns were not amused by these plans, and wished to discuss the matter. However, in Mombasa letters to and from London sometimes took several months, because they had to go through Bombay. In Cairo the conditions for correspondence were better.

Both Johannes and Emma gave lively descriptions of their adventurous voyage to Aden.[305] Their ship ran aground on a cliff. After ardent prayer they were saved by another ship. Leaving behind almost all their luggage, they went over to the other ship, which was carrying slaves, and waited for daylight before entering the harbour of the island of Lamu. The poor prisoners smelled so horribly that, advised by the captain, the Rebmanns decided to spend the night on a small island nearby! In Lamu the unfortunate travellers were helped with food and clothes by some European tradesmen and an American sea captain. Then an Arab ship took them to Mkule (Maralla), where they almost fell overboard and drowned when disembarking. Another ship took them to Aden, from where they reached Cairo by the end of November 1855. They were hospitably received by the Lieder family and other friends of Emma's former place of work.

Rebmann communicated to his employers in London that he was not pessimistic about the situation at his Rabai mission station, and about the danger of the Masai. Apparently he was able to explain that the robbers had not shown up, and that 'of course he could not completely leave the place'.[306] After some weeks the Rebmanns started to long for home. Meeting 'friends and civilisation' did not satisfy them. Emma said: 'We were not happy as if we could find no kindred spirit ... in the midst of it we felt alone and continually wished ourselves back again to our loved home in the wilderness.'[307] In January 1856 they left Cairo, and stayed for a few weeks in Suez, Aden and Zanzibar.

In April 1856 we see the couple back in Kisuludini, soon in their own quiet way involved in contacts with the surrounding Nika people and in

---

[305] Rebmann, *Briefe*, 30-11-1855; Rebmann/Tyler (née Kent), *Journal*, p. 6-8 (1855).
[306] Rebmann, *Briefe*, 30-11-1855.
[307] Rebmann/Tyler (née Kent), *Journal*, p. 8 (1856).

studying the languages of East Africa and, at a distance, of the land of Lake Nyasa. The Rebmann family had consolidated its position in East Africa, and the CMS mission station, largely unnoticed in Europe, had taken roots.

Helpers and visitors

After the departure of Krapf and Erhardt the Rebmann family were the only Europeans in the Mombasa area, apart from the brief visits by explorers and of the crews of British or sometimes American vessels sailing between Zanzibar and Aden. There was not much sharing of the burden of work and stress with others. The CMS Committee in London understood that the mission field in East Africa needed more personnel than just the Rebmanns.

Consequently in August 1856 their situation of relative solitude was changed by the arrival of Johann G. Deimler,[308] a fellow CMS-er and Basler brother. He was supposed to be a helper. Deimler understood newly invented photography, consequently we owe to him some photographs of the Mombasa Mission. Apart from that, he was not of much use. He could not bear the climate and was often sick. Apparently Deimler was not happy with his posting in East Africa. Going back to India, where he had worked for the CMS, was his ideal. Emma reported that he often talked about the promising mission field of Bombay and the hopelessness of East Africa. He said he was unable to live like the Rebmanns did, deprived of everything. Apparently he infected his host with these discouraging comments. It made Emma's idea of being useless more urgent. She started to feel old and dejected. If only they could go to India, then she would be revived. In India there is 'work, work, work'. So many 'fellow creatures are perishing for lack of knowledge', whereas they are open to be taught. 'There', she thought, 'I could do something.'[309] Deimler did not stay long. Early 1858 he seized the opportunity to leave East Africa and return to India. Within some years, from there he was going to play a role in CMS's new plans for Mombasa.

Sometimes European craftsmen came to Kisuludini. They were a combination of visitors and helpers. During their brief stay they wanted to be active, mainly as builders. The Rebmanns found it difficult to use these visitors because they often had no knowledge of the local languages and culture, and could not tolerate the climate. Moreover, the Rebmanns

---

[308] Johann Gottfried Deimler (1826-1899).
[309] Rebmann/Tyler (née Kent), *Journal*, p. 11-20.

5. From Cairo to Zanzibar (1851-1859)

could only offer them to share their small house and primitive living conditions. A group sent by the St. Chrischona Pilgrim Mission in 1854 was frustrated by the situation and left for Europe disappointed.[310]

Before the work at the mission station led to concrete results, the Rebmanns were to have some painful experiences. Publicity at home on the East African mission was not always all that positive. Some media overlooked the miracle of the beginnings of a Church among the Nika people.[311] Like many missionaries before and after him, Rebmann discovered that observers at a distance and visitors from the 'civilised' home situation can be a blessing and a curse at the same time. Some of them behave as if they know and understand everything without having seen Africa, or after a brief stay in the continent, or even after many years without being really engaged with the Africans. In his letter to Gundert he described this category of 'Africa-experts' ironically as 'the great and distinguished'. To them all mission work is foolish, annoying and costly. They do not understand that just as the Africans, they themselves, with all their education, are lost in sin, and 'do not rise above the lowest level in Islam'. The persons that were specifically meant by Rebmann included the British geographer William Cooley, who had publicly ridiculed his observation of Kilimanjaro and had made scathing remarks on the Bible.

Another visitor whose reports Rebmann criticised was Von der Decken. He was received with great hospitality by the Rebmanns several times, at Mombasa and in Rabai/Kisuludini. Yet in his account he misrepresented the situation of the mission station by describing it as a miserable ruin, also accusing Emma Rebmann, who in his eyes was not industrious and took too much time for Bible reading. The Rebmanns felt hurt, not in the least by the suggestion that Emma's place was just in the kitchen and the kitchen garden. Later, when he heard that Von der Decken had been murdered in Somalia, Rebmann's heart melted, and he honoured him in a poem on what he saw as Germany's calling for Africa.[312]

---

[310] Rebmann, Briefe, 22-4-1854.
[311] AMZ, 1874, S. 249, without referring to converts, reports that 'there is not much to be said on the Mombas Mission, after 30 years of labour', and minimises Rebmann's work: 'Old Rebmann has persevered, but due to health he has to return. His many years of language study can be used in translation work. But there is a danger that he will be disabled by blindness.'
[312] Rebmann, Briefe, 21-9-1871. '... O kommet ihr lieben Deutschen, und wehret diesem Leid. Ach kommet nicht mit Peitschen. Kommet mit Gerechtigkeit. Wohl habet ihr zu rächen, das Baron van der Decken, im Land der Sonnenglut. ... Doch ist die Rache Gottes ...'.

Rebmann also criticised Speke's companion Burton, because of his 'superficial and subjective' report, and his speculations on the financial aspect of the mission.[313] Moreover, Burton and Speke in their journals had pictured Rebmann as a worker for commerce, civilisation, and geographical exploration, without emphasising his paramount missionary objective of winning people for Christ.[314] In a letter to the Calwer Publisher Hermann Gundert, missionary Rebmann was unusually sharp. He felt that some visitors had attacked the essentials of his work in Africa. In a note he allowed Gundert to spread his comments, not to cause bitterness, but so that these 'great and distinguished' people would be ashamed.

Sometimes Rebmann had to defend himself against criticism from relatives and others at home in Gerlingen. At times his brothers and sister took his refusal to come home and rejoin the family as an indication of lack of interest and love. He used to answer sympathetically by asking intimate questions and showing knowledge of some details of their daily life. The above mentioned group of St Chrischona handworkers, Hagenmann, Kaiser and Metzler, who failed to be useful in Kisuludini, and were sent back by the Rebmanns, reported to the relatives in Gerlingen that their brother had become cold and arrogant. Rebmann showed understanding for the disappointment of the group and tried to explain that helpers and visitors can be useful in the mission field only after a long process of language learning and acculturation.[315]

Exile

Following the upsurge of Masai violence in 1855, in the beginning of 1857 the Masai threat had become urgent again. The violent nomads had penetrated into the Kamba country, driving ahead of them a lot of cattle and people, who entered the Nika country, where the population also started to move. Visiting explorers Burton and Speke warned the Rebmanns that it was time to leave.[316]

Moreover, there was a potentially dangerous political situation because of the death of Sultan Sayyid Said in October 1856, and the infighting among his heirs. When the old Sultan died, his realm was divided

---

[313] Rebmann, *Briefe*, 29-4-1864. AMZ, 1878, S. 570: Perhaps conscience-stricken by Rebmann's reproach, Burton to a General Mission Conference in London in 1878 did not forget to laud the work of Rebmann (and of Krapf).
[314] Cf. Speke, *Journal*, January 1857.
[315] Rebmann, *Briefe*, 21-4-1854; cf. *Briefe*, 18-9-1858. Later Peter Martin Metzler became a Chrischona missionary in Palestine. Cf. Eisler, *Metzler*.
[316] Rebmann/Tyler (née Kent), *Journal*, p. 21, 22 (1857).

5. From Cairo to Zanzibar (1851-1859)

among his sons. The sixth son, Sayyid Majid, became the Sultan of Zanzibar. There was uncertainty about the future of the Mombasa region, the position of foreigners, and there was a threat of civil war. In addition, many years of work in the East African mission field seemed to have remained without much fruit. Indifference and hardness of heart toward the Gospel, the evils of witchcraft and sexual promiscuity, and the enmity of Muslim agitators, had held the indigenous people from accepting Jesus as their Saviour.[317]

In this situation the discouraged missionaries suggested that the CMS Committee in London should rethink their policy and perhaps temporarily stop missionary activities in the Mombasa area.[318] The Committee, after considering the threats of invasion by the Masai, of the political instability of the Sultanate, and of the lack of visible results, decided not to close the mission field of East Africa, but to interrupt missionary presence. They wanted to withdraw Rebmann to Mauritius.[319] In the *Proceedings* of 1856-1857 the CMS declared the mission in East Africa, consisting of Rebmann (his wife is not mentioned!) and John G. Deimler, 'suspended', because 'the unsettled state of the country obliged the missionaries to remove to a place of safety'.[320]

In the meantime Rebmann had taken courage, and found this measure by London too drastic. He wanted to stay, but when Masai gangs really started looting and murdering in the coastal regions of the Nika and Kamba countries, the missionaries were urgently invited to board a warship. Deimler immediately accepted the invitation. The Rebmanns hesitated, could not get ready for it and waited. When the Sultan's Governor sent a boat for them, they realised that they too had to make a move.[321]

For this reason, in January 1858, reluctantly the Rebmanns left Kisuludini for relative safety on the Isle of Mombasa and then the Isle of Zanzibar. Emma went with mixed feelings, especially when she noticed that

---

[317] Cf. Scheffbuch, *Große Entdecker*, S. 90.
[318] Ledderhose, 'Rebmann', in: *ADB*, vol. 27, S. 487, 'In einer Denkschrift der Missionare vom Jahre 1854 an ihr Committee in London sprachen die Missionare es geradezu aus, daß nach ihrer Überzeugung die Zeit für eine Mission in Ostafrika noch nicht gekommen sei, daß sie jedoch auch bereit seien, in Geduld ihre mühevolle Arbeit fortzusetzen, wenn es das Committee wünsche.'
[319] Ledderhose, 'Rebmann', in: *ADB*, vol. 27, S. 487: The Committee stressed that seemingly fruitless periods in other mission fields had lasted much longer; *BMM*, 1858, S. 93-102.
[320] CMS, *Proceedings*, 1856-1857, p. xi, 50.
[321] Rebmann/Tyler (née Kent), *Journal*, p. 20, 21 (1857); cf. Ledderhose, 'Rebmann', in: *ADB*, vol. 27, S. 487, 488.

almost no one came to say goodbye, except those who wanted to be given a present: 'I loved the place. I would have loved the people if they would have let me. I loved my home so dearly, we had privations but truly we also had our blessings'.[322] In their temporary refuge in Zanzibar Rebmann worked on his three dictionaries, Swahili, Nika and Nyasa. He took time to learn some Arabic, 'much on account of the many Arabic words which have been received not only into the Kisuahili but even in the Kinika language'.[323] Concerning the Kiniassa Dictionary, he asked for Salimini to be sent to Zanzibar. From him he had collected vocabulary since January1854.[324]

> 'I requested the Governor of Mombas in a letter to send me the man, with whom four years ago, I began to study the Kiniassa, as I could find no man here, who spoke that language so well as he did. He arrived in July, and accordingly I have been engaged since with him'.[325]

The exile of the Rebmanns dragged on for almost the whole of 1858 and 1859. The prospects for return gradually changed for the better. Christopher P. Rigby the new British consul since 7 July 1858, was of the opinion that the political and military situation had improved, and was not prohibitive anymore to the presence of CMS missionaries in the land of the Nika people.

In November/December 1858 Johannes briefly visited the Mombasa area in order to check on the situation. He was accompanied by his Nyasa language teacher Salimini. The new Sultan and Consul Rigby encouraged them. For the Sultan's governor of Mombasa he had been given an introduction by Rigby. That this worked was to Rebmann a sign that the climate for mission in Muslim ruled East Africa was improving. The commander of the new Sultan's troops in Mombasa offered him the protec-

---

[322] Rebmann/Tyler (née Kent), *Journal*, p. 22, 23 (1857).
[323] Rebmann, *Briefe*, 18-9-1858; Letter from Rebmann in Zanzibar to the CMS (no name), 16 September 1858 [024]. In 1873 Sir Bartle Frere quoted Rebmann saying that 'if he were to begin again, he would commence with the thorough study of Arabic before commencing a critical study of the coast languages, and some Arabic scholarship is surely wanted on these coasts'. Bartle Frere added that some knowledge of 'Hindustani such as is spoken in Bombay' and of Guzerati was also required for new missionaries who were to work among 'the Indian merchants' in the Zanzibar Sultanate (Report of Sir Bartle Frere at HMS Enchantress to CMS Secretary Hutchinson, April 1873).
[324] Rebmann, *Briefe*, 20-9-1859, S. 1.
[325] Letter from Rebmann in Zanzibar to the CMS (no name), 16 September 1858 [024].

5. From Cairo to Zanzibar (1851-1859)

tion of a detachment of 50 soldiers. However, Rebmann refused the armed escort, because it would make a wrong impression, and neutralise his mission. He travelled without a rifle, only with an umbrella, not wanting to look like a slave-trader.

In Rabai and Kisuludini he observed some of the consequences of the violence and atrocities committed by the invading Masai robbers. Especially among the neighbouring Giriama people, who were overrun in the beginning of 1858, many men had been killed and many wives and children had been abducted and sold as slaves. The Nika people had mainly suffered by the pressure of the soldiers of the Sultan who had been sent against the Masai. They were forced to carry loads of provisions for them from the coast up the country, 'for a mere trifle'.[326] Normally the Nika despised this work, even if missionaries gave them good wages, as it was considered slave-labour.[327]

The mission's cottage at Rabai was one of the houses that were destroyed. Abe Gunja's house in Kisuludini was burnt. However, the building of the mission in Kisuludini, constructed by Rebmann and Erhardt, had remained largely intact. When he saw that the house had been spared, he remembered Krapf's and the Committee's objections against his intensive building efforts. 'I trust that the Committee will now be ready to acknowledge that Mr. Erhardt and myself did nothing wrong in building a somewhat substantial house. We now reap the benefit of it'.

Rebmann noticed that the crisis had brought about fundamental change in the people. Their attitude towards him had become different. During his absence some new converts had joined Abe Gunja, one of them Mua Muamba. He was respectfully received by the local chiefs in Rabai and Kisuludini and groups of attentively listening villagers. They asked him to come back soon, because apart from those who had already 'entered the Book', others waited for instruction from the missionary to take that step.[328] The melancholy situation of the mission had cleared up by the providential guidance of the Lord. 'He lays foundations and makes that people see that we are not here for own gain'. Rebmann gratefully observed that the people in the Mombasa area had discovered that the missionaries had 'had no selfish object in view in staying so long in their country, and that it cannot but be that we only wanted to teach the Wanika about the 'Book'.[329]

---

[326] Idem.
[327] Eber, *Krapf*, S. 102 (Krapf, *Reisen* I, S. 340, 341).
[328] Letter from Rebmann in Zanzibar to the CMS (no name), 15 December 1858.
[329] Letter from Rebmann in Zanzibar to the CMS (no name), 16 September 1858.

Rebmann had become convinced that the mission work in East Africa had to be resumed as soon as possible. Back in Zanzibar in December 1858 he wrote to the CMS that he wanted to return. He also asked the Committee to send an additional missionary, if possible a medical doctor 'to loosen the converts from the local medicine men'. He urged them to send the missionary soon, so that he could instruct him to temporarily take his place. Rebmann was ready to go on furlough to Europe, 'in two or three years', because of his health and because he wanted to organise the printing of his books, which were 'indispensable if the work in East Africa is to be carried on and extended'.[330]

Although the situation in Rabai/Kisuludini had considerably improved, the Rebmanns could not return at once. Zanzibar and its coastal dominions were still threatened by the new Sultan Sayyid Majid's brother the Sultan of Muscat and Oman, who especially wanted to take revenge against the European guests on the island who were thought to have been helping Zanzibar to maintain its sway over Mombasa. Until war ships of Majid's British allies neutralised Muscat, Mombasa was in danger of being attacked and occupied by Oman's troops and the missionaries had to remain in Zanzibar. Moreover, endangered Mombasa was hit by cholera and administrative chaos. In April 1859 Rebmann ventured to go to Mombasa. He wanted to check the mission's house, and found it badly damaged, because a garrison of Arab soldiers had lived in it.

In June 1859, Johannes, now together with Emma visited Kisuludini again. They found the Nika people in a peaceful mood, ready to welcome them again, and hear their witness of Christ.[331] This important change was confirmed by the events following the death in January 1859 of Mua Muamba, one of the first new members of the congregation. On the convert's urgent request the small Christian community held no heathen ceremonies over his grave, only the Word of God was preached.[332]

Finally, in December 1859 the Rebmanns were able to return and settle in Kisuludini again.

---

[330] Letter from Rebmann in Zanzibar to the CMS (no name), 15 December 1858.
[331] Rebmann, *Briefe*, 20-9-1859, S. 2.
[332] CMS, *Proceedings 1860-1861*, p. 55-59.

5. From Cairo to Zanzibar (1851-1859)

*Johann Gottfried Deimler
in 1855
(Basler Mission Archive:
QS-30.001.0267.01).*

*Johann Rudolf Gottlieb Lieder
in 1825
(Basler Mission Archive:
QS-30.001.0037.01).*

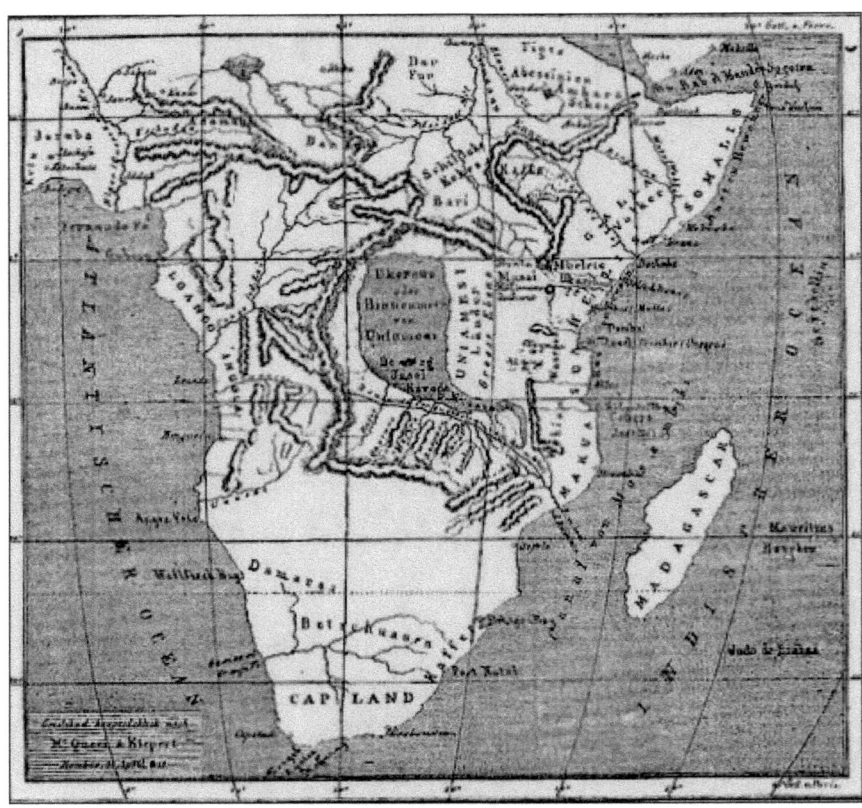

The map of Africa's interior according to the insight of Erhardt and Rebmann (published in the Calwer Missionsblatt of 1855).

5. From Cairo to Zanzibar (1851-1859)

*View of the harbour of Mombasa, a sketch made by W.B. Chancellor.
The three conical hills are called the Coronae. The hills behind are the Rabai-range.
The sailing route to Rabai is round the point in the left centre of the picture,
and up the River to the left. The mission boat is seen returning from Rabai.
The similar inlet to the right is merely a bend in the River.
The way out to sea is by the broad channel to the right
(CMS Gleaner, vol. 1, 1874, pp. 78, 80).*

6. Fruits and loss

Hopeful new start

Rebmann's misgivings with regard to the chances and opportunities of the mission field in East Africa had contributed to a misunderstanding on the side of his employers in London. For a time the CMS, discouraged by the absence of converts, the suffering of the missionaries and the disagreements between them, seemed to consider a complete stop of activities in the Mombasa area. This was not what Rebmann intended. His negative feelings concerning the position of the mission field were not caused by the primitive living conditions, the harsh climate, the deaths of his wife and some colleagues, the quarrels with Krapf, the lack of fruits in terms of the number of converts, or the threats by invading Masai. In his letters to the CMS he had not suggested to entirely terminate the work, neither had he agreed to abandon the field and to come to Europe. Rebmann had suggested a temporary interruption of outreach activities, and a concentration on linguistic preparations. He himself wanted to stay on his post until the main obstacle to mission would be taken away. In his view Christian mission was made almost impossible because for their safety the missionaries were dependent on the slave-trafficking Muslim government of the Zanzibar Sultanate, which through treaties had become an ally of Britain. In the observation of Africans the missionaries were on the side of islamic rule, slavery and slave-trade. That undermined their credibility and closed the hearts of Africans to the Gospel. An ineffective British consul in Zanzibar only made the situation worse. This was the dilemma which Rebmann and Erhardt had tried to explain to the CMS Committee in 1854.[333] The conclusion of the CMS was not in agreement with Rebmann's thought. They suspended the mission field, withdrew its personnel, and seemed to consider a close-down or a handover.

Soon after 1854 Rebmann realised that people in Rabai/Kisuludini were beginning to be more receptive. Later in his temporary refuge in Zanzibar, he continued to treasure his expectations for the mission. He eagerly waited for signs of decisive improvement of the situation, kept in touch, and looked for ways to return.

---

[333] Rebmann and Erhardt in an evaluation of 'ten years of labour', summarised by the CMS secretaries, point 9, November 1854.

By the end of the 1850s two important developments gave the Rebmanns new hope. First, British political resistance against the Zanzibar slave-trade had become more serious. Secondly, despite the temporary interruption of missionary activity, the Kisuludini/Rabai mission field had started to yield fruit. Rebmann observed a positive change of the official British attitude towards slavery and the slave-trade when he saw the determination and enthusiasm of the new consul Rigby, which was unknown to his predecessor. In a letter to the CMS he expressed his satisfaction:

> Rigby 'has taken an interest in East Africa. ... He appears all in acquiring foreign languages. Though he does not see the true nature and spiritual glory of the missionary work I have reason to hope that he will at least give us ready protection. In the few interviews I have had with him I found him a man of good common sense, courteous, affable, in this respect the very counterpart of his predecessor. He sees no obstacles in the way of resuming work among the Wanika. It will, however, be good if ... the Committee will recommend the East Africa [*mission field*] to his special attention and protection ..., as in fact he is the only true authority, not the Muhamadan ruler, under whom the existence of an East African Mission is at all possible'.[334]

Rigby on his own accord forced the Indians in the Sultanate – who were formally British citizens, hence under British anti-slavery law – to set free their slaves.[335] Rebmann rejoiced: 'For the first time a Consul ... really acts against slavery, in the sight of the Sultan he liberated 4950 slaves who had belonged to British subjects'.[336] In chapter 9 we will see that some of Rigby's successors definitely turned the tables on the Zanzibar slave-trade. A new era had started. These events demonstrated to the Arab slave-holders, to their Swahili-Arab and African allies, and to their African victims that Britain was not a friend of slavery and slave-trade, and that the CMS missionaries were no hypocrites. Messengers of the Gospel had gained credibility. For Rebmann 'the altered aspect of Muhamadanism ... re-established his 'belief as to the continuance ... and reinforcement of the East African Mission'. The Rebmanns felt relieved and encouraged.

The other reason for renewing hope and changing missionary policy was the continuation – during their exile – of a positive response from

---

[334] Letter from Rebmann in Zanzibar to the CMS (no name), 16-9-1858 [O24].
[335] CMS, *Proceedings 1861-1862*, p. 55-57; *Intelligencer*, December 1872; cf. Nwulia, *Britain, and Slavery in East Africa* p. 66, 67.
[336] Letter from Rebmann in Mombasa to the CMS Committee, 22 April 1861.

6. Fruits and loss

Africans in the Mombasa area. After making their definite comeback to Kisuludini in December 1859, the Rebmanns were happy to notice that during their absence the Holy Spirit had continued to work in the hearts of people who had received the seed of the Gospel. The crisis had made the hearts of many soft and receptive to the Word of God.[337] The conversion of Mua Muamba, his confidence in God when he died, and his Christian burial were signs of positive change among a lot of Nika and Giriama people.

In April 1860 Rebmann reported to the CMS Committee that the Nika people now were 'ready to abandon heathenism as falsehood', from which they only could be delivered by 'entering the book'. 'Many lay hold on the book and speak against heathenism now'. At the same time Rebmann warned not to be over-optimistic. The power of superstitions and pagan concepts remained strong. By God's grace individuals were converted and others were interested to get free from the bitterness of witchcraft and magic. People suffered. There was an 'unconscious general wish or yearning' for liberation. The system of falsehood had to be broken. Rebmann was still convinced that the hold of Muslim rulers, African chiefs, and magicians on the people had to be neutralised before there could be a general break-through of the Gospel.

Another basic problem for the young Christians was forgiving others. Rebmann mentioned as an example the story of two converts Mua Zuia and Lugo, whose niece was robbed by another clan. In return they wanted to take the daughter of the robber and kill her. When Rebmann persuaded them to abandon the plan and look for other ways, Mua Zuia and Lugo experienced the anger and threats of their relatives, and had to flee. At last a solution was found. The great enemy of souls had tried to rob sheep from the flock. But he had failed.[338]

The first one to be baptised was an old friend of Rebmann and Krapf, the lame Mringe, who had received the Lord long before, he was renamed Johanesi. On the day of Pentecost 27 May 1860 other early converts were baptised, Gunja and his son Nyondo, who received the names Abraham and Isaac. They had been willing pupils before Rebmann's temporary absence. Without the presence of his teacher, Isaac Nyondo had prepared himself for baptism by reading the Nika translations of the Gospel of *Luke* and the *Heidelberg Catechism*. Four more Nika were in the process of learn-

---

[337] Cf. Scheffbuch, *Große Entdecker*, S. 90.
[338] Letter from Rebmann in Mombasa to the CMS Committee, 13 April 1860 [O 24/36].

ing how to read and of preparing for baptism.[339] In subsequent years baptisms continued. Among the newly baptised were Mua Zua (David), Lugo (Jonathan), Zuia (Johannes), a Masai man (Joseph), a Nika man (Nathanael), an Upanga man (Gabriel). In a later stage also women were baptised, e.g. the widow of Mua Muamba. In general Rebmann baptised converts after 'a probation from 2 to 3 years'.[340]

Largely unnoticed by people at home in England and Germany among the Nika people of Rabai/Kisuludini a small congregation was taking shape. The members belonged to the very poor, barely able to cover their bodies. Rebmann reported that their huts were more miserable than those of surrounding Muslims, and that they were on their own unable to build a church or a small school. The Rebmanns joined deeds to words; activities for building houses, making clothes for the converts, and digging cisterns were developed.[341] To Rebmann these practical activities were an essential part of his mission. Working with mortar and bricks and spreading the Gospel belonged together. When they returned from Zanzibar they found some of the existing buildings needed repair whereas a new chapel, and new dwellings had to be built. In the more promising situation building was extra important because 'the East African mission must now become a permanent settlement'. Therefore Rebmann 'rebuilt the mission house with walls of stones in stead of unburnt bricks, and enlarged it for a fellow-labourer'.[342] For months this kept him very busy. In the evenings he was exhausted, and he would fall on his knees in prayer,

> 'Oh Lord thou alone knowest the whole history of my circumstances. Have mercy upon me. O have mercy upon me, and reveal Thy glory in the salvation of souls. I do all this because thou o Lord Jesus hast come down from heaven to save me. O help me, I am Thine.'[343]

Some Swahili carpenters and masons from Mombasa assisted, and at a later stage liberated African slaves, who had received a Christian education in Bombay, were brought in to help.

---

[339] Rebmann, *Briefe*, 20-9-1860.
[340] Rebmann, *Briefe*, 2-5-1861; Letter from Rebmann in Mombasa to the CMS Committee, 22 April 1861; CMS, *Proceedings1862-1863*, p. 51-53; Report by Rebmann (duplicated, by Sparshotts?) in Mombasa to the CMS Committee, 27 February 1866.
[341] Rebmann, *Briefe*, 2-5-1861. Emma Rebmann busied herself in making white 'Wämschen' (Kiswahili: visibao) for people to wear on Sundays.
[342] CMS, *Proceedings 1860-1861*, p. 55-59.
[343] Report by Rebmann (duplicated, by Sparshotts?) in Mombas to Committee, 27 February 1866.

6. Fruits and loss

From the beginning the young congregation was a Church Militant, as it was continually resisted, partly by weak missionary presence, as the CMS almost seemed to have forgotten Rabai/Kisuludini, but especially by the powers of darkness, tribalism, witchcraft, and Muslim rulers. Yet the church grew. The story of Abe Ng'owa is a helpful illustration. He belonged to the Giriama subtribe. He had inquired from Rebmann about the faith and had learnt from him how to read and write. In a later development he accidentally had severely wounded his wife. She died when the Bombayers Jones and Semler tried to care for her. Abe Ng'owa felt remorse. Stricken by guilt and grief he withdrew to a hut in the forest and started to read the Nika translation of the Gospel of *Luke*. Soon others joined him and together they listened to the Word of God. The Holy Spirit influenced their hearts, and instilled consciousness of sin and penance. Abe Ng'owa became one of Rebmann's early converts. Because of his responsibility for the death of his wife he was not accepted in his Giriama village anymore. He sought refuge with the Nika, but they suspected him of provoking rainfall through sorcery. He fled to the mission station, but Rebmann could not prevent the people from chasing him from there as well. These events helped Ng'owa to grow in understanding the meaning of the cross of Christ, and to be baptised. Reluctantly the Nika community accepted the Giriama finally, but only after Rebmann had refused to employ anyone who continued to threaten him. Ng'owa needed a new family, but he was only able to start one after Rebmann had bought a wife for him at the Mombasa slave market, an unusual step. Europeanised catechist Jones from Bombay was shocked,[344] but local Christians within the framework of time and place accepted what their acculturated missionary did. Ng'owa's witness gained new converts.

At first the Giriama people emphatically rejected the message of the missionaries. This changed after a group of *watoro*, escaped and fugitive slaves of different ethnic origins, had settled among them. Their chief Abe Sidi had been influenced by Rebmann. He reshaped his village Fuladayo into a Christian community. They attracted surrounding 'unreachable' Giriama, so that a growing number of them opted for a Christian way of life. There was also a community of Christian enquirers 'gathered around Mwaringa of Godoma', who read the Gospel of *Luke* to his group from his house in a tree.[345]

By the mid 1870s about 35 of Abe Sidi's village had become Christians, 'and many more adherents'. Sparshott and Rebmann strongly argued

---
[344] Reed, *Pastors, Partners, Paternalists*, p. 44.
[345] Sundkler and Steed, *A History of the Church in Africa*, p. 555, 556.

with CMS not to abandon the mission because of the 'steady growth of the Giriama church despite persecution by the Arabs'. Amazingly Reed uses this success story of the East African CMS Mission to degrade Rebmann's work. He argues that the progressive growth of the church had not taken place in Rabai and was not the result of Western missionaries.[346] Both arguments are void if one realises that humanly speaking Christianity at Godoma could not have emerged if the seeds had not been sown at a mission station and by the missionary at Rabai/Kisuludini.

Less sensational but equally miraculous was the conversion of Gabriel, the Upanga man 'whose heart was as dead as a stone but came to life', not long before his sudden death by smallpox.[347] He was baptised in January 1866, together with five others.[348] The congregation and the mission station also had to deal with periods of famine, when hundreds of Nika people asked for food and work. The young Christians had to consciously adopt a position towards the evil of local slavery, often a consequence of abject poverty and tribal wars.

Widening missionary interest

In 1860 some events, which happened far away from the Mombasa area, pertained to Rebmann in a special way. In London an English translation of Krapf's travel journal in two volumes was published.[349] The publication of this influential account, which contains information on Rebmann's work, was too early to have included a report on the important event of the first baptisms. However, the Kingdom does not depend on fame and publicity. Neither is the progress of the Kingdom stopped by setbacks. In the same year the Anglican bishop Charles Frederick Mackenzie started a mission in South Malawi, but he got surprised by the tricks and the violence of the invading Muslim Yao tribe and its practice of catching and selling slaves. The bishop failed and died, and his Universities' Mission to Central Africa (UMCA) had to withdraw to Zanzibar.[350] Also in the same year, near Nusewa at Rufuma River on the East side of Lake Nyasa a young German explorer was killed, Albrecht Roscher from Hamburg. He

---

[346] Reed, *Pastors, Partners, Paternalists*, p. 43, 44.
[347] Rebmann, *Briefe*, 2-10-1862; cf. 21-9-1863; cf. 26-9-1866; cf. Krapf, *Reise*, I, S. 361.
[348] In *Briefe*, 26-9-1866, Rebmann mentioned their names, new and old, Andreas Mzomba, Kigofi, Daniel, Josiak, and Lukas, 'a younger brother of Isaac ... the first boy who asked me for the Gospel of Luke'.
[349] Idem, *Travels, Researches and Missionary Labours during an eighteen years' residence in Eastern Africa*, Abingdon: Frank Cass/Boston: Tricknor and Fields, 1860.
[350] Cf. *Christianity in Eurafrica*, p. 451, 452.

6. Fruits and loss

had visited Rebmann, and observed Kilimanjaro. Rebmann thought a lot of him, and was very touched by the death of this 'excellent young man'.[351] He commemorated him in a poem in 1871.[352] In his view the murder could have a positive effect, by drawing the attention of the Christian world to Nyasa land, so that 'another large field for missionary labour is being added to the Lord's vineyard'.[353] A decade later Rebmann's Kiniassa Dictionary would be able to help explorers and missionaries of the UMCA on their return to Malawi be better prepared, and four years later emissaries of the Scottish Churches would travel in Malawi with Rebmann's dictionary in their luggage.

In addition to the work of Church planting and house building, Rebmann tried to continue his language studies for making 'a small grammar, a small dictionary and for finalising a translation of the Gospel of Luke'.[354] Intensive preparation including the acquisition of knowledge of the local language and culture is needed by any missionary. Rebmann had become convinced of this. Experience had taught him that lack of preparation leads to failure. He warned newcomers not to be trapped by this. For example, another group of Hermannsburgers, two missionaries and two craftsmen from Port Natal, who arrived with their ship the *Candace* in Zanzibar in August 1858, immediately wanted to proceed to Gallaland and start a mission station there. Rebmann advised them not to go to Mombasa at once, but to acclimatise first in Zanzibar, and learn at least Swahili, so that they would be less dependent on others, because 'in a strange land everyone who cannot talk with the people is like a child, and children you have to look after'.[355] He also advised the missionaries to let their two mechanics, who were not likely to learn new languages soon, go back to Port Natal, 'to make their first beginnings as easy and simple as

---

[351] Albrecht Roscher (1836-1860), a German physicist and geographer; Rebmann, *Briefe*, 20-9-1860, said the murderers, some Yao robbers, were extradited to Zanzibar where they were executed; cf. Letter from Rebmann in Zanzibar to the CMS (no name), 16 September 1858 [O24].

[352] Rebmann, *Briefe*, 21-9-1871: '... Auch is getödtet worden (ermordet) bei dem Niasa See Herr Roscher von dem Norden, leicht wie ein junges Reh. Doch ist die Rache Gottes ...'.

[353] Letter from Rebmann in Mombasa to the CMS Committee, 15 September 1860 [O24/37].

[354] Rebmann, *Briefe*, 20-9-1861.

[355] Rebmann, *Briefe*, 18-9-1858. The Hermannsburg group originally consisted of three missionaries and three mechanics; soon one missionary died and one mechanic left, leaving missionaries Filter and Frigge and two mechanics.

possible'.[356] Rebmann had experienced that ignorance of culture and language and exposure to diseases were the main reasons why so many of his co-workers died or had to leave.

At times the Rebmanns received visitors. Already during Rebmann's period together with Krapf some had dropped in on them. In May 1848 there were two officers of a French warship, and in 1849 they were visited by the Jewish convert to Christianity Bialloblotzky.[357] Triggered by the 'discovery' of Kilimanjaro and Mount Kenya by respectively Rebmann and Krapf, and the publication of the 'slug' map of the supposed features of the inland of Africa, which Erhardt and Rebmann had made on Arab information, the interest of various scientists and explorers was roused. The map was presented to the Royal Geographical Society on 10th November 1855, and it was included in a book by Krapf, published in 1856. In 1857 the Rebmanns were visited a few times by the British explorers Richard Burton[358] and John Hanning Speke.[359] They travelled from Bagamoyo to Lake Tanganyika in 1857/1858, and Speke also saw Lake Victoria. This expedition was followed by Speke's second journey, in 1860, in the company of James Augustus Grant,[360] to justify Speke's claim that the Nile River rose in Lake Victoria.

In 1859 after their return to Kisuludini the Rebmann couple had become the only CMS missionaries left in East Africa. This situation of relative solitude was briefly interrupted twice by visiting explorers. In 1861/1862 a German nobleman, Karl Klaus von der Decken,[361] stayed some

---

[356] Letter from Rebmann in Zanzibar to the CMS (no name), 16 September 1858 [024].

[357] Eber, *Krapf*, S. 105; The German Jew Christoph Heinrich Friedrich Bialloblotzky (1799-1869) became a Lutheran theologian, then turned a Methodist missionary, with a special interest in Africa. His journey included attempts to locate the source of the river Nile (cf. Nicolas M. Railton, Transnational Evangelicalism: The Case of Friedrich Bialloblotzky, 1799-1869, Vandehoeck & Ruprecht, 2002).

[358] Richard Francis Burton (1821-1890), a British army officer who is described as 'explorer, translator, writer, soldier, orientalist, ethnologist, spy, linguist, poet, fencer and diplomat, known for his travels and explorations within Asia and Africa as well as his extraordinary knowledge of languages and cultures'.

[359] John Hanning Speke (1827-1864), 'an officer in the British Indian Army who made three exploratory expeditions to Africa and who is most associated with the search for the source of the Nile'; cf. Ledderhose, *Rebmann*, S. 487; cf. Speke, *Journal*, January 1857.

[360] James Augustus Grant (1827-1892), a British army officer, biologist and plant collector in e.g. Ethiopia, Tanzania, Uganda.

[361] Baron Karl Klaus von der Decken (1833-1865), German army officer (Kingdom of Hanover) and explorer. Cf. Rebmann, *Briefe*, 20-9-1860, 2-5-1861, 20-9-1861, 2-10-1862.

6. Fruits and loss

periods with them, alternately accompanied by the English geologist Richard Thornton,[362] and a German scholar Otto Kersten[363] who was together with a Prussian military officer. Their primarily geographic explorations interacted with the activities of David Livingstone, who in 1866 set out on his last journey for Lake Nyasa. Livingstone's objective was not in the first place to find the source of the Nile, but to expose the horrors of the slave-trade and, by opening up legitimate trade with the interior, to destroy the evil at its roots. Livingstone's journey led to the expeditions of Henry Morton Stanley[364] and Verney Lovett Cameron, equally searching for the sources of the Nile.[365] Spurred on by Livingstone's work and example, a number of missionary societies began to take an interest in East Africa. This coincided with further travels by other explorers.

An example was Von der Decken, who in 1860 had explored the region around Lake Nyasa, only one year after David Livingstone had been the first European to reach the area. Thornton had been with Livingstone at the Zambezi. Von der Decken and Thornton experienced real snow at Kilimanjaro. Their published account took away doubts of opinion-makers with regard to Rebmann's earlier observations. Rebmann noticed that his guests were not born-again Christians, although they took part in daily house worship. In a letter to Gerlingen he shared his prayer for the visiting explorers with his relatives, 'that by observing the misery of the heathen they may come to recognise the truth and glory of the Gospel'.[366]

After Livingstone's death in 1873, missionary interest grew wider and stronger, first with the Scottish churches, who sent workers to Central Africa to the Nyanja, Yao and Tumbuka-speaking peoples in present-day Malawi.

---

[362] Richard Thornton (1838-1863), a mining geologist, who made many observations of the mountain, and estimated that it stood about 20,000 feet above sea level.

[363] Otto Kersten (1839-1900), a German chemist and African traveller, wrote a work of 6 volumes on his Kalimanjaro expeditions.

[364] Henry Morton Stanley (born in Wales as John Rowlands), 1841-1902, an American journalist and explorer. Rothe, 'Henry M. Stanley: Der Erforscher von Central-Afrika', in: AMZ, 1879, S. 143-160, says that the Roman Emperor Nero had already sent an expedition to search the sources of the Nile, and refers to Arab and Portuguese writers on the topic; cf. William Desborough Cooley, *Claudius Ptolemy And The Nile: Or An Inquiry Into That Geographer's Real Merits And Speculative Errors* (1854).

[365] Verney Lovet Cameron (1844-1894), English naval officer, and explorer.

[366] Rebmann, *Briefe*, 20-9-1861.

Shifting CMS positions

The signs of positive change in the political movement against the slave-trade, the first fruits in the Kisuludini/Rabai mission field, and consequent renewal of hope in the missionaries were not immediately followed by a change of CMS policies. For quite a long period the Committee seemed to have lost interest in the mission, making the impression that they wanted to abandon it, or hand it over to others. In September 1860 Rebmann complained that for two years he had not received a letter from the Committee.[367] The *Proceedings* of the CMS over the years 1856-1862 only offered a few brief articles on East Africa. In 1861 'a growing openness to the Gospel' and the first baptisms are reported, but this important news was not followed up in the *Proceedings* of 1862, which were completely silent on Rebmann and East Africa. Apparently the CMS Board, considering the threat by violent Masai and the political uncertainties of the Zanzibar Sultanate to which Mombasa belonged, was still to make a decision with regard to the future of the Rabai Mission. Would they add new missionary staff to Rebmann at Rabai/Kisuludini? Would they allow missions of other denominations to enter the same region, or vacate the Mombasa area in favour of them? Would they, in view of the growing number of uprooted ex-slaves in the region, devise a completely new concept and settlement that would surpass and bypass the Kisuludini station?

At first all options were kept open. In 1856 Deimler was sent to Rabai in support of Rebmann, but was soon to be transferred to India. Subsequently, much to Rebmann's disappointment the CMS seemed to bless the establishment early 1862 of an additional mission of a different denomination at Ribe, in the direct neighbourhood of Rabai/Kisuludini. The involvement of his friend and colleague Ludwig Krapf in this United Free Methodist enterprise[368] was particularly painful to Rebmann. His initial joy because of the unexpected appearance of Krapf's 'friendly and loving face'[369] soon vanished when he noticed what his arrival was about. Under Krapf's guidance missionary Thomas Wakefield settled at nearby Ribe.

---

[367] Letter from Rebmann in Mombasa to the CMS Committee, 15 September 1860 [O24/37].

[368] Eber, Krapf, 205, 206. The party of the United Free Methodists consisted of missionaries Thomas Wakefield and James Woolner, and St. Chrischona students Samuel Elliker and Johann Friedrich Graf. Woolner and the two St. Chrischona men were invalided soon and left for home the same year. In December 1862 Charles New was added.

[369] Cf. CMS, *Proceedings 1862-1863*, p. 51-53.

6. Fruits and loss

Krapf organised that materials for a house of corrugated sheet iron were transported from Europe and then from the coast to the new station. In July 1862 it was ready for the Methodist missionaries. To Rebmann this 'poaching' in CMS territory was symptomatic of 'Krapf's whole approach to pioneer missionary work', which he mistrusted.[370] In a letter to his fellow Basler Brother Hermann Gundert in Calw[371] he emphatically doubted the wisdom of establishing a station of Methodists near his own CMS station at Kisuludini, while the mission field of East Africa was very large. He complained that his report to the CMS on the conflicting situation was not published, and in an addendum he suggested that the hasty establishment of the new mission might have escaped their attention. Although agreeing that God is above denominations and sects, he stressed that in good order each should stick to its own area.[372]

Soon Rebmann's feelings about the Methodist station at Ribe were superseded by other worries. He remained opposed to the policy of establishing two missions of different denominations close to one another. Considering practical reality, however, he was ready to accept the presence of missionaries Thomas Wakefield and Charles New and other newcomers and visitors at nearby Ribe. At times the new station was a blessing in disguise. There was a need for mutual assistance when in both stations death entered. At Ribe the young missionary Butterworth died, just when the English consul paid a visit, and the assistance of Kisuludini was required.[373] A few years later Rebmann reported that the Methodists wanted to abandon their station at Ribe and sell it to the CMS.[374] In November 1865 Wakefield and New came to Kisuludini 'in order to confer about the continuance of their station'. They doubted the right place, because of the 'scarcity of population', and 'the proximity to CMS station'. Moreover, they wanted to move on to their original destination, Lamu and then Galla-land. Pending decisions at home, Rebmann practically took over Ribe. He put prominent Nika Christian Isaac Nyondo in charge: 'To the rough commencement of a station I should prefer our Wanika

---

[370] Cf. R.C. Bridges, 'A Manuscript Kinika Vocabulary and a letter of J.L. Krapf', in: *Bulletin of the Society for African Church History*, vol. 2, No. 4, 1968, p. 295.
[371] Hermann Gundert (1814-1893), German missionary and philologist in India (1836-1859), manager of the Calw Publishing House (1862-1893).
[372] Rebmann, *Briefe*, 29-4-1864; cf. *Briefe*, 20-9-1861, *Briefe*, 2-10-1862.
[373] Rebmann, *Briefe*, 27-4-1864.
[374] Rebmann, *Briefe*, 26-9-1866. Looking forward to a decision by the CMS Committee on this takeover, Rebmann appointed Nyondo and David to oversee the Ribe station, together with a guest at the station, St. Chrischona-brother Tiismann (or Tüsmann).

Christians'. He added to him George David, an African catechist from Bombay, who 'should not so easily be spared'.[375] He suggested to the CMS to buy the buildings, and thought '£ 120 a fair sum to be offered and paid at home'.[376] Apparently the CMS had not intended to disavow or hurt Rebmann by favouring the move of the Methodists to Ribe. They agreed to the take-over of the station, and the sum to be paid.[377] Quoting Krapf they continued to appreciate the 'promising prospects' of what 'God had wrought by ... Mr. Rebmann his humble servant'.[378] At the same time they prepared for Rebmann to go home.

In the meantime in London it had become logical that the Rabai/Kisuludini station was to be absorbed by a new and wider plan in which Empire and Church were going to cooperate, i.e. a settlement for liberated slaves in the Mombasa area. What would be the part to be played by the CMS in this new plan? New potential players in that ambitious concept appeared on Rebmann's doorstep, e.g. in 1864 the Anglican bishop William George Tozer of the High Anglican Universities' Mission to Central Africa (UMCA). After being founded in 1859 the UMCA in June 1861 had started a mission work in Southern Malawi, at Chibisa and Magomero, under the initial guidance of David Livingstone. However, due to violent behaviour of Yao slave-traders the enterprise failed. Charles Mackenzie the leading bishop of the party died on 31 January 1862. He was replaced by Tozer. In 1864 Tozer and his fellow-workers retreated from Lake Nyasa to Zanzibar. They prepared themselves for new tasks on the island and on the African mainland. Tozer and Rebmann met one another several times. Although the convinced classical Protestant Rebmann disagreed with High Anglicanism[379] and even mistrusted the UMCA's intentions as to the Mombasa mission field, there seems to have been a good personal relationship between him and Tozer. In November 1864 Tozer

---

[375] Report by Rebmann (duplicated, by Sparshotts?) in Mombasa to Committee, 27 February 1866.
[376] Idem.
[377] In a note from Mombasa, 6 May 1868, Rebmann urged the Committee to indicate whether they accepted the take-over, and in a letter from secretary C.C. Fenn to Rebmann, 26 August 1868 [C A5/I p. 6], the Committee accepted the transfer and was prepared to pay the 120 pounds for the building. 'They wrote this to the secretary of the Methodist Mission in Manchester, but they never collected the money'.
[378] CMS, *Proceedings*, 1863, On p. xii Rebmann is mentioned as the only CMS missionary of East Africa. Krapf is quoted on p. 51-53.
[379] High-Anglicanism, also known as Anglo-Catholicism, or Tractarianism, see, Paas, *Christianity in Eurafrica*, p. 247, 248.

visited him at Kisuludini for the first time. He was 'most kindly welcomed'. Rebmann felt honoured and encouraged because of the positive attention for his work by a leading church man. Tozer was impressed by Rebmann. After another visit to Kisuludini and Ribe in December 1865 he reported to his secretaries in England as follows:

> 'It was with very much pleasure that I made the acquaintance of all these devoted men on the occasion of my recent visit to Mombas. Mr. Rebmann, of whom I must ever speak with the deepest respect, has, as you are aware, been labouring among the Wanyika tribe for the past seventeen years, and few missionaries can have encountered the same amount of difficulty and discouragement, or exhibited such noble patience and perseverance, as this tried and eminent servant of God. He is now surrounded by a small but earnest body of native believers, the first-fruits, I cannot but think, of the whole Wanyika tribe'.[380]

When another group of players in the Mombasa mission scene arrived, even a kind of cooperation between Tozer and Rebmann developed. From 1864 African ex-slaves were taken to the Mombasa area from Bombay, British territory in India. Rebmann found it difficult to use them and he asked Tozer to train a few of them as missionary workers.

The Bombayers

The plans of the CMS to assist liberated African slaves were a direct consequence of the Evangelical revival or awakening that started in the Anglo-Saxon world in the 18th century and spread over the whole of Western Europe, where it was paralleled by revival movements in for example Switzerland, Germany, and The Netherlands.[381] This rejuvenation of Western Christianity led to an enormous enthusiasm for mission to the unreached peoples in Asia and Africa. It also led to a deep consciousness that slavery was a shameful practice and had to be stopped, not only on the coasts of the Atlantic Ocean, but also on the Indian Ocean. In 1787 William Wilberforce founded a Committee for the Abolition of the Slave-trade, which in 1807 was followed by a law against slave-trading, and in 1833 by the Slavery Abolition Act. During the 19th century British war-

---

[380] William George Tozer, Letter to the Secretaries, 24 December 1865, in: 'Letters of Bishop Tozer and His Sister together with some other records of the Universities' Mission from 1863-1873', edited by Gertrude Ward, London: Office of the Universities' Mission to Central Africa, 1902, p. 44.
[381] Cf. Paas, *Christianity in Eurafrica*, p. 249-258, 337f.

ships, first in the Atlantic and later also in the Indian Ocean, tried to stop slave ships, liberate the slaves, and take them to a safe haven.[382] With their plan of a settlement of ex-slaves at Mombasa, the CMS emulated what had happened on the West African coast, where in Freetown/Sierra Leone, liberated slaves had been assembled in a big colony under the British crown.[383] Similar colonies were to be organised at Africa's east coast. Most of the ex-slaves had become Christians, and the new colonies were expected to become important instruments to the Christianisation of Africa. The CMS plan for Mombasa was paralleled by High Anglican activities on Zanzibar, and a Roman Catholic plan for Bagamoyo, opposite Zanzibar, on the Tanganyikan coast.

The activities in the 1870s for establishing settlements of ex-slaves on the East African coast were preceded by a period, since the *Hamerton Treaty* of 1847, of taking recaptured slaves to the islands Mauritius and the Seychelles, and to India. British ships that arrested Arab slavers, and set free their cargo, could not take the ex-slaves to the Muslim-ruled coast of East Africa as there was no safe place for them. For this reason they transported the liberated Africans to British-ruled territories. A few hundred landed in India. Most of them were children. In Bombay the government sent them to the *Indo-British Institution* for learning agriculture and trade, subsequently the more clever ones went to the so called *Robert Money Schools*, modelled on the British public school system. In their formative teenage years they were thoroughly trained in various subjects of learning, and in the process they joined with the elite of India, and adopted Anglosaxon language and culture. On these anglicized African Reed comments: 'They would never be the same again'. The government cooperated with the CMS. The Indo-British Institution was run by a CMS missionary, George Candy. A very important part was played by CMS missionary Karl Wilhelm Isenberg. Like Rebmann and Krapf, he was a Basler Mission brother in the service of the CMS. Before being posted in India, he had been Krapf's colleague in Ethiopia. Isenberg taught religious education at the Money Schools; he received East African children in his house, and gave them a Christian home. Unexpectedly his previous experience in Ethiopia, and his knowledge of the Galla language, became useful again. A role was played by Johann Gottfried Deimler, former colleague of Rebmann at Kisuludini, but now a missionary among Muslims in Bombay.

---

[382] Cf. Paas, Paas, *Christianity in Eurafrica*, p. 339.
[383] Cf. Paas, *Christianity in Eurafrica*, p. 341, 342. 376.

6. Fruits and loss 127

The very young children were not yet ready for the Indo-British Institution and the Robert Money Schools. The government sent them to the CMS mission centre Sharanpur (*place of refuge*) at Nasik near Bombay. In 1860 this Christian industrial settlement for orphans started an African Asylum, for hosting East African children. The Superintendent of Sharanpur was the CMS missionary William Salter Price. Under his leadership children got a training for practical jobs and for the ministry. Later Price was posted to Mombasa, where he met some of his former students.

Missionary Deimler in Bombay assisted in training African catechists and teachers and in preparing them for work in East Africa.[384] Some of them received his special attention. Their African names got lost; they became known as William Henry Jones, Ishmael Semler, and George David. From 1859-1864 they were under Deimler's care; they were at the *Robert Money School* for two years. In 1861 Deimler sent them to Sharanpur to teach and to be taught. They helped in training the children, and themselves they learnt the trades of blacksmith, and carpenter, and in 1864 of coach-building and of how to work with a printing press. They married Galla wives, before they were the first to be sent from Bombay to East Africa for the CMS. Deimler also had under his guidance a number four boy, who was dismissed, and two Yao girls, who became wives of young Nika Christians in East Africa.[385]

The Bombayers were intended to become the nucleus of the newly founded Christian communities in the Mombasa region and subsequently in places of the interior of Africa. Jones, Semler and David belonged to the group of nine Africans that Livingstone in 1864 brought with him from Bombay to Zanzibar.[386] When they came to Rabai and Kisuludini the surrounding Nika people were much impressed when for the first time they saw educated African Christians. Rebmann was moved to tears when the group sang a hymn during their first worship in Africa.

In Rebmann's letters we notice that coaching and using these young people in the context of the mission field was not always easy. The ex-slaves came from different tribes and languages in a wide area of East and Central Africa. Some of them were from the 'far south', from tribes that Rebmann called Mgindo (or M'gnindo) and Idakiao. Jones and Semler were Yao. Their variety of backgrounds made it difficult for them to communicate with the local Swahili and Nika peoples. Moreover, in Bom-

---

[384] Cf. Scheffbuch, *Große Entdecker*, S. 97-99.
[385] The *Church Missionary Gleaner*, Volume I, 1874, p. 127.
[386] BMM, 1867, S. 429, 430.

bay they had become used to cultivated conditions of life, like good food, clothing, education, a reading culture, and Western manners. Life in Mombasa was much harsher. The practice of hard manual labour of building and cultivating at the mission station fell short of their expectation to be used as missionary workers. Sometimes this led to bitterness between the ex-slaves and their coaches. An extreme example was the conflict between a group of 16 liberated Africans, sent in 1866 by the CMS from Bombay through missionaries Deimler and William B. Chancellor.

There were a number of positive effects brought about by the newcomers. They showed that the Christian faith really changes man's life for the better, and is able to have victory over evils of tribalism and witchcraft. The influx of African ex-slaves was an important encouragement for the congregation. Some strangers showed that they felt at home when intermarriages took place between them and local Christian boys and girls. The first marriage was of newly arrived Polly Christian with local convert Isaac Nyondo. Other Bombay refugees intermarried among themselves, like George David, originally a Mgindo, who became a leading catechist, and Priscilla. These marriages strengthened the early Christian presence in East Africa. The newcomers were expected by the CMS to be co-workers of Western missionaries, like Rebmann, in carrying the message of the Gospel across the boundaries of culture and language to the hearts of the African people.[387]

Apart from the positive aspects of the presence of the Bombayers, there were also negative aspects. Rebmann had expected a lot from them. In 1859 during his exile in Zanzibar he wrote to the Committee: 'I believe the Africans in Bombay may still become an important help to us in East Africa. Let us work on humbly and quietly, and the glory of the Lord will appear unto His children'.[388] After 1864, when looking back at his first experiences with the Bombayers, Rebmann concluded that negative effects had outweighed some of the positive effects. If the CMS asked for his opinion, he would prefer for the time being not to have new groups of Africans from Bombay. Here are extracts from his report to the Committee in 1866.

> They are too different from Africa, have too much of the Indian and European civilisations. They are not used to the poverty. They are not really

---

[387] Rebmann, *Briefe*, 4-5-1865, 26-9-1866.
[388] Letter from Rebmann in Zanzibar to the CMS (no name), 15 December 1858, in a PS of 11 February 1859. He added that his translation of *Luke* would be printed in Bombay in 1860, and he expected that it would be useful for the 'Bombayers' in their preparations for Africa.

6. Fruits and loss 129

useful in general. In their trades, e.g. of carpenter and blacksmith, they are found deficiënt, they cannot replace the Muhamedan workmen. Some are perhaps more fit to be evangelists and teachers. However, some who are trained as such, like evangelist Jones, would be better placed in a school with English, but Nika people do not yet know enough English. Teachers must learn Kinika, but they still have not done properly. It will take them years 'before they speak the pure Kinika and the pure Kisuaheli which are in our position indespensable'. They are strangers twice over, by birth and by education.

Concerning their Christian witness, Rebmann had noticed that the Bombayers were less effective than the local Christians. To the question 'Have you given yourself to Christ?', Rebmann had expected a cheerful 'yes', but the Bombay girls remained silent, and the young men said 'that's my desire', or 'I hope so'.

'In their Christian character, they have not experienced trial. Their Christianity is 'put on rather than rooted, grown from within' in comparison with Nika Christians. The secret spring and the usefulness of a teacher/evangelist is having learnt to become and to stay a Christian against opposition and even persecution. This is found in Nika Christians, who in addition only have to learn how to read and write, they know the language and the culture already. In situations of 'the first rough commencement of a station I should prefer our Nika Christians'.[389]

Rebmann's relationship with the Bombayers had become tense. He found it difficult to delegate work to them, either in the 'secular' or in the spiritual field. His approach to them was not always found tactful. For example he unceremonially dumped catechist Jones with bishop Tozer in Zanzibar, who he normally would not have favoured, because Jones had been slow in learning Nika and Swahili, and consequently in Rebmann's view could not be used.[390] Reed does not explain why he thinks Rebmann's mo-

---

[389] Report by Rebmann, duplicated (by Sparshott?) in Mombasa to the CMS Committee, 27 February 1866.
[390] Cf. Note by Rebmann to CMS Secretary J. Mee, no date, announcing a 'letter to secretary C.C. Fenn in which he will explain why he sent Bombayer evangelist W. Jones to Zanzibar in UMCA service, whereas before he even refused to lend him'; According to the Report by Rebmann (duplicated, by Sparshotts?) in Mombasa to the CMS Committee, 27 February 1866. William Jones taught some younger boys, but the work was impeded and interrupted by lack of accommodation, the need for cultivating, insecurity and hostilities. That is why they were sent to Zanzibar to be supervised by Tozer.

tivation is 'somewhat unfair'.[391] An African worker not speaking an African language is less acceptable than a European missionary who has not yet managed to learn a relevant vernacular tongue. Other Bombayers went back to India. Ishmael Semler returned to Sharanpur after the death of his wife in 1866, the same year Rebmann's wife had died. In 1869 after his stay with the UMCA at Zanzibar, Jones went back to Rabai, and in 1871 after the death of his wife he too temporarily returned to India. Both came back to East Africa in 1874, for taking up tasks in the new CMS plan. Bartle Frere, the visiting British diplomat, gathered 'inferentially' from catechist George David, posted at Ribe, and his friends at Kisuludini, that although the Bombayers continued to love and respect Rebmann, they felt frustrated because of their 'forced inaction', which 'must continue so long as Mr. Rebmann directs the mission'.[392]

How important were the Bombayers for the emerging church in East Africa? A balanced view is needed. The East African Church had started before 1864 when the first Bombayers arrived. It had started long before some of them were ordained as the first indigenous pastors of East Africa. That happened after 1888 when a *Divinity School* was opened at Frere Town. Jones, Semler and Deimler were students.[393] Jones was ordained as an Anglican priest in 1895. By then the East African Church was well on its way. In 1898 Jones resigned for a better paid job with the government.[394] Yet Reed positions Jones, 'as the most influential of the early group of African founders of the church', and after him his fellow-clergyman Ishmael Semler. Another clergyman who he reckoned part of this group was Deimler, also enslaved near Lake Nyasa, who had not come through Bombay, but directly to Mombasa by a British warship in 1875.[395] Reed further adds to the group George David, an 'outstanding person', and Isaac Nyondo, one of Rebmann's earliest converts. He says: 'The whole Bombay group emerge as men and women of intelligence, integrity and sophistication. They were anxious to succeed and did so. They

---

[391] Reed, *Pastors, Partners, Paternalists*, p. 34.
[392] Report from Sir Bartle Frere at HMS Enchantress to CMS Secretary Hutchinson, April 1873.
[393] Sundkler and Steed, *A History of the Church in Africa*, p. 553, includes George David, who died in 1884, in the group of the nine first students of the Divinity School.
[394] Sundkler and Steed, *A History of the Church in Africa*, p. 554.
[395] Reed, *Pastors, Partners, Paternalists*, p. 2, 19, 'He was a clergyman of the Church of England, the first African to be ordained in Kenya after being educated entirely in East Africa'. Although he was named after Johann Gottfried Deimler, probably by Jones and Semler, he never met his namesake.

6. Fruits and loss

were anxious to serve and did so'.[396] He is of the opinion that these African Christians, rather than the missionaries, were the 'true' fathers of the church.[397] According to Reed in Euro-centric history writing the wrong impression is made that the missionaries were in the forefront. He admits that the Western missionaries significantly contributed, were devoted, and were used by God. However, in his view they were not very highstanding people. After stressing that he does not want to denigrate them, Reed sums up a long list of downgrading characteristics. The missionaries were transient, often not of great stature intellectually and spiritually, mainly ordinary people, often not well-educated, they were fallible, limited in vision and experience, they showed personal failings and insecurities, were prejudiced, and they were part of the whole expansion of British influence and power, and succumbed to imperialism.[398]

By degrading the missionaries and by defining the Bombayers as practically the main founders of the East African church Reed tries to correct an imbalance. Unfortunately he creates an opposite imbalance, which is more politically correct than historically justified. Essentially the Bombayers in East Africa were an elite of a foreign culture. Apart from their colour and birth they were not more African than the missionaries. It is impossible to criticise them or the missionaries for that. They were products of the history of the British Empire. However, because of their emphatic acculturation to a European lifestyle, culture, and language, they were less prepared for and less conscious of the need for adapting themselves to the African conditions of life. The local Africans saw them as strangers and at first could not understand them. For that reason Rebmann found them less useful.

The seeds of the Gospel had been sown by Krapf, Rebmann, Erhardt and other missionaries, and the first fruits had been harvested years before the first party of Bombayers arrived in Mombasa. The history of the East African Church continued through the witness of its very first local converts, Mringe, Gunja, Nyondo, Mua Muamba, Mua Zua, Lugo, the Upanga man, Ng'owa, Sidi, etc. Looking at the small number of early converts Reed deridingly remarks, that 'the Pietist Germans were probably happy with this outcome, but to other observers, there was little to show for twenty years of work'.[399] Yet the earliest history of the East African Church is not different from the inconspicuous ways of the emergence of

---

[396] Reed, *Pastors, Partners, Paternalists*, p. 29, 174.
[397] Reed, *Pastors, Partners, Paternalists*, p. 3.
[398] Reed, *Pastors, Partners, Paternalists*, p. 3, 12.
[399] Reed, *Pastors, Partners, Paternalists*, p. 33.

the Christian Church since the beginning of its existence. It is simply incorrect to classify the Bombayers as the originators of the East African Church. This is not to deny that after a troublesome period of reafricanisation some of them became important contributors to East African Christianity. Rebmann's hesitation about the usefulness of the Bombayers was not inspired by thoughts of white supremacy in a colonialist context. Rebmann and his Western colleagues lived and worked before imperialist powers orchestrated the 'scramble for Africa'; they cannot possibly have been part of it or have succumbed to it.

The CMS Committee did not answer to Rebmann's specific remarks on the Bombayers of 1866, nor to the copy of his report that was sent two years later.[400] It is possible that their silence was an indication of tension between the Committee and Rebmann on missionary policy. It could also be a sign of a change of thought in the CMS Committee with regard to the position of Africans in the mission. Gradually the attitude shifted from accepting Africans as fellow-missionaries to limiting their role to the pastorship of the local congregation.[401]

Emma's death

Death was a frequent visitor in the East African mission field, leaving the survivors alone in at their remote post. Attempts by the CMS to send new personnel in support of Rebmann failed more often than not. In August 1864 young James Taylor arrived at the station, much to Rebmann's joy. Bishop Tozer congratulated Rebmann, and called Taylor 'a missionary of great promise ... singularly fitted for the difficult task before him'. In December 1864 Taylor sailed to Mauritius to marry Ann Philipps, and to be ordained by a CMS Bishop. In January 1865 he was back in Kisuludini. A few months later, on his way in Zanzibar, he got sunstroke. On 8 March 1865 Taylor died in the house of Playfair the British consul.[402] Bishop Tozer erected a cross over his grave.[403]

---

[400] Margaret Sparshott in a note from Mombasa to the CMS Committee of 7-4-1868: 'Mr Rebmann received no reply to this letter, he concludes it has not been received and considering its contents important has requested me to copy it'.
[401] Cf. Reed, *Pastors, Partners, Paternalists*, p. 7.
[402] CMS, *Proceedings 1863-1864*, p. 76; *1864-1865*, p. 178-180; *1865-1866*, p. 172; cf. letter from Mary Ann Philipps, wife of James Taylor, from Colombo, Colpetty, 29 June 1865, on Taylor's death, referring to the welcoming attitude of Rebmann who sent an atlas of Africa, and to the books from the mission house in her cases which she was to take to Rebmann; Letters from Rebmann to the CMS Committee (summa-

6. Fruits and loss

Then Johannes Rebmann was hit by a very hard blow. On 8 November 1866 his wife Emma died. According to his own account his dear Emma passed away at 5 o'clock in the morning of the 8th day of suffering 'of what appeared to be an inflammation in the chest'. Fever, shortness of breath, pain, and sleeplessness had almost taken away her power of speech. Probably it was pneumonia.

> 'She took leave of me by a most affectionate smile lighting up her countenance only a few minutes before her happy spirit left its earthly tabernacle to be forever present with the Lord'. Her parting words were: 'Be always with the Lord ... farewell'.

Rebmann gratefully noted that in his grief he was assisted by a guest from the Methodist station at Ribe, one brother Tüsmann (or Tiismann), an Estonian sent by the Swiss St. Chrischona community. Tüsmann buried Emma the same day. He took over in the funeral service when Johannes broke down, who felt especially comforted when in the liturgy John 14: 1-3 was read. Tüsmann remained with him 'for nearly a week and was a great comfort' to him in his 'bereavement and sorrow'. At Ribe Tüsmann stayed until March 1867, and from there he continued to be 'an angel of comfort'.[404]

Although his relatives in Gerlingen had not known Emma face to face, Johannes honoured her memory in a letter to them.[405] The German content he translated for the CMS in London:

> 'I shall always look upon her as one who had been especially prepared for a situation which involved so much of privation and at a time when East Africa was still so much dreaded by Europeans. The Lord gave, the Lord hath taken away, blessed be the name of the Lord. Her memory will still be a blessed one for the East African Mission. Though from her advanced age as

---

rised by Margaret Sparshott), 3 July and 8 Sept 1865, with a reference to the erection of a cross on Taylor's grave.

[403] William George Tozer, Letter to J.W. Festing, 30 Nov. 1864, to the Secretaries, 24 Dec. 1864, of Miss Tozer, 24 August 1865, in: 'Letters of Bishop Tozer and His Sister together with some other records of the Universities' Mission from 1863-1873', edited by Gertrude Ward, London: Office of the Universities' Mission to Central Africa, 1902, p. 40, 44, 62, 63; cf. Johannes Rebmann, *Handwritten Half-year accounts and Journal notes*, from 19 Sept. 1861 to 14 June 1865 [City Archive Gerlingen No 76102a-c; Originals in Württ. Landesbibliothek].

[404] Rebmann, *Briefe*, 26-9-1866; letter from Rebmann in Kisuludini to CMS, 16 Nov. 1866 [CMS/B/OMS/C A5 O24/47]; cf. Rebmann, *Briefe*, 30-4-1868.

[405] Rebmann, Letter from Kisulidini of 16-11-1866 to CMS.

also a want of talent for language, she could not conquer the native tongue so far as to enter into easy conversation with the people, I can already see a greater willingness among the women to come to Christ'.[406]

Emma had been a missionary's wife, faithfully by the side of her husband. She also was a missionary in her own right. She had followed Johannes from Cairo, 'had persevered well in privations', and although she found it difficult to learn the regional Nika language, she had been in regular contact with local women, and 'prepared them to accept Jesus'.[407]

---

[406] Idem.
[407] BMM, 1867, S. 429, 430, referring to Rebmann, Briefe, 16-11-1866; Ledderhose, 'Rebmann' in: ADB, vol. 27, S. 488; cf. Jehle, Der Entdecker, S. 9.

6. Fruits and loss

Baron Karl Klaus von der Decken (1833-1865) (Wikimedia, public domain).

Sir Richard Francis Burton 1821-1890 (by Frederic Leighton, Baron Leighton © National Portrait Gallery, London).

Abe Gunja, the first convert baptised by Rebmann (Calwer Missionsblatt nro 7, 1858).

*John Hanning Speke 1827-1864
(Wikimedia, public domain).*

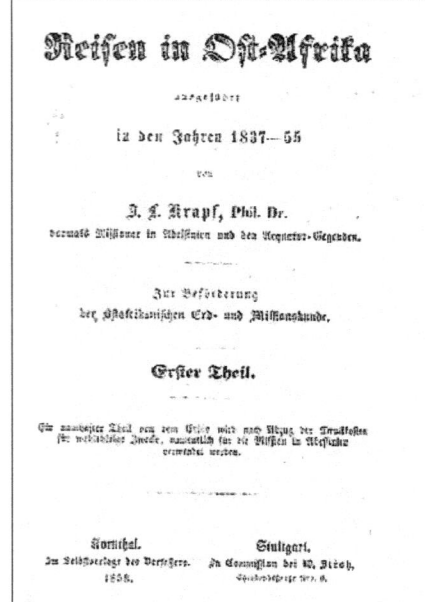
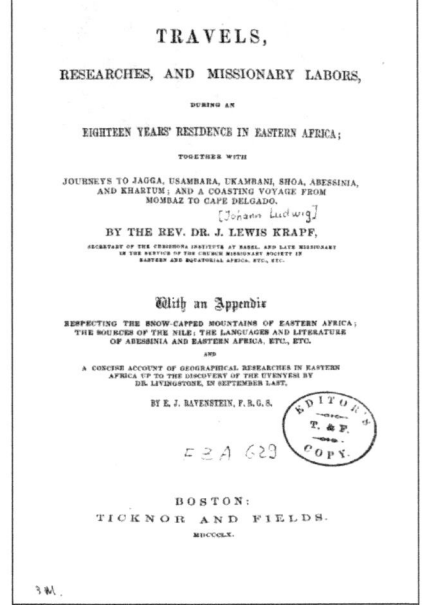

*Title pages of the German edition (1858) and the English edition (1860)
of Krapf's account of his expeditions, including Rebmann's of 1848/1849.*

6. Fruits and loss

'Bombayer' helpers of Rebmann, George and Priscilla David and their children (picture H.K. Binns appr 1875, Kenya National Archive).

David Livingstone, 1813-1873 (Wikimedia, public domain).

7. Lonely and enduring (1866-1875)

Rebmann in CMS policy

After Emma's death and the departure of his friend Tüsmann Johannes in 1866 Rebmann was in East Africa for another nine years. He persevered in Rabai and Kisuludini to prepare and hold the ground for his successors. Besides, there was a harvest of first fruits, the shaping of a tiny congregation, which was the foundation of the Church of East Africa. Rebmann rejoiced at the victory of the Gospel which had started to demonstrate itself by an increase of conversions in Rabai and Kisuludini.[408] At times Rebmann withdrew to Mombasa and Zanzibar, because of fits of ill-health and because of political unrest caused by tribal tensions and competing Sultans. Then he intensified his linguistic labours, translation work and the compilation of dictionaries.

Although the CMS Committee in London had allowed the work in East Africa to continue, its policy was undecided during most of this period. Three interrelated questions waited for answers. First, was it too soon for mission and church planting in East Africa? In other words, was mission expected to succeed in a country under Muslim and African traditional rule, or should it wait for a British political and military umbrella? Since the *Moresby Treaty* of 1822 between Britain and the Sultan of Oman and Zanzibar, British merchants and visitors in the Sultanate enjoyed a certain protection through the presence of British consuls at Zanzibar. However, for CMS mission and missionary personnel in the Mombasa area, at a distance of 250 kilometres from the British Consul's residence, the Consulate could only provide relative safety. Not all consuls were engaged Christians or felt sympathy for missionaries. Their influence was not strong in Mombasa where the Governors had less restraint and motivation to contain anti-Western or anti-Christian feelings than the Sultan. In Rebmann's experience Muslim rule of the East African coastal zone was an enormous hindrance to mission. The Swahili people on the coast were held back by their Islamic authorities. The Nika, Kamba, Samba, Jagga, and Galla peoples outside the Sultanate's corridor were in a different po-

---

[408] Note by Rebmann to Sparshott, 18 Sept. 1872: 'This day the sun rose upon our village as being entirely Christian. The last remnants of Islamism and heathenism were my cook Songoro with his wife Suria, and Abraham's heathen wife, the former were dismissed three weeks ago, the latter was buried as the sun rose. I feel as having gained the victory.'

sition, because they were ruled by their own chiefs and most of them did not belong to Islam. They were much more open to the missionaries and the faith. Yet the presence of Islamic power on the coast was destabilising and disrupting their development, which made Christianising them a difficult task.

> 'Although not civilised, they are not cut off from Christianity. However there is a wall of separation with Europe in the form of Muhamadan power on the coast. The Gospel among them is like a kernel without a shell. It needs a shell. Therefore the missionary has to do a lot of secular work, which may be undesirable in missionary reports'.[409]

In Rebmann's eyes, in East Africa the social, medical, and economical preconditions for mission were undermined by the ever present reality of slavery and the slave-trade under Islam and Muslim rule. He would prefer the power of this rule be broken, at least weakened.

The second question pertained to the 'Bombayers', the Christianised African ex-slaves from Nasik, India. Should more of them be brought back to Africa and would their presence in East Africa be helpful to mission and an emerging church? Although numerical Christian presence was strengthened by new groups of liberated Africans from India, their coming did not fit in Rebmann's missionary ideas. He feared that a clash of culture between 'Europeanised' Africans and local Africans would undermine Christian witness and damage balanced relationships in the Church. Rebmann's honest opinion on the doubtfulness of the effect of the Bombayers did not sound agreeable to the ears of London policy makers, either of the CMS, or the Government, or those who had been responsible for the training of Africans in India.

The third undecided question was related to the policy of the British Empire with regard to the fight against the slave-trade. Where should the slaves that were freed at sea by British warships be taken? What was the best place for the settlement of liberated ex-slaves and what role was to be played by the Church? Rebmann was not in favour of a settlement of ex-slaves in Mombasa as long as the area was under Muslim rule by the Sultanate of Zanzibar. He stressed that the situation was very different from West Africa/Sierra Leone, where ex-slaves were under British rule and free to return to their homes.

> In an East African settlement in the dominions of the Zanzibar Sultanate 'liberated slaves cannot go home, because of the distance and the wretched

---

[409] Annual Letter from Rebmann in Kisuludini to the CMS Committee, 24 Nov. 1868.

7. Lonely and enduring (1866-1875)

state of their homelands', which are Muslim ruled. In the East the slave-trade goes on, condoned by the British government. Its termination is far off. Stopping the slave-trade would be much better than educating liberated children. East Africa is still in the pioneer phase. In the West Missionaries can work among free people, here people are not free. In the West the ex-slaves are educated to be saved for Africa, here they are educated and get estranged from Africa. Some African ex-slaves were mistreated. Others have become arrogant, although poor and ignorant'.[410]

Rebmann was convinced that instead of playing with the thought of a centre for ex-slaves, the CMS should 'focus on spreading the Gospel to the tribes of East Africa!' In conclusion he said 'continuing this mission work is more important than starting the education of young people in a settlement for former slaves'.

The CMS Committee had not ruled out the Mombasa area to be in the picture for all the three questions. However, it took time before final decisions were taken. In the meantime Rebmann and his temporary helpers sometimes got the impression that the CMS was abandoning its position in East Africa, in favour of other missionary players, like the Roman Catholic Mission with their centre in Bagamoyo, or the High-Anglican Universities' Mission in Zanzibar. The crisis by the end of the 1850s caused a substantial interruption of Rebmann's presence in the Mombasa area, but also was used by God to turn the hearts of some Nika people to the Gospel. Since then he had become convinced that he and the CMS had to continue in East Africa. One should not look at outward appearances. Even in 1870 he did not regard 'East Africa as a field which justifies the expectations of great results in number of converts'. However, he stressed that the seed was being sown for a harvest in the future. 'We are in the time of preliminary labours'.

The CMS Committee in London did not always agree with Rebmann's conviction and motivation. Geographical distance, difference of character, and perhaps differences between German and British mind-sets, caused miscommunications and misunderstandings. The CMS looked at East Africa in the wider perspective of British presence in Africa and India, and wondered why the field of Mombasa, which after many years had not yielded much fruit, necessarily was the best vantage point for mission in the region. Also they realised that Rebmann had spent much of his strength and health. The Committee wanted him home in Europe, at least

---

[410] Letter from Rebmann in Kisuludini to Sparshott, 24 Febr. 1872 [sent by Sparshott to C.S. Royston in Greenock, 6-8-1872, indicating that it is a report which Rebmann sent him before he left Mombasa on 11-3-1872].

for a period, so that his health could be restored and so that they could discuss with him 'the best mode of preserving and utilising the fruits of his literary labours in the native languages'.[411] When new plans gradually took shape, Rebmann in their eyes seemed too old and too disconnected from general policy to play a leading role, and to continue as the head of CMS activity in East Africa. He had to be replaced.

Undoubtedly the Committee's dissatisfaction with some aspects of Rebmann's functioning was influenced by reports of a few players in the field who had not been pleased by him. Above we pointed to some visitors who at home coloured Rebmann's picture negatively. Apart from Krapf, there were other colleagues who distanced themselves from Rebmann's views and methods, and reported their criticism to London. Especially workers of CMS in India, who were proud of having trained African slave children at Nasik and Bombay, were offended by Rebmann's unwillingness to receive many of them. Some of their reports were second hand, like the one by John Barton, who himself had never seen Rebmann and East Africa. Here is an extract:

> Rebmann would have greatly benefitted from contact with West India and Nasik long before. This 'might have saved him from falling into that painful position in which he now appears to be. The accounts the African youths brought back from him and his mode of life are most deplorable, and whatever else is done it seems clear enough that the sooner he is brought away the better. It appears that not only he will not preach himself or attempt in any way to reach the heathen, but he would not even let them do so. When one of the Christians lost his wife he would not let them bury her in a decent coffin in the way they had been accustomed in India, but that it was quite enough to wrap the body up in a sheet as the heathen are accustomed to do. Worst of all he recommended one of these widowers to supply the place of the wife he had lost by buying (!) a heathen woman, a slave in fact, in the bazar'.

Barton realised the gossip character of his account, but this did not prevent him from trying to beef it up by mentioning some 'external witnesses'. He added a biting remark, advising the CMS to force Rebmann out in a most unfriendly way.

> 'No doubt these stories are to be received with some qualification, but the impression left on the minds both of Mr. Deimler, Mr Robertson and Mr Price, who know the man well and have had many opportunities of finding

---

[411] CMS, *Proceedings* 1870-1871, p. 206.

7. Lonely and enduring (1866-1875)

out the real facts of the case, is that poor Rebmann has sunk into a sad state and that the sooner he is removed the better it will be for the East African mission. I fear, however, there is little chance of moving him unless you stop his supplies; he says he is going but when it comes to the point, he cannot make up his mind to leave'.[412]

Of the three mentioned 'witnesses' Johann G. Deimler was the only one who knew Rebmann face to face. In the years 1856 and 1857 he was in Kisuludini where he found it too difficult to function and to share the primitive living conditions of the Rebmanns. Later in India, where he played a role in sending Bombayers to Mombasa, his uneasy feelings about East Africa were fed because he felt hurt by Rebmann's scepticism with regard to his protegees. In 1868 when temporarily at home in Germany, because of the illness and subsequent death of his wife, Deimler sent a letter to CMS secretary Henry Venn. In it he admitted that he had spoken with Krapf, and that they both agreed that Rebmann had to come to Europe to refresh and to publish the valuable books that he had compiled. In their view he should be replaced by unmarried missionaries. At that time Deimler still thought that Rebmann might return for another period, to be again with 'his dear East African children'.[413]

The CMS Committee seem to have been influenced by these voices. However, removing Rebmann, either temporarily or permanently, had to be done in a respectful way, without harming or damaging him. The task for new missionaries sent by the CMS to the Mombasa area gradually shifted from just assisting Rebmann to performing responsibilities independently of him, including the assignment of advising him to take a furlough. However, as in the past, the newcomers did not last long. The first one to assist, after the untimely death of James Taylor in 1865 and of Emma Kent in 1866, was E. Parnell. He was accompanied by his wife. Parnell was a clergyman who had studied Arabic and medical science. As such he was a perfect helper in Rebmann's situation of health problems and linguistic challenges. Unfortunately, however, Parnell got serious eye

---

[412] CMS, *Mission Book*, of documents received in 1871-1872, p. 245-246(2), letter, n.d., from J. Barton relating to the possibility of sending African ex-slaves trained at Nasik to Kisuludini to work together with other liberated slaves, i.e.15-20 educated as blacksmiths, carpenters etc., and a few as teacher-catechists, e.g. William Jones then with Deimler at Bombay [CMS/B/OMS/C MA M3].

[413] Letter from J.G. Deimler in Windesheim/Stuttgart to Venn, 20 August 1868 [CI3/O 25/13].

problems and had to give up, leaving Rebmann more lonely than before.[414]

Accused of stagnation

In April 1868 Thomas H. Sparshott and his wife arrived. Rebmann had organised a joyful reception by the Nika people of Rabai and Kisuludini. They sang several hymns which he had composed in their own language for the occasion, which William Jones had printed at Zanzibar.[415] The CMS had given Sparshott the responsibility to rejuvenate the CMS work in the Mombasa area, including the making of preparations for the planned settlement of ex-slaves. He was briefed to cooperate with Rebmann, but not to work under him.

The CMS Committee, in letters to Rebmann, expressed its 'deepest sympathy' with the loss of his wife, and then informed him about Sparshott's appointment and position. They also encouraged him to visit London and home.[416] Apparently they did not want Sparshott to follow Rebmann's line. In a separate letter to Rebmann the Committee gave some reasons. We have not found the literal content, but the gist is clear from Rebmann's written defence. Probably because of disappointing numerical growth of the East African Church, the Committee had concluded that there was 'spiritual stagnation in the mission field'. They also suggested a cause, wondering whether Rebmann spent too much time and energy on 'secular work'. Especially they pointed to his building activity, and his refusal to delegate that task to the Bombayers and to local Africans.

The suggestion of spiritual failure was a hard blow to Rebmann. He said that it made him weep. Yet he suppressed the inclination to conclude that the Committee implied 'a want of confidence and yielding', for that would mean that his 'position was not really understood at home'. If that were the case he would have to withdraw from his post at once. Rebmann preferred to take the words as a brotherly warning by his authorities in the great project of winning souls for Christ, in what they saw as errors. He had gone into judgment with himself and reported on the result of it. He was aware of his weaknesses even of his transgressions. 'I am willing to call myself an unprofitable servant, but the Holy Spirit is

---

[414] CMS, *Proceedings 1867-1868*, p. 139, 140; CMS, *Intelligencer 1866*, p. 266, 267; cf. letter from Rebmann in Kisuludini to the CMS Committee, 16 November 1866 [CMS/B/OMS/C A5 O24/47].

[415] Annual Letter from Rebmann in Kisuludini to CMS Committee, 24 Nov. 1868.

[416] Letters from CMS Secretary C.C. Fenn to Rebmann, dd. 17 July 1867 and 26 August 1868 [CMS/B/OMS/C A5/I, p. 3, and p. 6].

7. Lonely and enduring (1866-1875)

first of all the Spirit of truth'. In this light Rebmann wanted to comment on the 'all important subject treated in your letter'. There is stagnation indeed, but it should be considered positively not negatively. 'The stagnation is a slow but undeniable process of 'growth, be it materially or spiritually'. He called for patience.

The reproach of spending too much time on secular activities was not new. Already before the death of his wife he had had to defend himself in letters to the CMS Committee. In 1859 when returning to Kisuludini after the period of exile in Zanzibar, he found the station in ruins. He spent half a year on rebuilding and enlarging the houses, 'of burnt bricks now', so that the settlement would be a permanent one. Referring to Livingstone 'who also built houses for his people with his own hands', Rebmann stressed the missiological necessity of this work.[417] He realised the 'temptation of letting building be more important than preaching'. One should do both. Drawing a comparison with Paul as a tentmaker, he said:

> 'The spiritual work also in an African wilderness, will never be done except the missionary knows to unite it with proper time measure the secular work of not only building himself a proper house, but also of helping his poor converts to do the same, and bring in the very nature of Christianity to unfold and represent ... in civilisation'.[418]

Building 'is not rightly called mere secular work'. It belongs to the work that must be done. 'Even the apostles served at the tables when no other people were at hand.' Delegating this task he found impossible because local Africans were too poor for it and the Bombayers refused to emulate his example. All members of the congregation needed all their time and strength for cultivating their gardens in order to survive. He also pointed to Krapf, who in 1851 failed in Ukambani 'simply because he had found no house to live in, and would take no time to build one'.[419] The Sparshotts also soon discovered that working with mortar and bricks could not be evaded. It was one of the normal activities at the mission in Rabai and Kisuludini. In Rebmann's vision better houses were part of Christian ethics.

Troubled by fever and by the death of their new-born baby, the Sparshotts found it difficult to participate in daily life at the mission. Moreo-

---

[417] Letter from Rebmann in Mombasa to the CMS Committee, 13 April 1860 [CMS/B/OMS/C A5 O 24/36].
[418] Letter from Rebmann in Mombasa to the CMS Committee, 15 Sept. 1860 [CMS/B/OMS/C A5 O24/37].
[419] Letter from Rebmann in Mombasa to the CMS Committee, 2 May 1868 [CMS/B/OMS/C A5 O24/42].

ver, the local political situation had again become unstable and dangerous for the CMS workers. A war, not only of Giriama against Nika, but also of Kamba against Masai, and of Somola and Galla against Kamba, created unsettled conditions. He commented: 'There seems to be less prospect of extension of the mission into the interior than there was 20 years ago'. However, he faithfully added: 'There is the better and higher prospect of their extremity becoming God's opportunity'. The wars of the tribes had devastating consequences. Both sides seized wives and children and enslaved them. A lot of people were killed, and others withdrew into the 'kaya', that is behind the palisades of fortified villages. The small Christian congregation was affected by these troubles, but its growth was not stunted by them.

One of the problems of the missionaries was how to attract women to conversion and baptism. Until that time the congregation had no baptised women, apart from those from Bombay. Yet Emma Rebmann and others had not in vain sown the seed of the Gospel among the Nika women. In addition, Rebmann noticed that a general interest in the Christian faith had taken root. Even among the heathen harshness and cruelty in the relationships gave way to mutual respect.[420] Sparshott observed that the young native Church consisted of steadfast Christians, a lay teacher, 14 members and 7 communicants, 'proving themselves to be indeed the Lord's own people'.

Against vacating Mombasa

The hopeful signs of a growing impact of the East African mission were scarcely noticed by the CMS in London. It looked as if they were tired of the seemingly unyielding mission station in the Mombasa area. Rebmann had to come home, at least for a furlough, perhaps permanently. There were persistent rumours that the CMS would withdraw from the East African mission field, abandon it, or hand it over to the High Anglicans or the Roman Catholics. In 1870 they removed Thomas and Margaret Sparshott from Mombasa to the Seychelles, against their will. The CMS had the intention to give Sparshott a permanent job on those islands 'with the view of commencing missionary operations among the liberated slaves' there, 'with the hope that a basis may thus be obtained for evangelistic efforts on the continent'. The plan failed because the British government hesitated to opt for the Seychelles as an assembling point for ex-slaves. Zanzibar and Mombasa seemed more logical choices. The CMS

---

[420] Rebmann, *Briefe*, 23-11-1869.

7. Lonely and enduring (1866-1875)

sent the Sparshotts back, first to Mauritius, then to Mombasa, which according to CMS *Proceedings* 'should be for the present the head-quarters of the East African Mission'.[421] However, the status of headquarters could change soon, because in the observation of the CMS during these years the work at Mombasa – Rabai – Kisuludini was at its lowest ebb. The yearly *Proceedings* reflect almost no activity and no vision, apart from the Committee's instruction for Rebmann to visit Europe, and the suggestion that Sparshott had to go back to the Seychelles, because that island might after all become a centre of ex-slaves.

In 1872 the Sparshotts had to give up. Thomas' health had deteriorated a lot. Consequently he was 'medically ordered to return to his country'.[422] In May 1872, on board of the *Abydos* to Aden, on his way to London through Bombay, Thomas Sparshott emphatically protested against a letter of the CMS Secretaries, which according to him was 'perplexing, grievous and puzzling'.[423] He was especially grieved because the secretaries showed an 'apparent want of interest in East Africa'. He refused to go back to the Seychelles, and start a slave settlement there, because it would certainly fail. Not the Seychelles, but 'Mombasa will be a suitable place for a slave depot'.

In his report to the CMS Secretariat Sparshott showed unflinching loyalty to Rebmann. He appreciated that Rebmann at first had assented him to settle in Mombasa permanently. He supported his arguments for continuing the mission field, and not transferring it to others. The Kingdom roots in small beginnings. New converts, like Abe Ng'owa and seven others, were harbingers of more successes. He could not understand why the Secretaries continued to call Kisuludini 'an unfruitful soil', especially since he himself believed to be 'the first missionary spared to the Society who has been willing to stay and devote his strength to educational and evangelistic work', in addition to Rebmann's labours. Referring to the rumours that the CMS would abandon the mission field to others, Sparshott in support of Rebmann adroitly challenged the contemporary Low Anglican or Evangelical feelings of the CMS, which were opposed to the motives and objectives of 'romanised' High Anglicanism. Realising the sensitivity of the issue, Sparshott suggested that the secretaries might be influenced by the Anglo-Catholic bishops of the Universities' Mission Tozer and Steere, who in his mind from their location at Zanzibar had

---

[421] CMS, *Proceedings 1868-1869*, p. 173; *Proceedings 1869-1870*, p. 210; *Proceedings 1870-1871*, p. 206.
[422] CMS, *Proceedings 1871-1872*, p. 191.
[423] 'Annual Report', by T.H. Sparshott in Aden, to the CMS Secretaries, 6 May1872.

fixed their greedy eyes at the CMS possessions in the Mombasa area. He even called the bishops 'wolves, ready to go, to steal, to kill, and to destroy the precious lambs of Christ's fold', and he further said: 'I know they are most anxious to gain possession of our station and that of Ribe, and of Mr. Rebmann's manuscripts. May God forbid that the CMS should ever give one iota to such deceitful men. Giving it to them is giving up East Africa'. Secretary Henry Venn was reminded by Sparshott of having warned against the ploys of the bishops. 'I have thanked God continually that Mr. Venn told me before leaving him: Bishop Tozer's principles are not our principles and I don't want you to have anything to do with them'. He warned the secretaries that they could be used in the political game of the British government with the 'Romanists' who had already got Bagamoyo, and the High Anglicans who wanted Mombasa, whereas the CMS was wearing out and losing.

Sparshott, in his report to the CMS secretaries, shared Rebmann's scepticism with regard to the usefulness of the Bombayers. He informed them about his personal experiences, when he worked with the Afro-Indians. Apart from his observation that some of the boys 'were a disgrace', because of loose morals, e.g. drinking, he warned not to expect help from the Bombayers in the work of mission. They are 'so isolated in their affections', and do not want to be fellow-Africans. They are less useful than those Africans educated in their own African environment.

Sparshott, on his way to London, understood why Rebmann had not left his post, although he was exhausted and due to go on furlough. The lack of genuine interest and understanding of the CMS Committee, the relative ineffectiveness of the Bombayers, and the absence of a successor were among other reasons. The main reason, though, was the risk of losing the mission to others. He reported to the CMS secretaries: 'I could not help thanking God for the providence which he has retained Mr. Rebmann to keep them out. I sent him a cask of beer, and a case of port, which I knew he much needed, and which I felt convinced the Committee would justify.'

Another pressing reason for Rebmann's inability to travel home was his bodily weakness and illness. Sparshott said that he had left him in a very weak state. His 'failing health had almost entirely laid him aside from work for two years', and he would be unable to travel before the beginning of 1872. In addition, Rebmann was worried about his manuscripts. Sparshott:

> 'I urged him to allow me to carry him away and take him to Zanzibar and go home in the Abydos, but he has a number of papers, including some Ni-

7. Lonely and enduring (1866-1875)

ka hymns, which he feels he must arrange before leaving, which will take him a few months after his recovery. He therefore earnestly begs the Committee to have patience with him. He says: God willing they will see me in their presence'.[424]

Sparshott agreed that Rebmann should be replaced. Actually he proposed to the CMS secretaries to return to East Africa as Rebmann's successor, subsequently help him to go home, and then continue to assist the feeble emerging Church.

> 'I cannot withhold my conviction that Mr. Rebmann's work is done. His constitution is broken, and the effort to go home will be too much for him. ... I believe if the Committee allow me to see them, and will consent my returning to Mombasa to continue the work', Mr. Rebmann will not find it difficult to leave soon.[425]

Apart from Sparshot's offer, attempts had failed to move Rebmann away from East Africa and send him home. CMS secretary Hutchinson addressed Rebmann's erstwhile fellow-worker Johann Gottfried Deimler in Bombay. He begged him 'to go to Mombasa and bring away Mr. Rebmann'. Deimler refused. His motivation is interesting, apart from his explanations of the prohibiting conditions of the weather, due to the time of year.

> 'Again, knowing Br. Rebmann's character and habits ... I have not the least confidence that I shall prevail upon him to leave with me East Africa before Mr. Sparshott has actually taken charge of the East Africa Mission. ... I consider it very likely that even if the steamer were waiting for him at Mombasa to receive him on board he might tell me that he could not possibly leave the station before Mr. Sparshott arrived'. If you bring in Sparshott, then Rebmann has not the slightest reason to remain any longer. ... This is in my opinion the only effectual means for bringing Mr. Rebmann home, removing so to say the ground from under his feet and giving him no more any room in East Africa'.[426]

Deimler's letter undoubtedly strengthened Sparshott's position with the CMS Committee. They did not turn a deaf ear on Sparshott's protest, and allowed him to return to Mombasa, accompanied by W.B. Chancellor.[427]

---

[424] Sparshott, 'Annual Report', idem.
[425] Sparshott, 'Annual Report', idem.
[426] Letter from J.G. Deimler in Bombay to CMS, 12-5-1874 [CI3/O 25/18].
[427] CMS, *Proceedings 1873-1874*, p. 32, 33.

The missionaries were charged to reshape the East African Mission, and gradually take over from Rebmann. Sparshott was happy to be back, and marvelled 'to find so many still bright and rejoicing Christians in Rabai'.[428] Both missionaries got involved in new arrivals of African Christians from Bombay, and in new disappointing experiences. That was one of the reasons why again Rebmann 'could not be persuaded to return to Europe in the summer of 1873', nor in the following months. The Committee's *Proceedings* admitted that Rebmann 'felt with justice that it would be dangerous for him to return in winter', and be felled by pneumonia. A tragic aspect of Rebmann's position was that by then he had become visually handicapped. Probably, at last the need for an eye operation in Europe took away his resistance against the idea of going on furlough.

Bartle Frere's observation and advice

The years 1873 and 1874 mark a turning point in the East Africa policy of the CMS. Final decisions were taken to continue the East Africa mission field at Mombasa, to transfer as many Bombayers as possible to Mombasa, and to accept the British government's invitation of establishing a permanent settlement for ex-slaves in Mombasa. These decisive steps were not in the first place inspired by the outward appearance of the emerging East African Church and even less by Rebmann's advice and vision. To a great extent the CMS went by the observations and the advice of a high-ranking British diplomat, Sir Henry Bartle Edward Frere, former Governor of India.[429] In 1873 the British government sent Bartle Frere to East Africa to investigate the situation of the slave-trade, to evaluate the measures that had been taken against it, and to design a new plan for Britain's involvement in the region. Bartle Frere was happy to accept an additional assignment, from the CMS, to observe the East African mission field in the Mombasa area and to give advice. He also visited the Roman Catholic centre Bagamoyo north of Dar es Salaam, a small beginning settlement for ex-slaves, which had been established in 1868,[430] and the High Anglican training centre at Zanzibar. Although he thought their ap-

---

[428] Sparshott, in Mombasa, in a letter of December 1873 to: *The Church Missionary Gleaner*, Volume I, 1874, 79.
[429] Sir Bartle Frere (1815-1884) Governor of Bombay during the 1860s, High Commissioner for South Africa in 1877.
[430] Sundkler, *A History of the Church in Africa*, p. 526, 527.

7. Lonely and enduring (1866-1875)

proach was too academic, Bartle Frere did not hide his sympathy for 'Catholic' presence in East Africa.

In Bartle Frere's concept, the CMS like the other agencies was to play a major role in finding provision for the future and welfare of captured ex-slaves, i.e. the reception and training of slaves liberated by the British Navy. When the plan of assembling the ex-slaves on the Seychelles was abandoned, the Mombasa area was proposed. This implied the construction of a settlement of freed slaves under British supervision in a territory outside British jurisdiction, ruled by the Muslim-Zanzibar Sultanate. The presence of a mission station, as well as the desire of the CMS to incorporate the training and care of freed slaves in its East African mission, opened the door for cooperation between Church and State. The *Intelligencer* describes the Committee's thought on the issue.

> We need a settlement on the coast 'possibly not an English possession, but certainly under English administration'. Moreover, such a settlement 'needs Christian rule and example'. Leaving them in secular hand to their own religion, is leaving them to fetishism, jugglery, magic spells, poisoning, degrading superstition, witchcraft, etc., as negro settlements in Arabia show.' The course of the CMS is simple and clear: 'already has the Committee determined to open a special fund for East Africa.'[431]

These words show that the CMS had left its attitude of hesitation and doubt with regard to East Africa. They had decided in favour of continuation, in terms of a new strategy.

> It is not improbable that Mombas may be chosen for a settlement: that Mission is accordingly to be strengthened; it will be a remarkable coincidence if the place at which the Society has been labouring for so many years with so little success, should become the scene of more cheering labours. There is still the veteran Rebmann, a perfect master of all the languages of that part of Africa, and with him are a few converts, whose assistance might be had in commencing the operations, while skilled labourers might be imported from the Society's school at Nasik.'[432]

To an extent the interests of the Empire and the Church merged. However, would the CMS mission station, in its present setting with its present veteran missionary, fit in this plan? That question was in Bartle Frere's mind when he visited Mombasa, Rabai and Kisuludini. Some passages of

---

[431] CMS, *Intelligencer*, December 1872.
[432] Idem.

his report to the CMS Committee are unique as contemporary observations of Rebmann's personality by an outsider.

> 'We found Mr. Rebmann, living I should think, a most unwholesome life, in an old native house at Mombas, sadly in want of cleansing, whitewashing and ventilation. He seems utterly worn out, by climate, over-study, and solitude, and if he does not get a change, I fear he will certainly die. But he has entirely lost the power of making up his mind, and making preparations for a move; and he has for some months past given up his old occupation connected with the languages of the country – of his three great works, the dictionaries of the three great divisions of East African languages, and he told me, were fairly written out, and I should judge in a state which anyone less exacting as to perfection of work, than Mr. Rebmann himself, would consider ready for the Press. The third is still in the rough, but I should think complete as to materials, and only needing careful transcription. He told me he would, on no account part with them to anyone, and I feel sure that the only way to get these invaluable works printed and placed beyond the reach of loss, will be to get him to take them to Germany and print them there. I do not believe that there is any chance of their being added to, or further perfected, by his remaining at Mombas, for he told us that, for months past, he had done nothing connected with languages, being wholly absorbed in spiritual thoughts, connected with the Fall, the institution of the Lord's Supper, and other like subjects, regarding which he puts his thoughts in verse, in English or German. It really seems to me that the only chance of saving his life, and the results of so many years labour, is that you should send some discreet person, possibly a countryman of his own would be best, with no other duty to perform than to uproot him and bring him away. It will be no easy task, but unless it is performed, he may die any day, and all his papers be lost. He must be <u>brought</u> away, not <u>sent</u> away [underlined by B.F.]; for he is really no more fit to move himself, or to travel by himself in steamers and railways, than a child of 5 years old. His mental faculties are in many respects, as bright as ever, and his memory is wonderful, but solitude has reduced him more to the state of one in extatic trance than of an ordinary practical missionary. He has done great service, apart from his linguistic acquirements, by making a character for the mission and for all Europeans. This service is priceless, and he is regarded by all around him with great veneration as a holy man; but beyond the conviction that our religion can produce such beings, he really does not now promote your cause, as he has done in years past. Indeed while he remains at Mombas I see little chance of anyone else being able to do much for you, either at Mombas or Kisuludini. It is impossible to set aside Mr. Rebmann's authority, and equally impossible to move him to alter his views, or to get him to allow others to work. You probably know his extreme views regarding any admixture of

7. Lonely and enduring (1866-1875)

any but the highest and most spiritual teaching and motive. I have no doubt that one real convert he would make, in his own way, would be worth thousands of such as would satisfy ordinary missionaries, but I have met with very few men in my life, who could pass the rigid tests he would apply, and really can find in no history, sacred or profane, any accord of a province being converted by such means as he would permit of.'[433]

In brief, as a representative of the British Empire in India and Africa, Bartle Frere 'found little to admire' at the CMS mission station. At the same time personally he highly respected and valued Rebmann's work and person. Although Rebmann was 'feeble and quite blind' and there was 'little visible evidence of success', his significance did not escape him. Bartle Frere not only expressed this positive evaluation in his report to the CMS Secretariat, but he also published it for a wider circle of interested people, e.g. in an article in the *The Church Missionary Gleaner*:

'Mr Rebmann, whom I was sorry to find utterly prostrated in bodily strength by overwork and solitude, is a scholar of the highest repute, who has devoted his life to the study of the languages of East Africa. He has completed dictionaries of three of the most extended dialects, one of the tribes round lake Nyassa, another of the Suaheli or Coast dialect, and a third of the Nika, the first and last being ready for the printer, and the other requiring fair transcription ... . Much has been said at Zanzibar and elsewhere regarding the small number of converts, especially at the CMS station. But it seems to me that apart from their literary labours, if judged only by character, they have established among the people around them, Mr. Rebmann and his fellow-missionaries have not lived or laboured in vain. They seemed to me to be regarded as benificent superior beings, whose presence the simple tribes round were glad to secure, and whose precepts and example they would gladly follow.'[434]

Although he emphatically praised Rebmann, Bartle Frere realised that the missionary did not fit in his policy. Rebmann's target was the Kingdom of God, which did not necessarily run parallel with British interests. In Bartle Frere's mind Rebmann was too conservative and too unpractical for the realisation of British objectives in East Africa. Probably he envisaged German-British tensions in the area and did not prefer Germans to play a role in his plans. Bartle Frere expressed his opinion that Rebmann should now be helped to leave, to save his own life, and to make room for

---

[433] Report by Sir Bartle Frere at HMS Enchantress to CMS Secretary Hutchinson, dd April 1873 [CMS/G/Y A5/23].
[434] *The Church Missionary Gleaner*, vol. 1, 1874, p. 78-80.

a new missionary approach in East Africa. In the rest of the report he enveloped his descriptions of the task of the CMS in Africa by his general vision 'to speed up the end of slavery'. The establishment of a large settlement of ex-slaves, freed by British war ships, on the Mombasa coast, under the umbrella of the CMS was vital in this vision. He realised that the small number of converts should not be considered as an indication of failure, although he thought that Rebmann's criteria for admission to the Church were too strict.

As to the geographical position of the mission, Bartle Frere was of the opinion that it was 'extremely well chosen in every respect, for operating on the coast as well as on the interior'.[435] The insalubrity of the climate was only a problem on the coast, but in hills and the interior he found the climate healthy.

With regard to the intake of African ex-slaves, educated in Bombay, Nasik and other places in India, Bartle Frere emphatically differed from Rebmann.

> 'I would send to Mombas, as soon as Mr. Rebmann leaves, all the Africans who can be spared from Nassick, and at once set them to work, those who can do nothing else cultivating for their own subsistence, as the natives do. I talked the matter over carefully with George David, and feel assured that, if the management were left to him, he would make it a great success, with very little help from Europeans. But all will depend on your having a good practical large-hearted and energetic man, at the lead of affairs, out at Mombas.'[436]

Here Bartle Frere swept aside Rebmann's spiritual and practical objections against the immigration of Africans who had grown away from their own culture. The usefulness of the Bombayers for mission may be debatable, but in the diplomat's thought they were undoubtedly useful for the furtherance of the interests of the British Empire in East Africa. Although the CMS followed Bartle Frere in this issue and with regard to the settlement for ex-slaves, they did not slavishly accept all his proposals and qualifications. The diplomat's apparent admiration of 'the ef-

---

[435] Sir Bartle Frere, *Eastern Africa as a Field for Missionary Labour*, London: Murray 1874, review in: *CMS Intelligencer*, November 1874, Mombasa: about 2 miles long by two and a half broad, and is at its north-west point separated from the mainland only by a shallow ford. It is situated in an estuary which forms a harbour. 'Mombas presents the greatest advantage of all as a place for European settlement'.

[436] *The Church Missionary Gleaner*, vol. 1, 1847, p. 78-80.

7. Lonely and enduring (1866-1875)

fectiveness' of Roman Catholic policies and the 'successes' of the Universities' Mission did not sound well in the ears of the CMS Committee. Any present-day missionary with some experience at Africa's east coast would frown at his descriptions of African Traditional Religion, which he found 'not strong at the coast', and of Islam, which according to him was 'a decaying creed ... not a serious problem'. In his view of racial positions Bartle Frere was a characteristic product of paternalistic 19th-century Enlightenment belief in the superiority of Western culture and religion that had progressed above African primitivity. He saw in the East African tribes,

> 'backward intelligence of the negro races, a degraded moral and intellectual condition. However, there is a great potential. When educated they easily assimilate to any more highly-civilised race. They need a basis of moral law and such a bond of union as Christianity supplies.'[437]

At one point Rebmann and the CMS Committee undoubtedly fully agreed with Bartle Frere. The slave-trade had to be rooted out. CMS secretary Hutchinson had just published a book rousing the consciousness of the general public.[438] Christianity cannot exist where slavery is allowed to exist. The former treaties between Britain and the Sultan had not been helpful. Britain had to act!

The establishment of Frere Town

According to the *Proceedings* of the CMS by the end of 1874 Rebmann was 'in a physically prostrated condition'. Often he had to withdraw from Kisuludini to the slightly easier situation in the mission's house in Mombasa. Sparshott practically had replaced him as supervisor of the Bombayers, who outnumbered local Christians in the tiny East African Church. However, Sparshott's relationship with the Bombayers and with his colleague Chancellor went sour. To this complicated network in November 1874 another participant was added, with the arrival of William Salter Price (1826-1911). He was supposed to be the 'energetic man' suggested by Bartle Frere, who for the CMS was to translate Bartle Frere's ideas into deeds. Formally he became the new head of mission. Price was an experienced player in the India – East Africa scene of CMS activities. He was the former superintendent of the Nasik Asylum of Sharanpur near Bombay in Western India where the CMS christianised and trained liber-

---

[437] CMS, *Intelligencer*, November 1874.
[438] Edward Hutchinson, *The Slave-Trade of East Africa*, London: Sampson Low, 1874.

ated African slave children. With the help of Johann G. Deimler, who after his stay in East Africa, served as a missionary to Muslims in Bombay, Price had sent Nasik pupils from Sharanpur through Bombay to the Mombasa area. To them belonged the catechists William Jones, Ishmael Semler and George David, who Deimler had sent to Price for an extra training in the trades of blacksmith and carpenter, before they were sent to Mombasa.[439] Also Price's companion Jacob Wainwright was trained there. Wainwright was a former helper and pupil of Stanley. He had taken part in the burial of Livingstone, both of his heart at Ilala, present-day Zambia, in 1873, and his body in Westminster Abbey, London, 1874. Price was warmly welcomed by his ex-pupils and by the rest of the East African Church.

Price had not come alone. Apart from his wife, Wainwright, and six other missionaries had joined him: the ministers John Williams, David S. Remington, the mechanics Joseph T. Last, and John G. Pearson plus a female teacher. Price's main task was to receive liberated slaves from the British authorities and prepare a settlement for them on the mainland of Mombasa. The second task for the team was strengthening and expanding the work by the mission station at Kisuludini. In addition, they were assigned to establish new fields in the Interior, e.g. among the Jagga, and among the coastal Swahilis.[440] However, soon death, disease and disharmonies forced Price to slow down and moderate his expectations. Chancellor was moved to the Seychelles, Remington died, and Williams went home after his wife died. Other staff replaced some of them. Price himself in the beginning of 1875 was hit by malaria and nearly died. Charles New of the neighbouring Methodist Mission at Ribe died. Bombardment of Mombasa by a rebel force from Fort Jesus, and subsequent bombardments of the Fort by British ships, set Mombasa on fire and made it a dangerous place. The environment of Mombasa had also become dangerous, because of a war between the Nika and Kamba peoples. A description of these troubles concluded Price's interesting Diary, published by the *CMS Intelligencer*.[441] The problems did not take away his confidence that Western Christian mission would bring progress and prosperity to Africa. In a speech full of the rhetoric of 19th century Euro-Christian self-consciousness to the Nika elders, interpreted by George David, he said:

---

[439] *The Church Missionary Gleaner*, vol. 1, 1874, p. 127.
[440] *The Church Missionary Gleaner*, vol. 1, 1874, p. 128.
[441] *The CMS Intelligencer*, May 1875: Price's Journal, 14 Nov 1874-20 Febr. 1875. Price added pictures to his writings; he belonged to the rare possessors of a 'photo apparatus'.

7. Lonely and enduring (1866-1875)

'We have come for no other purpose than to do you all the good we can. God has greatly blessed us. He has given us knowledge of many things, and made us a happy and prosperous people, and our wish is to impart this knowledge and blessing to you. There is one thing above all others on which our happiness depends, and which we desire to communicate to you and your countrymen, and that is the knowledge of the true God, and of the way of life which we have learnt from God's Holy Word. This, if you will receive it, will make you happy, now and forever.'[442]

Independent from Price's speech, there was a break-through of a higher reality. God was at work in Mombasa and Kisuludini. New converts to Christ among the contacts of Rebmann came out into the open. More Bombayers arrived, who were supposed to help them. By the time of the arrival of Price their number had grown to over one hundred. They were an addition to the East African Church, which apart from them by that time had already grown to 73 native members, including three teachers and twelve communicants. More of the seed sown by Rebmann had begun to sprout.[443]

Price contributed to the work others had started. That was especially true for the establishment of a settlement for ex-slaves on the mainland opposite the Isle of Mombasa. Rebmann had held the ground until the CMS could develop a free haven for liberated slaves.[444] From the angle of missionary methods the settlement of ex-slaves was much more practical than Krapf's idea of a chain of mission stations.[445] In the 'cities of refuge' in the Mombasa region and elsewhere in Africa a strong Christianity developed, often referred to as 'kitoro' (*refugee*) Christianity, which produced East Africa's first Christian martyr David Koi, beheaded by the Arabs in 1883,[446] and other influential African Christians, such as William Henry Jones. The missionary concept of establishing cities for freed slaves interacted with anti-slavery policies of the British government. Sir Henry Bartle Edward Frere paved the way for the realisation of the CMS concept. As an envoy of the British government he concluded a new pact with the Sultan of Zanzibar, which reduced a lot of the external slave-trade of the Sultanate. Through the British consul he forced the Sultan

---

[442] Idem, reporting on 10 December 1874.
[443] CMS *Proceedings 1874-1875*, p. 37-40; *The Church Missionary Gleaner*, vol. 1, 1874, p. 80, 127.
[444] AMZ, Beiblatt, S. 24. In an article on Livingstone, Rebmann is referred to as the person who paved the way for the new activities by CMS and Sir Bartle Frere.
[445] Cf. Fiedler, *Story of Faith Missions*, 73-84.
[446] Cf. Hildebrandt, *History of the Church in Africa*, p. 183.

into acceptance by simply blockading the harbour of Zanzibar with gunboats until the Sultan gave in to his demands. The British government of Gladstone was not happy with this very direct approach, but the act was popular with the English and Scottish public, who had been fired up by the publicity of Livingstone's anti-slavery ideals, his adventures, and by his famous meeting with Stanley in 1872. Popular, at least with the leaders of the Evangelical Awakening and the anti-slavery movement in Britain, were the British warships that freed the slaves, who were smuggled by Arab *dhows* from Zanzibar and other places in the Sultanate to Arabia and Asia.

The sending of Bombayers to Mombasa by the CMS was a prelude to the settlement of ex-slaves, which was born out of an agreement between the British government and the CMS, condoned by the Muslim rulers of the Zanzibar Sultanate. In 1873 the CMS had sent William B. Chancellor to Mombasa to assist Rebmann with the African ex-slaves from Bombay who had already arrived, and to help with the establishment of the 'city of refuge'. The settlement was started in 1874 on the mainland, opposite Mombasa. In fact it was not the first one. In 1848, on his journeys to Jagga-land, Rebmann had already seen a settlement of ex-slaves, who had fled from their masters on the coast.[447] Others sprang up later, even near Mombasa. Chancellor first named the Mombasa settlement 'Venn's Town', after Henry Venn,[448] the secretary of the CMS, strategist of mission and opponent of slavery, who had died a few years before. However, history remembers the settlement as 'Frere Town', because Sir Bartle Frere designed the political and military conditions for its birth.[449]

Above we saw that preceding a large influx of freed slaves in Frere Town in 1875, the CMS in 1874 had sent William Salter Price to take over from Rebmann,[450] to 'revitalise' CMS work in the Mombasa region and include it in the wider concept of Frere Town.[451] Apparently he agreed to Rebmann's arguments not to establish the settlement at Kisuludini,[452] thus deviating from the original ideas in London.[453] On the mainland at

---

[447] Rebmann, *Tagebuch*, 10-6-1848.
[448] Henry Venn (1796-1873), http://www.dacb.org/stories/non%20africans/legacy_venn.html
[449] BMM, 1876, S. 152-154.
[450] AMZ, 1875, S. 428.
[451] BMM, 1876, S. 157.
[452] Statement by Rebmann to CMS Committee, reasons against choosing Kisuludini as a place of the settlement for liberated slaves [CMS/G/Y A5/1/1].
[453] In *The Church Missionary Gleaner*, Volume I, 1874, p. 80, the CMS Committee mentions Kisuludini as the place where Price was to establish an 'industrial Native

7. Lonely and enduring (1866-1875)

Kisownee, about a mile across the harbour, opposite the island of Mombasa, he bought a tract of land for the CMS from an Arab.[454]

Price's tenure of office lasted only two years. Tropical diseases weakened his health. After his return home he kept in touch with Frere Town. His place in East Africa was taken by CMS veteran missionary in West Africa, James Abner Lamb, who stayed for only a few years too.[455] By that time Frere Town counted 400 liberated slaves.[456] The CMS appointed Lamb as pastoral leader, for 'spiritual affairs'. For the civil administration and government ('secular affairs') of Frere Town they appointed a 'lay superintendent' or 'commander', William F.A.H. Russell. Hoisting the British flag, begun by Price,[457] laid a solid foundation in the political reality. The establishment had practically become a British enclave under the CMS in a Muslim-ruled Arab Sultanate.

Last years in Africa

From the early 1870s Rebmann gradually lost control of the centre of activities and responsibilities in the East African Mission. In part this was because of his physical problems, but it was also due to the shifting CMS policies that gave room to the involvement of others in the leadership of the mission. Sir Bartle Frere's visitation and advice brought about a new period, in which Rebmann was supposed to fade out. Sparshott and Price were to take over his task and to lead him out to Europe. There were still some fundamental uncertainties as to the future of the mission. Even though under the CMS and the British government Frere Town took shape, doubts remained whether the CMS and its Evangelical persuasion would remain the leading factors in emerging East African Christianity. How did Rebmann interact with this changing situation? There was an ambiguity in his vision. On the one hand he was ready to leave, on the other hand he was not.

Christian Colony', for the rescued children. The adult ex-slaves will be 'at or near Mombas where the Government is asked to constitute a free settlement'.

[454] Price's Journal, in CMS, *Intelligencer*, May 1875: 'I doubt if we can find any place more suitable than this for our settlement'. According to CMS, *Proceedings 1876-1877*, p. 39 Frere Town was 220 acres.

[455] CMS, Proceedings 1876-1877, p. 39, 40, summary of the work by Lamb; 1877-1878, p. 53, 54, Lamb left in 1878.

[456] CMS, *Intelligencer*, 1876, p. 436, 437 (July), p. 499, 500 (August).

[457] CMS, *Intelligencer*, March 1876, p. 181. The Sultan had given permission, but some Mombasa Arabs protested.

Rebmann had maintained remarkable good health during most of his years in East Africa. This is to deny Reed's implied claim that ill-health was a 'deeper reason' of his failing plans.[458] In this respect Rebmann had been different from many missionary workers who were sent to the mission station. Many left with broken health like Krapf, or died like Wagner, Taylor and Remington. However, his eyesight had been a problem already since his youth when he came to Africa.[459] For some years he had realised that the end of his time in Africa was drawing near, for example in a poem in 1871, of which the first translated lines run as follows: 'Now I am finally finished with my Africa. There my Germany is open to me, in full harmony.'[460] Apart from his visual handicap, his body was growing weaker. Reed likes to depict Rebmann unfavourably, partly deriving from Bartle Frere he says that in 1874 Rebmann was 'an old man in appearance and behaviour ... physically debilitated ... utterly prostrated by overwork and solitude, and totally blind'. Reed's information on Rebmann's health is not completely reliable. At least his eyesight had not entirely disappeared by that time. Moreover, Reed makes another mistake by giving him only 25 years in Africa in 1874.[461] Actually at that time Rebmann had been in Africa for 28 years. For a long time he had felt unable to answer to the challenge of travelling to Europe. In that critical period he often withdrew to Mombasa, because for a sick person life was a bit easier there than in Kisuludini, where the houses of the mission had become dilapidated.[462] In his loneliness and suffering he tried to continue his literary work.

In crises friendships are tested. Among the Africans Rebmann relied on the small circle of Christians, especially Isaac Nyondo. Among the Europeans he relied on Sparshott most. In a letter he thanked him for the beer and wine, which because of lack of mobility and illness he had not yet touched, although he was not a 'teetotaller by intention or resolution'. On a serious note he said: 'I could have left the mission in your hands with a good conscience'. However, Sparshott had fallen ill and his

---

[458] Reed, *Pastors, Partners, Paternalists*, p. 32.
[459] Rebmann, *Tagebuch*, 8-5-1848, when his companion saw a lake: 'meine schwache Augen reichten nicht so weit'; In a letter of 4-1-1849, he refers to spectacles; cf. Stutzmann, 'Johannes Rebmann: Leben und Werk des Missionars', Vortrag, S. 7.
[460] Rebmann, *Briefe*, 21-9-1871: 'Nun bin ich endlich fertig mit meinem Africa. Mein Deutschland steht mir offen, in voller Eintracht da.'
[461] Reed, *Pastors, Partners, Paternalists*, p. 48.
[462] Cf. Letter from Chancellor to CMS Wright, 4 Febr.1874. 'The cottages built by Mr. Rebmann are in a very dilapidated condition ... the house in which Mr R. lives is all built of stone with a flat roof but it sadly needs repairing. The walls are cracked in several places [C A5/05/8].

7. Lonely and enduring (1866-1875)

sick-furlough in England had made this impossible. Consequently, Rebmann postponed his departure. Now that Rebmann knew that Sparshott had gone home to England, he felt encouraged by God 'to remain still longer and wait patiently for His farther guidance in opening for me the way for going home, or wanting me to die at my post. Thy will be done!' Sparshott's absence, until 1872, did not prevent Rebmann from discussing with his trusted friend some views he knew they shared, and confiding to him some intimate experiences.

First, they were worried about the possible abandonment of the mission by the CMS. Both missionaries realised that in terms of visible successes the mission looked a failure, but the CMS should understand that appearances deceive and that the mission was promising. After Sparshott left, Rebmann informed him about new developments among the neighbouring Giriama, their leaders Abe Sidi, Wanje, Mrari and five young men wanted to join them 'under the book'. Sparshott was to pass this information to the Committee, so that they would be aware of 'this new quiet but important movement in favour of Christianity among an adjacent tribe', and be motivated not to give up the mission. This is how Sparshott wrote on the issue to the Committee (in extract):

> Someone has to be there, for example for the new Christians of the Giriama tribe, who now constantly go to Mr. Rebmann for religious instruction. They have to walk four hours. If there were no one there to meet them, would not the CMS be like 'the ostrich in the wilderness'?[463]

Rebmann added a personal note: 'After a man has devoted 23 years of his life to a mission, which for a time he himself had thought premature, the time is gone by for relinquishing it, even if we had not the prospect just opening before us of gathering in the first fruits from another tribe'.[464]

Rebmann shared with Sparshott his love of the theology of the 16th century Reformation, and his fundamental mistrust of anyone who seemed to betray that position. He was an ardent opponent of Roman Catholic theology and church policy. He belonged to the tradition that considered the Papacy as a greater danger than Islam.[465] Rebmann also

---

[463] 'Annual Report', by T.H. Sparshott in Aden, to the CMS Secretaries, 6 May1872.
[464] Letter from Rebmann in Kisuludini to Sparshott, 24 Febr. 1872 [Sent by Sparshott to C.S. Royston in Greenock, 6-8-1872, indicating that it is an account, which Rebmann sent him before he left Mombasa on 11-3-1872].
[465] Rebmann, *Tagebuch*, S. 148 'However, the Papacy in its relationship to God and fellow-men is 'lügenhafter, greulicher und abscheulicher als selbst der Mohammedanismus'.

opposed the High Church section of Anglicanism, which in his opinion was an imitation of Rome. In addition he suspected the CMS, notwithstanding its Evangelical-Reformed stance, of secretly selling the East African mission field to the High Anglican Universities' Mission (UMCA). Commenting on the position of the CMS in the Church of England, Rebmann pointed to the 'conflict between the Evangelical and Romish elements', and said (in summary):

> In order to preserve union and prevent a rupture of the Church of England the CMS could feel obliged to make a sacrifice to please the other wing. 'Both parties idolize the Common Prayer Book', and want 'with all might to be right with it'. This leads to the question whether the East African Mission 'in its hitherto seemingly unfruitful aspect ... will be found or has already been selected as the lamb most suitable for the sacrifice to bring about a reconciliation, which wanting in truth, will after all never be realised.'

Rebmann was not aware of a comity agreement between the CMS and the UMCA, and he seriously considered the possibility of betrayal by the CMS of his beloved East African mission to the High Anglicans.[466] His suspicions were questionable as he knew that already in 1865 Bishop Tozer had suggested leaving the territories south of the equator to the CMS, and 'the country and tribes bordering on Lake Nyasa' to the Universities' Mission.[467] Yet the thought of losing the mission field to others remained in Rebmann's mind, and made him and Sparshott agree on postponing his departure. He knew that Sparshott would never cooperate in such a handover, and he trusted that under Sparshott in the East African Church 'the pure Gospel of our Lord and Saviour Jesus Christ will continue to be taught, without allowing mere rites and ceremonies to assume a dangerous importance'. However, Sparshott had gone, and he might not return. What to do now? If challenged to vacate the mission in favour of a takeover by the High Anglican bishops, Rebmann would refuse. He felt that as long as he would hang on, the bishops would not dare to come and take

---

[466] Rumours about the East African mission being abandoned by the CMS to the Universities' Mission or being grasped by the Universities' Mission were laid to rest in *The Church Missionary Gleaner*, Volume I, 1874, p. 78, with information on a comity agreement between the UMCA and the CMS. The UMCA 'will we believe extend its operations from Zanzibar in the direction of Livingstone's later journeys; and the CMS is about to do its utmost to strengthen its band of labourers further northward, toward the snow-capped mountain Kilimanjaro'.

[467] Report from Rebmann in Mombasa to the CMS Committee, 27 February 1866 (duplicated, by Sparshott?).

7. Lonely and enduring (1866-1875)

possession of the mission. The following, summarized, passage shows an enormous tension between Rebmann's loyalty to the CMS, and the identification of himself with the East African Mission.

> 'I cannot trust it [= the mission] to those who ... regret the Reformation and put it in question'. They put the Church in between the sinner and Christ. This is perversion of the Gospel. Of course a missionary society [the CMS] is free to handover a mission to another society. But the East African Mission is special: 'The only missionary left in it, is in a most providential manner, against his own will, in the face of the kind invitation from the Committee to come home after so many years of ..., interrupted only by two short visits to Egypt (in 1851 and 1855), one of its founders, and has given his life for it, in a sense to an extent which certainly is rare in the missionary history of the Christian Church in all ages. He stands to this mission in the relation of a father to his child. Thus his claim to it is established as the first no less than the best, his right and claim appear in fact as a sacred duty' [words underlined by Rebmann].

In rejecting a possible handover of the mission Rebmann adopted the view that he was almost its owner, at least had a right to define its future destiny. That he meant business is proved by his willingness to accept the financial consequences. If he were forced to take the mission upon himself, he was going 'with the help of God' to finance it by selling the little property he had at home in Gerlingen, 'a few small pieces of fields, vineyards and meadows'. He admitted that selling these would be difficult, and would cause great perplexity to his brothers. But it could be done, and the money 'may be enough until the mission can be taken over by some German Evangelical Society, or perhaps the Basler Mission'. In case the money from Germany could not be made available fast enough, Rebmann 'was ready to borrow the money from the Hindu merchants in Mombasa'.[468] In a later stage he saw a better way. If the CMS allowed him to 'continue drawing money on them through their Bombay Secretary', Rebmann promised that he would pay back as soon as his properties were sold and the money was available'. Also he wanted to remain 'in friendly connection by way of correspondence' with the CMS.

The letter in which Rebmann shared these far-going plans with Sparshott was mistakenly forwarded to Deimler in Bombay. Deimler immediately reacted in a letter to Sparshott, advising him not to support the idea of 'good brother Rebmann' of going independent. He hoped that the CMS would do neither the one thing nor the other, 'not abandon the East Afri-

---

[468] Letter from Rebmann in Kisuludini to Sparshott, 14 Sept. 1872.

can Mission and not have Mr. Rebmann appropriate it'. He agreed that Rebmann was one of the founders of the mission, 'and that the Romish should not have it'. He thought the CMS should not only continue the station, but also put a lot more money and energy into it. Remembering his motivation for leaving Kisuludini in the 1850s he reiterated his opinion that 'the Mission field of East Africa is not less promising than any other', and added: 'only let it be worked up' by the CMS. Concerning Rebmann, he stressed his noble character, and repeated that he should go to Europe to be bodily and spiritually refreshed'.[469]

These last years of bodily exhaustion, suffering and solitude sometimes strangely brought about in Rebmann a psychological state of enthusiasm or spiritual enlightenment, which enabled his mind to extranormal activity and capacity. He told Sparshott about an experience in 1872.

> 'I was held up by an enormous pain in my feet above the ankles. When this pain subsided I was held up by a special activity of my mind on Biblical and religious subjects. Sometimes my thoughts so thronged upon each other that I could hardly be quick enough in writing, losing one at the time, then finding it again. I wrote day and night, several times it occurred that daybreak still found me at my table with my lamp or candle. What I wrote is all in poetry, in hymns, in metrical composition or blank verse, in English, German and Kinika. This special activity of my mind lasted till about the middle of last month ceasing gradually, having begun in May'.[470]

Rebmann had gradually become worn out by bodily pains and psychological tensions. By 1875 he had spent his strength and energy. The time for departure had come.

---

[469] Letter from Deimler in Bombay to Sparshott, dd 14 Oct. 1872.
[470] Letter from Rebmann in Kisuludini to Sparshott, 14 Sept. 1872.

7. Lonely and enduring (1866-1875)

Johannes Rebmann, back in Germany in 1875, almost blind, and his friend Isaac Nyondo, who guided him on the journey home (Basler Mission Archive: QS-30.003.0178.01).

An Arab slave dhow being chased and arrested by a British warship in the Indian Ocean (S. Paas).

Sir Henry Bartle Frere (1815-1884), who was instrumental to the establishment of Frere Town a refuge of ex-slaves at Mombasa (Wikimedia, public domain).

8. The last passages (1875-1876)

Back to Europe

Before ill-health forced Price to leave East Africa, he succeeded in persuading Rebmann to take the concrete step of going home. Leaving had become a necessity because of his ever-decreasing eyesight. By mid-1873 he had become at least half-blind.[471] Gradually he became almost unable to read and write. In one of the last letters by his own hand to his brothers and sister in Gerlingen he gave a moving comment on his situation: 'I have become blind, but I say everywhere: God is faithful. Whoever is His, will not get lost, he is chosen for life. God is faithful. I want to be a little child in the arms of my Saviour ...'.[472] The very last letter from Africa to Gerlingen, announcing his coming home, he dictated to catechist George David in English, and a German translation was added.[473]

On 12 March 1875 Johannes Rebmann boarded ship at Mombasa. All his belongings he left behind, including a considerable number of books.[474] He was accompanied by Isaac Nyondo. Rebmann trusted Nyondo as much as his own eyes. He was convinced that Nyondo would be able to take him home safely, and to bridge the gap between the cultures of Africa and Europe.[475] On 12 April they arrived in England. He was kept in London for some months by the CMS Committee. They trusted that his

---

[471] The CMS was aware of the problems. See an almost illegible letter of 26 Dec. 1873 to H. Wright of the CMS Committee, by N.E. Malcolm, whose cousin, one Captain Malcolm had asked his brother in-law Mr Davies to announce a visit by Rebmann to eye specialist Dr. Rudolf Berlin (b.1833) in Stuttgart [G/AC4/1/129]; cf. *ADB*, 1902, Berlin became known as the medical scholar who coined the term 'dyslexia', in 1887.
[472] Rebmann, *Briefe*, 20-8-1874, '... Ich bin ein blinder Mann geworden. Doch sage ich an allen Orten: Gott ist getreu ... Wer Sein ist, der geht nicht verloren, zum Leben ist er auserkoren. Gott ist getreu. Ein Kindlein will ich seyn in meines Heilands Armen ...'[cf. Matthew 18:2].
[473] Rebmann, *Briefe*, 21-8-1874.
[474] Cf. an attachment to the certificate of marriage between Johannes Rebmann and Luise Däuble, April 1876, with an estimation of the value of this library, of 1000 Marks.
[475] Letter from Rebmann to the CMS, 12 December 1875: 'In ihm [Nyondo] hat Ostafrika Europa gründlich verstanden. Er ist ebenso verständig als er aufrichtig und treu ist. In ihm blüht nicht nur seinem eigenen Volke sondern auch andern Völkern Ostafrikas die Hoffnung eines neuen Lebens. Gott behüte ihn in der Einfalt seines Sinnes'.

eyesight would be restored, and 'that he may do further service ... in making available for other labourers the fruits of many years of painstaking linguistic toil'.[476] Apart from suffering from sickness because of the change of climate, Rebmann continued to be troubled by his eye-problem. On 12 May he managed to write his last letter to his brothers and sister. It was written with pencil in irregular script with disconnected characters. He announced that he would come home as soon as possible after an operation on his eyes.[477] The operation took place, but did not improve the situation.

Finally, the CMS bade him and Isaac Nyondo farewell home to Germany. They were guided by one Mr. Jonas, who functioned as a messenger between the CMS and its relations on the European mainland.[478] When Johannes Rebmann arrived in Gerlingen he was received by his brothers Johann Georg, and Gottlob, his sister Katharina Margarethe, and their families.[479] Gerlingen was his physical and spiritual home where once the Lord, through Pastor Stange and others, had spoken to him, and called him to the mission field.

Dependent on Krapf

Another operation, financed by the CMS, now in Stuttgart, only 'imperfectly and temporarily' restored some of his eyesight.[480] For a time it 'enabled him to see people to whom he is joined now and recognise others'. In February 1876, through Krapf, he informed the CMS about the conclusion of oculist Rudolf Berlin in Stuttgart that there 'is no hope of recovery', and that he would be unable to return to Africa.[481] The Committee expressed its 'regret that the attempt to restore Mr. Rebmann's eyesight

---

[476] CMS, *Proceedings 1874-1875*, p. 37.
[477] Rebmann, *Briefe*, 12-5-1875.
[478] In a letter to CMS secretary Hutchinson of 17 Nov. 1875 Rebmann abundantly thanked Mr Jonas, 'who performed his duty faithfully and even used his own money'.
[479] His sisters in-law and brother in-law were respectively Anna Maria Heck, Maria Magdalena Wagner, Lorenz Roth. Consequently these names belong to Rebmann's family tree. See: http://www.johannes-rebmann-stiftung.de/de/missionare/rebmann/Rebmann-Verwandte-18-11-2008.pdf
[480] In a letter from Korntal to CMS Secretary Hutchinson, of 17 Nov 1875 Rebmann thanked the CMS for paying the occulist. He would have liked to pay himself, but that 'would have taken almost all his possessions'. Cf. Preface, in: *Dictionary of the Kiniassa Language*, p. viii.
[481] Letter from Krapf in Korntal, 10-2-1876 to CMS Secretary Henry Wright [CMS/G/AC 4/2/207].

8. The last passages (1875-1876)

proved unsuccessful.' Yet, they did not stop expecting output from their valued ex-employee. Krapf had to be instrumental in this.

> 'The past year has witnessed the return home from East Africa after thirty years patient and uninterrupted service, of the veteran Rebmann, the founder of the Mission jointly with Dr. Krapf. The two fellow-labourers are now living near each other in Germany; and their untiring labours in investigating and reducing to writing the languages of that part of Africa are now, it may be hoped, about to bear valuable fruit.'[482]

Visually handicapped, Rebmann had become dependent on others. That was an enormous challenge. For many years he had been used to be on his own and to function independently. Now he needed help for being guided from spot to spot and for provision with the daily practical necessities of life. More painful to him was the inability to read and write. He had come to the CMS in London with his manuscripts, which had to be edited and published. The documents had become a very important part of his life. Mr. Jonas was charged to bring them from the CMS office to Germany. Rebmann's instructions illustrate the importance he attached to the documents.

> 'In this connection you will perhaps excuse me if I speak of my manuscripts as another kind of treasure in the possession of the Society, which, to me at least, is of greater value than all the gold and silver of England, you can truly say, than all the earthly riches of the whole world' ... 'I would add the wish that the tin box containing them be put into a strong case of wood for greater safety.'[483]

The literary work required correspondence with publishers, the CMS, and colleagues. The help of his trusted friend Isaac Nyondo had been indispensable during the passage from Africa and thereafter. However, in this respect Nyondo's assistance was limited because he was a stranger in Europe and not trained for working on literary products. Moreover, he was to return to Mombasa,[484] although his departure was postponed for con-

---

[482] CMS, *Proceedings 1875-1876*, p. 53, 54.
[483] Letter from Rebmann in Korntal to CMS Secretary Hutchinson, 17 Nov 1875 and a PS of 24 Nov. 1875.
[484] From Korntal Krapf had a finger in the pie with regard to many issues. Cf. letter from Krapf in Korntal to CMS Secretary Henry Wright dd 23 Febr. 1876 [G/4/A5/1/21], suggesting that Jonas should fetch Isaac Nyondo and take him to London to join a group of missionaries that were scheduled to travel to Mombasa

venience sake a number of times. Rebmann's relatives were farmers, specialised in winegrowing, and unable to assist in work requiring knowledge of foreign languages.

In this difficult situation Johann Ludwig Krapf's advices seemed acceptable. Krapf had settled in Korntal, at a short distance from Gerlingen. His suggestions went very far. They put Krapf in a controlling position, and entailed practically the whole of Rebmann's personal and professional life. First, he advised his former colleague to come and live in the same village. Secondly, he arranged for Rebmann to marry a woman he knew. Thirdly, he volunteered to edit Rebmann's manuscripts.

Rebmann's experiences with Krapf had not been altogether positive. The two missionaries differed in character, in missiological method, and in theological persuasion. Sometimes Rebmann had been disappointed by Krapf's lack of loyalty. However, he had no choice. In general he trusted Krapf, together they had represented the Kingdom of God in a hostile environment, and survived during many years in difficult situations. He once called him his 'faithful guide on earth'[485], and he had given him the position of godfather of his son. Moreover, it seemed practical to live close to Krapf, and follow his advice to marry. He had become blind and helpless, Krapf's suggestions seemed to be a way forward. Perhaps he did not realise that once married the wife Krapf suggested and moved to Krapf's village, he had practically surrendered control of his life and work to his former colleague.

Krapf's correspondence with the CMS shows that he had taken over the initiative. In a letter to secretary Henry Wright he claimed 'having been commissioned by my dear former colleague Mr Rebman to communicate his wishes to you for the information of the Committee'. He was sure that the Committee would 'do all they can to ease his situation', now that Rebmann had become blind and had to part with his guide and nurse Isaac Nyondo. 'Before dismissing Nyondo, Rebmann needs help, a family for feeding, helping and nursing him'. Apparently the CMS had not yet made a permanent financial arrangement for its veteran worker. Krapf broached the sensitive subject, and asked for financial support, Rebmann now being a 'superannuated missionary', who was entitled to a kind of pension.[486] He also suggested the amount to be given to Rebmann, 'the

---

on 30 March 1876. No problem if Isaac would not catch up with the group, because 'he wants to stay longer for learning more English' etc.
[485] Rebmann, *Briefe*, 3-7-1845.
[486] Letter from Krapf in Korntal, 10-2-1876 to CMS Secretary Henry Wright [CMS/G/AC 4/2/207].

8. The last passages (1875-1876)

sum which in my opinion might be voted for Mr. Rebman', i.e. half the amount he received in the mission field, which would be 150 pounds per year. In passing Krapf mentioned the amount he himself received from the CMS at his dismissal in 1856 'a lump sum of 400 pounds.'[487]

The mission bride

Krapf's most sensational intervention in Rebmann's life was his role as marriage broker. He was instrumental in Rebmann's marriage with Luise Friederike Däuble. 'Mission bride', that's what Luise was called, because of her eventful life of previous marital relations. The Däuble family were special. Out of the eleven children of father Jakob and mother Luise, three sons became missionaries, and two daughters missionaries' wives.[488] One of them was Luise Friederike. She was born in Sindelfingen in 1835. Before marrying Rebmann she had lost a prospective husband and a husband. The first mentioned was G. Kammerer, a missionary in India, sent by the Basler Mission. He had worked on the Dravidian language Tulu, of South-Indian Tulu Nadu.[489] She got engaged to him, and went on her way to India. However, before she arrived the young bridegroom had died, in 1858. Subsequently the Basler Mission decided to employ the gifted widow on the spot in an orphanage and as a teacher of catechism classes in Mangalore.

---

[487] Letter from Krapf in Korntal to CMS Secretary Henry Wright, 23 Febr. 1876 [G/4/A5/1/21]. Probably the amount of 400 pounds was for the period between Krapf's 'valedictory dismissal' in 1851 and his final retirement from CMS activities in 1856, see his letter from Korntal on 22 May 1856 to the CMS [CMS C A5/O16/121]. According to Eber,*Krapf*, S. 180, 181, the amount he received from the CMS was 700 pounds, apart from the pension of 500 Swiss francs per year from the St. Chrischona Pilger Mission.

[488] Cf. http://www.johannes-rebmann-stiftung.de/en/missionaries/gerlingen_missionaries.html, where their names are given. Rebmann, *Briefe*, 30-11-1855 indicates that he corresponded with a Däuble, which may be one of them; cf. 'Gerlinger Heimatblätter: Gerlingen Missionare', nd., S. 22, 26.

[489] Kammerer had made the Tulu language printable by changing its original script to the Kannada script, which was used by the Basel Mission Press in Mangalore. He collected Tulu words and their meanings until he died. His lexicographical activity was continued by fellow German missionary (Jakob Friedrich ?) August Männer, who published in Mangalore a Tulu-English dictionary (1886) and an English-Tulu dictionary (1888), printed by the Basler Mission Press. http://en.wikipedia.org/wiki/Tulu_language. In the Preface of the 1886 publication, on p. iii, Männer says that he added to a compilation of about 2000 words, made by G. Kammerer.

There she met August Hermann Finckh, born in Calw in 1831, like her from Württemberg. Finckh was trained as a missionary by the Basler Mission. Luise and August Hermann married at Mercara in 1859.[490] Two children were born to them in India, Selma (15 April 1861), and Paul (1863); the latter soon died. In 1865 Luise was pregnant again when she, her husband and Selma travelled from India to Europe for a furlough, first by ship to Suez, then by train to Alexandria, and finally by the Austrian steamer Jupiter to Europe. Unfortunately August Hermann fell ill and he died in February when they were off the Greek coast at Korfu. The body was taken from the ship and buried, in her absence. Back in Germany, Louise settled with her parents-in-law; she gave birth to a son, Paul August, on 15 March 1865. Her brother Louis Däuble from Sindelfingen became guardian of the children. However, the baby boy died shortly afterwards, on 2 August 1865.[491] A few days later Luise informed the BM-B Inspector of the death of her child and said that she would move to Heslach and set up a household together with her eldest sister.[492]

Luise was the lady Krapf presented to Rebmann and then to his former employer the CMS. At least she would be able to replace Nyondo as nurse and guide, who had to return to Africa.[493] He dealt with the sensitive issue carefully, step by step, and first only talked about her as a host for Rebmann.

> 'There is Mrs. Finck, widow of late Rev. Finck, who for many years was the principal of the Catechists' Institution at Mangalore, in connection with the Basler Mission'. She had taken up her abode in Korntal. 'She would indeed be the proper person for taking care of Mr. Rebmann. She is a pious and accomplished lady, who would also be able to carry on Mr. Rebmann's correspondence in German and English, and to assist him in printing his East Africa manuscripts. She has a daughter of 14 years, who was born in

---

[490] City Archive Gerlingen keeps some documents, letters and articles on her and Finckh, KAT 5/17.1/07 (Missionar August Finckh und Luise Friederike Finckh geb. Däuble – Indien).

[491] *DGB* 170, S. 144, http://worldroots.com/ged/andreae/@I19031@.html; Personenstammkarte August Hermann Finckh, http://www.wucherer-wolfgang.de/Reutlingen/Karte_2152.htm; Scheffbuch, *Große Entdecker*, S. 49, 50.

[492] Letter from Luise Friederike Däuble in Untertürkheim to the Inspector of the BM-B, 8 August 1865.

[493] On 29 February 1876 CMS Secretary Wright had ordered Nyondo to be fetched by Jonas, and be back to London on 18 March 1876. This did not happen because Nyondo's presence was 'a case of necessity' for Rebmann until the officiation of his marriage with Luise. On 14 March 1876 Krapf sent an apology to Wright.

8. The last passages (1875-1876)

India. Mrs. Finck would provide Mr. Rebmann with the necessary rooms, with food etc., I believe at very equitable terms.'[494]

A few weeks later Krapf suggested the next step to the Committee. As 'friends of Rebmann' they had come to the conclusion that marriage would be better ... if the Committee will sanction.'

> 'When we conversed with Rebman on the subject, he quite revived and said he would never have ventured to express such an idea to anybody, as he being a blind man could not expect that a female should have the self-denial being requisite for marrying a blind man. However, he would take it as a great and undeserved [gift] at the hand of God, if He would incline the heart of Mrs. Finck, and if the Committee would sanction such a step, which in every respect will render our dear brother happy and comfortable. His treatment is in many points so delicate that no female who is not his own wife could accomplish it fully.'[495]

Krapf must have felt rather sure that his plan would succeed. It would relieve the CMS of the moral duty of taking care of their blind veteran missionary.[496] Rebmann had no choice, for he was in a vulnerable position. Krapf knew Luise, as she was almost his neighbour in Korntal.

> 'When we the friends of Mr. Rebman the first time were suggesting this matter to Mrs. Finck, she was quite puzzled, but soon composed herself by saying, that she would take time for considering it and to bring it before God in prayer. When we alluded to the great self-denial which her being married to a blind man would impose upon herself, she replied that if it be the will of God to [join] her with Rebman, his divine strength will not fail her under all trials that may await her'.

Father Däuble was a schoolteacher. In 1841 the family had moved to Gerlingen. By that time Johannes Rebmann had already gone to the Basel Mission Seminary. Ledderhose claims that Luise, when she was a small child, had got to know Johannes.[497] She must have seen him in 1846, when he had finished his training at the Basler Mission Seminary, and was in Gerlingen for a few weeks, before travelling to London. Luise was ready

---

[494] Letter from Krapf at Korntal, 10 February 1876, to CMS Secretary Henry Wright [CMS/G/AC 4/2/207].
[495] Idem.
[496] The answer came pretty soon for already in his letter of 2 March 1876 to Wright, Krapf thanked the Committee for permitting Rebmann to marry.
[497] Ledderhose, 'Rebmann', in: ADB, vol. 27, S. 489.

to nurse the 15-years-older ailing missionary. It is not strange that she needed time for thinking when she was asked to marry him. Undoubtedly she remembered the traumatic experience of losing a fiancé and a husband within seven years. Krapf reported to the CMS that to Rebmann's joy Luise finally agreed to marry him.

> 'After some time of consideration and prayer Mrs Finck gave an affirmative answer, by which Rebman was almost moved to tears in view of the infinite goodness of the Lord who cared for him so graciously.'[498]

The engagement took place on 2 March 1876. To the BM-B Inspector Luise explained the reasons why she had decided to accept the proposal of marriage. Basically she called her marriage to the disabled and helpless Rebmann an act of obedience to God.[499] The marriage followed on 16 March.[500] A month later a contact with some remarkable details was added to the marriage certificate. In the presence of witnesses the spouses stated that their individual possessions would remain their own, and that their common household would be financed by the fruits of these possessions. Probably the agreement was inspired by a conspicuous difference in wealth between husband and wife. Rebmann possessed practically nothing apart from some doubtful claims. He brought in his CMS pension. Luise Däuble possessed a nice sum of 8,000 Marks, and brought in the fruits of this capital. She also brought in the income of a legacy to her daughter Selma from her parents-in-law. These details of Luise's relative wealth stand in contrast to her complaints to the BM-B, which suggest that she was poor and destitute.[501] About the remaining years of Luise's

---

[498] Letter from Krapf in Korntal, 23-2-1876, to CMS Secretary Henry Wright [G/4/A5/1/21].

[499] Letter from Luise Friederike Däuble in Kornthal, 6-3-1876, to the Inspector of BM-B.

[500] See the relevant Hochzeit Register of 16 March 1876, No 4 of Kornthal. Krapf and two of Luise's brothers Christian Ludwig and Louis Eberhard were witnesses. The last mentioned was added because of Rebmann's inability to read the documents. 'Da der Bräutigam seit einiger Zeit das Augenlicht beinahe verloren hat, wurde als dritter Zeuge zugezogen und erschien: ... der Louis Eberhard Däuble Stadtpfleger der Persönlichkeit nach bekannt und fünfzig Jahre alt wohnhaft zu Sindelfingen'. The Evangelische Brüdergemeinde Hochzeit Register of 16 March, No 2, refers to Familienregister 339.

[501] Cf. letters from Luise Friederike Däuble in the Gerlinger City Archive, transcribed by Imanuel Stutzmann, to the BM-B Committee, from Heslach 16 July 1866 to the Inspector, from Korntal, 15 March 1873 to the 'Comittee'. In a letter from Kornthal 10 June 1875, she referred to the bodily weaknesses of herself and of her daughter Selma, which necessitated her to spend money on thermal baths. She

8. The last passages (1875-1876)

life not much is known. From October 1879 to July 1880 she was back in her birth place Sindelfingen for a brief stay. According to the City Archive of Korntal-Münchingen in 1885 she moved to a home of the Herrnhuters in Gnadenfrei, Silesia (now: Pilawa Górna), where she stayed until an unknown date. In 1914 at the age of 79 she died, either in Gnadenfrei or in Stuttgart, where at any rate her daughter Selma had settled.[502]

The manuscripts

Reportedly Rebmann had brought with him, on his return in 1875, a lot of material, e.g. diaries, letters received from friends, and copies of letters he sent to friends and others.[503] His manuscripts, a bookcase full ('eine Kiste voll') of them, must have been left in the custody of Luise, or of the Gerlinger relatives, or of both. In all likelihood after the marriage she became the main custodian of what Johannes had left. What happened to these papers? Eventually a lot of them got lost. Did this happen during or after Luise's lifetime?

Krapf must have had access to at least a considerable part of Rebmann's literary legacy. This included the content of another consignment of Rebmann manuscripts that arrived from London in March 1876.[504] Krapf had emphatically requested the CMS to send the manuscripts,[505] which he supposed to be contained in a bag,[506] and he promised to send to London a list of the documents in it. At last a box arrived, not a bag. Krapf reports to the CMS:

> 'In the presence of Mr. Rebman, Isaak, and of Mr. Jonas, I have looked over the manuscripts contained in Rebman's box. The result of the investigation was, that only the Gospel of St Luke and the Kiniassa Dictionary are in a state of fitness for being printed immediately, but the Kisuahili and Kinika

---

claimed that the money received from BM-B was not sufficient and prayed for a 'way out'.

[502] Cf. Irmgard Großmann, 'Louise Friederike Däuble verh. Finck/Rebmann, 1835-1914: Eine Frau in der Mission', in: Dagmar Konrad, *Missionsbräute: Pietistinnen des 19. Jahrhunderts in der Basler Mission*, Münster/New York, München/Berlin, 1999; cf. Scheffbuch, *Entdecker*, S. 50, 51.

[503] Cf. Letter from BM of 24-5-29 to one R.F. Merkel.

[504] In a letter to the CMS of 4 October 1876, at Rebmann's death, Krapf in Korntal confirms that he possesses Rebmann's manuscripts.

[505] Noted by Rebmann in Korntal in a PS of 24 November 1875 to his letter of 17 Nov. to CMS Secretary Hutchinson.

[506] Letter from Krapf in Korntal to CMS Secretary Wright, 2 March 1876. 'Mr. Rebman's manuscripts will be attended to as soon as they are in our [hands]. We will send you the precise list of the content of the [...] we found in the bag'.

Dictionaries require long preliminary labour before they can be sent to the printer. In the present form they are in fact an immense bulk of materials for compiling Dictionaries in Kinika and Kisuahili. There you see a great number of sheets stitched together containing words and sentences exemplifying the meaning of the words. It is a great pity that these materials have not been sifted and arranged. If Mr. Reb. who is in great love with these valuable materials will allow me to prepare and arrange them for the press, I will perform the task and read him the result of my labour, whether he approves of it for printing.'[507]

Krapf was asked by the CMS Committee to edit Rebmann's manuscripts. Finally he only prepared the publication, under Rebmann's own name of his Swahili translation of *Luke* and of his *Dictionary of the Kiniassa Language*. At the time Krapf started work on them Rebmann was still alive. A short time before his death, he dictated a letter to Krapf on the origin of the Kiniassa dictionary.

Rebmann at first consented to Krapf's position as editor of his work. However, as soon as he noticed that Krapf took the liberty of making a large number of changes, he felt very unhappy. Especially they clashed on the orthography. Rebmann preferred a spelling based on German sounds, close to the system of Lepsius, which was at that time still generally accepted by scholars, whereas Krapf with his premonitions of changing political realities in Africa preferred a spelling based on English sounds. Krapf took the liberty of cutting deep into the lifework of his blind friend. In anglicizing every detail he even changed Johannes Rebmann's name into John Rebman. This affected the whole of Rebmann's oeuvre and public presentation. Probably the English CMS sympathised with Krapf, although they were careful not to side with him openly. Rebmann's German ex-colleagues Erhardt and Deimler opposed Krapf.[508] Rebmann himself was barely in the position to protest. As to the translations Krapf simply forced Rebmann to comply to many alterations, even when he 'saw him weeping bitterly' after he had 'told him that his orthography was untenable'.[509] As to Rebmann's dictionary work Krapf's changes are perhaps less numerous.

---

[507] Letter from Krapf in Korntal to CMS Secretary Henry Wright, 14 March 1876.

[508] Cf. Letter from Erhardt in Secundra Orphanage at Agra, to CMS, 8 March 1877 [CI/O 103/8]; Letter from Deimler in Nuremberg to CMS Secretary Fenn, 1 Nov. 1879 [CI3/O25/29].

[509] Letter from Krapf in Korntal to the CMS Committee, 5 February, probably 1877, anyway not 1876, because written after Rebmann's death [G/4/A5/1/21: the code is confused with the code of Krapf's letter of 23 Febr. 1876].

8. The last passages (1875-1876)

It seems strange that Krapf showed little respect for work by a scholar who he recognised as more able than himself with regard to East African languages. When the CMS asked him for a translation into Swahili of letters to be sent to King Mtesa of Uganda, he had to transfer the work to Rebmann and Nyondo, 'who have more time and ability for doing this work than myself being pressed by various and numerous matters'.[510] Krapf realised that his Swahili translations of Scripture were not good enough. He urged the CMS to let them be improved by some people of Frere Town, or even by Bishop Steere, whom he otherwise mistrusted and accused of 'plagiarism.'[511]

Apart from his annoyance with regard to the contents and the order of Rebmann's manuscripts, Krapf did not always enjoy working with the papers as such. In June 1877 he reported to the CMS that he had become literally sick through them.

> 'I have [to tell] that I have been severely ill (since February) in consequence of catarrh and fever, which latter the physician declared to have taken rise from the putrid air which I had been inhaling in using Rebman's manuscripts, which were locked up for so many years. The Doctor said there were certain animalculae productive of fever after they got into a state of putridity. It is true; the smell of the leaves was often almost unbearable. The Doctor therefore interdicted using the MSS until they have been completely sulphurated. Had I known this, I might have saved much pain, much time, and much money for medical treatment.'[512]

Luise Däuble and Krapf knew one another and were almost neighbours. He himself said that after Rebmann's death, Luise showed him a bundle of letters her husband had written to the CMS Committee for East Africa during the period 1850-1855.[513] We can be sure that Krapf saw more than the contents of the case during the time from Rebmann's arrival and death until his own death in 1881. In the Introduction to his Swahili Dictionary, published in 1882, he mentioned a version of the manuscript of

---

[510] Letters from Krapf in Korntal to CMS Secretary Henry Wright, 2 and 24 March 1876.
[511] Letters from Krapf to CMS Committee of 22 May and 19 June 1877. Steere, UMCA bishop in Zanzibar, was on furlough in London at that time. Krapf wanted him to help, but was 'not sure whether we might not get into difficulties with him', and added: 'At all events, if the Bishop corrects my translation I beg you concernedly, that the corrections may be shown to me before the translation is being printed'.
[512] Letter from Krapf in Korntal to CMS Committee, 19 June 1877.
[513] CMS, *Intelligencer*, 1876, p. 696, 697: 'The Late Rev. John Rebmann', quoted by Krapf in his Preface to Rebmann's *Dictionary of the Kiniassa Language*, London/St. Chrischona, 1877, p. vi.

Rebmann's Kinika Dictionary, which was more advanced than the disorderly heap of papers he claimed to have seen in Rebmann's case in 1876. Krapf must have written this in about 1880. In 1886 Robert Cust visited Luise on behalf of the CMS in search of Rebmann manuscripts. He found Rebmann's bookcase in disarray; of the Kinika manuscript there were only a few scattered pages.[514] Would this mean that Luise for some reason had not taken good care of the part of her husband's literary legacy that was entrusted to her? Probably in the first ten years after Rebmann's death many of his writings had already gone astray.

Rebmann's death

By the end of 1875 Luise accompanied her husband to the thermal springs of Bad Liebenzell, where he stayed for several weeks to become healthy and strong again.[515] All looked well when together with Isaac Nyondo he was able to attend a mission feast of the Basler Mission at Leonberg, and express in public his gratitude to God for 29 years of labour in Africa.[516] He explained why he had stayed in Africa for so long despite his blindness. He wanted to prevent the mission station from being taken over by non-protestant hands ('unevangelische Hände'). He also informed his German audience about hopeful new developments of the mission among the Giriama people.[517]

Unfortunately after some weeks Rebmann was brought down again, first by a serious cold, then by inflammation of the lungs.[518] Luise noticed he was dying, but he himself apparently did not realise this and asked why she was weepingt, because he would not die, for a lot of work was waiting for him. He did not speak much during his illness, but on the day before his death he said to his wife: 'Now the Word is more true than before: praise the Lord.'

> On his death-bed he exclaimed, 'Now it is time to say, praised be the Lord!', and then again, thinking he might recover: 'There is still work before me: trust and be not afraid'. But it was not to be.[519]

---

[514] Cf. next chapter.
[515] Letter from Krapf to the CMS, 20 November 1875 [CMS C A5/O16/144].
[516] Cf. Stutzmann, 'Johannes Rebmann: Leben und Werk des Missionars', Vortrag, S. 9.
[517] Oskar Rebmann, 'Missionar Johann Rebmann', S. 147, 148 quotes an anonymous attendant at the mission feast.
[518] Cf. Oskar Rebmann, S. 149-151.
[519] Letter from Krapf to the CMS, 4 October 1875 [CMS C A5/O16/147]; Obituary by the CMS, in: Rebmann, *Dictionary of the Kiniassa Language*, p. viii.

8. The last passages (1875-1876)

On Wednesday 4 October 1876 at 08.45 hours in the morning death took him away. Johannes Rebmann was 56 years, 8 months and 18 days old.[520] It seems only Luise was present when he passed away. Krapf was one of the first to be informed by her.[521] Rebmann was buried in the cemetery, now 'der alte Friedhof',[522] of the Congregation of the Evangelical Brethren (*Evangelische Brüdergemeinde*) in Korntal. The funeral took place on the 'next Thursday', which was probably the next day. On his tombstone are the English words, 'Saved in the arms of Jesus'. Luise, the 'mission-bride', was a widow again.

---

[520] Sterberegister 4-10-1876, Nr. 20, Korntal, signed by Daur; cf. Abschrift 24-8-1965, signed by Nachtigall; Evangelische Brüdergemeinde Register 1876, Nr 801, referring to Familien Regisrer 339.
[521] Letter from Krapf to the CMS, 4 October 1874 [CMS C A5/O16/147]: reference to a message from Mrs Rebmann informing him on the death of her husband in the morning at 09.56.
[522] Cf. Karl Götz, 'Auf dem alten Friedhof in Korntal', *Ev. Gemeindeblatt*, 22 Nov. 1959.

August Hermann Finckh (1831-1865),
Luise Däuble's first husband
(Basler Mission Archive:
QS-30.001.0322.01).

Johannes Rebmann, briefly
before his death in 1876
(Basler Mission Archive:
QS-30.009.0021).

Johann Ludwig Krapf at old age
(Basler Mission Archive:
QS-30.016.0064).

8. The last passages (1875-1876)

*Family Däuble, appr. 1848. The girl in front in the centre is Luise.
The others are, from the left:
Johannes Zimmermann, Rosine Däuble, Christian Däuble, Luise Friederike Däuble,
Johann Jacob Däuble (Father), Gottlob Christoph Däuble Theodor Däuble (in front),
Maria Christiana Däuble (Mother), Wilhelm Däuble,
Jakob Däuble (teacher in Gerlingen 1894), Karl Gustav Däuble
(Gerlinger Heimatblätter – Gerlinger Missionare, p. 23.)*

9. Language Worker

Two tragic aspects

The language work of the 19th-century missionaries in Africa originated in their main task, the communication of the Bible, the Gospel of salvation of Jesus Christ, to the peoples. Consequently the histories of mission and of linguistics are intertwined to a great extent. Western missionaries compiled most of the lexicographical collections, and made most of the translations, while Africans assisted as informants, and became the first readers. Often the encounter between linguistically interested missionaries and their informants took place during critical situations, e.g. war, slavery, migration, diseases. Their informants were often uprooted people, displaced persons living far from their homes. That the missionaries were foreigners and strangers to the African culture contributed to the obscurity that had to be clarified, and emphasised the cultural gap that had to be bridged.

In 1874 Sir Bartle Frere found Rebmann in Kisuludini, 'surrounded by translated manuscripts on which he had worked for decades'[523] Apart from his correspondence, Rebmann's literary work comprised prose and poetry, translations and lexicographical work. Of what survived, some Nika hymns a Nika translation of the *Heidelberg Catechism* (made together with Krapf), a translation of the *Gospel of Luke* into Swahili, and lexicographical collections of Swahili, Nika and Kiniassa are best known.

There are two aspects of tragedy to Rebmann's literary legacy. First, a lot of it got lost. We can be sure that correspondence, biographical material, journals by him and his first wife Emma Kent, meditative notes, translated material, and lexicographical collections were transferred into the custody of the Basler Mission, the Church Missionary Society, his close relatives in Gerlingen, and his second wife Luise Däuble in Korntal. There was also correspondence with friends, e.g. BM's director Hoffmann, Ludwig Krapf, and probably Gerlingen's Pastor Stange, and its local teacher. Important references to Rebmann documents might be unearthed if we could find Emma Kent's correspondence with her relatives and friends, e.g. her sisters and her friend Alice Lieder-Holliday. Most of this literary material is not available at present. For this reason we sometimes have to resort to indirect evidence.

---

[523] Ringwald, *Rebmann*, in: 'Ludwigsburger Geschichtsblätter', 29/1977, S. 108.

The second tragic aspect is that Rebmann's literary legacy was overwhelmed and partly absorbed by the fame and ambition of Johann Ludwig Krapf, his colleague. Krapf's travels and researches were widely published, in both German and English.[524] His enormous literary productivity impressed the world of scholars and explorers in the West, and put Rebmann's contributions in the shade. Some history writers even referred mistakenly to Krapf as the 'discoverer' of Kilimanjaro.[525] Moreover, Krapf sometimes minimised the significance of his friend's research, either by including his results in his own publications, or by making disparaging remarks, e.g. in the preface to Rebmann's work that the CMS had asked him to edit. Krapf was more able, had more opportunity, and probably was more willing to work on his public relations than Rebmann. His sixteen years in Africa, of which he spent nine years in the Mombasa area, are a much shorter period than Rebmann's twenty-nine years. Unlike Rebmann, who stayed in Africa all the time, he at times commuted between Europe and Africa, and developed contacts with the elites in England and Germany. After he left Africa in 1853, he came back only for short spells, and until his death in November 1881[526] he resided and worked in Korntal. While Rebmann was far away from the publishing houses of Germany and England, and after his return in 1875 due to his blindness and early death could not prevent many of his documents from getting lost, Krapf produced a large oeuvre, and became widely known.

Krapf on Rebmann's work

Krapf was a diligent writer and collector. His most recent (2006) biographer Jochen Eber says that almost 700 original writings by Krapf are

---

[524] Krapf, *Reisen in Ostafrika*, ausgeführt in den Jahren 1837-1855, 2 Teile, Hrsg. u. Einf. Hanno Beck, Korntal 1858; Krapf, *Travels, researches, and missionary labours, during an eighteen years' residence in Eastern Africa*, London, 1860. In a letter of 5-12-1857 to CMS secretary Henry Venn [CMS/G/AC 16/138], Krapf in Korntal reported that he was working on his Travels, and had 850 pages, but now missed the Journals of his Nov/Dec 1847 and Febr.1848 expeditions respectively to Patta, and to Ribe, Jagga, Kauma and Emberria, and asked Venn to send them.

[525] Knauß, 'Krapf', in: *BBKL*, vol. 4, S. 606. 'Auf Reisen entdeckte er 1848 den Kilimandscharo und 1859 den ebenfalls schneebedeckten Kenia'; Elizabeth Isichei, *A History of Christianity in Africa*, p. 137, describes Krapf as a visitor to Kilimanjaro without mentioning Rebmann; Werner Raup in his announcement of the 1994 re-edition of Krapf's Reisen says: 'Zusammen mit seinem Mitarbeiter Rebmann entdeckte er als erster Europäer den Kilimandscharo und den Mount Kenya', http://www.lit-verlag.de/isbn/3-8285-2081-5

[526] Eber, *Krapf*, S. 237.

9. Language Worker

known.[527] This he had already shown in his Ethiopian period, before 1844, when he started to publish his dozens of publications in and on mainly the Amharic and Galla languages.[528] After his arrival in Mombasa, May 1844, he immediately set himself to the study of Swahili and the Nika language families, paying special attention to the Kamba dialect. He profited from the colloquial Arabic that he had learned in Egypt, Ethiopia and Arabia. He discovered that the Swahili and Nika languages belong to the large family of Bantu languages, which extends from the Equator to the Cape of Good Hope, and that with 'their eight classes, each having its own euphonical concord', they were 'a key to all the dialects inland'. Before Rebmann's arrival in 1846, Krapf had already sent to London a Swahili vocabulary, a grammar outline, and a translation of some Gospels. In subsequent years he seems to have made attempts to translate almost the whole New Testament. A note by the CMS secretary of 1876 says that 'in the possession of Dr. Krapf are all the portions of the translations in Kisuaheli, from Epistles of the *Romans* to *Revelation*, except the Epistles to the *Corinthians*'.[529] He also translated Bible stories.[530]

A grammar by Krapf, with a vocabulary, enlarged to 5 columns including Swahili, Nika and Galla, was printed in Tübingen in 1850.[531] In 1849 he sent to London a Yao vocabulary 'spoken by the Kamanga tribe, on the south eastern bank of the Lake Nyasa, which he collected two years ago from a slave in Mombas',[532] and he continued working on a Kamba list.[533] After he left East Africa in 1853 plans for his 'large Suaheli Dictionary' could not be materialised without his colleagues. Erhardt got a copy and made contribu-

---

[527] Eber, *Krapf*, S. 7; cf. S. 117, 219-228.
[528] Cf. Bibliographies of Krapf's Works in: Catherine Griefenow-Mewis, 'J.L. Krapf and his role in researching and describing East African Languages', Paper at the Swahili Colloquium at Bayreuth, AAP, 1996, p. 161-171; Clemens Gütl, 'Literaturergänzung', in: Karl Knauß, 'Johann Ludwig Krapf', *BBKL*, vol. 4 (1992) col. 606-608; M. Louise Pirouet, *The Legacy of Johann Ludwig Krapf*.
[529] Letter from Krapf in Korntal, in German, to an unknown addressee at the CMS, 18 March 1876 [G/4/A5/1/2]; Cf. Letters from Krapf in Korntal to the CMS Committee of 22 May 1877 and 19 June 1877, referring to Swahili translations of books of the New Testament.
[530] Letter from Krapf in Korntal to CMS Secretary Wright, 2 March 1876, asking for his 'manuscript of Dr Barth's Bible stories in Kinika', which he had sent to the CMS in 1854.
[531] Cf. Krapf's *Briefe* 24 November 1857, on: Krapf, 'Elemente von Kinika', 1850; CMS, *Proceedings 1849-1850*, p. xcv-cvii, quotes Krapf who is 'thankful to have at last succeeded in transcribing my Suaheli and Kinika Dictionary in 595 quarto pages'.
[532] CMS, *Proceedings 1849-1850*, p. cvi-cvii
[533] Idem, p. cvi.

tions. Krapf also left a copy in the hand of Deimler, who handed it to Rebmann in Zanzibar in 1857.[534] In 1861, before going to Africa to help the Methodists, he sent the original of his collection to Venn in London.

Apart from making his Swahili translation of *Luke,* Rebmann had already started his own lexicographical collection of Swahili, which he used when he checked and added to Krapf's beginnings. Copies were made by Wakefield at Ribe in 1861, Sparshott in 1868, and Price in 1874. Whether this material was mainly from Krapf has become increasingly doubtful. Apparently, Krapf came to recognise that there was a separate Swahili Dictionary by Rebmann. In 1876, when Rebmann's manuscripts were in his hands, he asked the CMS for 'the original of my large Dictionary in Kisuahili, that I took with me to Kornthal in 1861, and that I sent to Venn ... I would like to compare it with Rebman's Dictionary'.[535]

There is ample proof that Krapf and the CMS secretaries were well aware of the fact that for many years Rebmann was active in making translations into Swahili and in producing a very large collection of Swahili vocabulary. Throughout the years the CMS *Proceedings* reported on Rebmann's labours in Swahili. In 1858 during Rebmann's exile in Zanzibar they referred to his 'being desirous of completing a grammar and a dictionary of the Suaheli language for the use of missionaries whenever the country shall be sufficiently settled to allow the resumption of a mission'.[536] In 1859 and 1860 they mentioned the progress of his Scriptural translations in Swahili and were satisfied with his application of the orthography of Lepsius.[537] In 1876 Krapf wrote to London:

> 'When this [Rebmann's translation Luke into Swahili and the Kiniassa Dictionary] has been done we will think of printing the Kisuahili and Kinika Dictionaries of Mr. Rebman. But the materials of the Kisuahili Dictionary are so [*immense*] that one might almost be frightened from putting one's hands on the enormous task. However, it will be mastered if the Lord spares my life and grants health. An estimate of that work cannot yet be given, as it is not yet ready for the press.'[538]

There is impressive evidence of Rebmann's lexicographical work in Swahili and there is also a strong indication of its superiority to Krapf's lexi-

---

[534] Letter from Krapf in Korntal 5 December 1857 to CMS secretary Henry Venn [CMS/G/AC 16/138].
[535] Letter from Krapf in Korntal to CMS secretary Henry Wright, 2 March 1876.
[536] CMS, *Proceedings 1857-1858*, p. 65.
[537] CMS, *Proceedings 1858-1859*, p. 56-57; *Proceedings 1859-1860*, London, p. 60.
[538] Letter from Krapf in Korntal to CMS Secretary Henry Wright, 27 March 1876 [II].

cography in Swahili. Despite this Rebmann's lexicon was not published, but Krapf's was. Who was the main contributor to the first published Swahili Dictionary? Krapf had referred the CMS to Rebmann's statement that his (Rebmann's) 'large Dictionary ... is the foundation of Krapf's'.[539] Yet Krapf published the work in his own name and the CMS allowed him to do so. Probably Krapf's Swahili Dictionary is his best-known publication. It went through various stages before it was finally printed and published in 1882, one year after his death. Though it started in the early 1850s with Krapf's English-Swahili-Nika vocabulary that was left in the hands of Rebmann, the final product undoubtedly to a great extent came from Rebmann's collection. However, Rebmann was humble enough to write to London that the original list was not his own work, thus perhaps giving the wrong impression that his own contribution was inferior to Krapf's. In his preface to the dictionary Krapf did not have much to say in appreciation of his friend's assistance.

It cannot be denied that all Krapf's Swahili and Nika output after Rebmann's arrival in June 1846 bears the marks of input by Rebmann. In 1848 Rebmann and Krapf made their first joint publication, a book on the spelling of the Nika language, and a translation of the *Heidelberg Catechism*.[540] However, Rebmann was not always credited for his contributions. After Rebmann's early death Krapf became the editor of his work. That explains why bibliographies of Krapf's literary legacy often overlook that some publications include Rebmann's work, even when Krapf contributed little.[541]

---

[539] Cf. note by the CMS secretary in the margin of a letter from Krapf in Korntal, in German, 18 March 1876 [G/4/A5/1/2]. Cf: CMS, *Intelligencer*, February 1849, page 20.

[540] Cf. Krapf's *Briefe* 24 November 1857, on: Krapf and Rebmann, 'Buchstabierbuch in Kinika dazu Heidelberger Katechismus', 1848.

[541] Cf. Clemens Gütl's bibliography, in: Knauß, 'Johann Ludwig Krapf', *BBKL*, vol. 4 (1992) col. 606-608; Krapf, 'Three Chapters of Genesis translated into the Sooahelee Language, with Introduction by W.W. Greenough'. In: *Journal of the American Oriental Society*, vol. i, 1843-9, 1847: 261-274; *Krapf, *Evangelio za Avioandika Lukas* [Kinika translation of Luke], Bombay 1848; *Krapf and Rebmann, *The Beginning of a Spelling Book of the Kinika Language, accompanied by a Translation of the Heidelberg Catechism*, Bombay 1848; Krapf, *Evangelio ta Yunaolete Malkosi* [Kamba translation of Mark], Tübingen 1850; Krapf, *Outline of the elements of the Kisuaheli language [with special reference to the Kiníka dialect]*, Tübingen 1850; Krapf, *Vocabulary of six East African languages [Kisuáheli, Kiníka, Kikámba, Kopokómo, Kohiáu, Gigálla]*, Tübingen 1850; Krapf, *Mémoir on the East African slave-trade etc.*, 1853, in 80 pages quarto [CMS, CA5/O16/179]; Krapf, *Salla sa sabuci na jioni sasalli waso katika kiriaki ja kienglese siku sothe sa muaka* [Swahili translation of morning and evening pray-

Krapf criticised Rebmann's orthography, e.g. accusing him of 'confounding letters b and p, d and t'. Krapf said that he changed the spelling which was used in Rebmann's translation of the Gospel of *Luke* into Swahili, and in his contributions to the manuscript for the Swahili Dictionary.[542] Rebmann had followed the so called 'General Alphabet' or 'Standard Alphabet' which was devised by Karl Richard Lepsius[543] and published in 1855.[544] It was intended for reducing unwritten languages to writing. However, missionaries with an Anglo-Saxon background found the system unfit for that purpose, because it was based on German sounds, and because of the 'enormous number of new types of diacritical marks' that Lepsius reportedly used to supplement the Roman alphabet. Krapf wanted to please his Anglo-Saxon friends, which led him to publicly reject Rebmann's spelling. Krapf said he adopted the spelling system suggested by the Anglican bishop Edward Steere, based on the English pronunciation.[545] He thought that 'this mode of writing should be universally introduced in Eastern Africa'. He took for granted that the missionaries and missionary societies 'are all English, and therefore the English pronunciation should have the preference to the German or any other mode'.[546] In a

---

ers in Anglican liturgy], Tübingen 1854; *Krapf (ed.) and Rebmann, *Dictionary of the Kiniassa Language*, London and St. Chrischona 1877; *Krapf, *A Dictionary of the Suahili Language: with Introduction containing an Outline of a Suahili Grammar*, London, 1882 [new print 1964]; *Krapf and Rebmann, *A Nika-English Dictionary*, edited by Thomas Henry Sparshott, London 1887 [391 pages]; Krapf, 'Chuo cha utenzi. Gedichte im alten Suahili: Aus den Papieren des † Dr. L. Krapf, herausgegeben von Carl Gotthilf Büttner', in: *Zeitschrift für afrikanische Sprachen*, 1. Jg., Okt. 1887 bis Juli 1888, 1-42, 124-137; Krapf, 'Deutsch-Kikamba-Wörterbuch von Krapf, herausgegeben von Carl Gotthilf Büttner', in: *Zeitschrift für afrikanische Sprachen*, 1. Jg., Okt. 1887 bis Juli 1888, 81-123.

[542] Krapf in: Rebmann, *Dictionary of the Kiniassa Language*, p. iii.

[543] Karl Richard Lepsius (1810-1884). 'Standard Alphabet for reducing unwritten languages and foreign graphic systems to a uniform orthography in European letters', in: *Amsterdam Studies in the Theory and History of linguistic science*, I: Amsterdam Classics in Linguistics, vol. 5, Amsterdam: John Benjamins, 1981, p. 39.

[544] Letter from Rebmann in Zanzibar to the CMS (no name), 15 December 1858. In a PS to that letter, of 11 February 1859, Rebmann reported that he had completed his translation of *Luke* into Kisuahili, and that he had 'adopted the Standard Alphabet of Dr Lepsius as nearly as that language admit it'. He said that he wanted to add to the translation two pages with an explanation of the spelling. 'Every consonant (with but few exceptions) being followed by a vowel in this language, a quick boy will learn to read within a month's time, as I have had several proofs among the Wanika, and also among the Suahilis.'

[545] Krapf refers to Steere's *Handbook of the Swahili Language* (2nd ed.), p. 8.

[546] Letter from Krapf in Korntal to CMS Secretary Henry Wright, 14 March 1876.

bombardment of letters to the CMS, who had charged him to edit Rebmann's work, Krapf condemned Rebmann's orthography and urged them for permission to make changes, especially in Rebmann's translations of Scripture.[547] Whether the CMS explicitly allowed Krapf to change Rebmann's work is doubtful. They certainly did not want to offend their faithful missionary of many years.[548] Apparently Krapf was not very sure about his mandate, because when finally he took the liberty of applying his preferred spelling to Rebmann's translation, he begged the CMS with regard to the result 'to state that it is in perfect harmony with that of Dr. Steere'. Finally Rebmann's translation of the Gospel of *Luke*, published in 1876, after modifications by Krapf, became a disorderly mix of spellings, so that some considered it as 'of little use'.[549]

Apart from his criticism of Rebmann's spelling, he also criticised Rebmann's translations and sourly remarked: 'There are many words in Mr. Rebmann's manuscripts which require a closer examination; but I did not think it right to leave out such words, though they are inexplicable at the present stage of our knowledge of Suahili.' This comment was strange

---

[547] Letter from Krapf in Korntal, in German, to an unknown addressee probably at the CMS, 18 March 1876 [G/4/A5/1/2]. In the margin notes were made in English: Rebmann's spelling would create confusion, as 'there would be two systems of orthography in different portions of the Bible published by the same society'. In a letter of 24 March 1876 to CMS secretary Wright: 'I beg you will soon send me the result of your decision in reference to the orthography, which shall be used in printing Mr. Rebmann's translation' of Luke in Swahili. In two letters of 27 March 1876 to Wright he repeated his request.

[548] Letter from Krapf in Korntal, in German, to an unknown addressee probably at the CMS, 18 March 1876 [G/4/A5/1/2]. In a note the CMS secretary indicates that he does not prefer Rebmann's spelling in the translation of Luke. Yet he suggests: 'would the Society like that only say a few hundert copies be first printed, in order not to offend Mr. R., and so procure the translation as Dr. Krapf thinks it very good one, and at a later period it could be altered in the second edition and a greater number could conveniently be done at Mombas'.

[549] *Engili ya Lukasi : Iliofasirika kua Maneno ya Kisuaheli* (= The Gospel according to St. Luke, translated into the Suaheli-language by J. Rebman [sic], missionary of the Church Missionary Society in East Africa St. Chrischona: British and Foreign Bible Society, 1876). A copy at Cambidge University Library has MS corrections by bishop E. Steere. In the library's Catalogue there is the following remark: 'Translated by John Rebmann of the Church Missionary Society, in 1860 and revised by him and J.L. Krapf of the Church Missionary Society. Though J.L. Krapf had modified J. Rebmann's spelling, yet the orthography remained so irregular that the book proved of little use'. Rebmann's translation of Luke was again revised by bishop E. Steere who included it in his Swahili translation of the New Testament, published in 1883.

in view of Krapf's own limitations. Later we will see that he was criticised with regard to the quality of his translations, his lexicographical method, his inaccuracy, and his spelling.

Finally, in 1882, one year after the death of Krapf his Swahili-English Dictionary was published.[550] Rebmann's name was not on the title-page; only his own name was there. From Krapf's beginnings Rebmann had worked on the Swahili lexicon for decades, yet until after Rebmann's death Krapf was adamant in refusing to him even the co-authorship.[551] He left it to Robert Cust of the CMS Committee to stress in the introduction that 'the Dictionary was his [i.e. Krapf's], and that of his lamented friend Dr. [sic] John Rebmann'. In the same Preface Krapf attacked the Anglican bishop Edward Steere, considering the question whether he had committed plagiarism in his *Handbook of the Suahili Language* (1870), 'if he were not a Christian'. 'The form of the book is the bishop's, while the essence of the grammar and the dictionary are in the main my work.'[552]

Krapf's most painfully unfriendly remark on his former colleague appeared in the Preface of Rebmann's *Dictionary of the Kiniassa Language*, which was printed for the first time and published in 1877, one year after Rebmann's death. This publication was entirely the work of Rebmann, although sometimes Krapf is mistakenly called (co-)author.[553] Although Krapf had not contributed anything to its contents, he was asked by the CMS to edit the book. It was simultaneously brought out in two places, St. Chrischona, Switzerland, and in London. The content was exactly the same except for two additions. First the following rather biting words in Krapf's Preface, which were only included in the version published by the St. Chrischona Pilger Mission, where Krapf had a lot of influence:

---

[550] Johann Ludwig Krapf, *A Dictionary of Suahili language*, containing an Outline of a Suahili Grammar, Edinburg: Ballantyne & Hanson/London: Trübner, 1882 [Cust's Introduction, p. v, vi; Krapf's Preface, p. vii-xii; Outline Grammar p. xiii-xxxx, Lexicon, p. 1-431].

[551] In a letter to the CMS of 19 December 1876 Krapf reiterates his claim that the Swahili dictionary is not Rebmann's [CMS C A5/O16/148].

[552] Letter from Krapf in Korntal to the CMS Committee, 5 February, probably 1877, anyway not 1876, because written after Rebmann's death [G/4/A5/1/21: code confused with code of Krapf's letter of 23 Febr. 1876]. K. Knauß, *BBKL*, vol. 4, 1992, S. 606-608. <http://www.bautz.de/bbkl/k/Krapf.shtml>; L.Pirouet, 'The Legacy of Johann Ludwig Krapf', <http://131.111.227.198/CKrapf.htm>.

[553] Cf. *Dictionary of the Kiniassa Language* (Paperback), by Johann Ludwig Krapf (Author), John Rebman (Author), http://www.amazon.com/Dictionary-Kiniassa-Language-Johann-Ludwig/dp/1145318991.

9. Language Worker

> 'Pleased as we may be with Rebman's linguistic labours, yet we cannot forbear thinking, that his memory would be by far more blessed by the millions of East Africans, if he during his 29 years' stay in East Africa had made a correct translation of the Bible in Kisuaheli or Kinika. In point of translations Rebman has left nothing behind him but an excellent translation of St. Luke in Kisuaheli which has been printed in July last. Except this translation together with the Kiniassa Dictionary, and the numerous additions, with which he enriched the Editor's large Dictionary of the Kisuaheli and Kinika languages, Mr. *Rebman* has brought to Europe nothing of any great value in regard to Philology.'

In the Preface to Johannes Rebmann's special work Krapf was 'not wishful of making any remark' on Rebmann's life, which means he refused to publish some personal words to the memory of his old friend; he just referred to the formal obituary by the CMS. The CMS in the Preface complied by briefly commending Rebmann as a faithful worker, persevering in a lonely post where he was instrumental in the establishment of the beginnings of the Church. As for his language work the CMS added:

> 'His work was mainly a preparatory one: he compiled a dictionary in Kiniassa, and improved with numerous additions the Dictionary of the Kisuaheli and Kinika languages, which Dr. Krapf had first reduced to writing between 1844-1853, labours of which future Missionaries will reap the benefit.'

In Krapf's opinion these words, although few and plain, gave too much personal honour to the late Rebmann. Therefore in the St. Chrischona version he made another addition, in brackets after the name Krapf: '(the real author of this Dictionary).'

In 1880, a year before his death, Krapf wrote the Preface to his Swahili Dictionary. By then he somehow realised that his disparaging comment on Rebmann was unjustifiable. He apologised, saying that at the time of his remarks in 1876, he had not seen and read the manuscript of the Nika Dictionary. He did not want to give in too much, though, and stressed that Rebmann had compiled the Nika collection 'on the basis of my own Kinika work.' Yet, with regard to the Kiniassa Dictionary he admitted:

> 'I regret that I had not seen and read the scattered manuscripts of this great work, or I should not, in the year 1876, when I edited Mr. Rebmann's Kiniassa Dictionary, have made in the preface the desultory remark.'[554]

---

[554] Krapf, *A Dictionary of the Suahili language*, Introduction, p. x.

Rebmann on Krapf's work

Rebmann's low profile in comparison to Krapf's fame was partly due to the relative shortness of his life, which he mainly spent far from the network of contacts that counted for publicity and authority. However, that remark is not decisive for the quality of the work of both missionaries. Apart from the moral aspect, Krapf's degrading comments on Rebmann's linguistic work were strange in view of his own limitations. In the previous chapter we noted that Krapf had to recognise Rebmann's greater ability in Swahili and Nika. Hence there is no reason to assume that the spelling and the translations of the vocabulary Krapf contributed himself needed less improvement than the labours of Rebmann's.

How did Rebmann himself look at the work of his former colleague? His experience on the spot with African languages lasted much longer than Krapf's. After Krapf's departure in 1853 he continued the translation of the Scriptures and the collection for the dictionaries of the Swahili and Nika languages, soon to be followed by the Nyasa language. He added to the material in Swahili and Nika that Krapf had prepared either on his own, or in cooperation with Rebmann. In 1858 during his exile in Zanzibar Rebmann fully concentrated on his linguistic tasks. It stands to reason that with the growing output of his own work, Krapf's contribution grew less significant. In addition, Rebmann found some difficulties in the translations and collections of Krapf. When Deimler urged him to send translated Bible portions and vocabulary lists in Swahili to Bombay for the training of African Christians, he had to say that Krapf's material was not good enough. This pertained to Krapf's translation into Kinika of the Gospel of *Luke*, to his translations of books of the New Testament into Swahili, and to his Swahili dictionary.

By that time Rebmann had started revising his own translation of *Luke* into Swahili in Mombasa with the help of a Muslim kadi, 'with the Arabic New Testament in hand', to prevent misunderstandings, e.g. of a literal translation of *Luke* 12:49, which 'says just the contrary of what it wants to say'. Rebmann saw similar problems in Krapf's Kinika translation of Luke, e.g. 'the two debtors in *Luke* 7:41 are represented as demanding money instead of owing it'. He concluded: 'I see more and more how much care and time is needed to make a correct intelligible translation into a language, the only source of information about which is the mouth of the natives.'[555]

---

[555] Letter from Rebmann in Mombasa to the CMS Committee, 16 Sept. 1859.

9. Language Worker 193

Rebmann also worked on his own Swahili dictionary, but its completion 'had to wait a few years longer'. Could Krapf's material be used in the meantime? When the Hanoverian missionaries, preparing themselves in Zanzibar for work in mainland Africa, asked him for learning tools for Swahili, Rebmann hesitated to recommend the use of Krapf's Nika and Swahili products. He explained why:

> 'Already at the time when Dr. Krapf departed for Europe I had begun to see that all was not right, neither in his grammar, nor in his other linguist labours. God has hitherto so wonderfully preserved my health and strength and has given me the requisite leisure, especially during my residence here, that I have been enabled, while studying the Kinika and the Kiniassa, the latter of which I could only do through the medium of the Kisuahili, to perfect my knowledge of this also so far as to see in the translations etc. the mere exercises of the beginner of a new language. By the Hanoverian missionaries asking me for some means of studying the Kisuahili I had the occasion to look over the [*columns*] of the languages in his "Vocabulary of six East African languages", and found it so full of inaccuracies that I actually sat down and began working [*on*] them [*for making*] a new copy, my wife writing for me the English [*part*].'[556]

In Rebmann's observation Krapf's work suffered from three weaknesses, a wrong method, undue haste, and faulty translations. First he concluded that Krapf's failing lexicographical method was the cause of many mistakes. He had followed the wrong order. He had not started by collecting Swahili words and subsequently trying to translate them into English, but he had taken English as his starting point, trying to translate English terms into Swahili.

> 'Dr. Krapf from the beginning [*has had*] a most unfortunate mode of studying this language, in setting himself the task of translating the English dictionary into it, not omitting even such words of which he knew perfectly well that no corresponding word could [*possibly*] be found in Kisuahili. ... This was only spending one's time and strength for nought. The true mode of coming to a correct knowledge of an unwritten language is evidently that adopted by Mr Kölle and this has also been mine, though I had never conferred about it with him. We must learn from them and ascertain the true and exact meaning of every word they mention, and especially learn their way of expressing themselves with their interesting proverbs and proverbial sayings, in one word the genius of a language, and not try to

---

[556] Letter from Rebmann in Zanzibar to the CMS (no name), 16 September 1858 [024].

teach them what they might possibly call this and that of things they never heard of and are not likely soon to get acquainted with.'[557]

Rebmann said that 'even in the early years' of his being together with Krapf he had often tried to persuade him to change his method, but to no avail. 'I had many a controversy with him on this subject, but he was so firmly fixed in the pernicious mode of working he had adopted that I did not succeed in persuading him to alter it.' In a separate note Rebmann discussed the motivation which Krapf offered for his method.

> 'The argument by which he always defended himself was this, that Europeans in their intercourse with the natives should be enabled to explain to them in their own language every English word, denote it a subject foreign to them or not; as also that Suahilis learning English will be in want of having every English word rendered into their tongue.'[558]

Rebmann rejected Krapf's reasoning, and stressed that in lexicography the foreign language always should be the starting point.

> 'The fact is that Europeans want first to know the meaning of the words they hear from the natives, and the wants of these are certainly most unduly anticipated by explaining words to them, many of which are in fact foreign even to the English dictionary (I mean the technical ones).'

Remarkably Krapf abandoned his method of working from the most familiar language to the target language in the 1882 publication of his Swahili Dictionary. The order was Swahili-English like the large collection of Swahili-English vocabulary, which he found in Rebmann's luggage in Korntal in 1875/1876. If he had persisted in his usual order of English-Swahili the inclusion of Rebmann's work would have been more difficult.

Krapf's method sometimes had strange consequences for the Swahili words used in their translation. Rebmann said that Krapf had invented artificial Swahili terms.

> 'This officiousness betrayed him into another great error, viz. of forming a great many new words, [which] certainly as to form, are allowable, but are never used. It is as if an Englishman would affix the terminations, 'ment',

---

[557] Idem; Sigismund Wilhelm Kölle (1820-1902), a German fellow CMS missionary, trained by the Basler Mission, who worked among freed slaves in Free Town, Sierra Leone. He was a pioneer scholar of African languages. His most important work, Polyglotta Africana (1854) contains word lists of many African languages.
[558] Idem.

9. Language Worker

'ion' etc. etc. to any word according to his fancy, as if the words of a language could be multiplied almost at random.'[559]

The second 'element destructive of accuracy' of Krapf's linguistic work, in Rebmann's opinion, was 'his haste and anxiety of looking more to the quantity than to the quality of work done'.

'If it had not been for this, he might still have produced a useful work, after I had arranged the Kisuahili alphabetically from his great English-Kisuaheli Dictionary, during his absence in Europe in 1850. By this process the language became at once stripped of that fake appearance which it bore when placed behind the English and the real task could no more be mistaken. But instead of bestowing upon it that patience of research, which is alone sure of accuracy, he finished off in a few months what ought to have taken him almost as many years. Besides, he goes into particulars on subjects and words where they are not needed, and only impart to the language the appearance of a degree of obscenity, as if almost a third part was made up of it.'[560]

Thirdly, according to Rebmann Krapf offered weak translations, which Krapf sometimes admitted. According to Rebmann it showed that Krapf was only a beginner in the Swahili language.

'In his translations he is particularly unfortunate in the use of the tenses, and the working of the sentences in general is accordingly heavy and awkward. ... [Only] the words but not the grammar can be called Kisuahili. I feel in fact something like a disgrace that after we have been so many years on this coast there does not yet exist even a good vocabulary of the language, which would be a book [useful] not only to freshly coming missionaries and travellers, but also to the merchants on this island and I do hope that as soon as I shall be permitted to visit Europe I shall be enabled to bring home not only my works of the Kinika and Kiniassa but also one of the Kisuaheli language.'[561]

As to the translations of Scripture, Rebmann seems to have preferred the work by Bishop Steere to Krapf's. In 1870 he received copies of the Gospel of *Matthew* in Swahili, probably translated by Steere. The translated text was difficult to understand for the Nika readers, but there 'was no better available'.[562]

---
[559] Idem.
[560] Idem.
[561] Idem.
[562] Letter from Rebmann in Korntal to CMS Secretary Hutchinson, 17 Nov. 1875.

Rebmann defended

Some former colleagues noted Krapf's inferiority as a scholar in comparison to Rebmann. The first one was Jakob J. Erhardt, who had closely co-operated with Rebmann in Kisuludini. He had also seen Krapf at work, and had personally experienced some painful consequences of Krapf's missiological approach. He expressed his worries about Krapf's interference with Rebmann's documents, and his attempts to appropriate work that was not his own. Writing about his own collection of Swahili, Erhardt said:

> 'A very short time before my dear brother Rebmann's death he sent a very sad message to me, dictated as the writer remarked under tears, lamenting that all his linguistic labours had to fall into Dr. Krapf's hands. ... Dr Krapf [*made a start*] at ever so many languages, but never had the patience to learn one African language properly. Mr Rebmann worked very carefully, and I cannot help [*sobbing*] with him on the result of Dr Krapf's doings. If he confined himself to Mr Rebmann's manuscripts I have no [*doubt*] something solid and real would be published. But he should never correct him and [*learn*] his own out.'[563]

In addition Erhardt reported to the CMS that not only Rebmann, but also he himself had contributed to the Swahili vocabulary that Krapf claimed for himself. He attached the vocabulary list that he had compiled himself.

> 'The vocabulary which I forward is in part Dr. Krapf's. I had copied his. Mr. Rebmann and myself had agreed that one of us should take the Kinika the other the Kisuaheli, the latter I had taken. I had taken and enlarged the vocabulary into what it is now. After I had undertaken the Usambara mission and settled at Tanga Mr Rebmann copied my vocabulary.'[564]

Another former colleague of both Rebmann and Krapf in Kisuludini was Johann G. Deimler. He had left East Africa for India with mixed feelings. After having returned to Germany, Deimler looked back and equally ex-

---

[563] Letter from Erhardt in Secundra Orphanage at Agra, to CMS HQ in London, 8 March 1877. The document is severely damaged and only partially legible [CI/O 103/8]. The last words of the quotation are in faulty English, but serve to emphasize that in Erhardt's view Krapf should have respected Rebmann's way of writing and should have learnt from it.

[564] Idem. In a letter of 19 June 1877 to the CMS Committee Krapf confirmed the reception of 'the Suaheli Dictionary of Mr. Erhardt, and I hope to find some valuable additions as in that of Mr. Rebman'.

9. Language Worker

pressed to the CMS his misgivings about Krapf's involvement in Rebmann's literary legacy.

> 'I understand that Dr. Krapf has prepared for the print several of the late Mr. Rebmann's dictionaries and that these dictionaries are to be printed by the Society. I do not exactly know in what this preparation consists, though I am surprised that Dr. Krapf should give a finalising stroke to any dictionaries of Rebmann ready as manuscripts. I think that excepting the rendering of soft and hard d and t sounds, Rebmann is ... the authority in East African languages.'[565]

That Deimler took position as a defender of Rebmann is the more worth noting as he was not Rebmann's friend and had kept up a relationship with Krapf, who he sometimes met after his return from India.[566] His ambiguous position explains why Deimler, though he definitely considered Rebmann's work as foundational, made a suggestion to the CMS to recognise Krapf's contribution too:

> 'I would therefore in the interest of the Society and of scholars who will have the use of these dictionaries, very strongly suggest, as the best plan to secure the most reliable and correct edition of these dictionaries, that by all means Rebmann's manuscripts should be preserved along with those of Dr. Krapf, and both be submitted to a missionary competent in an East African language, who if ever possible, assisted by clever natives, should revise these dictionaries and prepare them for the print.'[567]

Krapf's biographer Eber says that he went into history as pioneer of African linguistics.[568] Sundkler says that Krapf's 'work on the Gospels into Swahili and on a dictionary of this language and related East African languages' was basic to subsequent Bible translations into Swahili and into other leading East African vernaculars.[569] However, witness by close contemporary observers like Deimler and Erhardt should be taken into ac-

---

[565] Letter from Deimler in Nuremberg to CMS Secretary Fenn, 1 Nov. 1879 [CI3/O25/29].

[566] Cf. letter from Krapf in Korntal to CMS secretary Henry Venn, 5 Dec. 1857, pleading to give some work to Deimler, who had stayed in his house on the occasion of his wedding [CMS/G/AC 16/138].

[567] Letter from Deimler in Nüremberg to CMS Secretary Fenn, 1 Nov. 1879 [CI3/O25/29].

[568] Eber, *Krapf*, S. 241, quoting CMS *Intelligencer and Record NS 7, History of the Church Missionary Society*, II, 124-136, 428-429: 'Als Pionier auf dem Gebiet afrikanischer linguistischer Forschung hat er kaum Konkurrenz'.

[569] Sundkler and Steed, *A History of the Church in Africa*, p. 517, 518.

count to adjust this one-sided picture. Church historian Reed looks back at Krapf and Rebmann, and thinks that they 'provided basic knowledge which other Western people could use', but he concludes that 'Krapf's Swahili works were later regarded as of little use, his spelling being eccentric and his grammar inaccurate.'[570] As to spelling, probably Reed condemned the systems of Rebmann and others. However, he realised that Krapf's own orthography smacked of opportunism. Unfortunately Reed does not mention linguistic or historical arguments for his conclusion, nor does he look for traces of Rebmann's research in Krapf's Swahili Dictionary, or explain why Krapf put Rebmann in the shade.

The Kinika Dictionary

According to SIL's *Ethnologue* the Nika language, also known as Nyika, is similar to Swahili. The name Nika is not in use anymore, because it means 'bush people' and is considered to be a derogatory indication today. At present it is named *Mijikenda*, referring to the nine ethnic groups along the coast of Kenya, from the border of Somalia in the north to the border of Tanzania in the south. It is spoken in the Coast Province of present-day Kenya, especially in the Kilifi and Kwale districts, north of Mombasa. The dialects in question are Chonyi, Digo, Duruma, Giriama, Jibana, Kamba, Kauma, Rabai, Ribe (or Rihe). An alternative name for the language is Kigiriama after its most prominent dialect. The Digo dialect is also found in Tanzania.[571] His Nika-English Dictionary, his Niassa Dictionary, and his work on the Swahili Dictionary, were Rebmann's most important linguistic work. The first effort to reduce the Nika language to writing was started two years before Rebmann's arrival at Mombasa by his colleague Krapf, who had come in 1844. The work was followed up by Rebmann over a period of twenty-nine years. He considered it his own work.[572] On the frontispiece of the first printed edition of 1887, however, both Krapf and Rebmann are mentioned as compilers, alphabetically.[573] Krapf's prominent position on the title page suggested that he was the main author. However, the work was essentially Rebmann's, who had used

---

[570] Reed, *Pastors, Partners, Paternalists*, p. 32.
[571] http://www.ethnologue.com/show_language.asp?code=nyf; http://en.wikipedia.org/wiki/Mijikenda_peoples;
[572] Rebmann, *Tagebuch*, 4-11-1848, 'all the time that was not occupied by visitors, I worked on my Kinika-English Dictionary'.
[573] J.L. Krapf and J. Rebmann, *A Nika-English Dictionary*, edited by T.H. Sparshott, London: SPCK, 1887 [391 pages]. Preface by Robert Cust (p. iv), and Introduction by Sparshott (p. v, vi). Digitised by Google and published on the internet.

9. Language Worker

Krapf's incentive.[574] During Rebmann's lifetime the dictionary remained unnoticed by the general public, and he received no credit for it. Even worse, the work was almost lost.

Before he left the mission field in 1875 Rebmann had sent the manuscripts of the three dictionaries to the CMS in London.[575] Subsequently 'fatality seemed to attend' the Nika manuscript. These words were written by Robert Cust, a member of the CMS Committee for East Africa, and representative of the Society for Promoting Christian Knowledge (SPCK), which finally printed and published the book. Cust added a Preface explaining why it had taken an 'extraordinary delay' before the book was given to the public. 'A fair copy', even neatly bound, 'ready for the printer had been prepared by Rebmann, and had been seen and handled by many missionaries. It is presumed to have found its way to the CMS office at Salisbury Square, but there is no further trace of its existence.' Only much later was the loss of the manuscript noticed. The fair copy was never found.

In October 1886, ten years after Rebmann's death, Cust went to Korntal to see his widow Luise Däuble. He checked 'the book-case' of her husband. Apparently the bookcase full of material spoken of in Merkel's letter of 1929 ('eine Kiste voll') was still there in 1886. However, its contents were apparently in disarray, because Cust only 'brought away some scattered leaves of manuscript'. The 'bound volume' of the Nika dictionary had disappeared. Fortunately a rough copy was found among the papers sent to London, of which several pages were missing. Cust asked missionaries who had succeeded Rebmann in East Africa to work on the lacunae. The challenge was accepted by Rebmann's friend and colleague Thomas H. Sparshott, who edited the whole work. In his introduction to the work,[576] Sparshott described how he had spent a lot of time and energy correcting the 'very imperfect' manuscript, and put in place 'notes on scores of odd pieces of paper.' He inserted meanings, made remarks on the pronunciation, especially the accentuation, and found it particularly difficult to decide on the transliteration.

The Kiniassa Dictionary

Rebmann's meeting with a slave Salimini, from present-day Malawi led to the compilation of the first Chichewa or Chinyanja Dictionary. In this way Johannes Rebmann, after the Portuguese army officer Antonio C.P.

---

[574] Cf. AMZ, 1899, S. 181.
[575] Cf. Jehle, *Der Entdecker*, S. 15.
[576] Robert Cust, in 'Preface' to *A Nika-English Dictionary*, p. iv.

Gamitto and his Portuguese-Chichewa compilation of 1832,[577] became an early father of Chichewa lexicography. The book was published in printed form in 1877, a year after Rebmann's death, simultaneously at St. Chrischona near Basel, and in London. Rebmann's former colleague Johann Ludwig Krapf edited the book and included a Preface and some remarks on spelling. Very shortly before his death, on Krapf's request Rebmann dictated to his wife some details about his first meeting with Salimini, and his surprise on hearing the 'Kiniassa' spoken.

> 'One day while he was at work with my servants in building an appendage to our dwelling-house, I heard him talk with them in a strange language. On inquiry I was told it was Kiniassa, i.e., the language spoken in the neighbourhood of the lake Niassa (Nyasa/Nyassa).' I at once felt the wish to learn so much of it as to be able to judge about its relationship with the Kisuaheli and Kinika and some other dialects spoken inland of Mombas with which I had got more or less acquainted.'

What was Rebmann's motivation for compiling the *Dictionary of the Kiniassa Language*, and when did he start the work? Undoubtedly he agreed with Krapf, who found that 'the Kiniassa language, which is spoken in the region of the Niassa Lake, is most interesting, as it contains the roots of the Kisuahili and other dialects spoken on the coast'.[578] Rebmann's motivation went deeper than a philological interest, and his vision went further than the coastal regions of East Africa. Even before the famous explorer Livingstone had touched the area, Rebmann foresaw that in subsequent decades missionaries would enter the region of present-day Lake Malawi. He felt called to make a contribution to paving the way for them linguistically.

Emma reported that her husband 'this year' [i.e. in 1854] began 'the study of a most interesting language', Kiniassa, and that Salimini was instrumental in it.[579] Rebmann's engagement in the study of that language, in cooperation with Salimini, would last until at least the end of the 1850s. In 1858, when in exile in Zanzibar and working on the Dictionary, he asked for Salimini to be sent to him, because he 'could find no man here, who spoke that language as well as he did'.[580] The Rebmanns were of

---

[577] See Appendix II, 'A History of Chichewa Lexicography'.
[578] Letter from Krapf in Korntal to CMS Secretary Henry Wright, 27 March 1876 [II].
[579] Rebmann/Tyler (née Kent), *Journal*, p. 3 (1854).
[580] Rebmann, *Briefe*, 20-9-1859, S. 1. Letter from Rebmann in Kisuludini, to CMS secretary Henry Venn, 27 January 1854. Letter from Rebmann to the CMS (no name), 16 September 1858 [024].

9. Language Worker

the opinion that God had guided Salimini to their place, so that linguistic preparations could be made for future missionaries to reach out the Gospel to as yet unknown peoples of Central Africa. Emma wrote: 'I believe his coming is quite in the order of Providence, for the knowledge of this immense lake throws much light on the unknown interior of this Continent.'[581] Johannes, when going deeper into Salimini's stories about the people and the land of Lake Nyasa, felt like going there himself: 'I might mention many more names referring to regions of inner Africa, but the great thing is to go and see with your own eyes, and whenever I make inquiries about those unknown regions, I feel as if I must go and visit them.'

Apparently Krapf had not been aware of the Dictionary. When he was charged to edit it Rebmann was still alive, but he had become blind and was very sick at times. As to the state of Rebmann's manuscript there is a strange discrepancy between Krapf's evaluation and how Rebmann described the way he compiled the dictionary. Krapf reported to the CMS:

> 'Furthermore Mr. Rebman has delivered over to me the manuscript of his Kiniassa Dictionary. Unfortunately on close examination I found that it requires a great deal of labour before it can be printed. I have to make a copy of the whole and arrange it more alphabetically; else the printer would not find his way through the bulk of notes and slips of paper.'[582]

Krapf implicitly suggested that Rebmann's manuscript was in a disorderly state, but he may have just been dissatisfied with Rebmann's methodology. With regard to lexicographical method, Rebmann was convinced that he had to work from the unknown to the known, i.e. from the subject language (Kiniassa) to the explanatory language. He first collected Kiniassa vocabulary and then translated it into Swahili. In a later stage he fixed the meanings in English. At this point he disagreed with the method Krapf applied to his Swahili Dictionary. Krapf did not start by collecting Swahili terms, but he translated English words into Swahili.

After Rebmann's death, Luise showed Krapf a small bundle of copied letters which her husband had written to the CMS Committee for East Africa during the period 1850-55. In a letter of 13th April 1854, he said that the collection of Kiniassa vocabulary had progressed as far as the letter M. On 19th September 1854 Rebmann had 'gathered about 2,500 words of the Kiniassa language' and had 'arranged them alphabetically'. In his view this activity had to take place first.

---

[581] Rebmann/Tyler (née Kent), *Journal*, p. 3 (1854).
[582] Letter from Krapf in Korntal to CMS Secretary Henry Wright, 27 March 1876 [II].

'Before this is done no real insight into a language is afforded. I therefore look on all vocabularies which only follow the alphabet of a European language as most unsatisfactory half work. Words which should stand together in a group with the root at the top are there unintelligibly scattered about.'[583]

Gradually Rebmann discovered the richness of the Kiniassa language. The work continued to absorb him for more than a year; it went on during his stay in Cairo in 1855, and thereafter. In a letter from there, of 27 November, he wrote to the CMS Committee:

'Excepting the time I spent with Abbe Gunja every morning in reading and praying with him, I was exclusively engaged in studying the Kiniassa language. The Vocabulary which I had originally intended to form, growing under my pen to a Dictionary, finding as I gradually did, to my great astonishment, that language to be nearly as rich in words as the Kisuaheli, with all that the latter has borrowed from the Arabic, and almost richer in grammatical forms of a most curious kind. The importance of that language in its relation to the great south African family of languages can scarcely be overrated, when it is known that it contains the *fundamental meanings* of a great number of words, not only in Kisuaheli, Kinika, Kisambara, &c., but even in the Caffre language. It was with the profoundest interest that I traced the various forms and particles of speech which elucidated what had still remained dark and unaccountable to us in the other dialects. I fully believe that the language spoken to the west of the lake Niassa holds the same central position in the great south African family of languages, as the people who occupy that part of the Continent do, in a geographical point of view, for no sooner had I got an insight into it, than the dialects with which I had previously made myself more or less acquainted, appeared to me rather as so many rays of one and the same light. My study of the Kiniassa was to me such a continual intellectual feast, that days and weeks fled so quickly as I never remembered they had done before, and it was with great reluctance that I tore myself from it when we had to get ready for our voyage to Aden.'

Evidence for early use of Rebmann's manuscript is given by McIntosh, in his study on Robert Laws. He reports on the first party of Presbyterian missionaries from Scotland, who travelled in Malawi in 1875, in preparation for the establishment of their respective missions. Among them were Robert Laws, Henry Henderson, Duff MacDonald, James Steward, Alexan-

---

[583] Half-year account by Rebmann in Kisuludini to the CMS, 19(?) September 1854 [O24/16A].

9. Language Worker

der Riddel, and Edward D. Young etc. McIntosh says: 'On going out to Africa the party had been supplied with short vocabularies and grammatical notes prepared by two members of the Universities' Mission to Central Africa (UMCA), and a dictionary published by a Mr Rebman of Mombasa. These were the only language tools available in Chinyanja.'[584]

Rebmann's handwritten manuscript could have been used before 1875. There is no evidence that the Dictionary was available to two early activists on the Malawian scene, David Livingstone and Charles Frederick Mackenzie. If Livingstone possessed a copy, it would explain why the famous explorer showed some command of Chichewa during the last few of his five journeys in Malawi in the years 1858 and 1867.[585] There are no indications that Bishop Mackenzie and his party of the Universities' Mission to Central Africa (UMCA) used Rebmann's vocabulary during their first Anglican attempt for mission in Malawi in 1861-1863. Horace Waller, a member of the party, seems to have collected vocabulary speaking to the Mang'anja people through an interpreter.[586] After their withdrawal to Zanzibar under Bishop William George Tozer in 1864 the UMCA-ers communicated with Rebmann and must have used his work.

We do not know about the whereabouts of Rebmann's original manuscript that Krapf worked on in Korntal, nor of the hand-written pages that were used in Malawi. The book that was edited by Krapf is still available in printed form. It is entitled *Dictionary of the Kiniassa Language*. Kiniassa is the Swahili name for Chinyanja. It was printed and published in St. Chrischona, near Basle, in 1877. Rebmann's employer, the Church Missionary Society, had paid for the expenses. In 1877 the book was also printed and published in England,[587] directly by the CMS.[588] Where did the

---

[584] McIntosh, *Robert Laws*, p. 81 [quoted from: FGGA Reports 1884, p. 102].
[585] Cf. P.A. Cole-King, *The Livingstone Search Expedition 1867*, Department of Antiquities, No 2, 1968, re-issued by The Society of Malawi 1984.
[586] Horace Waller, Vocabulary list English-Chichewa, Archive Rhodes House, Oxford, 'Horace Waller's Papers', Mss. Afr s.16, 10 vols; Horace Waller diaries, 11 vols (1860-1864). Elias Mandala who is transcribing the papers thinks Waller's work 'to be very original not copied from any other source beside the people he was listening to', through a Zulu interpreter.
[587] John Rebman, *Dictionary of the Kiniassa Language*, edited by L. Krapf, London: CMS/Basel: St. Chrischona (at the request and the expense of the Church Missionary Society), 1877. The title page of the Chrischona edition has the following details: *Dictionary of the Kiniassa Language*, by the Rev. John Rebman, late Missionary in Eastern Africa. Edited by Ludwig Krapf. Published by: St. Chrischona, near Basel, at the request and expense of the Church Missionary Society, 1877. The book has pages i-viii, and 1-184. [NB. His real name is Johannes Rebmann. Krapf anglicized it, John Rebman].

printed copies go? Some remained in Europe. I consulted a copy in the Archive of the *Basler Mission*, where Rebmann trained to become a missionary. Many of the books are likely to have been shipped to Malawi. Krapf expected that the missionaries would be very interested in using and financing the dictionary.

> 'The Scotch missionaries and their friends, whose eyes are happily turned to the Niassa region, will be glad on hearing that the Dictionary is about to be printed. No doubt they will give you [= the CMS] a handsome contribution toward the printing expenses.'[589]

After 1877 Presbyterian missionaries in Malawi must have used printed copies of the Kiniassa Dictionary. When the Anglicans under bishop Tozer returned to Malawi in 1881, they probably used the printed book by Rebmann, who after all was an employee of a fellow-Anglican mission organisation.

Today Rebmann's book is relatively unknown in Malawi. Some archives and individual persons possess copies.[590] On the internet I found digitised copies of two editions, available to be downloaded.[591] A facsimile

---

[588] The book is similar to the Chrischona print except for the publisher. On the title page it says: London: Church Missionary Society, Salisbury Square, Fleet Street, 1877.

[589] Letter from Krapf in Korntal to CMS Secretary Henry Wright, 27 March 1876 [II]. Krapf said that the printer had estimated the cost of 1000 copies at 100 £ and of 2000 copies about 125 £.'

[590] In the 1970s D.D. Phiri observed in the *National Archives* in Zomba a vocabulary book that was probably Rebmann's work. However, when he checked later he found that the copy had got lost (D.D. Phiri, 'The Synod's Public Records', in: *The Nation*, 27-2-07). Also Louis Nthenda says he saw a copy in the National Archives 'as late as 1966'. S. Chavula, who once worked for the National Archives, says that the work is amongst the Livingstonia Synod papers, particularly those of Dr. Robert Laws' (S. Chavula and Louis Nthenda on 10 February 2011 in a discussion following my article 'Chichewa in Progress' in the *Nyasa Times* of 9 February 2011.) Menno Welling, a Lecturer of the Catholic University of Malawi, mailed me the frontispiece of a copy that had been in his possession for some time. In January 2011 I saw a copy in the Archive of the Society of Malawi in Blantyre.

[591] The digitised book can be found by entering 'Rebman Kiniassa Dictionary' (so spelled) into a search engine. Both prints the Chrischona one and the London one have been digitised by Google, from copies found in the Archives of the Universities of Harvard, Michigan, and Virginia. http://www.archive.org/stream/dictionarykinia01socigoog#page/n36/mode/1up>.

9. Language Worker

of the St. Chrischona version was made in 1967.[592] The words in the Dictionary can be easily recognised as Chichewa/Chinyanja; often the descriptions are accurate and detailed. Apparently it is the language that was spoken in central Malawi in the first half of the 19th century. There are several differences with present-day Chichewa, in both grammar and orthography.[593] Some of these characteristics, such as ni and na for ndi, plurals in (b)vi-, concords with bu-, 'pamanga' for maize, and class prefix tu- for ti- were also found in the Kasungu Chichewa of Kamuzu Banda described by Mark Hanna Watkins in the 1930s.[594] The dictionaries of Laws and Scott-Hetherwick, on the other hand, adopted the Southern Region dialect of Chinyanja, which (with one or two modifications such as yake for yache 'his', and the substitution of z- for dz- in plurals like dzaka 'years') forms the basis of standard Chichewa today.[595]

Some of Rebmann's explanations remain an enigma. He said that the peoples living on the shores of Lake Malawi call the lake *niansha* or *niancha*, which according to him means: ni (me) yancha (love) = love me, 'of which the Suaheli evidently made Niassa.'[596] To my knowledge this explanation is wrong. Niassa, Niasa, Nyasa are just other versions of Nyanja, meaning: *lake*.

Another remarkable thing is that the dictionary does not include references to Rebmann's faith or theological convictions. There is no explanation of Christian and Biblical terminology in it. For that matter there are no references to Islam either. On the other hand the dictionary has some words that convey meanings in animism, i.e. the concepts of African Traditional Religion, like the paramount being, ancestral spirits, offerings and ceremonies to appease the spirits, sacred forests and rivers representing the sprits, sanctuaries, magic and witchcraft.[597] Msidu wa

---

[592] On page ii it says: Repuplished [sic] in 1967 by: Gregg Press Limited, Westmead, Farnborough Hants, England. Printed in Germany.
[593] For details see appendix I.
[594] Watkins, Mark Hanna, 'A grammar of Chichewa: a Bantu language of British Central Africa' *Language*, vol. 13, No. 2, Language Dissertation No. 24, 1937. This work, which used Kamuzu Banda as its sole informant, was written when Banda was a student in Chicago.
[595] Robert Laws, *An English-Nyanja Dictionary*, Edinburgh 1894; David Clement Scott & Alexander Hetherwick, *Dictionary of the Nyanja Language*, London and Manchester 1929 (based on Scott's original of 1892).
[596] Rebmann, *Dictionary of the Kiniassa Language*, p. iv, 135.
[597] Rebmann, *Dictionary of the Kiniassa Language*, see entries like: kakisi (= kachisi) 'temple', manda 'tokens of mourning, burial and ceremonies to appease the spirits', msidu (= msitu) 'forest'; the entry includes a description of a certain forest 'of about 15 miles in length and 5 or 6 in breadth, the trees, of which are said to

Guwa (Msitu wa Guwa) or 'forest of the shrine' is a specific sacred forest mentioned by Salimini.[598]

Moreover some impolite words and terms referring to sexuality were included.[599] Apparently Rebmann, as the first person (excepting the Portuguese traveller Gamitto) to reduce Chichewa to writing, just wanted to record the existing language and not the desired language. The content of the Kiniassa Dictionary was meant as a reflection of the language of the resource person.

---

be all of one kind, of about 18' in height and presenting a perfectly level surface at the top, and standing so close to each other, that neither animal nor man can enter. Inhabitants of the country keep it sacred, no tree ever being cut down of it, though they are much in want of fuel. Their sacrifices for rain &c. are also offered in its neighbourhood'; ndsembe (*nsembe*) 'offering for the *wazimu* i.e. the spirits', ufidi (*ufiti*) 'witchcraft, sorcery'. Other entries: Chambebe (*Chambepe*) 'an apparition confined to Lake Niassa', Chiuda (*Chiuta*) 'God', psidi psidi (*psitipsiti*) 'an apparition' (the entry also mentions other kinds of ghosts), chiwanda 'an evil spirit, demon, spectre', chambu 'a charm to prevent stealing from gardens'.

[598] It is said by Rebmann in another entry to be in the country of 'Msincha' (*Msinja*). It can thus be identified with the Dzalanyama mountain forest, on the border between Malawi and Mozambique. Here holes in a rock called Kaphirintiwa were thought to be the footprints of the first man and woman. The Chewa made sacrifices for rain here, presided over by the Makewana (high priestess). (See: J.W.M. van Breugel, *Chewa Traditional Religion*, Kachere, p. 34, 45-47).

[599] E.g. mbina = an uncommon projection of the bottom; mchimba = hard shitting; nia ((*ku*) *nya*) = to emit/to void by stool; ku nia liwewe = to emit or speak lies; maniamia [sic] (*manyanya/manyi*) (obscene from ku nia); dóira (obscene) = *towira* = to make sexual movements with the hips'; ana mpongo = he is a whore-monger; kisende (*tchende*), kinda/kindana (*chinda/chindana*); gnini (*nyini*) (no translation given).

9. Language Worker

Johannes Rebmann's grave in Korntal,
'Saved in the arms of Jesus' (Stadtarchiv Gerlingen).

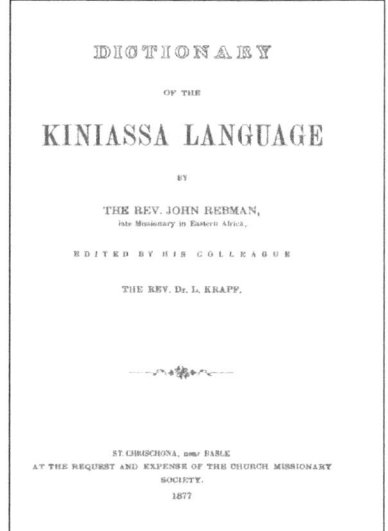

Title page of Rebmann's Kiniassa
Dictionary, St. Chrischona print, 1877.

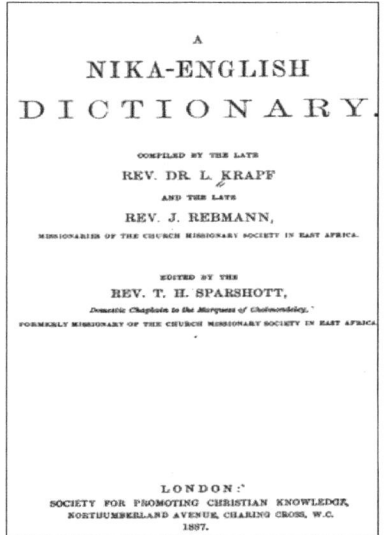

Title page of Rebmann's Kinika
Dictionary, 1887.

10. The context of Muslim Slavery

Nofa and Salimini as types

Johannes Rebmann lived and worked in the context of slavery and slave-trade. Only by the end of Rebmann's 29 years in Africa did the British Government manage to force the Zanzibar Sultanate to close its slave market. Day by day the Rebmanns were confronted with the presence around them of men and women who were owned by their slave masters. Many belonged to the age-old phenomenon of internal African slavery. Prisoners taken in wars with nearby tribes lost their freedom, and were used as workers, wives or soldiers. Others were captured in the African interior, at the end of long-distance trade lines. For centuries Africans had been sold into slavery to the East African coast, and from there to the Arab-dominated world and the Persian Gulf, often as domestic servants, concubines, and plantation workers. Amongst these slaves were people from present-day Malawi and neighbouring countries. We know two by their names, Nofa and Salimini. Nofa was a slave girl briefly referred to in Emma Kent's Journal. About Salimini we know more. He assisted Rebmann by serving as an informant for the Kiniassa Dictionary, apparently the only one. In this chapter Nofa and Salimini stand for all the slaves of East Africa in Rebmann's time. They personify a very important aspect of the environment of 19th-century mission in Africa.

Britain and the slave-trade

By that time in Europe the Evangelical and Pietist *Awakenings* had led to the public will and the political decision to make an end to slavery. In the British Empire the slave-trade ended in 1807, and slavery as such had been prohibited since 1833. In West Africa the anti-slavery movement led to earlier results than in East Africa. With regard to the East African slave-trade, Britain had to deal with its main perpetrators, the Portuguese in the South, and the Sultanate of Oman and Zanzibar in the North. Originally the Sultan's capital was at Muscat in Oman, but Sultan Sayyid Said shifted his residence to Zanzibar, and after his death Zanzibar became a Sultanate in its own right.

In 1822 the British made a pact with the then ruler of Muscat, the *Moresby Treaty*. It was the first formal British anti-slavery treaty with rulers of Africa's east coast, not regarding the Portuguese south. The treaty forbade external slave-trade, particularly the trading and transporting of slaves from Oman/Zanzibar to British-ruled territories in India. Internal slave-trade, i.e. within the dominions of the Oman/Zanzibar Sultanate, was permitted. On a cynical note, the Sultan was left free to receive slaves from the interior of Africa, keep them in his dominions, and to trade them to Asia, except British India. The treaty did not force the Sultan to acknowledge 'the principle that slave-trade is a crime against humanity'. The Sultan had to accept, though, the presence of a British consul 'to observe and report on the external traffic'.[600] The consul was mandated to direct the British warships, which were to seize and confiscate ships that illegally transported slaves. However, for a long time the naval squadrons existed mainly theoretically, in practice Arab slave-trade was not really affected.

One of the first British consuls in Zanzibar was Atkin Hamerton. He gave his name to the *Hamerton Treaty* of 1845. The new treaty prohibited all slave-trade by the Sultanate to Asia, but it continued legal recognition of slave-trading within the islands and coastal regions of the Sultanate.[601] Practically nothing changed. In 1858 Hamerton was succeeded by Christopher P. Rigby, who noticed the smuggling of slaves in open violation of the *Hamerton Treaty*. Rigby learnt 'that no slave ship had been captured ... for at least eight years'. He stressed the need for strengthening the naval squadron with more warships, and he forced the Indians of Zanzibar to free their slaves.

Of all the British consuls in Zanzibar,[602] perhaps Henry Adrian Churchill, 1867-1870, was the one who definitely wanted the end of all slavery and slave-trading. After the death of Sultan Majid, Churchill helped Majid's brother Barghash to the throne. He expected a lot from Barghash, who was trained in Bombay under the British educational system.[603] However, the new Sultan refused to cooperate. The one who made him bow was John Kirk, a medical officer, who was frequently acting consul in the period 1866-1873. He forced Barghash to accept a treaty that ended

---

[600] Moses D.E. Nwulia, *Britain and Slavery in East Africa*, Washington: Three Continents Press, 1975, p. 41-54. Joe Khamisi, *The Wretched Africans: A Study of Rabai and Freretown Settlements*, Plano, Texas: Jodey Publ., 2016, especially chapter 12 (p. 201ff), 'Finally Slavery Abolished'.

[601] Nwulia, *Britain, and Slavery in East Africa*, p. 60. Khamisi, *The Wretched Africans*, p. 203.

[602] The others mentioned by Nwulia are: Lewis Pelly, acting consul 1861-1863 (p. 79, 106, 107), Playfair, consul 1863-1865 (p. 79), G. Edwin Seward, acting consul 1865-1867 (p. 106), Prideaux, acting consul, 1874 (p. 140).

[603] Nwulia, *Britain, and Slavery in East Africa*, p. 92.

10. The context of Muslim Slavery

the legal slave-trade by the Sultanate. Instructed by Sir Bartle Frere, a visiting British envoy with a powerful mandate, Kirk threatened the Sultan with a full-scale naval blockade. Consequently, on 5 July 1873, Barghash issued a proclamation that closed the Zanzibar market and prohibited slave-trading in his dominions. However, the treaty 'depended on the active cooperation of the Sultan and the effectiveness of the enforcement machinery.'[604]

During the 19th century, despite the anti-slavery treaties, restrictions and humanitarian propaganda, slave-traffic in East Africa persisted and grew. Nwulia says that demand was the main cause, including demand by Western merchants. He thinks that 'British policy and attitudes facilitated the satisfaction of that demand.' Nwulia points to the following aspects. First, the British Navy did not provide effective naval and financial support to the squadrons that patrolled the African coast. Secondly, 'the consuls before Churchill generally winked at the Arab slave-trade', visiting explorers like Grant, Speke, Burton, 'themselves used slaves', and 'even the British men-of-war were coaled by slaves on contract.' Thirdly, contradictions in British policy practically left slave-traders off the hook. Lastly, Nwulia thinks that public opinion in the West was rather indifferent toward slave-trading in East Africa, because people presumed that Muslim slavery was milder than slavery for which the Western 'Christian' nations had been responsible.[605] On this point, perhaps Nwulia overlooks or underestimates the effect on public opinion by David Livingstone in his reports on the horrors of slavery and slave-trade. During his earlier travels, 1849-1856, Livingstone saw more of the Portuguese side than of the Arab and Swahili-Arab involvement in the slave-trade. When he made his journeys farther north, especially the four forays to the region of Lake Nyasa in the period 1858-1867, he discovered the devastations caused by the slave-trade triggered by the Zanzibar Sultanate, and reported on it. After Livingstone's death public opinion shifted to support of mission and humanitarian action in the lake region of the interior of Africa.

Long-distance slave routes

Formal termination of the slave-trade on the coasts of the Atlantic and Indian Oceans did not bring slavery in the interior of Africa to an end.

---

[604] Nwulia, *Britain, and Slavery in East Africa*, p. 81, 82, 137, 138. Khamisi, *The Wretched Africans*, p. 204,205.
[605] Nwulia, *Britain, and Slavery in East Africa*, p. 104-111. Khamisi, *The Wretched Africans*, especially chapter 13, 'Free but not yet free', p. 227ff.

The African demand for Western commodities, like manufactured cloth and firearms, continued. This required more production for exports. For this reason Africans turned enslaved labour to the production of articles demanded by Europe and the Arab world, e.g. ivory, beeswax, palm oil. Slaves were exported in the same way, but on a fairly small scale. The exportation of slaves had not dominated East African trade until the mid-18th century. Then the situation of moderate long-distance slave-trading changed for the worse. The first cause was the increased demand for slaves on the sugar and coffee plantations of the French Indian Ocean colonies of Mauritius and Réunion. Secondly, Brazil could not find enough slaves in the West because of the British anti-slavery squadron on the Atlantic coasts, and because they had expanded their sugar plantations. That's why they turned to East Africa for buying slaves. Thirdly, the new clove plantations of Zanzibar and Pemba demanded an increase of slave labour.[606] The Swahili islands and cities along Africa's east coast were under Portuguese control until 1698. Then the Arabs forced them out, and since the early 19th century the coastal region and its islands had been part of the Muscat-Oman Sultanate of Sayyid (*Lord*) Said. When Zanzibar's economy started to flourish, the Sultan moved in 1840 his capital to the island. Under him Zanzibar became the largest slave market in East Africa. Many men and women who were captured in the interior passed through Ibo and Kilwa before reaching Zanzibar.

Before the eyes of the powerless missionaries the shameful trade developed. In September 1854 Rebmann was in Mombasa. He reported that 1,500 to 3,000 new slaves, mainly women and children, had arrived from Kilwa. In one house he saw 15 of them and in another house 100. He was deeply touched, and tried to help five children by buying them from an Indian trader. Four of them were from somewhere near Lake Nyasa, one of the Manga tribe, and three of the Yao (Wahiao) tribe, at 30 days' distance from Kilwa. The Yao boys described the horrors inflicted by the Biti (Wabiti), who had attacked their village and killed the men. On their way to the coast with the mothers and children the Biti had also killed the babies, by binding them to the branches of trees over big fires. Rebmann addressed some slave-traders: 'I spoke to them freely about the sin and the curse of this trade, which for men and God is shameless, and said that the judgements of God were liable to hit not only the Christian world but also them.'[607] Unfortunately some time later he had to return the boys to

---

[606] Kevin Shillington, *History of Africa*, London: Macmillan, 1995 (first: 1989), p. 256, 257, p. 251, 252.
[607] Rebmann, *Tagebuch*, 18-9-1848.

the Indian slave-trader. Krapf had turned against the idea of buying slaves free with money and teaching them, as in his view this distracted from their 'calling to preach to the Nika people in diaspora.' Moreover, the British consul in Zanzibar pointed out to Rebmann and Krapf that British law, which protected them, did not allow the selling or buying of slaves.[608]

Between the 1860s and 1880s East African slave and ivory markets expanded considerably. The trade's agents penetrated far into the interior. This changed the character of the traditional long-distance trading, causing it to become dominated by the slave-trade. Although public opinion in Europe gradually was becoming conscious of the horrors of slavery and slave-trade in East Africa, including the Zanzibar Sultanate, and the antislavery squadron with its limited means tried to stop slave ships, in the 1860s about 70,000 slaves a year were exported from East African slave markets. Even after 1873, when the British forced the Sultan to close the market in Zanzibar, slavery and slave-trade went on. The increased European demand for ivory was one of the reasons. It indirectly promoted slavery, because the traders needed porters for carrying the ivory to the coast.

In the organisation of the slave-trade the slave markets played a key role. They encouraged the long-distance trade of slaves and ivory. The African east coast from Sofala in the south to Lamu in the north was controlled by two slave-trading powers, the Portuguese and Arabs. In the south, along the coast of present-day Mozambique, Portuguese and Indian traders were based especially in the ports of Quelimane, Angoche and Mozambique. In the north, along the coasts of present-day North Mozambique, Tanzania and Kenya, Arab and Indian traders had their markets, especially in Kilwa and Zanzibar, under the aegis of the Arab Sultanate of Muscat-Oman-Zanzibar, to which the African coast north of the Portuguese area of influence belonged. From the ports of these market towns the slaves were shipped overseas, either to the Arab-controlled African coast or elsewhere in the Arab or Muslim world. The conditions on those ships were miserable.

Emma and Johannes Rebmann once witnessed the plight of this living cargo when they were shipwrecked on their way to Aden and were picked up by a small ship with 100 slaves. The horribly smelling people were 'closely huddled together, mostly children', though they were well-fed. Among them there was a little girl who was sick and died. The Reb-

---

[608] Rebmann, *Tagebuch*, 11-11-1848.

manns felt powerless and frustrated. They could do nothing to help.[609] Another example was reported by a Roman Catholic priest on one of the islands of the Sultanate. He visited an Arab chief who held some 800 slaves in a palisade of bamboo. They were naked in the cold and the heat, a branch of fork-like shape was attached to their necks; others were chained in groups, could not stand because held down by dead bodies. They were very hungry, a girl had just delivered.[610]

Slaves were captured and transported to the coast by violent middlemen. In the Portuguese south these intermediary slave-traders were the *Prazeros*, of mixed African-Portuguese descent. Along the entire coast to the north they were the mixed Arab-African *Swahilis*, or *Swahili-Arabs*, who in their turn used African tribes, for example the Yao, the Nyamwezi, and the Kamba. There were various long-distance trade routes from the interior to the East African coast. They can be indicated by the geographical names of the regions, from south to north, where slaves were captured.[611]

In the Lower and Middle Zambezi Valley up to Tete and Cabora Bassa the *Prazeros* had been taking slaves since the 18th century. Originally they only needed them as porters of ivory and as soldiers in their armies. In the 1860s-1880s when external demand grew, e.g. with the high prices paid by Brazilian traders, they increasingly sold slaves, at times even their own subjects or soldiers, as an item of export. Their agricultural centres (*supra-prazos*) Makanga, Massangano, and Massangire became important markets.

On the south coasts of Lake Malawi and in the Shire Valley the Yao and Swahili-Arabs were active. From the 1850s, many Yao migrated to southern Malawi. Together with accompanying Swahili-Arab traders they started to capture slaves and to shoot elephants for ivory.[612] The Swahili-Arab traders stayed in the Yao villages, and their hosts caught the required commodities for them.[613] The Yao thought that the Swahili people of the Indian Ocean coast had a culture and a religion that was worth learning from and imitating. When David Livingstone visited the area to the south east of Lake Malawi, he commented on how the Yao chose to copy the coastal customs in their ways of dressing, house-building and

---

[609] Rebmann/Tyler (née Kent), *Journal*, p. 6, 7 (1855). 'I would gladly have had her to lie down by me, if I had dared, for we had a space allotted to us in the cabin, but to have interfered would not have been wise'.
[610] CMS, *Intelligencer*, April 1869.
[611] Shillington, *History of Africa*, p. 246-249.
[612] Desmond Dudwa Phiri, *History of Malawi*, Blantyre, 2004, p. 196.
[613] Bone, *Muslims*, p. 15.

even in cultivating crops. The Swahili-Arabs possessed the skill of reading and writing. This the Yao chiefs considered most valuable as a tool of trading and of controlling their large territories. By the 1870s many Yao chiefs had turned to Islam and had resident Swahili *Waalim* as their scribes.[614] The conversion of Yao chiefs accelerated the Islamisation of ordinary men and women.[615] There was a problem in the combination of slave-hunting and trying to find converts for Islam. The Qur'an forbids the enslavement of fellow Muslims. This is one of the reasons why some African tribes were lured into adopting Islam. Conversion took away the danger of slavery. The Yao chiefs went further along that line, thus confirming their alliance with the Swahili-Arab slave-traders.

Being guided by the Swahili-Arab traders, the Yao gradually developed from specialist ivory-hunters into full-time long-distance slave-hunters. Originally they were a trading link between the Shire valley and the Portuguese-controlled coast, especially the port of Mozambique. Later they shifted routes to the Swahili port of Kilwa, belonging to the Zanzibar Sultanate. The reason was that the French, who first bought slaves on the Mozambique and Quelimane slave markets, turned to Swahili-Arabs at Kilwa and Zanzibar. Many slaves in their ever expanding plantations on Mauritius and Réunion had died due to cruel treatment. It was up to the Swahili-Arabs and their Yao allies to replenish the perished slaves and add to their numbers. The Yao were ready to comply, and even sold many fellow-tribesmen. They extended their catchment area to the Bisa people in the centre of present-day Zambia. Raids by Mozambican Prazeros and invading Ngoni in the southern part of the Lake Malawi region were added to the violent Yao activity.

In the area of Lake Tanganyika the Nyamwezi developed and dominated the trading routes. There were regular caravans between their capital Tabora and Zanzibar. From Tabora they penetrated north to the Buganda on Lake Victoria, and south to the Bemba and the Kazembe (Lunda) of northern Zambia.

In the coastal region of Mombasa in present-day Kenya the Kamba people of Ukambani were the main trading nation. They linked trade between the Kikuyu and the coast. However, Masai domination of the central rift frustrated Kamba access to Lake Victoria and Buganda.

---

[614] Bone, *Muslims*, p. 115, 116.
[615] Phiri, *History*, p. 196.

Domination by the Swahili-Arabs

The intermediary slave-trade was increasingly dominated by the Swahili-Arabs. By their African appearance and Arab education and descent they were ideal middlemen between the coast and the interior. Their caravans were financed by Arab and Indian merchants in Zanzibar and other slave markets. They were the leaders of the trading expeditions. For the violent part they relied on the African allies they had hired, especially the Yao, the Nyamwezi and the Kamba peoples. The caravans consisted of hundreds of well-armed men. First the Swahili-Arab traders only followed the routes of the Yao and the Nyamwezi, respectively to the Lake Malawi and the Lake Tanganyika areas. Subsequently, from the 1850s they established permanent bases on the shores of those lakes and deeper in the African interior. Gradually the Swahili-Arabs pushed their African allies out of control, and hunted themselves for slaves and ivory from their own establishments. Since the 1840s they established for example the base of Msiri among the Yeke people west of the Luapula River, in the copperbelt area of Bunkeya in present-day Zambia. Another base was at Ujiji on the east shore of Lake Tanganyika. The notorious Hamed Muhammad, known as Tippu Tip, established a Swahili-Arab base west of Lake Tanganyika at Nyangwe and Kasongo on the Luabula (upper Zaire) River. From the 1860s he did not buy slaves, just stole them, and killed many. Other Swahili-Arabs settled in the Buganda capital, northwest of Lake Victoria Nyanza. Others took over Tabora from the Nyamwezi people. The region of Lake Nyasa was targeted by the Swahili-Arabs not only for slaves but also for making converts to Islam. In 1854 Jakob J. Erhardt had already reported that many slaves in the slave markets 'from Mosambique to Mombasa were from the tribes of Lake Nyasa.'[616] Swahili-Arab involvement is exemplified by the history of their settlements on Lake Nyasa.

Salimini's history as a slave began with the Swahili-Arabs who had come to the Chewa- or Nyanja-speaking peoples west of the Lake. Since the 1840s the town of Nkhotakota and its surrounding area had been under the control of a dynasty of Swahili-Arab traders, known as the Jumbes of Nkhotakota.[617] The first Jumbe was Salim bin Abdallah. He arrived at

---

[616] CMS, *Intelligencer*, April 1855, p. 96: Report by Erhardt after he had left Tanga (Usambara) in October 1854; Cf. Steven Paas, *Beliefs and Practices of Muslims: The Religion of our Neighbours*, Good Messenger Publications, Zomba: 2006, p. 125-133 ('History of Islam in Malawi').

[617] G. Shepperson, 'The Jumbe of Nkhotakota', in: Lewis, *Islam in Tropical Africa*, London: Oxford University Press, 1966, pp 193-203.

10. The context of Muslim Slavery

Nkhotakota when the Yao people invaded Southern Malawi from Mozambique. The Jumbe got permission from chief Malenga to start a trading post. Through careful diplomacy he convinced most of the local people that he meant no harm, while at the same time he was acquiring slaves and enlarging his village. Soon slaves and ivory were being dispatched to the coast in return for guns, gunpowder and cloth. He built large *dhows* and sent trade caravans to the coast. Nkhotakota was now linked in direct trade with Ibo, Kilwa, Zanzibar and other islands on the east coast. Traders from Zanzibar and the East Coast came to Nkhotakota. Some went into the interior as far as Kasungu and Marambo. Together with the trade, also Islam was being established. By the time of the arrival of the Christian missionaries in Nkhotakota, Islam had already gained roots and spread around the area through its *Waalim*.[618] The last Jumbe of Nkhotakota was deposed by the British government in 1895.[619]

In the meantime, in the 1880s, the Swahili-Arab trader Mlozi bin Kazbadema settled in the Karonga district, on the north-west coast of Lake Malawi, among the Nkhonde people. He came to trade in ivory, but later he turned to the slave-trade. He came at a time when the Scottish missionaries of the *Livingstonia Mission* (later: *Church of Central Africa Presbyterian* – CCAP) and the *African Lakes Company* (ALC) had made their centres there. Mlozi was too late, because he had to compete with the approaching powers of colonialism. Rivalry developed between him and the ALC, which turned into a war in 1887. Mlozi was defeated by the British government in 1895, and was captured and hanged by the Nkhonde people. The Swahili Community he established, though confined to a few villages, still retains its Islamic identity.[620]

Apart from the Swahili-Arab dominance of the slave-trade, tribes like the Yao, the Nyamwezi, the Baganda, and the Kamba continued to enslave fellow-Africans, use them for their own purposes, or sell them to the East African coast. The hunting and trading of slaves uprooted a great many people,[621] and caused a tremendous lot of instability and corruption. The bloodshed, and the robbery of people and goods not only dis-

---

[618] *waalim* (Swahili) singular *mwalimu* – lit.: teachers, particularly teachers of the Qur'an, from Arabic *mu'allim*.
[619] M.K. Mtumbuka, 'History of Islam in Malawi and the Christian Answer', Zomba: ZTC, 2004 [unpublished].
[620] David S. Bone (ed.), *Malawi's Muslims: A Historical Perspective*, Blantyre: Kachere/Claim, 2000, p. 14.
[621] Michelsen, W., 'Der Sklavenhandel in Ostafrika', in: AMZ, 1876, S. 383-393, describes the moral corruption through slavery and the need for establishing settlements of ex-slaves.

rupted the lives and health of many, but also affected the environment and economic prosperity. It changed the whole fabric of society and individual psychology. Fear became the ruler of the hearts of people, who had to live in stockaded villages for their safety.

Public opinion in the West became alerted by accounts of travellers. Above we referred to David Livingstone, who on his second series of expeditions into Africa, 1858-1867, covered the upper Zambezi and Shire River valleys, and the adjoining shores of Lake Nyasa. In his *Narrative of an Expedition* he exposed the horrors of the slave-trade. When seeing a slave caravan he noticed that many were children, a smaller number women, and almost no men.

> 'Those taken out of the country are but a very small section of the sufferers. We never realized the atrocious nature of the traffic until we saw it at the fountain-head. There truly "Satan has his Seat." Besides those actually captured, thousands are killed and die of their wounds and famine, driven from their villages by the slave raids proper. Thousands perish in the internecine war waged for slaves with their own clansmen and neighbours, slain by the lust of gain, which is stimulated, be it remembered always, by the slave purchasers of Cuba and elsewhere. ... Two of the women had been shot the day before for attempting to untie the thongs. This, the rest were told, was to prevent them from attempting to escape. One woman had her infant's brains knocked out, because she could not carry her load; and a man was dispatched with an axe, because he had broken down with fatigue.'[622]

Salimini was captured more than two decades before Livingstone saw this. The narrative depicts what he must have experienced, and with him many thousands of contemporary Nyasa people. Some charged that Livingstone had exaggerated his information on the slave-trade, i.e. on the mortality rate attending their capture, and their sufferings on the journey down to the coast. However, Sir Bartle Frere, reporting the results of his thorough investigations in 1873, found that details given by interviewed ex-slaves 'fully confirmed the statements made by Livingstone.'

> The tale of the liberated slaves almost always was: surprise, kidnapping, murder, indescribable suffering on the way down to the coast. On the dhow voyage there was overcrowding, starvation, lack of water, even on the short 'and legal' voyage from Kilwa to Zanzibar. The Arabic domestic slave, even if it is true that he is well treated, became a slave because his

---

[622] David Livingstone, *Narrative of an Expedition to the Zambesi and its Tributaries ... Lakes Shirwa & Nyassa, 1858-1864*, London: John Murray, 1865, p. 412-413, 378.

Salimini and the Rebmanns

parents were murdered and he was kidnapped. The East African slave-trade especially grew in the last half-century.'[623]

From Krapf's Preface of the 1877 editions of the Kiniassa Dictionary, which quotes from two letters from Rebmann, we can infer that Salimini was born in approximately 1824, and was sold as a slave about 1844. How did he and the Rebmanns meet? Both Emma and Johannes Rebmann described how they got to know Salimini.[624] In the entry of her journal of the beginning of 1854, Emma wrote:

> 'It seemed the merest accident that it was brought to his [i.e. Rebmann's] notice; and yet of what immense value may it become! A man one day brought a cow to sell and at the same time begged for work. He was kept for a few days when his strange dialect struck the ear of his master, who immediately asked where he was from. He found that he was a Kiniassa man, who had been seized when about 20 years old.'

In a letter of to the CMS Committee, which is included in Krapf's Preface of the *Dictionary of the Kiniassa Language*, Rebmann gave his own version of their first meeting with Salimini:

> 'In the latter end of 1853 a Suaheli man from Mombas passed at my station (Kisuludini) with a head of cattle. At that time it had been my purpose to bring in cattle for labour, for the benefit of the Mission and by way of an example for the natives. So I bought a young heifer for a few dollars and a fraction, cattle in East Africa at that time being very cheap. The fraction, however, I could not pay for want of change. So I proposed to the owner to do a few days' work in order to complete a full dollar. He agreed to do so. One day while he was at work with my servants in building an appendage to our dwelling-house, I heard him talk with them in a strange language. On inquiry I was told it was Kiniassa, i.e., the language spoken in the neighbourhood of the lake Niassa (Nyasa/Nyassa), the most southern of the great inland lakes. I at once felt the wish to learn so much of it as to be able to judge about its relationship with the Kisuaheli and Kinika and some other dialects spoken inland of Mombas with which I had got more or less acquainted. ... My informant is a slave from Mombas, who came into our

---

[623] CMS, *Intelligencer*, November 1873.
[624] Rebmann/Tyler (née Kent), *Journal*, p. 3 (1854); Rebmann, letter of 13-4-1854 to CMS Committee, in Krapf's Preface to Rebmann's *Dictionary of the Kiniassa Language*, p. iii (in: Letters to the CMS Committee 1850-1855).

service before I knew anything about his origin, which I rather accidentally discovered when I heard him once speak to one of his fellows in a strange dialect. On enquiry, I was told that he was a Mniassa.'

Where was Salimini from? Johannes Rebmann noted some details from his mouth. To his ears ten years after Salimini's abduction, remembrance of his country and language was still very distinct. His native territory Salimini calls Kumpande two days West from the lake, which by the tribes who live on its banks, is called Niansha or Niancha, ... of which the Suahelis evidently made Niassa.'

> 'From that part of the lake's banks he used to come to from his home, the opposite side cannot be seen, but a boat starting at day-break will reach it at sunset. Their boats are, however, not provided with rudders, wherefore they only use oars. Following the margin of the lake to the South through the territory of Maravi for a few days, its breadth seems gradually to decrease, till, as my informant expressed himself, people on the one side are within call of people on the other side, but of its extent to the North he and his countrymen have no idea. They only know that it gets much broader there than it is with them, so much that they are deterred from fording it, because they lose sight of the banks, and therefore only go to neighbouring islands for fishing. During the cold or rainy season the lake is said to be extremely boisterous, but during the hot season quite calm.'

Judging from the letters and journal of the Rebmanns and from information in some entries of the *Dictionary of the Kiniassa Language*, Salimini came from a place east of Lilongwe, possibly Kamphande, which was two days' journey from the coast, and two days east of the river Bua. As to the climate of the region where he was born, Salimini gave an interesting detail. 'When my informant spoke of the cold in his country, he described the water as getting a hard crust during the night, which of course can be nothing else but ice, called 'kungu' in their language.[625] This, however, is only found in small collections of standing water, and never in the lake Niassa.' Salimini's home was high up on a plateau. He says there was sometimes ice at night. Salimini must have come from the Central Region, probably from just east of Lilongwe.[626] The reference to ice may

---

[625] In modern Chichewa khungu = 'skin'. In *The Nyasaland Journal*, vol. 10, no.1 (January 1957) R.G. Willan says that 'frost occurs ... in most years at Lilongwe'. Although at present ice is not found in most parts of Malawi, it does apparently still occur occasionally in some of the higher regions, such as near Ntchisin mountain.

[626] See Appendix I, footnote 852.

10. The context of Muslim Slavery

have slipped in from accounts by travellers to higher regions of Malawi. At that time explorers and missionaries only guessed and dreamt about Unyamwezi, a country on the shores of a large African inland sea.[627] What did Salimini say about the ethnic groups living in his native country? The Rebmanns reported:

> 'The Wahiao (not Wahiau) are spread on the Eastern banks of the lake; to the south and south-west are the Wamaravi, and north from these the Wakamdunda, of whom the Wakumpande and Wapogera are only subdivisions. The name Maravi, which in older maps is given as the name of the lake, I had never heard before from a native. Salimini, my informant, never applied it to the lake, but to a large territory bordering upon it, and in fact forming its South-western banks. The occupants are called Wamaravi, and these, together with the Wakamdunda and perhaps still other tribes, are by the Suahelis on the coast generally comprised under the common name of Waniassa. The Wakamanga, whom on the map of 1850 I have placed to the east of the lake, are, according to Salimini, to be placed even to the west of the Wakamdunda, to whom they stand in the same relation as the Wakamba to the Wanika inland of Mombas ... From all that he tells us respecting his country people etc. they must be far superior to the peoples around us.'

The Rebmanns appreciated the honesty of the lake people, which was reported by Salimini. According to him 'among his people lying is spoken of in the most contemptuous way possible.'[628] Rebmann defined the potential of the economy of Salimini's country: 'It appears a most fruitful land – fruits and vegetables abounding', and he noted the economic significance of the lake.

> 'Salimini ... states that he used to go very often to the lake in search of Mia (pl. of Mua), a species of palm, of the leaves of which the natives make mats, bags, &c., as also to buy cotton, which is grown near the lake, and of

---

[627] BMM, 1861, S. 33. In an article on the expeditions of Burton and Speke, considering supposed details of the large African inland sea, Rebmann is said to have received information on it from a man who 'lived as slave in Mombas and whose home was two days from a lake that is called Nianscha oder Nyanja. He himself had often gone to the lake to look for a kind of palm tree the fibres of which are used to make mats or sacks or to buy cotton that grows near the lake and is used to make a kind of cloth'.

[628] Rebmann took from Salimini a term for the emphatic rejection of lying and included it in the Kiniassa Dictionary: 'ku nia liwewe (to emit or speak lies). The expression betrays a very strong moral sense, by speaking of lies in the most contemptible way.'

which they weave a coarse kind of cloth, while their better articles of clothing, as also their beads, brass wire, and especially their guns (called fudi in their language) they buy from the Portuguese, who seem to have some settlements at no great distance from them, called 'Kubale' and 'Kumkoma'. The Portuguese are called by them 'Wakigunda', while the name generally given by the East Africans to Europeans is 'Wazungu'. Salimini also referred to the economy of the Wandsunsi people, near the Watemba 'who, from an abundance of iron in their country, seem to be the principal blacksmiths among all the tribes around. On being applied to for hoes by people, who have come from a distance with a cow or goat for their barter, they will work all the night at their fires.'

His abduction into slavery, when he was 20 years old, was a painful landmark in Salimini's life. Rebmann quoted from his mouth that 'slavery casts a dark shade over all. ... So constantly are they exposed to it that in building their cottages they always make a secret door, plaister it over so that to a stranger it is invisible, by which they may escape at a moment's warning.' However this measure did not save Salimini.

'In consequence of international expeditions for slave-catching, [he] was seized by a tribe called Wapogera, who sold him to the Wamaravi, and these to the Suaheli slave merchants, who had come from Uibu. At Uibu, which was reached after two months' travelling at a very slow rate (in effective march only half the time is wanted), he was at last bought by slave merchants from Mombas. This, he thinks, happened about ten years ago, while he is now a man of about thirty years of age.'

Salimini's abduction and enslavement led him to the island of Uibu. This is Ibo, one of the Quirimbas Islands in the Indian Ocean off northern Cabo Delgado in the north of Mozambique. It grew as one of the Muslim ports for the slave-trade, in importance second after Mozambique Island. From Ibo Salimini was sold to a slave master in Mombasa, probably through Zanzibar. Except for some cursory notes in Emma's journal, we know almost nothing about Salimini's daily life as a slave in the Mombasa region. In August 1856 she noted: 'Salimini has had to flee, it seems owing to the debt of his masters, he is to be sold to another man. This he does not like, so he is off.'[629] A month later Emma reported that Salimini had returned. 'He has been sold to another man for 30 dollars.'

Subsequently he and his new owner, together with Rebmann's houseboy Hamedi, went to Ukambani for ivory.[630] The Rebmanns were disap-

---

[629] Rebmann/Tyler (née Kent), *Journal*, p. 12 (1856).
[630] Rebmann/Tyler (née Kent), *Journal*, p. 13, 14, cf. 17 (1856).

10. The context of Muslim Slavery

pointed that Hamedi wanted to leave them, and had made an agreement with Salimini's new master. They were successful in convincing him that Salimini had to stay and accompany them to Zanzibar.[631] In October of the same year Emma mentioned Salimini again. Johannes and a group including Salimini had visited Mombasa. On their return Salimini ran ahead carrying a large turkey, a present from the Governor, destined for her, in order to kill it for dinner.[632] In the same month there is another reference to Salimini's going to Ukambani.[633]

Was Salimini the only informant or resource person for Rebmann's Dictionary? We are sure there were more slaves from Malawi in the Mombasa area at that time. There were the slave boys whom Rebmann had bought in Mombasa. The three Yao could not be helpful for the Dictionary as their language was different. Perhaps the other one, the Manga boy Pakaya, could have assisted. Unfortunately Rebmann had to let them go back into slavery. Emma Rebmann tells us about Nofa, a slave girl from Salimini's homeland. She was forced to be the second wife to Hamedi, a houseboy of the Rebmanns', but ran out on him when she was beaten by the first wife. Both wives of Hamedi were slaves; he had to pay a fee to their owners, and the full price if they escaped. The Swahili-Arab laws did not allow Emma to help the poor girl. At last she was sold to some Arab owner overseas. Probably Nofa was from the south of Malawi, because before being transferred to the Swahilis, 'she was taken by the Portuguese, with whom she lived some time.'[634] Salimini and Nofa were certainly not the only slaves from Nyasaland in Mombasa. Today some descendants of liberated Malawian slaves can still be found in Kenya.[635]

---

[631] Rebmann/Tyler (née Kent), *Journal*, p. 19 (1857).
[632] Rebmann/Tyler (née Kent), *Journal*, p. 15 (1856).
[633] Rebmann/Tyler (née Kent), *Journal*, p. 18 (1856).
[634] Rebmann/Tyler (née Kent), *Journal*, p. 15, 16, 17 (1856); *Journal*, p. 20 (1857).
[635] Khamisi, *The Wretched Africans*, p. 287-303 ('History and family trees of slaves and their descendants') and p. 305-312 ('Selected List of African Slaves') concludes that of the 242 selected slaves in his list 123 were 'Bombayer' (seechapter 6). Among the other people of the list 27 were Mnyasa and 25 were Yao; both groups orginated from Nyasaland (present-day Malawi) The Kenyan author Khamisi belongs to their descendants; most descendants still live in Kenya. Cf. Kevin Mwachira, 'Remembering East African slave raids' http://news.bbc.co.uk/2/hi/africa/6510675.stm

Salimini as a person

The name Salimini is not of Nyanja or Chewa origin. It is a Swahili derivation from the Arabic word 'salam', and it means: 'safely' or 'in perfectly good order.'[636] Salimini presumably abandoned his original Nyanja name to adopt a Swahili-Arab name. We can only guess the reason. Perhaps he was forced to do so by his Muslim slave-masters. Maybe he voluntarily adopted that name in order to be accepted by his Swahili-Arab cultural environment. Perhaps he only began to use the word at a later stage, referring to the relative safety of his present situation, whereas Rebmann mistakenly thought he had heard his real name. He was not a Christian. The first missionaries had not yet arrived in Malawi when he was carried off to the coast. Would it be possible that Salimini changed his name because he had become a Muslim? At any rate it is unlikely that he was a Muslim before his abduction into slavery. The Muslim Swahili-Arabs who bought him from the Maravi middlemen were undoubtedly aware of the Islamic ban on selling or buying fellow-Muslims.

The information in some entries that he fed to Rebmann concerns aspects of African Traditional Religion. Like his forefathers he must have been an animist. Probably he belonged to the Nyau cult. Salimini was not a soft-willed person who had lost initiative because he was owned by someone else. Apparently he had some freedom of movement. Within the limitations of his position as a slave he tried to lead his own life. Sometimes he resisted, for example when his owner wanted to sell him. As for his character we have only one non-flattering witness, Emma's journal: 'Salimini is in himself a bad troublesome man, a thief and a liar.'[637] Anyway, Salimini is entitled to a place in history because of his significance for the beginnings of Chichewa lexicography.

---

[636] The word occurs in the expression: *salama salimini*, for example in Luke 15:27, Huyo mtumishi akamwambia: 'Ndugu yako amerudi nyumbani, na baba yako amemchinjia ndama mnono kwa kuwa amempata akiwa *salama salimini*.' = And he said to him: 'Your brother has come and your father has killed the fatted calf because he has received him *safe* and *sound*'. The word itself means: in perfectly good order/safely. Example: Wasafiri walifika *salimini* = The travellers arrived safely.

[637] Tyler (née Kent), *Journal*, p. 3 (1854).

10. The context of Muslim Slavery

*A slave market in 19th century Zanzibar
(Shillington, p. 251).*

*East African slave attached to a
fork-shape branch
(CMS Gleaner, vol. 1, 1874, p. 79).*

*A Yao slave-trader in Southern
Malawi, in the 1860s
(Shillington, p. 248).*

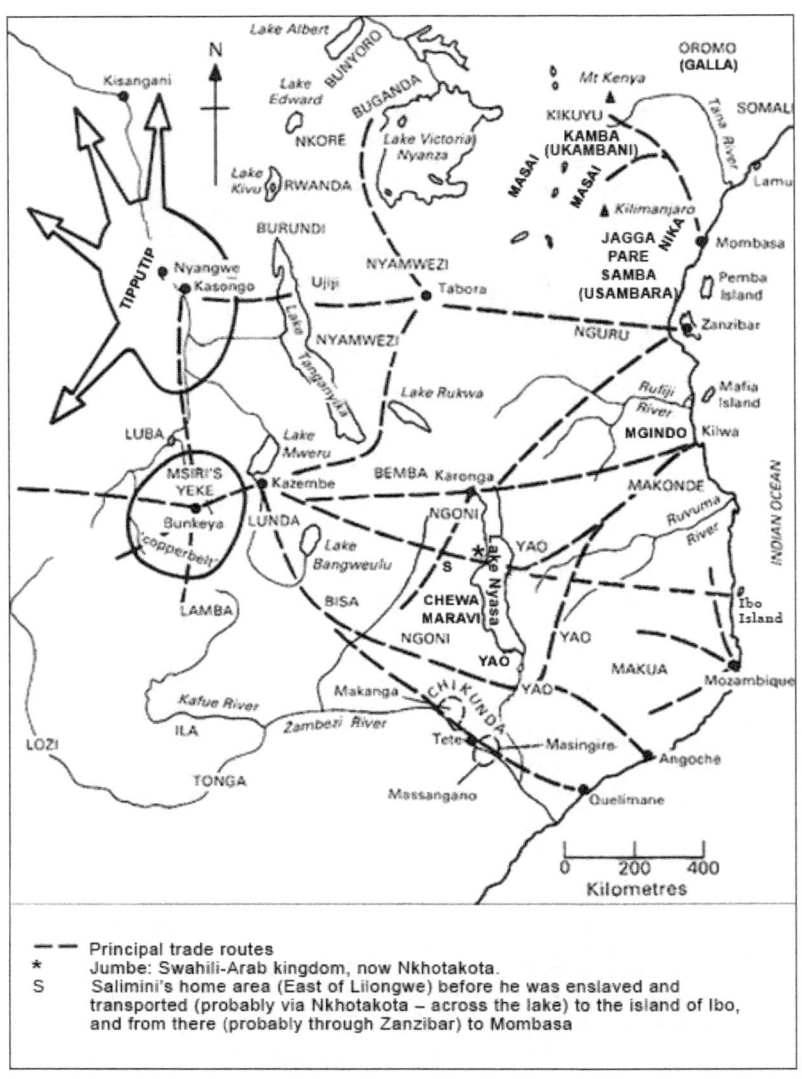

*Long-distance slave-trading routes in East Africa in the 19th century
(cf. Shillington, p. 249).*

11. Missionary

Character

The best way of getting an impression of Rebmann's character is to listen to those who knew him best. His teacher at school in Gerlingen described him as a well-behaved quiet child. However, Johannes later admitted that he had rebelled against this definition and that it drove him to be less socially acceptable. Perhaps these two sides to Rebmann's character prevailed throughout his life. On the one hand ready to please, to serve, and to sacrifice himself, on the other hand side persevering to the edge of stubbornness in being on his own, having not much rapport with the ideas of colleagues, the policies of the CMS in London, and of his loving family who wanted to have him back in Germany. The Basler Mission Seminary assessed his character. The *Protocols* of 1839 say that he

> 'is a serious Christian with a very fine balanced character. ... He goes his way quietly and very humbly, finds it difficult, however, to talk intimately. He is determined to become a missionary, but not without being tempted.'[638]

In 1842 the *Protocols* add that he is 'very honest' (*sehr aufrichtig*). His tendency to be introverted was sublimated by a very strong fixation on a target. He was determined and faithful to his task. Krapf who for seven years lived very close to him, also in times of personal crisis and conflict, called him 'a saintly character.'[639] In 1846 when Rebmann arrived Krapf was very sick and almost unable to receive his younger colleague, let alone help him when they had to build a new house in Rabai. In Krapf's eyes Rebmann acted favourably in the new situation:

> 'When I am attacked by fever, he makes my bed for me, cooks clear soup for me ... repairs broken chairs, plays his clarinet, learns the language to

---

[638] Quoted by: Stutzmann, 'Johannes Rebmann: Leben und Werk des Missionars', Vortrag, S. 5, from BM *Protokollen* XIV, 211: 'Bauer 19,5 Jahre alt. Urteil: ein gründlicher Christ von äußerst gesetztem feinem Wesen. Geht seinen stillen Gang in aller Bescheidenheit, hat aber etwas schwer sich traulich zu äußern. Unter den Brüdern steht er fest und liebreich. Missionssinn entschieden, aber nicht ohne Anfechtung'; cf. Jehle, *Der Entdecker*, S. 3.
[639] Through C.G. Richards, *Ludwig Krapf: Missionary and Explorer*, Nairobi: East African Literature Bureau, n.d. p. 49.

win souls for Jesus. He is so patient with the people and their shameless demands and tricks.'[640]

Rebmann had a gift of musicality and poetry. With his clarinet he would accompany the singing at the station, and he also made the first Christian hymns in the Nika language.[641] He also made hymns in his mother-tongue, German.[642] Apart from this, and his love of languages, he had a practical ability to consider things from a down-to-earth angle. If observers have looked upon the early East African missionaries as 'somewhat impractical'[643] they were mistaken concerning Rebmann. He was able to use his hands in constructing and repairing things. When houses were built, either for the Europeans or for the African converts, Rebmann participated. To her amazement Emma saw that he was not only involved in devising the plan, but also in executing it as a carpenter, mason or just a worker.[644]

In Krapf's observation another characteristic of his colleague was revealed, his patience. Rebmann undoubtedly was a very patient person.[645] Emma sometimes found it difficult to understand and accept the patience of her husband, when in her observation the people in their African environment showed 'apathy and indifference.' The missionaries gave themselves spiritually and materially, the receivers showed no satisfaction, not even by 'a small gift'. She 'was most painfully struck by the selfishness and coldheartedness' of a crippled Nika boy, who was helped a lot by them, but showed no real interest in 'the great truths out of the Book', and in Emma's view continued to consider them only as a source of material benefits.[646] Persevering in such situations not only required patience, but also love and humility. Rebmann loved the people to whom the Lord

---

[640] Krapf, letter of 26-11-1846, in: Fischer, 'Extracts from Krapf's Letters'.
[641] Cf. Eber, *Krapf*, S. 101, 104; Krapf, *Reisen*, I, S. 366, the first German hymn Rebmann translated into Nika was: 'Jesus Christus mache / Mein Herze neu; / Du bist mein Heiland, / Du hast mir meine Sünde vergeben. / Jesus Christus mache / Mein Herze neu'.
[642] E.g. in Rebmann, *Briefe*, 20-8-1874, 'Gott ist getreu / Sein Herz, Sein Vaterherz verläßt die Seinen nie ... Ein Kindlein will ich seyn in meines Heilands Armen', etc.; Oskar Rebmann, 'Missionar Johannes Rebmann', S. 151, 152, 'Einst fuhren wir vom Vaterlande / Auf Schiffen weit ins Meer hinaus ... Geh es zum Leben und Tode / Er tue was Ihm wohlgefällt / Wer is Jesu Christi treue Bote', etc.
[643] Oliver, *The Missionary Factor*, p. 6.
[644] Rebmann/Tyler (née Kent), *Journal*, p. 8 (1855); cf. Stutzmann, 'Johannes Rebmann: Leben und Werk des Missionars', Vortrag, S. 6.
[645] Cf. Weishaupt, *Rebmanns Reisen im Dschaggaland*, S. 5, 39.
[646] Rebmann/Tyler (née Kent), *Journal*, p. 12, 13 (1856).

had sent him. He targeted their interests. There are no indications that he ever put himself in the foreground to the detriment of others. Together with the other characteristics this made him suitable for the work of a missionary. That was what his pastor Stange in Gerlingen and his teachers in Basel had already observed. It was confirmed by his wife, after having been with him during five years of marriage: 'he has a truly missionary spirit.'[647]

Krapf's character was more or less the opposite of Rebmann's. He was restless, impulsive, quick to become enthusiastic, also quick to anger, and sometimes too fast in his decisions and actions.[648] Krapf referred to the weaknesses of his own character, and stressed the need for love, especially in situations of suffering and danger of life.[649] Krapf was active on many fronts, all bound together in one great vision. Only after leaving Africa and settling down in Korntal did he seem to find more rest, perhaps because of the quiet Pietist atmosphere in the Brüdergemeinde.[650] He was an extrovert, lively, more easy-going, but not very practical. At times he was selfish and overbearing. Eber's suggestion that Krapf's Christian character was on the whole 'loving', 'exemplary', 'humble' and without ambition can be debated.[651] By the end of the 19th century an observer of contemporary history would compare Krapf and Rebmann: 'Krapf had too much of a restless spirit than that he himself would have persevered at the post in Mombasa that he occupied, or also only would have used his influence to provide strong support for the lonely workers there, especially Rebmann. It remained a lonely and neglected post of the

---

[647] Rebmann/Tyler (née Kent), *Journal*, p. 11 (1856).
[648] Eber, *Krapf*, S. 32, 107 ('unchristlicher Zorn'), 120 (anger when there are no quick results), 238. Weishaupt, *Rebmanns Reisen in Dschaggaland*, S. 5: 'Die beiden Männer ... waren zwei sehr verschiedene Naturen, Krapf geistprüfend und anregend, von heiligem Optimismus getragen, von Großen, weittragenden Ideen erfüllt, unbekümmert um ihre Ausführbarkeit. Rebmann dagegen mehr der nüchtern abwägende, dem erreichbaren Ziel zutredende, dabei praktische Mann.'
[649] Eber, *Krapf*, S. 120, 121.
[650] Scheffbuch, *Große Entdecker*, S. 75, thinks that Korntal had a 'beruhigende Einfluss' on Krapf, and tamed the 'Sprunghaftigkeit seines Wesens ... mit seinem Unruhegeist'.
[651] Eber, *Krapf*, 238-241. On S. 241 he quotes Hanno Beck: 'Bewunderungswürdig ist die völlige Freiheit dieser Missionare von Rekordsucht und Ehrgeiz, die ihre Entdeckungen mit Seelenruhe als ein Geschenk Gottes hinnahmen', and he claims that also Claus, Ledderhose and Vortisch have presented Krapf's life as a Christian example.

English CMS on the isle of Mombasa and on the mainland in Rabai.'[652] Krapf's character did not suit long and tiresome efforts to consolidate Christian presence in a remote location at Africa's east coast.

Calling

Rebmann was convinced that he was called by God to be a missionary, not an explorer, even less an adventurer, not a scholar, a linguist, or a geographer. In the 19th century, the age of revival and discoveries, public sympathy and support were focused on missionaries and explorers. Attention was roused by a mixed interest in sensational geographical and anthropological findings, the spread of Western culture and power, and the conversion of people to Christ. In order to be favoured by politics, the media, including mission magazines, gave the impression that a missionary had to be an explorer at the same time.[653] The publicity about Livingstone's journeys and about Krapf's travels and researches stimulated this idea. According to his latest biographer Krapf himself considered his explorations and discoveries in connection with salvation history.[654]

Rebmann, although he was conscious of having 'discovered' Kilimanjaro, and reduced unknown languages to writing, consistently refused to win popularity by allowing the missionary be pushed behind the explorer.[655] He emphasised: 'We came to Africa without the thought or desire of making geographical discoveries. Our great objective was the extension of the Kingdom of God.'[656] In a letter to his father, brothers and sister, he commented on the silver medal received from the scholars of the Geographical Society of the *Institut de France* in Paris:

> 'I didn't come here to make geographical discoveries, but to uncover the release and the salvation in Jesus Christ for the people who sit in darkness and the shadow of death.'[657]

---

[652] AMZ, 1895, S. 375.
[653] Paul Richter, 'Geschichte', in: AMZ, 1897, S. 518, 519, refers to the great importance of the translation work of Rebmann and Krapf, which was 'even superseded by' ('noch übertroffen durch') their geographical discoveries.
[654] Eber, *Krapf*, S. 119.
[655] BMM 1862, S. 54, 54 reviews: Karl Andree, *Forschungsreisen in Arabien und Ostafrika nach den Entdeckungen von Burton, Speke, Krapf, Rebmann, Erhardt, und Anderen*, 2 Bände, Leipzig 1861. This article, in a mission magazine, shows that discoveries were the main interest of the reviewer.
[656] AMZ, 1882, S. 194; cf. Scheffbuch, *Große Entdecker*, S. 82, 83.
[657] Rebmann, *Briefe*: letter dated 1-10-1853; Rebmann/Tyler (née Kent), *Journal*, p. 2 (1853).

Being the first European to see Kilimanjaro to him was not an act deserving honour, but an accidental event. Also his employer the CMS did not want to be popular by acting as an agency for explorations and discoveries. CMS secretary Henry Venn emphasised that secular objectives should not be confused with the Great Command of winning people for Jesus.[658] Nor should private relations have higher priority than that Command. After 19 years of being away from his beloved Gerlingen, Rebmann wrote to his brothers and sister: 'I am happy because of your desire to see me again, but I can't yet satisfy it. I have to fulfil a task in East Africa, which will not allow me in the next years to visit my dear old place of birth.'[659]

Methods

Patience and a deep consciousness of being called by God to approach lost people with the saving Gospel of Christ were the parameters of Rebmann's missiological methods. To Rebmann personal Bible reading, meditation and prayer were the first and foremost methods of his missionary approach. A missionary should not only witness to others, he should first himself have and maintain peace with God. He has to find his strength in God, and also his protection. A missionary can be tempted by his own evil heart, and by sinful attractions in the world around. In his journal on one of his first journeys into the interior, observing the immoral behaviour of his Muslim carriers and women of the villages, Rebmann admitted that 'without the spirit of Christ even the most moral traveller with a healthy body' within a week would indulge in sexual immorality.[660] The missionary can feel distressed, discouraged, spiritually dead, miserable, empty, having lost the feeling of love and the consciousness of faith. Rebmann described how for four or five days he was in such a desolate spiritual state during one of his journeys. In me the flesh attacked the spirit, and in this way the devil wanted to destroy my work.[661] However, when such attacks by Satan occurred and captured his feelings, he resorted to prayer, and the Spirit led him to use his rationality and continue to do what he was supposed to do, i.e. 'to witness the way of salvation to a crippled person' and 'to a few who asked me about it', and 'to explain to someone what is the source of all suffering'.[662] In other words, a believer is weak in

---

[658] Cf. Scheffbuch, *Große Entdecker*, S. 83, 84.
[659] Rebmann, *Briefe*, 4-5-1865.
[660] Rebmann, *Tagebuch*, 22-12-1848.
[661] Rebmann, *Tagebuch*, 6/9-9-1848; cf. *Tagebuch*, 16-7-1848.
[662] Rebmann, *Tagebuch*, 20/22-7-1848; 23-7-1848; 27-7-1848.

himself and can lapse into sin, but resorting to genuine faith helps, because faith is stronger than temptation, because it works through the obedient-making grace of the eternal power of God, even when feelings are corrupted or when they try to pull man into disobedience.

Rebmann was convinced of the necessity of long and diligent study of the linguistic and religious situation of the local people. Scheffbuch defines Rebmann's conviction: 'Whoever in Africa wants to win people for the faith in Jesus should work thoroughly, and should long and patiently persevere in the same place and live there together with the people.'[663] One of the consequences Rebmann drew is that a missionary has to stay on the same place for a long time.[664] You have to live where the people live, not detached from them, but as close as possible to the place where you can meet many of them in daily life, you have to live among them.[665] Go from hut to hut, talk to people and help them, be at the markets, because they are suitable places for getting into contact with people.[666] Although similarly convinced of the need for knowledge of the local language and culture, Krapf's approach was different. In his grand design of a chain of mission stations, 'a missionary should remain mobile ... not stationary, ... and he should not settle nicely'.[667] Krapf's approach does not leave much room for in-depth inculturation, and is rather characterised by confrontation.[668]

Knowing and using the language of the people is one of the most important methods. Rebmann and Krapf were exemplary in demonstrating this missionary method. They learnt the languages of the peoples who they dealt with, they preached and taught[669] the Gospel in their vernaculars, reduced languages to writing, and translated the Bible and other writings. Their impressive intellectual linguistic work was not an effort on its own, but an essential missionary method to reach the hearts of the African people and the depth of their culture. Rebmann did not always like helpers or visitors to stay in Rabai/Kisuludini, especially if the guests

---

[663] Scheffbuch, *Große Entdecker*, p. 88.
[664] Kustermann, 'Johannes Rebmann', in: *G.H.: Gerlinger Missionare*, p. 17, quoted missiologist Johannes Maisch: 'Rebmann understood very quickly that if you really want to win people in Africa for the Christian faith, you have to stay very long and very patiently at one place, struggling for these people'.
[665] Rebmann, *Tagebuch*, 23-4-1848, 7-5-1848;
[666] Rebmann, *Tagebuch*, 9-6-1848; cf. Kusterman, Johannes Rebmann', in *G.H.: Gerlinger Missionare*, p. 15.
[667] Scheffbuch, *Große Entdecker*, p. 78.
[668] Eber, *Krapf*, p. 99.
[669] Cf. Rebmann, *Briefe*, 2-5-1861.

were unable or unwilling to learn Swahili or Nika. Some Bombayers and some craftsmen from Port Natal and from Germany were even sent back home.[670] He experienced that the mother tongue is the vehicle through which the real meaning of the Gospel can reach the ear, and that God's Spirit takes the truth from there into the heart.[671]

Cultural and linguistic barriers are less prohibitive when African Christians reach out to fellow-Africans. Rebmann preferred the mission work gradually being taken over by Africans. 'It is not European Missionaries who are wanted in any number in East Africa, but native agents under the influence of active Christianity, as in the West African Mission'. Because of this, Rebmann at first expected a lot from the Bombayers, and was very disappointed when they did not comply to his expectations.[672]

Rebmann realised that using linguistic methods is not holy in itself. The Swahili, Nika and Nyasa languages reflected cultures without God. The contents of the dictionaries he made showed this. There was no Christian or Biblical terminology in them. Learning languages and making dictionaries and translations may be intellectually attractive, but these activities can only be effective if they are blessed and consciously used as instruments in spreading the Gospel of Jesus Christ.

Rebmann knew that fruitful mission to the peoples of East Africa required a holistic approach. In this concern he did not distinguish between spiritual methods and secular methods. All the work for the Kingdom is holy, whether spiritual or secular. Not only preaching the Gospel but also living the Gospel is necessary to convince the heathen of the realities of sin and grace, of death and life, of judgment and freedom. In addition to the missionaries of the Word, the mission organisation should send medical doctors and craftsmen, and make settlements of Christian families.[673] The settlers should not expect luxury!

> 'A variety of labourers will be required. They are useful if they can teach and can adapt themselves. Many don't like to stay in this to them dreary place.'... In this part of the world in the outset we must learn to look less to foreign and polished and more to the rough ... instruments for the work of its evangelisation'.[674]

---

[670] Rebmann, *Briefe*, 18-9-1858.
[671] Rebmann, *Tagebuch*, 21-12-1848.
[672] CMS, *Proceedings 1863-1864*, n.d., p. 75, 76.
[673] Rebmann, *Tagebuch*, S. 96; cf. Scheffbuch, *Große Entdecker*, S. 89.
[674] Report from Rebmann (duplicated, by Sparshotts?) in Mombas to the CMS Committee, 27 February 1866.

To Rebmann missionary work included not only telling the Biblical message, but also teaching how to read it. Education in the basic subjects of knowledge belonged to mission. For that reason right from the beginning Rebmann started schools for children and adults. One of the problems was that at first pupils wanted to be paid.[675] It took time before people understood that education was profitable to their spiritual and economical development.

Rebmann stressed the necessity of building good houses for the missionary personnel at the station and for the people that had converted. All means must be used. The Semites wanted a sign, the Japhethites wisdom, but the Hamites ask for clothes and medicines.[676] They may be only interested in material things. Yet, their desire is a Macedonian voice begging Christianity to come over and help. Give naked Ham not only the Gospel but also give clothes. That is our slave's service for Africa, because of our Saviour, who served us long ago on the cross until death.[677] The Christian faith should be presented spiritually, and in its practical, bodily consequences (leibhaftig angeboten).[678] Rebmann derived this order from the Lord's Prayer, where the need for bread precedes the needs of the soul.[679] He thought that Christian life 'could not remain at home' in the small dirty, dark huts of the people. Christian morals need good houses.[680] For that reason he started the building of 'civilised dwellings' for the baptised. Only then they would be fully liberated from heathenism.[681]

At this point Krapf disagreed with Rebmann's missiological insights. He was of the opinion that Rebmann's ideas on secular work in general and on the necessity of building houses in particular would shift the activities of the mission to a process of colonisation, and would distract missionaries from the central task of 'preaching the Word of the cross of Christ'.[682] He said that nicely settling with study, and writing books in good houses was likely to exclude real mission work.[683] Eber supports

---

[675] Cf. Krapf, *Reisen* I, S. 369-371.
[676] Rebmann, *Tagebuch*, 7-1-1849.
[677] Rebmann, *Tagebuch*, 9-1-1849.
[678] Cf. Stutzmann, 'Johannes Rebmann: Leben und Werk des Missionars', Vortrag, S. 8.
[679] Rebmann, *Briefe*, 21-9-1871.
[680] Rebmann, *Briefe*, 23-11-1869.
[681] Rebmann, *Briefe*, 21-9-1863.
[682] Cf. Walter Ringwald, 'Johannes Rebmann 1820-1876: Missionar – Entdecker Sprachforscher', in: *Ludwigsburger Geschichtsblätter*, Nr. 29/1977, S. 95. 96; Krapf, *Reisen* II, 55f.
[683] Eber, *Krapf*, S. 150, 151 (Krapf, *Reisen* I, S. 141f).

11. Missionary

Krapf's claim that Rebmann's missiological concept, including his vision of railways, the settlement of Christian families, handworkers and farmers, was directed at colonisation.[684] However, in the end it was Krapf, not Rebmann, who withdrew to Europe as a 'Frühpensionierter',[685] and did the nice settling for study and scholarly work. Rebmann has never worked out a plan for colonisation. His inclusion of practical assistance in mission reflects his desire to join the saving words of the Gospel to the deeds of Christian love. Bartle Frere claimed that Rebmann condemned an 'industrial element' in missionary teaching, and withheld Bombayer George David and others from operating a farm.[686] Here the British diplomat made a mistake. 'Secular work' like building, agriculture, medical care, education in crafts etc. was emphatically promoted by Rebmann and put into practice. However, he rejected the identification of mission as social welfare activities disconnected from the message of the Gospel, which would weaken the call for individual and personal conversion.

Undoubtedly Rebmann's missionary method was directed at personal conversion of the individual who is lost in his or her natural state. If Oliver is right in saying that Rebmann and Krapf 'were Lutherans, Pietists of the old school who saw the negro primarily as fallen man',[687] it must be added that they applied the state of being fallen also to their natural self. There is no salvation without personal conversion. The Kingdom of God lives in the hearts of those who have personally surrendered to Christ, have received forgiveness of sin and the gift of new life. Reed considers this belief the main reason for Rebmann's 'lack of conspicuous success.' In his view Rebmann was not a real strategist. He 'did not capitalise on contacts with people', as 'a Pietist of the old school' he had no attention for the institution and community character of the church and for African society as a 'communal and corporate activity.'

According to Reed Rebmann considered industrial and social activities of the church as worldly affairs, an imitation of the materialism of the Western world and the corruption of the organised church. Reed tries to create a contradiction between 'the African' seeking holistic involvement with the community and 'the German' seeking personal conversions.[688] I think these disqualifications of Rebmann's missiological method rest on a

---

[684] Eber, *Krapf*, S. 129 (Krapf *Reisen* II, S. 24, 33, 42, 45, 95, 104).
[685] Eber, *Krapf*, S. 180, Frühpensionierter = person retired at an early age.
[686] Report of Sir Bartle Frere at HMS Enchantress to CMS Secretary Hutchinson, dd April 1873; cf. Reed, *Pastors, Partners, Paternalists*, p. 46.
[687] Oliver, *The Missionary Factor*, p. 9.
[688] Reed, *Pastors, Partners, Paternalists*, p. 32, 33.

misunderstanding of the working of faith, which in the first place is a personal relationship with God from which a Christian community springs, and on a misrepresentation of Rebmann's motivation and efforts. A holistic approach was essential in his methods, but only as belonging in the missionary framework that is directed at converting individuals in the first place. Here Reed misses the secret of Rebmann's missionary work. Krapf too believed in the priority of individual conversions, but he had no place for time-consuming holistic approaches and in-depth contacts.

To an extent the work of Rebmann and Krapf can be considered as a prelude to British and German colonialism in East Africa. Did they consider Western political and military rule as a welcome support to mission or even as a method of mission? Fiedler asked the question in general. Were Christian mission and Western colonialism soulmates or antagonists?[689] He answers that they were neither, because of three indisputable facts, first mission preceded colonialism, secondly mission and colonialism both cooperated and collided, thirdly mission and Church survived colonialism. I think Fiedler's conclusion is applicable to both Rebmann and Krapf, although in different shades. It should not be overlooked that they were never in any direct contact with colonialism in East Africa, because their missionary presence preceded British and German colonial rule over present-day Kenya and Tanzania. This means that they could not have had an exact idea of what colonialism was going to be. Yet they sympathised with the preparations for its advent. In their view Western countries were called to do away with the evil of slavery and the political and military structures of Islam in Africa. Both were convinced that Western powers were called to break the external unity and 'political existence' of Islam before the Gospel could win influence among the masses of Muslims.[690]

---

[689] Klaus Fiedler, 'Christian Mission and Western Colonialism: Soulmates or Antagonists?', in: Kenneth A. Ross (ed.), *Faith at the Frontiers of Knowledge*, Blantyre: Claim/Kachere, 1998, p. 218-234; cf. Paas, *Christianity in Eurafrica*, p. 394, 395.

[690] Fischer, 'Extracts from Krapf's Letters of 1837-1858', letter of 10 April 1846: 'Der Muhammedanismus hat nichts Belebendes, sondern ist eine abgefallener Gegensatz, innerlich verwandt mit der antichristlichen Bildung Europas ohne eine göttliche Widerstandskraft. Der Muhammedanismus muss seine äussere Einheit verlieren durch den Verlust seiner politischen Existenz, die sich in Constantinopel concentrirt. Erst dann kann das Evangelium auf Einzelne und ganze Scharen Einfluss gewinnen'.

11. Missionary

Krapf perhaps sometimes seemed a bit indifferent as to 'whether Europeans take possession of East Africa or not',[691] but in general he was more outspoken in favour of interference by Western states than Rebmann. For that reason some called him 'a pioneer of colonial expansion', or even 'a hero of German imperialism', with a suggestion of unhealthy racial preferences. Perhaps the aggressive title and some of the content of 'A Marshal Forward' (*Ein Marschall Vorwärts*) of Krapf's biography by Vortisch has contributed to bias.[692] 'He tried to promote the idea that Germany should establish a strong influence in the South of Ethiopia, convert the Galla or Oromo people to Christianity, and support them to establish a state Ormania, in order to have a strong bulwark against Islam.'[693] At least Krapf's missionary strategy for the Galla people had a nationalistic tinge. 'I consider them destined by Providence after their conversion to Christianity to attain the importance and fulfil the mission which Heaven has pointed out to the Germans in Europe.'[694] He also welcomed British imperial influence. Desiring to keep French-Roman Catholic influence out of Ethiopia, he advised the ruler of Shoa to come 'in some closer connection with the English government'. Crummey ascribes to him the following blunt colonialist formula: 'The British must become the guardians of Abyssinia whatever measures must be applied whether they are of a forceable or a peaceful nature.'[695] Krapf served as a translator in a British expeditionary force that beat the Ethiopian army in 1868. His largely utopian ideal, of a chain of mission stations across Africa, would only be possible if colonial rule took away the circumstances that barred its realisation.

---

[691] Isichei, *A History of Christianity in Africa*, p. 92, quoting from Krapf, *Travels, Researches*, p. 512, 513.

[692] Hermann Vortisch, *Ein Marschall Vorwärts der Mission: Dr. J.L. Krapf*, Stuttgart: Ev. Missionsverlag/Basel: Basler Missionsbuchhandlung, 1927. In Prussian militarist terminology war-like people were sometimes called 'Marschall Vorwärts'. On S. 11 it says that a 'schmierige Jude' (greasy or filthy Jew) overcharged Krapf for lending a book on Ethiopia that was much desired by the future missionary. The biography has a post-war edition, of 1954, now entitled more politically correct, 'Bahnbrecher in Afrika'. On S. 13 the Jew has changed into 'geschäftstüchtige Jude' (business-minded Jew).

[693] Cf. Catherine Griefenow-Mewis, 'J.L. Krapf and his role in researching and describing East African languages', paper at Swahili Colloquium, Bayreuth, May 1996.

[694] Krapf, *Travels, Researches*, p. 72.

[695] D. Crummey, *Priest and Politician*, London, 1972, p. 47, 53, quoted in Isichei, *A History of Christianity in Africa*, p. 370, and in Sundkler, *A History of the Church in Africa*, p. 156.

In his work for the English CMS Rebmann very rarely showed German nationalist sensitivity. In the period when he doubted the faithfulness of the CMS to the Evangelical cause he was prepared to call in German Evangelical Missions to take over. In a letter to Sparshott he pointed to the 'most remarkable' fact that for a long time the East African Mission, first in Egypt and the Abessinia, then here, had only German missionaries.'[696]

For Rebmann it was only the expected spiritual consequence of colonial rule, breaking heathen and Muslim structures of hostility against the Gospel, that motivated him. He thought that 'countries seem to prosper only according to the degree in which Christian power has been extended over them.' He meant 'power in general, not exactly political' or military power.[697] Rebmann was convinced that the Gospel cannot really do anything with most Muslims 'until the sword comes over them'[698] to break the 'imaginary dominion' (*Scheinherrschaft*) of Islam.[699] Emma more than agreed with her husband. She was appalled by the cruel despotism of the Muslim rulers, their shameless slave-trade, the misery they left their subjects in, and their obstruction of the missionaries' 'work of love to the poor heathen.' She drew some extreme conclusions: 'The more I see, the more I am convinced that the missionary ought not to be here. Leave them alone until some European power takes, subdues, and crushes them, and then let the messengers of peace follow. And they will find the way and the people prepared, and become as little children in willingness to listen and learn'.[700] Confronted with reports on the immense cruelty of the slave-trading Wabiti tribe Rebmann hoped that the time was near for them to be ruled by a small 'woman, who by her white colour' will be different from them, but who can be 'a real warrior'. Of course he meant Queen Victoria, and the imminence of British colonial rule that would end slave-trade and slavery.

From another angle Rebmann connected the possible interference by Western powers to the severe judgments of the Lord that in his view would precede and pave the way for the victory of the Gospel.[701]

---

[696] Letter from Rebmann in Kisuludini to Sparshott, 14 Sept 1872.
[697] Rebmann and Erhardt in an evaluation of 'ten years of labour', summarised by the CMS secretaries, point 9, November 1854.
[698] Rebmann, *Tagebuch*, 13-11-1848.
[699] Rebmann, *Tagebuch*, 2-1-1849.
[700] Rebmann/Tyler (née Kent), *Journal*, p. 4 (1854).
[701] Rebmann, *Tagebuch*, 29-11-1848; 13-1-1848, God's judgment on the heathen consists of e.g. dirt, pestilence, hunger, bad houses.

'Man ... is never changed by gentle measures. Crushed he must be first and trampled upon, before he bows to ... a Saviour'. They despise love, grace and mercy under their law ... They must discover that they are dust and ashes, miserable forever without Him, discover that 'Thy judgements are true and righteous.'[702]

The idea of imminent judgment Rebmann not only applied to the Muslims, but also to the poverty of 'Ham',[703] to adherents of African traditional religions, including their sorcerers, magicians, witches, and the habit of lying and theft. Actually some of God's judgments have already come in the suffering because of the dirt, the pestilence, the hunger, the cruelties, the injustice of slavery and the trade in slaves and ivory. Much of it can be summarised by the attitude of unfaithful and despotic chiefs. These chiefs who misuse what God's children have given, 'should fear us, not we them'.[704]

Here the Rebmanns were unable to see the consequences of their desire for Western interference. Shillington rightly says that the missionaries' plea for intervention by European powers did not end the misery of Africans but was the beginning of a new phase of it. Missionaries failed 'to replace the violence of the slave and ivory trade with Christianity and commerce'. Then they appealed for British government intervention. As such they paved the way for colonialism, giving European powers an 'opportunity and an excuse to intervene in the region'.[705]

However, the thought that the depravity in traditionalist and Muslim Africa first required God's severe judgment did not control Rebmann's concept of missionary methodology. He realised that his desire for judgment was caused by discouraging experiences, and not by Scriptural content. He continued to heed the spiritual lessons of his Gerlinger pastor Stange. We are not called to convert people by inciting judgment's fire from heaven, but by applying the love of Christ, who taught us to love even our enemies.[706] Rebmann realised that in the African culture not only the satanical element, but also the christological connecting point is present. Their desires, sacrifices, prayers to the God of their imagination

---

[702] Half-year account from Rebmann in Kisuludini, to CMS, 19 (?) September 1854 [O24/16A].
[703] Rebmann, *Tagebuch*, 29-5-1848.
[704] Rebmann, *Tagebuch*, 14-12-1848.
[705] Shillington, *History of Africa*, p. 256, 257.
[706] Stange, 'Predigt am Feiertag Johannis', on *Luke* 9:51-56 (cf. KJV), where the Lord reproaches John and James who wanted fire from heaven to punish the Samaritans who had refused board and lodging to Jesus.

and ancestors offer a lot of opportunities that should be used. That's why Rebmann, even in times of extreme threat by Islam and African traditionalism, did not want to wait for Western invasions, divine judgments, or even a full green light from the CMS. He felt God wanted him to do right away everything he could to learn the language, to make and translate books, to teach people how to read and write, and to instil the Gospel in them.

How did Rebmann address people? All opportunities for teaching, preaching or just witnessing, he tried to use. Often they were limited to personal contacts, either brief encounters during journeys, or longer sessions when at home in Kisuludini and Rabai or during stays at Mombasa or Zanzibar. There were many one-to-one meetings. Jagga-King Mamkinga, chief Manika, the chief's wife and his mother, chief Munandoru, his guide the caravan leader Bwana Kheri, sorcerer Muigni Wasiri, language helper Salimini, and hundreds of other individual Muslims or African traditionalists heard from Rebmann about salvation for the soul through atonement by Jesus, and in most cases the listeners heard his prayer for their conversion. Rebmann would not take leave of anyone he accidentally met before having witnessed to him Christ as the way of salvation.[707] He often talked with individual beggars, and he found them more receptive to the Gospel than others. Apparently to him this had a special spiritual dimension, reminding one of Luther's final words, 'we are beggars and that is true'.[708] Those who are not (spiritual) beggars often pay no attention to the Word.

More often he spoke to small groups, to his employees, to slave-traders,[709] guarding soldiers, fellow-travellers, chief's counsellors, sailors. Almost always meetings were informal, and they were often characterised by discussion. They could be brief, in passing, but sometimes they lasted for many hours, even until late at night, as the one with some local Muslim leaders in 1848 did.[710] There were the daily house-worship or prayer meetings, the catechism classes, and the Sunday morning and afternoon[711] services of the small congregation at Rabai, first at home and

---

[707] Rebmann, *Tagebuch*, 21 to 23-4-1848.
[708] Martin Luther, 'Table Talks', No. 5468, 1546-02-16, in: James A. Kellerman, *Dr. Martin Luthers Werke*, Weimar: Hermann Boehlaus Nachfolger, 1909, vol. 85 (TR 5) 317-318.
[709] Rebmann, *Tagebuch*, 18-9-1848. He explained to them the sin and curse of the slave-trade, and that judgment would follow.
[710] Rebmann, *Tagebuch*, 9-5-1848.
[711] Rebmann, *Briefe*, 2-10-1862.

later in a chapel, or the ad hoc worship sessions[712] somewhere in a hut. The house-worship meetings had an edifying character, and may have reminded Rebmann of the conventicle meetings of the *Stundenleute* at home in Gerlingen. Sometimes the Nika people tried to involve the missionary in their own large meetings, and challenge him to give them benefits. However, he refused to make the impression that he wanted to buy them to 'go into the Book', i.e. to become Christians on their own conditions, and thus become part of their opportunistic scheme.[713] He found that addressing large meetings of Muslims or traditionalists may look like a quick way to success, but in practice it does not work out much. His preferred method was patiently building personal contacts with individuals and small groups and sowing the seed of the Word during these encounters. Subsequently, with regard to the yielding of fruit, everything waits for the work of the Holy Spirit.[714]

He often experienced among his African audience a chilling indifference to the higher things that are related to God and eternity, and an unbreakable hardness of heart towards the love of Christ,[715] accompanied by a silent refusal to obey the call for repentance and conversion. However, he knew that this was the natural state of fallen men, and that renegade Europeans turning against their Christian background were even harder.[716] Finally, Rebmann realised that the love of Christ Himself and the tender inward work of His Spirit breaks the hardest hearts, and challenges His servants to radiate Christian love. This supersedes any missionary method.

Message

Rebmann's message reflected his godliness. Much more precisely it was what he found in the Bible. The Holy Scriptures played a key role in the various ways he communicated with others. He became known as the man of the Book, because the Bible was the very first thing he would show to his listeners.[717] Subsequently he would explain that it is the Book of life, which contains the way of salvation to eternal life. He had come to Africa as a pilgrim, to share the wonderfully joyful contents of the Book

---

[712] Rebmann, *Briefe*, 23-4-1848.
[713] Rebmann, *Briefe*, 20-9-1861.
[714] Rebmann, *Tagebuch*, 31-7-1848.
[715] Rebmann, *Tagebuch*, 26-4-1848.
[716] Rebmann, *Tagebuch*, 30-12-1848.
[717] Cf. Rebmann, *Tagebuch*, 14-5-1848.

with them. People had to know that he hadn't come for ivory or slaves,[718] for commerce or discoveries,[719] but only for telling them about the Book, to translate it into their language, and to teach them how to read it. To a group of chiefs and elders, who had explained that in their concept the word *Mulungu* means both God and heaven, he said: 'We have come to teach how to recognise God in the Spirit'.[720] God has expressed Himself in Christ and 'the birth of Christ is the reason for my journey' to you.[721]

Concerning the material gifts that people expected so much from visitors in return for hospitality and protection, they should understand that Rebmann was ready to give beads[722] and other gifts, but not as a payment, and not disproportionally. To him the exchange of modest gifts was just a means to create a climate for communication of the good message of the Book. 'We have not come to give earthly goods, but to preach the need for penance and faith in Christ.'[723] Consequently, those who started to believe Rebmann's message metaphorically were called people who 'had gone into the Book'. Rebmann realised that he could only communicate the Book to others if his life was in agreement with it. For that reason personal meditation was part of his daily programme, and as we saw before, basic to his missionary methodology. In the way of Bible study the Holy Spirit fed him spiritually, so that he would gather personal faith, strength, courage and wisdom, and also be able to share the Word of God with others. This he considered to be essential in the life of a Christian in general and of a missionary in particular. That is why the Rebmanns felt deeply offended, when Emma was criticised by a visiting explorer because of taking much time for Bible reading.[724] Johannes' letters and journal contain several references to pericopes, which apparently played a special role during some events in his life.[725]

---

[718] Rebmann, *Tagebuch*, 24-11-1848.
[719] Rebmann, *Tagebuch*, 3-5-1848, 'I have not come to see your land, but to teach you the Word of God'; cf. *Tagebuch*, 15-5-1848, 21-5-1848, 24-5-1848.
[720] Rebmann, *Tagebuch*, 18-11-1848.
[721] Rebmann, *Tagebuch*, 25-12-1848.
[722] Rebmann, *Tagebuch*, 11-12-1848, on one of the listeners who when Rebmann talks to them about God, have 'more attention for beads'.
[723] Rebmann, *Tagebuch*, 1-4-1848.
[724] Rebmann, *Briefe*, 29-4-1864.
[725] In his *Briefe* he quoted e.g.: *Genesis* 6:9, 18-22; 32:10; *Deuteronomy* 1-5; I and II *Samuel*; *Psalms* 23; 37; 51:10; 90; 91; 103; 105:7; 111 esp. 6; *Proverbs* 13:12; *Isaiah* 1:10-15; 2:18; 43:2; 52:7; *Zechariah* 14; *Malachi* 3, 4; *Matthew* 12:18-21; 13:24-29; *Mark* 16: 15-20; *John* 12:28; *Acts* 7; 27:4; I *Corinthians* 1:18-2:5; *Galatians* 5:13; *Hebrews* 12:5,6; *James* 5:14, 15.

11. Missionary

The next element in Rebmann's communication was prayer. Reflection on the Scriptures and prayer belonged together. All could happen in private,[726] but reflection could also directly lead to public prayer. There were the prayers for his own spiritual and bodily life, e.g. for forgiveness and daily conversion, 'create in me a pure heart o God' (*Psalm* 51),[727] for a strong faith so that he would not surrender to temptations,[728] or for wisdom in addressing people, 'God, give me your grace', as you have given before, to speak 'to these Muslims.'[729] The desire for salvation and conversion of people was central in Rebmann's prayers. 'God be merciful to us and bless us, and cause your face to shine upon us. That Thy [Name] may be known upon the earth, Thy salvation among all nations.'[730] In his intercessory prayers unconverted European visitors[731] and unbelievers at home were not forgotten. However, the main thrust of his prayers was for the salvation and conversion of African Muslims and traditionalists. He prayed for those who were 'in thick darkness of paganism, magic and sorcery.' They expected from him something that was stronger than these phenomena. Rebmann trusted that 'Christ is stronger, and will destroy their weak means, the Sun of Righteousness will be the light in the dark.'[732] He also prayed for the arrival of helpers; he was often the only missionary in East Africa, felt weak, and realised that his task required the work of many Christians. 'Oh Lord of the harvest, call, choose many faithful workers to bring this ... people to the light of the Gospel.'[733] Requests to the CMS for additional workers were added to his prayers. Once, feeling weak and downtrodden, he even prayed that one of his brother Gottlob's sons would come over to help him. He needed the warm closeness of relatives, because he felt 'bad and miserable', though conscious of living from grace only.[734]

Bible study and prayer used to lead Rebmann to praise. Actually praising 'the God of my life', 'the Name of my God' was part of his prayers.[735] Prayer and praise fused in a special way when Rebmann felt lonely, be-

---

[726] Rebmann, *Tagebuch*, 4-6-1848; 10-6-1848;
[727] Rebmann, *Tagebuch*, 19-2-1848.
[728] Rebmann, *Tagebuch*, 6/9-9-1848.
[729] Rebmann, *Tagebuch*, 9-5-1848.
[730] Rebmann, *Tagebuch*, 14-1-1849.
[731] Rebmann, *Briefe*, 20-9-1861: prayer for the conversion of visiting Von der Decken and Thornton.
[732] Rebmann, *Tagebuch*, 27-12-1848.
[733] Rebmann, *Tagebuch*, 6-1-1849.
[734] Rebmann, *Briefe*, 2-5-1861.
[735] Cf. Rebmann, *Tagebuch*, 12-5-1848; 13-5-1848.

cause he missed praise among the people around him. 'I lifted up my heart to God, because there is no one here to praise Him.'[736] When a protective squad of soldiers of the Jagga king, guiding him, burst out in a marching song, Rebmann prayed that 'these soldiers singing for their king will soon sing to the glory of King Jesus.'[737] The utterance of praise to God, either in private or in public, either in prose or in hymns, was the bridge to the communication of the Gospel to the surrounding world. Praise paved the pilgrim's way to prepare himself for reaching out to other people. At the beginning of his career as a missionary he exclaimed with the Prophet *Isaiah*, 'How beautiful on the mountains are the feet of those who bring good news.'[738] As a pilgrim he praised the Lord like Jacob, who realised that he as an unworthy creature only received God's kindness because of grace,[739] and like David, who rejoiced, 'Praise the Lord my soul ... and forget not all His benefits, who forgives all your sins.'[740] With praise he would express his unreserved trust in Jesus Christ. For example on board the *Arrow* heading for East Africa on Easter Day 1846: 'The crucified and resurrected Saviour is with me, even though passing through waters' (cf. *Isaiah* 43:2),[741] and much later in Kisuludini, 'The faithful Lord, who bought us with His dear blood to be His possession, has helped me thus far. I trust Him until the end.'[742] 'He is my Rock.'[743] Being musically gifted, he liked singing. For example the song derived from *Hebrews* 16:9 on Jesus, the anchor of the soul,[744] hymns of Doddridge on the healing love of Christ, 'He comes the broken heart to bind, the bleeding soul to cure',[745] of Gerhardt on God's enduring care for his children,[746] and on the

---

[736] Rebmann, *Tagebuch*, 28-1-1849.
[737] Rebmann, *Tagebuch*, 6-1-1849.
[738] *Isaiah* 52:7.
[739] *Genesis* 32: 9,10.
[740] *Psalm* 103:1-3; cf. Rebmann, *Briefe*, 3-6-1845.
[741] Rebmann, *Briefe*, 13-4-1846.
[742] Rebmann, *Briefe*, 21-9-1863.
[743] Rebmann, *Tagebuch*, 21-11-1848.
[744] Rebmann, *Tagebuch*, 30-12-1848, 'Now I have found the ground/where sure my soul's anchor may remain,/the Lamb of God who for my sin/was from the world's foundation slain./Whose mercy shall unshaken stay/when heaven and earth are fled away' [original in German, by Johann Andreas Rothe, 1688-1758].
[745] Rebmann, *Tagebuch*, 14-12-1848; cf. Philip Doddridge, 'Hark the Glad Sound! The Savior Comes', in: *The Handbook to the Lutheran Hymnal*, Hymn 66: 4.
[746] Rebmann, *Briefe*, 8-10-1845; cf. Paul Gerhardt, 1607-1676, Befiehl du deine Wege / Und was dein Herze kränkt / Der allertreusten Pflege / Des, der den Himmel lenkt: / Der Wolken, Luft und Winden / Gibt Wege, Lauf und Bahn, / Der wird auch Wege finden, / Da dein Fuß gehen kann. [One of the possible translations:

11. Missionary 245

radiance of God's eternal glory,[747] or Preiswerk's mission-song 'Lord Jesus Christ, the cause is Thine.'[748] A moving prayer or hymn possibly by Christian Adam Dann, expressing the desire to die with Jesus and to be resurrected with Him played an important role in Rebmann's spiritual life.[749]

Demonstrating the Book of life, personal meditation, praying, praising, and singing were accompanied by Rebmann's communication of the message to others. What was the content of his sermons, lessons, reports and correspondence? In the Rebmann material that is left to us, these categories are mixed. Separate sermons have not been found. Through letters and the only existing journal representative elements of Rebmann's witness have come to us, explanations, exhortations, and words of comfort, either to ignorant African traditionalists and Muslims, or to cultivated European Christians and unbelievers.

When he witnessed to Africans Rebmann showed that he had a detailed knowledge of African Traditional Religion (ATR). A key item in ATR was the supposed presence of ancestral spirits among the living and the vague consciousness of a remote Supreme Being. Spirits were good or evil. Through an intermediary priesthood, and a variety of witches, sorcerers, magicians, and herbalists, people sought blessing from the good spirits and protection against the evil ones. Much of daily practice was controlled by fear of the powers of darkness. Tribal hatred, envy, distrust of neighbours, and the desire for revenge played a dominant role.[750] Rebmann was con-

---

Entrust your way / and what grieves your heart / to the most faithful care / of Him who governs heaven! / He who gives to the clouds, air and winds / their way, course and path / will also find a way / where your feet can go.]

[747] Rebmann, *Briefe*, 13-4-1846; cf. Paul Gerhard, 'Die güldne Sonne' [The golden sun], esp. v. 8, 'Alles vergehet, Gott aber stehet' [Everything is transient, but God stands].

[748] Rebmann, *Tagebuch*, 20-12-1848; cf. Samuel Preiswerk (1799-1871), 'Die Sach ist Dein, Herr Jesu Christ' GCAK No. 683,1.

[749] 'Laß mich, o Jesu mit Dir an Deinem Kreuz täglich sterben / und mein Gewand in Deinem Blute färben / damit ich dort mit Dir auch möge erben. / Durch Kreuz un Todt kommt man zu Gott. / Durch Spott und Hohn zur Ehrenkron'. Rebmann quoted it in *Briefe* 2-10-1862, and mentioned Dann as its composer. Possibly he meant Christian Adam Dann, 1758-1837. However, we have not found the prayer/hymn with Dann, but almost the same words with Christian E. Göring, *Täglicher Wandel des Christen ... zum thätigen Christenthum in Lehren und Regeln, mit Gebeten und Liedern ...*, third edition, Nördlingen: Beck'sche Buchhandlung, 1847, S. 267 (under: Sterb-Gebete: Evangelische Sterbekunst). The first edition, of 1838, does not contain it. This suggests that the prayer/hymn was composed in the period 1838-1847, or collected from earlier composers, possibly Dann.

[750] Rebmann, *Briefe*, 2-10-1862; *Tagebuch*, 17-11-1848.

vinced that their gloomy situation was going to change. 'Christianity is going to take flesh and blood among the people of Ham', and that Europeans were called to be messengers, 'Japheth must mediate to Ham the spiritual body of Christ.'[751] Although Satan tries to prevent it, they 'soon will see the victory of Christ's Kingdom.' 'As long as Jesus remains Lord, every day is more glorious, and the kingdom of the Devil goes down evermore.'[752]

Optimism about the advancing victory of God's Kingdom in Africa did not close Rebmann's eyes to the stubbornness of everyday reality. The great majority seemed to be indifferent to his message. He often noticed that the people he talked to did not show a trace of conversion. He realised that a change of heart and morals could not happen before they really understood Christ. As for now, it was very dark in their souls; they were estranged from higher and godly things, showing that they were living under God's judgment.[753] Even when they aimed at higher levels, when praying to their ancestors and their god, they only wanted material things. In their selfishness they did not know anything of absolute truths. That's why they did not see any problem in lying. The sorcery they adhered to in principle rested on lies. It was connected to the evil spirits and the Devil, who adroitly misused some powers of nature, as shown by the Egyptian sorcerers in Moses' day.[754] The African chiefs and their counsellors used to laugh when Rebmann said he had come to make them stop lying to one another and to God. Rebmann felt that in their blunt rejection of the Gospel and in their continued reliance on magic, they were trampling on the truth and the foundation of the Gospel. He often repeated that they should not fear sorcery and evil spirits but God, and he warned them that they were challenging God, thus confirming God's present judgment, and preluding further and more severe judgment. Sometimes he found his own words too sharp. Then he would humbly admit that only Christ's Spirit brings truth in the hearts. He would continue to say that he only feared God, who was his friend, and that God also wanted to deliver them from fear of darkness. Rebmann trusted that hearing the voice of Christ could instil in the hardest hearts some idea 'of the meaning and the direction of truth, and a certain love for it.'[755] He believed that the African culture, despite all its darkness, harboured elements of light, which were connecting points to the truth of God.

---

[751] Rebmann, *Tagebuch*, 25-12-1848.
[752] Rebmann, *Tagebuch*, 1 and 2-1-1849.
[753] Rebmann, *Tagebuch*, 14 and 29-5-1848.
[754] Rebmann, *Tagebuch*, 14-1-1849.
[755] Rebmann, *Tagebuch*, 20 and 21-12-1848; 17-11-1848.

Rebmann was much more critical about Islam than about ATR. Both were characterised by a 'selfish lying spirit' that was to be broken by God's special judgment, before the Gospel could advance,[756] but there was an important difference. 'Heathenism' was only against God's revelation, but Islam had turned against God himself. More than the African traditional religionists the followers of Islam had made a caricature of God. In addition Islam had damaged the image of man, making man boast of a 'proud and lying nature.'[757] They often call the holy name of God, but have 'no idea' of how unholy and how 'hateful to fellow-men' they are themselves. The hope Rebmann had for Africans in general he also had for the Muslims. Both will be blessed by 'the seed of Abraham', and ultimately 'run against the Rock of promise', Jesus Christ. He already saw the harbingers of a new time, 'after the night of heathenism and Islam', the 'spiritual spring flowers of the dawning Kingdom of God.'[758] Yet for now Rebmann experienced resistance by Islam, the religion of the Muslim rulers of Zanzibar, on whose hospitality he depended. Muslims spread the story that he was a kind of sorcerer and the Bible some harmful substance that would make people sick. In answer to the accusation Rebmann would hand out some medicines and stress that the true medicine against Satan is God, who wants them to stop sinning and to love their neighbours.[759] He saw that Islam had made people proud and hostile towards Christianity. Yet he freely talked with Muslims about Christ and Muhammad, the true and the false prophet. He explained to them that Jesus is the only Saviour of the world, and that He does not promise victory to those who use violence or lies, but that 'the meek will inherit the earth.' Often they only wanted to listen to him in passing, when they knew he would leave their village soon. Rebmann knew that they would remain blind to the truth, until Jesus Himself touched their eyes.[760]

In general Rebmann avoided sharp words. He was a humble and meek person, respectful to the African traditional religionists and Muslims among who he lived for nearly thirty years. In his attitude he reflected Jesus' attitude of love, even love of enemies. Yet his words could bite, especially when he protested against pride and dishonesty. His sharpest reaction was not directed against Africans, but against fellow Europeans. Earlier we saw how, with an apparent desire to have his words published to the German mis-

---

[756] Rebmann, *Tagebuch*, 19-12-1848.
[757] Rebmann, *Tagebuch*, 18 and 19-12-1848.
[758] Rebmann, *Tagebuch*, 3-1-1849; 14-12-1848; cf. *Briefe*, 2-5-1861.
[759] Rebmann, *Tagebuch*, 7-1-1849.
[760] Rebmann, *Tagebuch*, 7 and 14, and 31-7-1848; cf. 3-6-1848; cf. 26-5-1848;

sion-minded public, he reported to the Calw Publishing House on those Europeans who felt themselves 'great and distinguished.' Apparently he meant the explorers and commercialists who wanted to exploit the Africans for the benefit of their own pockets or honour. To them money is more than the soul of a 'dirty negro'. At the same time in these words he indirectly criticised some fellow-missionaries who lacked love, probably even Ludwig Krapf, who had bluntly established another mission station very near to Rabai. Reacting to European arrogance and rudeness he said:

> Let us remember that man cannot see the Kingdom of God unless he is born again. We become missionaries only when we have owned salvation in Christ, and in His love have learnt to love all people, also those who offend us, even our enemies. ... This Christian love is not selfish, targets the lost, knows and recognises the true dignity of man, in any appearance, enjoys truth, not injustice. This love elevates us to a spiritual level that cannot be reached by any other education or science.[761]

Rebmann realised that the world does not understand the Kingdom of God and despises its structure of love: 'Whoever wants to be wise concerning salvation, should expect to be called a fool in the world.' The world may even cause suffering and death, which foremost happened to Christ Himself. However Christ uses all this to multiply His glory in the lives of converts and in ruling the world.[762] He quoted Pietist preacher Ludwig Hofacker who warned that being blessed by God does not mean that materially all will go well. If that were so all people would be eager to be called by the otherwise despised names of Pietist or Christian.[763]

Theology

Man finds forgiveness, peace, righteousness in God's gift through Christ. Man's chief end is to follow Christ, to live to the honour of God by loving Him and his neighbour, and to extend God's Kingdom. Undoubtedly Rebmann was inspired by the unreserved trust in God in the meditations and hymns of the Pietist writer Karl Friedrich von Bogatzky, which he loved to read.[764] In 1845 from Islington he wrote to his father in Gerlingen, who had celebrated his 60th birthday:

---

[761] Rebmann, *Briefe*, 29-4-1864, summarised.
[762] Rebmann, *Briefe*, 20-9-1861; 2-10-1862;
[763] Rebmann, *Briefe*, 18-9-1858.
[764] Cf. Rebmann, *Briefe*, 23-11-1869, quotation from a hymn by Bogatzky: Du wirst Dein göttlich Werk vollenden, der Du der Welten Heil und Richter bist. Du wirst

> God's grace in Christ is the source of all peace and comfort. We serve one another in love, the more so in the love of Christ, for that love gives eternal life. We live, suffer, die, in Him, who died and resurrected from the grave. In this is your and my thankfulness and joy.[765]

These words represent Luther's stress on justification, Calvin's complementary stress on sanctification, and are inspired by the Pietists' stress on evangelism and mission. Principal elements of the confessions of Augsburg, and Geneva, and the Hofacker mainstream of Württemberg Pietism have merged in Rebmann with the revived Reformed Evangelicalism of the Anglican Church. Rebmann knows that man in his original state is born in sin and is lost in death. The righteousness God wants from men He gives in Christ, to anyone who is contrite, confesses his sins and surrenders to Christ, the embodiment of God's grace. God pronounces just who surrenders in faith. Christ is burdened with my sin, I am allowed to receive His righteousness. God's act of justification is followed by the process of sanctification in the whole of a Christian's life. Sanctification, similarly to justification, is only to be found in Christ. The life of reborn man is that of a pilgrim, a stranger in a foreign land. Such a life is characterised by gratefulness to Christ, in the midst of troubles, suffering, and struggle against sin, readiness to live entirely for Him, expressed by growing in faith, and by lovingly sharing the saving truth of Christ with others. There is a great reverence for the Word of God in which Christ becomes visible through His Spirit, which makes a Christian's life dependent on Scripture reading, meditation and prayer. Special emphasis on keeping the Sunday as a day of rest and worship belonged to this.[766]

These indicators of his theology we can find in Rebmann's letters and journal. Let us look at the more doctrinal comments in his teaching, preaching and personal reflections. Referring to the baptism of Gunja and Nyondo on 27 May 1860 he summarised salvation theology as follows, indicating four aspects:

> It is Christmas when poor human beings, (1) who have in them only death and depravity, (2) accept the Saviour in their hearts, (3) and faithfully fol-

---

der Menschheit Jammer wenden, so dunkel jetzt dein Weg, o Heiliger ist. Drum hört der Glaub nicht auf zu Dir zu flehen, Du tust doch über Bitten und Verstehen'.

[765] Rebmann, *Briefe*, 10-5-1845.
[766] Krapf, *Reisen*, I, S. 494; Eber, *Krapf*, S. 96, Krapf and Rebmann did not allow the people of Rabai to start the work of building a hut for them on the Sunday after they arrived in 1846.

low the voice of the Shepherd, (4) and when they as former unbelievers through baptism have been included in the Church.⁷⁶⁷

The centrality of Christ and the Cross everywhere prevails in Rebmann's theology. When waiting in vain for a message from unfaithful king Mamkinga, he meditated for his helpers:

> We will enter heavenly Canaan not through our own righteousness but Christ's. We must do what God wants, that is to seek our righteousness in Christ, if separation from God is to end. In the Old Testament people had to be obedient to end separation from God, but they could not reach God, so that their desire for Him grew. In the New Testament He Himself ends separation. In Christ God is nearby again. This act of reconciliation we cannot do. We are not able to do that good work. However, He gives us the work of faith, which is the only source of our good works.⁷⁶⁸

Reconciliation with God is through the cross. This moving truth made Rebmann's language teacher Muidani weep, shedding tears of sadness on understanding that his sins had put Jesus on the cross, and shedding tears of joy because now his sins were forgiven.⁷⁶⁹ Reconciliation by Christ was also the topic which captured the attention of the boat's people during one of Rebmann's voyages along the Mombasa coast in 1848.⁷⁷⁰

Why has God decided to save sinners? In answering this question Rebmann avoided speculations. We can only know what Scripture reveals. First there is the covenant of grace, which God in his 'unchangeable faithfulness' has concluded with the world. In the covenant God promises salvation to anyone who believes in Christ. Without Christ the world would be cursed eternally. Christ is the rock on which the covenant rests.⁷⁷¹ Secondly there is the truth of God's election. God's decision to save people is hidden in His will. However, to us His will is revealed in Christ. In a hymn he rejoices because of God's faithfulness. Whoever is Christ's possession will not get lost, he is elected to life.⁷⁷² The hymn contains the sentence in English translation 'As child I want to be in the arms of my Saviour.' The essence of this sentence is on his tombstone in Korntal. He could not have more clearly expressed how he unreservedly trust-

---

⁷⁶⁷ Rebmann, *Briefe*, 20-9-1860, summarised.
⁷⁶⁸ Rebmann, *Tagebuch*, 27-12-1848.
⁷⁶⁹ Rebmann, *Tagebuch*, 6-4-1848.
⁷⁷⁰ Rebmann, *Tagebuch*, 18-7-1848.
⁷⁷¹ Rebmann, *Tagebuch*, 1 and 3-12-1848.
⁷⁷² Rebmann, *Briefe*, 20-8-1874, 'Gott ist getreu ... Wer sein ist, der geht nicht verloren, zum Leben ist er auserkoren'.

ed that God faithfully keeps His promises in Christ and the covenant of grace.

The worldwide impact of God's covenant led Rebmann to a mission-centred theology. Missiology was the heart of his theology. This remained so even in periods when his work was on the verge of failure. He quoted Krapf: 'Even if all missions were to collapse, I would still continue to do missionary work, because it is Jesus' command, and He promises victory. To understand the glory of the cause of mission one should be converted and be converted evermore.'[773] Rebmann approved of Krapf's conviction, although his understanding of mission was less rooted in his experience of conversion or sanctification, than in being assured that a sinner's justification is rooted outside himself in God's grace through Christ.

Mission to the Jews played a pilot role in his missiological thought. That was in line with the Pietism of his Gerlinger pastor Stange, the Pietistic climate at the Basler Mission Seminary of Spittler and Wilhelm Hoffmann, and the Puritan-Reformed Whitefield-oriented revivalism of the Church Missionary Society and the Society for the Propagation of the Gospel. They followed the old Puritan view that by the end of the age the conversion of the Jews would greatly promote the cause of mission to the whole world. Some became known as the Jerusalem Friends (*Jerusalem Freunde*) of the Württemberg Pietism. Rebmann spoke positively of them.[774]

At the same time he observed judaizing tendencies with the *Kirschenhardthöfer*, later called the *Tempelgesellschaft* (Temple Society), a sect of enthusiasts. Confusingly they had a Hoffmann as well, and also used the same name *Jerusalem Freunde*.[775] They claimed that the literal fulfilment of God's promises to Israel was at hand in Palestine. Some settled in colonies at Haifa and Jaffa, 'to live there without dogma, expecting the Second Coming of Christ', and the establishment of the Kingdom of God. In a development after Rebmann's departure from Africa, when Germany colonised part of East Africa, a number of Palestine Germans settled in the Kilimanjaro region.[776] Due to the world wars the British deported *Templers*

---

[773] Rebmann, *Briefe*, 3-6-1845; Krapf, *Briefe*, 1843, in: *Extracts from his letters of 1837-1858*, BM-B.
[774] Rebmann, *Briefe*, 2-10-1862.
[775] Gottlob Christoph Jonathan Hoffmann, 1815-1885, brother of Wilhelm Hoffmann, the one time director of the Basler Mission Seminary; Stutzmann, *Johannes Rebmann im Spiegel seiner Briefe*, Teil IX, 8-4-1998.
[776] Helmut Glenk, Horst Blaich, Peer Gatter, *Shattered dreams at Kilimanjaro: An Historical Account of German Settlers from Palestine, who started a New Life in German East Af-*

from Palestine and Africa, respectively to Australia and Germany. In his time Rebmann warned against the noisy prophecies of the *Templers*. They should be quiet, not run ahead of God and they should expect the heavenly Jerusalem first.[777] Rebmann's distrust was confirmed long after his death. They had adopted a liberal theology, rejecting the divinity of Christ. By 1933 when the Hitler era began, the Templers had secularised to a great extent. In the process their political views radicalised, and gradually many of them turned to national-socialism.[778]

As with many 19th-century missionaries, Rebmann's missiology was coloured by his anthropology, which considered the peoples of Christian Europe (and America) as the source of spiritual and economic progress. He did not escape from paternalism, the idea of being in a parent-child relationship to the African. One of the consequences was that converts had to wait for years before Rebmann would allow them to be baptised. He was extremely careful. Baptism took place after a long period of teaching and other preparations. Mringe, the crippled Nika, was the first one. He and his mother had been thoroughly taught by both Krapf[779] and Rebmann. Even after Mringe had discovered that 'Christ is more than beads', had confessed that 'he had received a new heart', and had shown his joy because of the Bible stories and his ability to praise the love of Christ in prayer, Rebmann postponed baptism for a while.[780] Another example is (Abe) Gunja. Two years before his baptism on 27 May 1860, the *Calwer Missionsblatt* in a long article already described him as a Christian.[781] His son (Isaac) Nyondo was baptised after being able to read Scripture, e.g. the Nika translation of *Luke*, and also English portions, and studying the translated *Heidelberg Catechism*. After years of 'going into the book' and of catechising Gunja's stepson Hasani was not yet baptised.[782] A

---

rica in the late 19th and 20th Centuries, Trafford, 2011. For the role played in Palestine by Peter Martin Metzler, who once was Rebmann's short-time assistant, see: Eisler, *Metzler*.

[777] Rebmann, *Briefe*, 18-9-1858; cf. Krapf's criticism of the Templers, Eber, *Krapf*, S. 234, 235.

[778] Ralf Balke, 'Hitlerjugend in Haifa: Ein unbekanntes Stück Nahostgeschichte – Die NSDAP-Landesgruppe Palästina, *Jüdische Allgemeine*, 8 July 2004; Ralf Balke: *Hakenkreuz im Heiligen Land: die NSDAP-Landesgruppe Palästina*. Sutton, Erfurt 2001. Karl Ruff was one of their leaders. The British deported them to Australia and many returned to Germany after the war.

[779] Rebmann, *Briefe*, 7-9-1848, Krapf taught Mringe from the New Testament and prayed with him.

[780] Rebmann, *Tagebuch*, 18 and 31-7-1848; 1, 21, and 27-8-1848.

[781] 'Abe Gunscha' in: *Calwer Missionsblatt*, 1-4-1858, Nro 7, S. 29-32.

[782] Rebmann, *Briefe*, 20-9-1860; 4-5-1865.

tendency to a one-sided exegesis of the positions of Noah's sons Japheth and Ham in *Genesis* 9 contributed to this, apart from the optimism of technological and philosophical progress and the enthusiasm for new discoveries that had taken hold of Western man. In this framework fitted a certain acceptance of the expansion of Western political and military influence in Africa. In Rebmann's opinion the West was called to end slavery, and to break Islamic rule and other power structures that hindered the progress of the Gospel.[783] Yet Rebmann's paternalism was paralleled and even superseded by his love for the African people, for many of their customs and for their languages. He felt more at home with Africans than in secularised circles of Europe. 'These heathen are nearer to us than the most civilised and cultured European who does not believe in God!'[784]

Rebmann and Krapf

The differences between Rebmann and Krapf as missionaries are reflected by their theologies. In Rebmann's theology I have not met with any trace of the speculations on the future of Hahn and Oetinger. Krapf was influenced by both.[785] In the final analysis it should be realised that Rebmann and Krapf belonged to different spiritual climates which led to different theological positions, and consequently to different missionary motives and objectives, rooted in different expectations from God's power. Rebmann realised this:

> 'I was quite one with Dr. Krapf, with whom I lived and worked together for the first 5 years I was in East Africa in [*expecting*] all my salvation [*from*] a crucified Saviour, and ever being in consequence a living sacrifice for Him, but I differed from him in the manifest confidence in Divine power which ... marked the first missionaries of the Gospel of Christ, and which I will add [*has*] sustained me in East Africa for 22 years, which repeatedly I have been not only the only missionary on this whole coast, but for hundreds of miles off at Zanzibar the only European – the English lady excepted who for 15 years was my devoted [*helpmate*]. I was different from my older colleague in the way in which I expected Divine power to be exercised.'[786]

---

[783] Cf. Rebmann, *Briefe*, 2-5-1861.
[784] Rebmann, *Tagebuch*, 30-12-1848.
[785] Scheffbuch, *Große Entdecker*, 75.
[786] Letter from Rebmann in Mombasa to the CMS Commitee, 2 May 1868 [O24/42].

Krapf was a faithful member of the *Hahnische Gemeinschaft*. As Trautwein shows the Hahner are a heterodox body within the general movement of Pietism, joining together a theosophical system and an ascetical ethics. There is an element in it of the old *Gnostics*, who thought that the soul, when liberated out of its sinful body by death, would return to its eternal home with God. There is no eternal condemnation of a sinner, because finally in eternity, he or she will be restored to God. In this thought Christian mission is not meant to save people from eternal death. In the end, after death, all will come to recognise their sin, turn to Christ and be saved. That's why prayer for the dead fits in Hahn's system. It is important that people convert to Christ before their death though, not necessarily to escape eternal condemnation in hell, but to be equipped for doing good in this life for God and man, to be elevated to Christian civilisation that fights against evil in this world.

In this struggle, according to Hahn's theological concept, there is a lot of suffering, related to a process of conversion. Krapf said that in mission 'the first unbeliever who has to be converted is the missionary himself.'[787] He stressed that his spiritual life needed purification, including sickness to qualify his vocation. Referring to 1 *Samuel* 2:6 he said: 'Let Him bring me to the grave. He can bring me up. Nothing can hurt me. Be prepared to drink the cup of suffering.'[788] Here the suffering of man in salvation tends to take the place of the suffering of Christ. Despite this, in Hahn's missiology Christ is central, even His cross. However, a consequence of his logic is that the decision to believe in Him and be saved can be postponed, until long after death. Even in eternity the blood of Christ is able to cover and take away all guilt of 'repentful souls.'[789] Consequently, Christ is not the Saviour from God's wrath here and now. He is rather the Example who man should emulate, to live an ethical life of obedience to God.[790] In Krapf's theology priority is not justification but sanctification. Striving for personal holiness here and now precedes the reception possibly in eternity of Christ's righteousness earned on the Cross.

---

[787] Eber, *Krapf*, S. 120.
[788] CMS, *Proceedings 1852-1853*, n.d., p. 52-60.
[789] Eber, *Krapf*, S. 234. He complains that so many sins, active and of negligence, have remained in him, that have to be taken away by the blood of Jesus. 'Es kann dem Herrn nich genug verdankt werden, dass es in der Zeit *und Ewigkeit* noch ein Mittel gibt, das alle unsere Schulden decken und wegnemen kann, nämlich eben das teure und kostbare Blut des Sohnes Gottes, das sich gerne von den bußfertigen Seelen fassen läßt' [italics by S.P.].
[790] Cf. Trautwein, *Die Theosophie Michael Hahns*, S. 39, 40, 47, 111, 178, 244, 260.

11. Missionary

Looking for signs of salvation in man himself supersedes looking for salvation outside of man in the crucified and risen Christ. In a note written not long before his death, Krapf said in the short period of life that was ahead of him he should have his eyes fixed on his 'own inward life' in order to have and keep an 'assured hope of eternal life'. There should be a 'lively, pure, complete, inward, thorough communion with the Lord and his Word'. One should not go for anything 'useless or entertaining', but only do what is 'useful and enjoying in eternity.' He should be searching his past life and put everything under God's judgment.[791] Practically in Krapf's theology there is not necessarily a turning point of rebirth through God's salvatory act in man's life before his death. Throughout Krapf put a lot of stress on his own sinfulness. He wanted to guide sinners on the road to righteousness.[792] This road in his thought leads to the Lamb of God, who is ready to receive struggling sinners even after millennia in hell.

We do not know to what extent Krapf expounded these thoughts in his teaching in East Africa. He claimed that the birth of a Christian congregation in East Africa was the most important result of his missionary work.[793] However, he seemed to forget the much longer and much more intensive input by Rebmann on the East African scene. Krapf himself perhaps turned only one or two persons to the Christian faith during all of his missionary life.[794] His visions may have influenced some strategist of Christian mission, but also met with fundamental criticism.[795]

Johannes Rebmann, in line with Hofacker, who represented mainstream Württemberg Pietism, and the orthodox Lutheran-Calvinist teaching of the Reformation, believed that in life before death the decision is taken on man's eternal destination. That's why Christ first of all has to be presented as the Saviour. In Christ God saves all who have believed in Him during their lives on earth. When receiving of forgiveness of sins, they receive new life and become new creatures. The blood of Christ has reconciled them to God, death and sin do not dominate them anymore, they have become children of God. Salvation is decisive and it

---

[791] Eber, *Krapf*, S. 236, quoting from Krapf's earliest biographer Wilhelm Claus (1882); cf. Eber, *Krapf*, S. 197.
[792] Cf. Eber, *Krapf*, S. 71, 72, quoting from a fetter from Krapf to BM Inspektor Hoffmann.
[793] Eber, *Krapf*, S. 239, writes in italics: '*Die Entstehung christlicher Gemeinden in Ostafrika war für Krapf selbst das wichtigste Ergebnis seiner Missionstätigkeit*'.
[794] Cf. Griefenow-Mewis, p. 161.
[795] Eber, *Krapf*, S. 238, admits that 'manches in seiner Theologie uns heute fragwürdig scheint'.

starts here and now, in man's earthly life. Only saved people really follow the example of Jesus, and in Him escape God's eternal wrath. Rebmann's pastor Stange in Gerlingen, preaching on *Luke* 9:55 and 56, asked his congregation which spirit they had. In Rebmann's missiology this is a central question. Those who have the Spirit of Christ are eternally saved, and by definition are witnesses of Him. This was Rebmann's theological and spiritual position as a missionary.

11. Missionary

*Rebmann preaching to the Nika-people
from the roof of his mission station in Kisuludini
(Basler Mission Archive: QQ-30.006.0105).*

*Mission station at Rabai in 1850
(Gehörloseninstitut, Bönnigheim).*

12. Herald

Ploughmen and sowers

Johannes Rebmann's 29 years in Africa remind us of the Apostle Paul's vision of the mission field. He sowed the seed, Apollos watered it, and God made it grow.[796] The whole process of cultivation until harvest is God's work, although He employs men as ploughmen, sowers, planters, irrigators, harvesters.[797] Ploughmen and sowers may not see the harvest, but they are as much used in the mission field as the harvesters. Rebmann and the few colleagues, who joined him at times, mainly sowed and also watered. For that reason we cannot agree to those who say that these 'other-worldly men achieved no great evangelistic success.'[798] It is true that only after 1860 Rebmann could reap a modest visible harvest. A small congregation emerged. However, he trusted that others would build on his work. He paved the way for future missionaries in Africa to be Christ's instruments, to gather in the rich harvest of God's elect. Without the preparatory work by Rebmann, mission in East Africa would have taken a different course. He laid the foundations of mission on both sides of boundary that after 1885 would divide East Africa into spheres of English and German influence.

This is the primary significance of his life and work. During his lifetime the world did not see many results of what he performed. Today in the West mission has become an interest of a decreasing minority. Public opinion in the 21st century may consider Rebmann as a somewhat tragic figure, who failed to succeed, a queer and 'worn out' hero for a lost cause, buried in his primitive remote outpost, far from the civilisation and culture that count. Others find a reason why they want to 'save' him. They point to what he did as a geographical explorer and a language researcher. Oliver while picturing Rebmann and Krapf as somewhat clumsy 'other-worldy' figures, praises their 'vision, tenacity and boundless courage', and stresses that their 'linguistic work laid a solid foundation for all who

---

[796] 1 Cor. 3: 5-9;
[797] Cf. Stutzmann, 'Johannes Rebmann: Leben und Werk des Missionars', Vortrag, S. 10.
[798] Oliver, *The Missionary Factor*, p. 6, refers to the British Consul Playfair who saw only 6 baptised converts and six under tuition, and semi-completed well-built and commodious houses, when he visited the station in 1864.

came after.'[799] Rebmann's failure or insignificance as a missionary makes him greater (*'um so größer'*) at the front of the expansion of scientific knowledge.[800] That may be so in the thoughts of secularised observers. To the scope of their eyes, limited by the sky of this-worldliness, Rebmann's dictionaries would be wasted effort if they had not been useful to colonial administrations and economic or educational development. In a perspective that includes the reality beyond the sky, however, Rebmann's life and work have been useful to the Kingdom of God.

The scramble for Africa

Rebmann and Krapf were exponents of Western presence in 19th-century Africa. They were heralds of the Kingdom of God to a continent that had largely been unknown to Church and Christianity. At the same time they were citizens of countries that wanted to extend their political and military power to Africa. As such they were part of a dramatic change in the relationship between Europe and Africa. Since the Middle Ages the old imperialism of the Arabs, the Portuguese, the Dutch, and the English had affected parts of Africa. By the end of the 19th century economic and other interests enticed countries like France, Germany and Belgium, preceded by Britain, to colonise the whole of Africa. At the *Berlin Conference* (15 Nov. 1884 – 26 Febr. 1885) of the foreign ministers of 14 Western states a plan of partition was made. This initiated the *Scramble for Africa*. Before 1880 only 10% of Africa was controlled by European Powers. By 1902 only Ethiopia and Liberia had remained free of European control.[801]

Before the *Berlin Conference*, the British had already acquired spheres of influence in West and Southern Africa, and they had become the most powerful force in Egypt. After 1885 they pushed south and Anglo-Egyptian Sudan was established. To secure the sea routes to India and the Far East, the British considered it necessary to colonise Somalia. In the same period they established their control over the islands and coastal regions of the Zanzibar Sultanate. In 1887 the *British East Africa Company* secured the lease of a coastal strip from the Sultan of Zanzibar. On 25 May of that year the administration of Mombasa was relinquished to the company. In 1898 the Sultan formally surrendered Mombasa to the British.

---

[799] Oliver, *The missionary Factor*, p. 6, 7.
[800] Anonymous, 'Johannes Rebmann, Missionar in Ostafrika und Entdecker des Kilimandscharo', in: *Gerlingen: vom Dorf zur Stadt*, 1983, S. 107.
[801] Paas, *Christianity in Eurafrica*, p. 361-372 ('Eastern Africa 1800-1900'), p. 373-389 ('Africa's Old Colonizers after 1885'), p. 381- 388 (('Africa's New Colonizers after 1885').

The Germans also wanted concessions. In exchange for the possession of Tanganyika they agreed with British claims to Mombasa island and mainland, and that the British company's lands spread from the coast up to Ethiopia in the north, and Lake Victoria in the west. In an Anglo-German treaty of 1890 Uganda was assigned to Britain. The *East Africa Company* placed Buganda and other parts of present-day Uganda under its control. In respectively 1894 and 1895 these territories became British Protectorates.[802]

By then the British had already extended their power base in South Africa. It was the vision of Cecil Rhodes that the whole of Africa eventually would be under British control. He was a financier, statesman, and philosopher of mystical imperialism. Eventually Botswana, Southern Rhodesia (later Zimbabwe), Northern Rhodesia (later Zambia), and Nyasaland (later Malawi) were added to the British sphere of influence. Malawi, the land of Rebmann's Kiniassa Dictionary, became a British Protectorate in 1891.

Missions before 1885

Rebmann's departure in 1875 marked the beginning of a new period of mission in East Africa. First, the harvest, which he had expected for such a long time, began to show its fruits. After he left, the small young Church continued to experience the wonderful work of the Holy Spirit. In 1878 at the new CMS mission centre Frere Town 45 catechumens were confirmed by the Anglican bishop of Mauritius.[803] Before that, more Giriama people had begun to go to missionary Price to be baptised. Price sent a teacher, who found some 30 people, who the whole day were meditating on the Word and praying for forgiveness of sins.[804] Conversions and baptisms continued to take place. The young Giriama church was exposed to persecution and suffering. Their leader Abe Sidi was considered a rebel by the Muslim rulers of Mombasa. In 1883 Fuladayo was obliterated by a Swahili-Arab attack, and 'Abe Sidi was killed, becoming a Christian martyr'. The British at Frere Town did not help as they depended on friendly relations with the Governor of Mombasa.'[805]

---

[802] John Baur, *2000 Years of Christianity in Africa: An African History 62-1992*, Nairobi Paulines Publ., 1994, p. 257, 258.
[803] Scheffbuch, *Große Entdecker*, p. 91
[804] Jehle, *Der Entdecker*, S. 15, 16.
[805] Sundkler and Steed, *A History of the Church in Africa*, p. 556.

When Rebmann left, informally the CMS had already started its new strategy for East Africa, concentrating on Frere Town, the establishment of liberated slaves on the coast, and on preparations for penetration into the interior. Parallel to this, the congregation at Rabai/Kisuludini expanded by a surprising increase of new conversions, and by the addition of more Christianised Africans from Bombay. After meeting with Rebmann in London, though more precisely after his death in 1876, the wider plan for East Africa was worked out in further detail. It was as if a new era had arrived with Rebmann's death. The Committee's obituary, almost described it as an event of Providence.[806]

> 'Very remarkable are the coincidences of missionary history. But few have been more remarkable than that furnished by the death of John Rebman, just at the present moment. Blind, and infirm, and prematurely aged (he was but fifty-six when he died), the solitary veteran clings to his post at "the entering in of the gate" of Equatorial Africa, even after thirty years of trial and hardship, unbroken by a single visit to Europe; and it is only when at length a strong missionary party arrives to occupy the post, that he is persuaded to come home. Scarcely has he settled down in the retirement provided for him, than a sudden providential call, loud and clear, announces to the Church Missionary Society that the time has come for making a vigorous attempt to carry the Gospel into those very regions – the great Lake districts of Central Africa – the first accounts of which he himself conjointly with his colleagues Krapf and Erhardt sent home twenty years ago. An expedition is organised and dispatched. It arrives on the coast. It starts for the interior, commissioned to plant a mission on the shores of the missionaries' inland sea. Truly he might well say, "Lord, now lettest Thou Thy servant depart in peace"; and so it comes to pass. The veteran's work is done, and in peace he departs, to receive at the Master's hand the reward of his faithful service.'[807]

From February 1875 to March 1877 Frere Town grew by the reception of 456 freed slaves.[808] Time had come for realising plans to establish mission stations in the interior of present-day Kenya, Uganda and Tanzania. In a sense CMS-ers tried to put Krapf's plan into practice, although they limited it to a number of mission stations across Kenya to Uganda. John

---

[806] Rebmann, *Dictionary of the Kiniassa Language*, p. viii.
[807] Idem.
[808] Statement of freed slaves received by CMS, Mombasa, 1875-1877 [CA5 O: Original papers O25 Kenya Mission, Part 16, Reel 326, item 28; cf. Church Missionary Society Archive, Section IV: Africa Missions, Parts 16-19, Adam Matthew Publication, London 2004, p. 64].

Mackay reached Uganda in 1875 as the first CMS missionary. Before him Henry M. Stanley, the explorer-journalist, had done some work in preparation for mission among the Baganda. The CMS did not remain the only agency. Different missionary societies were encouraged by the publications and proposals of Krapf to work in East Africa, e.g. the *Swedish Evangelical Mission*, the *Methodist Mission*, the *St. Chrischona Mission*, and the *Hermannsburg Mission*. In 1879 the Roman Catholic *White Fathers* entered Uganda. They started work near the Protestant stations. Competition between Protestants and Roman Catholics was found confusing, and led to some serious setbacks. The first Anglican bishop in East Africa for the CMS was James Hannington. He was ordained in 1884, and briefly visited Frere Town in 1885. In October of the same year he was murdered in Uganda by the new king or *kabaka,* Mwanga II, who had turned very hostile against Christianity. The king also ordered the death of three African CMS Christians in 1885. In 1886 he burnt 31 Roman Catholics and Protestants in the capital, and had many others killed in other parts of the country.[809]

The *Universities Mission to Central Africa* (UMCA) had withdrawn to Zanzibar after an initial failure in Malawi. After Livingstone's appeal in 1857, they had started a mission in southern Malawi under Bishop Mackenzie, who collided with the Yao slave-traders.[810] The early attempt miscarried, and under Bishop Tozer the UMCA went to Zanzibar in 1864. In 1869 the UMCA moved to mainland Tanzania, establishing centres for freed slaves at Magila (1868), Masasi (1876) and Newala (1878).[811] In 1881 they were back in Malawi, starting from Likoma Island. They were preceded by other missions at the Zambezi and Shire Rivers, and at Lake Nyasa in 1874.[812] A party of missionaries consisting of missions of the *Church of Scotland* and the *Free Church of Scotland*, e.g. Riddel, Laws, Henderson, and Duff McDonald, scouted parts of southern Malawi including the lake shore, in preparation for permanent settlement.[813] A hand-written version of Rebmann's Kiniassa Dictionary was one of their tools. The Nyasa missions seemed to Krapf part of a fulfilment of his desire for a chain of missions.

---

[809] Louise Pirouet, *The Witness of the Ugandan Martyrs*, Kampala: Church of Uganda Literature Centre, 1969; cf. Hildebrandt, *History of the Church in Africa*, p. 187-189.
[810] Adrian Hastings, *The Church in Africa 1450-1950*, Oxford: Clarendon Press, 1996, p. 268, 286, 293.
[811] Hastings, *Church in Africa*, p. 257.
[812] *AMZ*, 1882, S. 164-175, 414-415; *AMZ*, 1888, S. 386-388, a brief survey of the continuation of mission in East Africa and the beginning of mission in Malawi.
[813] *AMZ*, 1882, S. 415, 416.

This he expressed in the Preface to Rebmann's Kiniassa Dictionary in 1877.

> 'The Editor of this Dictionary ardently wishes that the tribes of the Wakamdunda in the West may still be found existing and not have been entirely annihilated, as has been the case with many tribes of that quarter. The Author and the Editor, as well as the Society which has liberally offered the means for giving publicity to the Dictionary, would consider themselves amply rewarded, if the publication of this work would induce a few or many Missionaries to convey the tidings of salvation to the Wakamdunda and the other tribes residing in the West and especially in the region where Dr. Livingstone breathed his last, so that also in the latitude of the Lake Niassa, a chain of Mission-Stations between the East and West coasts of Africa might be established, as the Editor has proposed (since 1844) a line of Missions under the Equator (the so-called Equatorial Mission chain). Whether this Dictionary will be of any real use to the Missionaries of the Church Missionary Society, proceeding to Karague and Uganda, remains to be seen, but in a general way it will be useful to all Missionaries and travellers, who have to do with the people of the great Southern family of African languages.'

How useful was Rebmann's handwritten Kiniassa Dictionary for early missionaries in Malawi? They must have found it difficult to read Rebmann's handwriting, and as Anglo-Saxons they may have been somewhat confused by Rebmann's use of the German-oriented spelling system of Lepsius. After 1877 the printed version became known in Malawi, and must have been helpful to missionaries and language workers.[814] Soon Scottish missionaries started their own collections. In 1880 Alexander Riddel published a Chinyanja-English vocabulary, which was followed in 1892 by the large Mang'anja-English Dictionary by David Clement Scott. In respectively 1892 and 1894 Margaret Woodward and Robert Laws published English-Chinyanja vocabularies.[815]

Undoubtedly Rebmann and Krapf were significant figures in boosting public opinion in the war against slavery.[816] Krapf expected that the Nyasa Missions and Rebmann's Kiniassa Dictionary would contribute to the end of slavery and the slave-trade in Central Africa.

---

[814] Cf. F.M. John of the CMS, in an article on mission in the Nyasa, Shire and Zambezi valleys, in: *BMM*, 1883, S. 414-416.
[815] Cf. Appendix II, 'A History of Chichewa Lexicography'.
[816] *AMZ*, 1900, S. 339-348.

'Let us hope and pray that this monster of slavery and all other gross heathenism may soon be put down by the light and power of Christianity and Christian civilization, which is happily beginning to be inaugurated in that dark region by the noble enterprise which the various Scotch churches have directed toward the Southern end of lake Niassa, whilst the Universities' Mission at Zanzibar no doubt will occupy the North-eastern shore of that great lake.'

Missions after 1885

After 1885 the character of mission changed. The emphasis shifted from Western mission characterized by much desired contributions of Africans to mission of independent operations by Western missionaries. The presence of many missionaries, colonial civil servants and soldiers made missionaries feel less dependent on cooperation with the representatives of African culture and traditional religion than Rebmann was.

Also the cooperation between English and German missions became more difficult. The colonial border between German Tanganyika and British Kenya and Uganda frustrated interdenominational mission and international cooperation. The German Lutheran Rebmann, trained in a nondenominational institution in Switzerland, employed by the English Church in pre-colonial Africa, belonged to a different era. That's why the influence of Rebmann and contemporary missionaries on missionary approach and method declined after 1885. By the end of the century the number of missionary organisations in Kenya and Uganda had grown considerably. For example the *Church of Scotland Mission* (CSM), pioneering in the interior of Kenya. They worked hand in hand with the Anglicans of the CMS.

On the Roman Catholic side the *Holy Ghost Fathers* came to Kenya. They arrived in 1889, temporarily withdrew, and started work among the Gikuyu in 1899. They were followed by the *Consolata Fathers* in 1902 and then *Mill Hill Fathers* in 1903.[817] The completion of the Uganda railroad in 1901 made it much easier for missionaries to enter the interior.

The Germans followed the example of Britain and other colonizers. Otto von Bismarck felt that colonisation in Africa would give the recently unified German state due respect in the world. German colonial presence concerned territories in South, West and East Africa. One week after the *Berlin Conference* ended, on 26 February 1885, Germany took possession of Tanganyika, the land south of Kilimanjaro, henceforth called *German East*

---

[817] AMZ, 1895, S. 375.

Africa, present day Tanzania. Before German rule in Tanganyika began, the CMS, through Rebmann, Krapf and others, had been working in Zanzibar and on the coast south of Mombasa since 1844. The Roman Catholics were already at Bagamoyo, opposite Zanzibar; the *Holy Ghost Fathers* made a refuge there for freed slaves. They also established missionary stations along the coast and around Kilimanjaro. Christian communities of ex-slaves and others were also established by the *White Fathers* of Cardinal Lavigerie, who arrived at Lake Tanganyika in 1879.[818]

The establishment of German colonial rule was followed by the arrival of German missionary organisations. Before the First World War German missionaries were active for the classical German Protestant missions in various parts of Tanzania. In 1885 the CMS started to work among the Jagga in the Kilimanjaro region. First it seemed that the English could continue their work in German Tanganyika. There at the foot of the mountain, in Moshi, CMS bishop Hannington appointed a missionary.[819] However, the German Governor closed the CMS station in 1892, and in 1893 the work was taken over by the *Leipzig Evangelical Mission*, which had come to Tanzania in 1891. In 1886, stimulated by Krapf and Rebmann, the Bavarian pastor Max Ittameier founded the Protestant-Lutheran *Hersbrucker Mission* in the Kilimanjaro region.[820] On their arrival in 1891 the *Leipzig Mission* took over the work of the Bavarians. Later Bruno Gutmann would work for them among the Jagga. Other German organizations in Tanzania were the *Berlin Evangelical Mission* working in the coastal areas, the *Bethel Mission*, and the *Moravian Mission*.[821] The *Neukirchener Mission* had started work among the Kamba people in Ukambani, which came under British jurisdiction. In Usambara and further to the South the *Bielefelder Mission* and the *Berliner Mission* deployed.

The missions related to mainstream churches in Europe were named *Classical Missions*. Towards the end of the 19th century the classical missions slowed down in reaching out to new mission fields, because they had run out of money and personnel. However, other Protestant bodies took over the initiative. In general they were private organisations, independent of denominational structures and clergy. As such they were

---

[818] Paas, *Christianity in Eurafrica*, p. 365, 384ff. ('The Germans')..
[819] AMZ, 1894, S. 139, 509.
[820] Cf. Eber, *Krapf*, S. 240.
[821] Klaus Fiedler, *Christianity and Culture: Conservative German Protestant Missionaries in Tanzania 1900-1940*, Blantyre: Kachere/Claim, 1999 (first published by Brill, Leiden, in 1996); cf. Hildebrandt, *History of the Church in Africa*, 181-183; cf. Griefenow-Mewis, 'Krapf and his role', AAP 47 (1996) S. 161.

sometimes called *Post-Classical Missions* or more often *Faith Missions*.[822] The first one to arrive in Africa (1878) was the *Livingstone Inland Mission*, founded by Fanny Guinness. In British East Africa the first one was the *Africa Inland Mission* of Cameron Scott (1895).[823] They more or less restored the climate of international and interdenominational cooperation that had existed in the situation of Rebmann and Krapf.

To the memory of Rebmann

How should Johannes Rebmann be remembered by posterity? The few nice lines to his memory in Binders *Heimatbuch*[824] may have reached schools in Rebmann's home district in Württemberg for decades, but they fail to position him for today. Some have compared Rebmann to Livingstone,[825] others to the heroes of faith in *Hebrews* 11.[826] There is some truth in both comparisons, although Rebmann himself would have considered them exaggerations. After his death the significance of his life and work continued to be overshadowed by Ludwig Krapf. Rebmann's humility and shunning of publicity were among the reasons why contemporary and later observers have underrated him in comparison to Krapf. An example is the text on the big cross in memory to Krapf in the harbour of Mombasa. It was put there in 1944 by the British.

> 'Dr. Krapf and his wife landed in Mombasa in May 1844, but in July she died, and from her grave (near to this place) she called on the Church to attempt the conversion of Africa. As a scholar, language researcher and traveller he discovered together with Rev. Joh. Rebmann the Kenya and Kili-

---

[822] Paas, *Christianity in Eurafrica*, p. 389ff ('Mission and Colonialism 1885-1960'), p. 421ff ('Faith Missions').

[823] Cf. W.B. Anderson, *The Church in East Africa 1840-1974*, Nairobi/Dodoma/Kampala, UZ.I.M.U/CTP/CPH, 1981 [1977].

[824] Johannes Binder, *Heimatbuch für den Bezirk Leonberg*, Leonberg: Reichert, 1924, include a section on 'Johannes Rebmann', which familiarised many pupils on the region with at least the missionary´s name.

[825] J.M. Zahn, 'Die neueste Missionsunternehmungen in Ostafrika', in: *AMZ*, 1881, S. 241-264. Almost the whole article is on Rebmann and the co-workers who left him (Krapf, Erhardt, Deimler, Parnell), or died (Wagner, Pfefferle, Taylor), the fruits of their faithfulness, and on p. 245 a comparison noting similarities between Rebmann and Livingstone.

[826] *AMZ*, 1885, Beiblatt, S. 1-6. Under the title 'Fortsetzung von Hebräer elf', referring to their observation of mountain tops, lakes, the dawning liberation of slaves etc. the writer says: 'By faith Krapf and Rebmann have persevered in their post at Mombas.'

manjaro mountains. Like Dr. Livingstone he died on his knees in prayer, on 26 November 1881.'

Here Rebmann is not given separate attention, a few words on him are just included as an adjunct to the definition describing Krapf's importance.[827]

Should we fight for Rebmann's place in history the way his great-nephew Oskar Rebmann[828] did in the 1930s? Oskar was convinced that his great-uncle had been neglected by the CMS and that he was held back by Krapf. He did his utmost to assemble the material that he could find. He was optimistic about the lost biography and diaries. In a letter to secretary Leuschner of the Basel Mission he expected that these papers would turn up one day. The secretary lauded him because of his collection activities, and thought there might be some truth in his suspicion. Oskar had developed contacts with Arthur Jehle, who was a former missionary for the Basel Mission in Ghana. Later Jehle became a pastor and administrator in Stuttgart. He remained highly interested in mission and published some biographies, including a brochure on Johannes Rebmann.[829] Oskar got angry because in his view Jehle had not honoured Rebmann properly for his work and had given Krapf part of the honour. Subsequently Jehle terminated his relationship with Oskar, finding him too much of a burden. He only wanted to consider the importance of Rebmann's literary legacy on the basis of objective methods and of available Rebmann manuscripts.[830]

Jehle was of the opinion that Rebmann and Krapf deserved equal honour. Both were pioneers, pathfinders (*Pfadfinder*), or heralds. This he expressed when Sir Harry Johnston, Governor of British Nyasaland and former Governor of Uganda, in 1910 was in Stuttgart to campaign for a

---

[827] Cf. Jehle, *Der Entdecker*, S. 16.
[828] Oskar Rebmann (born 1901), grandson of Johannes Rebmann's brother Gottlob and Magdelene Wagner, through their son Immanuel and Emilie Schwinghammer. Cf. Rebmann Verwandte18-11-2008: www.johannes-rebmann-stiftung.de. The website of the Rebmann Foundation has published portions of a manuscript by Oskar Rebmann, which starts as follows: 'Für die Leser der Lebensgeschichte unseres Miss. Past. Johannes Rebmann. Vorliegende Arbeit empfangen Sie in 3 Lieferungen, sie umfasst 250 Seiten [the Website has 362 pages], und gibt einen grossen Einblick in das Lebenswerk dieses vielfach verkannten Mannes ...'.
[829] Gustav Arthur Jehle (1874-1957), see: http://bmpix.org/bmpix/controller/browse.htm? summary=INDIVIDUAL&mode=search&nodeIds=19863.
[830] Cf. correspondence on the issue: Oskar's letter to BM Basel of 14-1-28, letter of BM Basel's secretary to R.F. Merkel of 24-5-29, Jehle's letter to BM Basel of 26-1-34, letter of BM Basel to the Machame Mission 22-2-1940, letter of BM Basel, secretary to W. Oelschner, 23/3/1948.

plaque (*Gedenktafel*) to the memory of Krapf and Rebmann.⁸³¹ On Rebmann Sir Harry said:

> 'By his holy life Rebmann has earned for mission and Christianity insurpassable respect. His 29 years of uninterrupted work in East Africa drew the eyes of Christianity to that region.'⁸³²

Such praise is not attributed to everyone's great uncle! Before claiming that collective memory has been cruel to Johannes Rebmann we should realise that history has not been completely silent about him. In 1900 one of the glaciers of Kilimanjaro was named after him. In 1933 the Leipzig Mission erected a Rebmann memorial stone in Kalali (Tanganyika) at the foot of Kilimanjaro. In 1957 Gerlingen, newly elevated to city-status, erected a memorial statue for Rebmann in the main street (*Hauptstraße*), a gazelle of bronze, made by Fritz von Graevenitz.⁸³³ In 1961 a Krapf-Rebmann memorial church was opened in Kilifi (Kenya). In 1976 the City of Gerlingen, 100 years after Rebmann's death organised a solemn event (*Festakt*) in memory of its great son. The previous year the family of Gerhardt Rebmann in Esslingen transferred the hand-written letters to the City Archive. In October 1993, on the occasion of 100 years of the *Leipzig Mission* in East Africa, a *Johannes Rebmann Memorial Library* was opened at Kalali.⁸³⁴ On the occasion missionary Klaus-Peter Kiesel in Moshi reminded attendants and others of the three journeys by Rebmann to the area in the period 1848/1849.⁸³⁵ In Germany there are Johannes Rebmann street names in at least Freiberg/Neckar, Gerlingen, Korntal, Lübeck, and Stuttgart.⁸³⁶ There is a Rebmann statue in the Gerlingen City Hall, and a bronze plaque on the wall of the house where he was born. Apart from Rebmann documents and other memoralia in Basel, Birmingham, Cambridge, etc., in the *City Archive*

---

⁸³¹ Jehle, *Der Entdecker*, S. 2.
⁸³² Through Scheffbuch, *Große Entdecker*, S. 92.
⁸³³ Anonymous, 'Gerlingen ehrt seinen Größten Sohn: Enthüllung des Denkmals für den Missionar und Afrikaforscher Johannes Rebmann', Gerlinger Anzeiger 13/1957.
⁸³⁴ The initiator of the library was Peniel R. Shali. The opening ceremony was attended by thousands of locals, and by numerous guests of honour, e.g. Gunnar Staalsett (the Norwegian General Secretary of the Lutheran World Alliance), the Anglican Bishop of Moshi, the Pastor of Kalali, Helmut Luckert (Pastor of the *Petruskirche* in Gerlingen), Christian Haag, and Markus Rösler, representatives of the Rebmann family (*Rebmann Verwandschaft*).
⁸³⁵ Cf. Letter from missionary Klaus-Peter Kiesel in Moshi, 5 Nov. 1993 [City Archive Gerlingen].
⁸³⁶ Cf. Stadtsanzeiger Stuttgart 10 Nov.1934 [City Archive Gerlingen].

of Gerlingen there are letters, a journal, a picture drawn in 1844, photos, maps, a biography, etc. of Rebmann.[837] In the *Tanzanian National Museum* of Dar es Salaam, in the first section, there is an exhibition in memory of Johannes Rebmann.[838] The house he and Krapf built in Rabai is said to be still in existence ('soll bis heute erhalten sein').[839]

Of the 500 or so relatives of Johannes Rebmann descending from his brothers and sisters several bear the name Rebmann,[840] and a few of these are still living in Gerlingen. Some other names related to the Rebmann family are: Draack, Graser, Haag, Jamecsny, Knoblauch, Maisch, Rösler, Schrade, Zipfel.[841] Since 1996 in Gerlingen public consciousness of the significance of Rebmann has increased. When the 16th-century house, Kirchstraße 18, where he was born was planned for destruction and replacement by a modern building, a group of Rebmann friends (*Rebmann Haus Freundeskreis*) was formed to save the house. Chairman was Imanuel Stutzmann. City archivist Agnes Maisch started a series of articles on Rebmann's Letters (*Briefe*) in the local paper, the *Gerlinger Anzeiger*. She noted a controversy with regard to the future of the Rebmann house, which disturbed the minds of the people of Gerlingen.[842] Unfortunately Agnes Maisch died soon afterwards. The series on Rebmann's *Briefe* was continued by Stutzmann. From February to May 1998 twelve articles were published.[843] Finally in 1999, after some judicial procedures, by the joint effort of the stakeholders, the Rebmann house was saved from demolition. Since 12 July 2002 there has been a *Johannes Rebmann Foundation*,

---

[837] http://www.johannes-rebmann-stiftung.de/en/traces_rebmann.html; Ringwald, Johannes Rebmann, in: *Ludwigsburger Geschichtsblätter*, Nr. 29, S. 108; Stutzmann, 'Vor 150 Jahren sieht Missionar Rebmann den schneebedeckten Kilimandscharo', in: *Schwäbische Heimat*, 1998/1 Januar-März, S. 55; Stutzmann. 'Johannes Rebmann: Leben und Werk', in: Brochure of the *Rebmann Stiftung*, 2003, S. 8; Stadt Gerlingen, *Festschrift zur Stadterhebung* 1958, last sentence. Christian Haag, 'Johannes Rebmann: sein Wirken heute', in a brochure of the *Rebmann Stiftung*, 2003, S. 9-10.

[838] Scheffbuch, *Große Entdecker*, S. 86.

[839] Markus Rösler, 'Johannes Rebmann Kompakt', Stand 24-7-2007 [Zusammenfassung].

[840] Markus Rösler, Idem: 'Today about 500 hundred relatives of the missionary are alive, descendants of his sister and two brothers ('Nachfahren von drei seiner Geschwister').

[841] Peter Kustermann, *Johannes Rebmann, Missionar und Entdecker*, in: *1200 Jahre Gerlingen*, S. 797-1997.

[842] Quoted by Stutzmann, 'Johannes Rebmann im Spiegel seiner Briefe: Auszüge aus den Briefen von Johannes Rebmann', in: *Gerlinger Anzeiger*, Teil I, 12-2-1998.

[843] Stutzmann, 'Johannes Rebmann im Spiegel seiner Briefe', Februar-Mai, 1998.

12. Herald

established by various stakeholders.[844] The first activity was to buy the Rebmann House.[845] The Foundation liaises with the City of Gerlingen and its Archive. Since 2002 they have developed a website including all missionaries who originated from Gerlingen, which has widened the circle of Rebmann friends.[846] Growing interest in Rebmann was symbolised by the German President Horst Köhler and his wife Eva Luise Köhler, who visited the Rebmann House in December 2008.[847]

---

[844] The Rebmann Foundation (*Johannes Rebmann Stiftung* – JRS) at Rathausplatz 1, Gerlingen, is a fully private organisation, registered with Notary Ziegler in Gerlingen, on 12 July 2002, as Urkundenrolle II Nr. 566 /2002. It consists of: I. The Chairmanship of the Foundation (*Stiftungsvorstand*), responsible for the activities, consisting of three members, currently Mr. Christian Haag, Mrs. Martina Koch-Haßdenteufel, and Mr. Jürgen Schilbach. II. The Board of the Foundation (*Stiftungsrat*): chairman Mr. Georg Brenner, the Mayor of Gerlingen, and the following members: a. The local *Evangelische Petruskirche*, Pastor Dr. Martin Weeber, Mr. Michael Bühler, Mr. Helmut Gruber, Mr. Werner Lachenmayer, Mr. Ulrich Stirner-Sinn, and Mr. Christoph Zimmermann. b. The City of Gerlingen: (former) city-councillors Mr. Horst Arzt, Mr. Ulrich Knoblauch, Mr. Andreas Lederer, Mr. Nino Niechziol, and Mrs Ulrike Stegmaier. c. Relatives (*Rebmann Verwandschaft*): Mr. Dr. Markus Rösler. d. Society for Home Care (*Verein für Heimatpflege*) Gerlingen: Mrs. Dr. Catharina Raible, Mrs. Brigitte Fink Brigitte Fink. e. Friends of the Rebmann Foundation (*Freundeskreis JRS*): Mrs Irmgard Schopf, Mr. Werner Schmidt. f. Private persons: Mrs Uta Grob. III. Office Manager of the Foundation (*Geschäftsstelle der Stiftung*): Mr. Tobias Schölkopf. Besides, there are some other involved persons (*Beteiligten*), who support the foundation, e.g. *The City Archive, led by Mr. Klaus Hermann. Archivists are Mrs. Beate Wagner and Mrs. Carla Kastner. *The Württemberg bodies for safeguarding historical monuments (*Landesdenkmalamt*, and *Denkmalstiftung*), who sponsored the Foundation. *Regional and local banks, *Stefan Rösler, and his wife Aita Koha (who are involved in projects in Rebmann places in East Africa).

[845] The first publication of the Foundation, *Johannes Rebmann*, 2002, is introduced by Klaus Herrmann, Leiter des Stadtarchivs on S. 2, and Mayor Georg Brenner on S. 3. To the initial activities belonged Imanuel Stutzmann's presentation in the City Hall on 11 May 2003 ('Johannes Rebmann: Leben und Werk des Missionars'), the opening of a special room in the Rebmann House (*Missionarsstube*) on 9 January 2004, a visit by representatives of the Foundation to the graveyard in Korntal where Rebmann was buried in 2007 (cf. Manuel Liesenfeld, 'Johannes Rebmann verbindet Gerlingen mit Korntal'), journeys to Rebmann places in Tanzania and Kenya, in February 2007 by Stefan Rösler and Aita Koha, and in August/September 2009 by a group of Christians from Gerlingen, led by Markus Rösler and Wilfried Braun (cf. Franziska Kleiner, 'Ein Beitrag zur Völkerverständigung', in: *Strohgäu Extra*, 24-8-2009).

[846] http://www.johannes-rebmann-stiftung.de/en

[847] Cf. *Stuttgarter Zeitung* 29 Nov. and 2 Dec. 2008, *Ludwigsburger Kreiszeitung* 2 Dec. 2008.

These commendable activities have done a lot to restore to Rebmann his rightful place in history, distinguished from his famous colleague Johann Ludwig Krapf. Both have become known as earliest missionaries in East Africa. However, in the final analysis Rebmann and Krapf belonged to different spiritual climates, which led to different motivations and objectives.

Again, how should Johannes Rebmann from Gerlingen be remembered by posterity, by us? Undoubtedly he is one of the founders of African Studies,[848] especially in the Swahili and Mijikenda cultures, and an early father of Chichewa Lexicography. In particular I am convinced that he should live on in our memory as a son of the powerful movement of the Protestant Reformation and of the tradition of Württemberg Pietism, who with his limitations, as an ordinary human being but a saved sinner, was a faithful servant of God, and was used to be founder of the Church in East Africa, and pathfinder for mission in Central Africa.

---

[848] According to the anonymous article 'Gerlingen ehrt seinen Größten Sohn: Enthüllung des Denkmals für den Missionar und Afrikaforscher Johannes Rebmann', Gerlinger Anzeiger 13/1957, er gilt 'neben Krapf als Begründer der deutschen Afrikanistik'.

12. Herald

Preaching in an East African Village (CMS Gleaner, vol. 1, 1874, p. 126).

*Rebmann memorial in Gerlingen 1957
made by Fritz von Graevenitz (G.H. p. 18).*

In 1933 the Germans erected a Rebmann memorial stone at Kalali, Tanzania. Since 1993 there is also a Rebmann Memorial Library (Pfr. Luckert, Stadtarchiv Gerlingen).

The Krapf-Rebmann memorial church, in Kilifi, Kenya, opened in 1961 (Stadtarchiv Gerlingen).

Since 1944 at Mombasa harbour there has stood a memorial cross, dedicated to the memory of Krapf and indirectly Rebmann. The plaque in Swahili and English, says: 'Dr. Krapf and his wife landed in Mombasa in May 1844, but in July she died, and from her grave (near to this place) she called on the Church to attempt the conversion of Africa. As a scholar, language researcher and traveller he discovered together with Rev. Joh. Rebmann the Kenya and Kilimanjaro mountains. Like Dr. Livingstone he died on his knees in prayer on 26 November 1881.' Next to the cross there are four graves, of Johannes Rebmann's wife Emma, of their only child Samuel, and of Krapf's wife and daughter.
(Stadtarchiv Gerlingen)

Bibliography

Original sources

Correspondence by and to Rebmann, and other manuscripts pertaining to him, in English, collected in: CMS Archive, Section IV: Africa Missions, Parts 16-19, London: Adam Matthew Publications, 2004. Most relevant Rebmann documents are in Part 16, Kenya Mission 1841-1888. They are available on microfilm: Reel 316. See: CMS/B/OMS/C A5 O24 (55 documents), CMS/B/OMS/C A5 O23 (76 documents, especially: /17a-b), CMS/B/OMS/C A5 O5 (8 documents, especially: /7-8), CMS/B/OMS/C I1 O103 (24 documents, especially: /8), CMS/B/OMS/C I1 O306 (96 documents, especially: /20), CMS/B/OMS/C I3 O25/1-48 (48 documents, especially: /8, /13, /18), CMS/B/OMS/C MA M3 (1 volume, especially pp. 245, 264, 274).

Rebmann manuscripts in German, collected by the Basler Mission Archive, now Mission 21, especially in the file: Betriebsdokumentation Rebmann BV 246. In addition about 70 letters from Krapf [BV 110] and a bundle of letters from Luise Däuble are waiting for being transcribed and accessed.

Briefe. Since 2017 the majority of Rebmann's German *Briefe* (26 letters, of which 25 are addressed to his relatives) and 15 of his English *Letters* to the Church Missionary Society (CMS) in London have been made accessible on the website of the Johannes Rebmann Stiftung (JRS) [http://www.johannes-rebmann-stiftung.de/cms/missionare-aus-gerlingen/johannes-rebmann/rebmann-johannes-dokumente/briefe-von-johannes-rebmann/].

Almost all Rebmann's German letters are addressed to his closest relatives in Gerlingen. We know of only one that was addressed to someone else, to Gundert. Most German letters are kept by the Stadtarchiv of Gerlingen [KAT 5/17.1/21, No 873] and by the BM-B [BV 246]; those with an asterisk were found only in the BM-B Archiv. These are the German letters on the JRS site: 27-7-1844, from London; 10-5-1845 from London; 3-6-1845, from Islington; 8-10-1845, from Islington; 13-4-1846, from the Arrow; 31-7-1846, from Mombasa*; 20-4-1847, from Rabai*; 11-11-1847, from Rabai*; 11-3-1848, from Mombasa*; 4-12-1851, from Cairo (to Christian Gottlob Barth in Calw)*; 1-10-1853, from Kisuludini; 21-4-1854, from Kisuludini; 10-9-1854, from Kisuludini*; 19-9-1854, from Kisuludini; 30-11-

1855, from Cairo; 18-9-1858, from Zanzibar; 20-9-1859, from Mombasa; 20-9-1860, from Mombasa; 2-5-1861, from Mombasa; 20-9-1861, from Mombasa; 2-10-1862, from Mombasa; 21-9-1863, from Mombasa; 27-4-1864, from Mombasa; 29-4-1864, from Mombasa (to Hermann Gundert); 4-5-1865, from Mombasa; 26-9-1866, from Mombasa; 30-4-1868, from Mombasa; 23-11-1869, from Mombasa; 21-9-1871, from Mombasa; 20-8-1874, from Kisuludini; 21-8-1874, no place mentioned; 12-5-1875, from Islington; NB: The Gerlinger *Briefe* file contains an additional letter, of 19-11-1976, from Gerlingen, by which Berta Rebmann transferred the letters that were kept by the family Rebmann to Stadt Gerlingen.

Tagebuch, Diary of 1848-1849 in German, entitled *Tagebuch des Missionars vom 14. Februar 1848-16. Februar 1849,* Veröffentlichung des Archivs der Stadt Gerlingen vol. 3, Herausgegeben vom Stadtarchiv Gerlingen, 1997 [Transcribed by Edelgard Frank, edited by Pfarrer Klaus-Peter Kiesel, missionary in Moshi, Tanzania, who added explanatory notes, KAT 5/17.1/23 No 875].

The Beginning of a Spelling Book of the Kinika Language, Accompanied by a Translation of the Heidelberg Catechism, with Johann Ludwig Krapf, Bombay: American Mission Press, 1848 [78 pages, 18 cm.]. p. 5 Alifu ya Kinika za kuamba – Harufu sa Maneno ga Kinika; p. 6 Mavokali/Makonsonanti; p. 7 Matabo etc.; p. 12 Katexismo zakuamba Kandi ya Mafunsio ga Axrisiano, gago ikoa luasu Kua Maneno Mafuhi ga ku USA na ku uza ku Funsia Anika enjira ya usima wa Milele; p. 68 Masalo a tembe, II Masalo ga Diramuko, III Masalo ga Ziloni, IV Kua Madira ga ku Henda Kasi, V Masalo gahedoago kua utu wa Mazuso ga moyo, VI Kua utu wam ambo gossi ga atu, VII Sukuru, VIII Neno ra Mulungu Rorokarasoa, IX Kua utu wa zumwe; p. 75 Viuo Via Neno ra Mulungu Riihoaro Biblo; p. 77 Vio via Uhadi Uvia.

Map of Africa's Interior, 'Sketch of a Map from 1 & deg; N. to 15 & deg; S. Latitude and from 23 & deg; to 43 & deg; E. Longitude delineating the probably position and extent of the Sea of Unyamwezi as being the continuation of the Lake Niasa and exhibiting the numerous heathen-tribes situated to the East and West of that great Inland-sea together with the Caravan routes leading to it and into the interior in general. In true accordance with the information received from natives – Representatives of various inland tribes – and Mahomidan inland traders. By the Revd. Messrs. Erhardt and R. Rebmann, missionaries of the Church Miss. Society in East Africa, Kisuludini, March 14, 1855. Under this title the map was presented to the Royal Geographical Society on 10th November 1855'. Further details were given in a paper published in German: J. Erhardt, 'Mémoire zur Erläuterung der von ihm und J. Rebmann zusammengestellten Karte von Ost- und Zentral Afrika' [Auszug aus: Mitteilungen aus Justus Perthes' Geographischer Anstalt über wichtige Erforschungen aus dem Gesamtgebiet der Geographie von Dr. J. Petermann, Gotha, 1856].

'Narrative of a Journey to Jagga, the snow country of Eastern Africa, CMS *Intelligencer*, vol. 1, No. 1, May 1849, pp. 12-23; 'Journal d'une excursion au Jagga le pays des neiges de l'Afrique Orientale, Nouvelles Annales des Voyages et des sciences géographiques, Tome 2eme, 1849.

'Abe Gundscha', in: *Das Calwer Missionsblatt: herausgegeben von mehreren Missionsfreunden*, 31. Jahrgang, nro 7, 1 April 1858 [picture and biographical sketch of Rebmann's first convert, who he also presents as important assistant to his work on the Kinika dictionary].

The Gospel of St. Luke translated into the Suaheli language, St. Chrischona: Financed by British and Foreign Bible Society, 1876 [Rebmani Yohanes, Engili ya Lukasi iliofasirika kua Maneno ya Kisuaheli], [135 pages, 16 cm.].

Dictionary of the Kiniassa Language. Details on title page: *Dictionary of the Kiniassa Language*, by the Rev. John Rebman, late Missionary in Eastern Africa [John Rebman is an anglicised version of his real name: Johannes Rebmann]. Edited by Ludwig Krapf. Publ. by: St. Chrischona, near Basle, at the request and expense of the Church Missionary Society, 1877. The book has pages i-viii, and 1-184. On page ii it says: Repuplished [sic] in 1967 by: Gregg Press Limited, Westmead, Farnborough Hants, England. Printed in Germany. The book was also printed in England in the same year. It is similar to the Chrischona print except for the publisher. On the title page it says: London: Church Missionary Society, Salisbury Square, Fleet Street, 1877. Digitised copies of the book can be found on a website by entering 'Rebman, Kiniassa Dictionary', or 'digitized Rebman Kiniassa' (so spelled) into a search engine. On this website we find first the Chrischona print, digitised by Google on 30-8-2007, from a copy found in the Archive of the University of Michigan, and from a copy found in the Library of the University of Virginia, digitised 10-3-2007. There is also a copy of the CMS print, found by Google in Harvard College Library and digitised on 14-1-2008.

A Nika-English Dictionary. The title page says: Compiled by the late Rev. Dr. L. Krapf and the late Rev. J. Rebman, missionaries of the Church Missionary Society in East Africa. Edited by Rev. T.H. Sparshott, domestic chaplain of the Marquess of Cholmondeley, formerly missionary of the Church Missionary Society in East Africa, London: Society for Promoting Christian Knowledge, Northumberland Avenue, Charing Cross WC, 1887.

Handwritten Half-year accounts and Journal notes, from 19 Sept. 1861 to 14 June 1865 [City Archive Gerlingen No 76102 a-c; Originals in Württ. Landesbibliothek].

Rebmann's Contemporaries

Gilbert and Rivington, 'The Missionary Career of Dr. Krapf', in: CMS *Intelligencer*, London: February and March 1882.

Gossner, J. (ed.), *Martin Boos der Prediger der Gerechtigkeit die vor Gott gilt, seine Selbstbiogr.*, Leipzig: Tauchnitz, 1826;

Gossner, J. (ed.), *The Life and Persecutions of Martin Boos, an evangelical preacher of the Romish Church*, chiefly written by himself, London: Seeley and Burnside, 1836;

Hoffmann, W., *Elf Jahre in der Mission: Ein Abschiedswort an den Kreis der Evangelischen Missionsgesellschafft zu Basel*, Stuttgart: Steinkopf Verlag, 1853.

Krapf, Johann Ludwig, *Briefe*: Extracts from his letters of 1837-1858, by Fischer in 1948 [B.M. Archive 14.IX 48; vgl. F2.Abtg III, no 7], 10-4-1846; 26-11?-1846; 24-11-1857.

Krapf, Johann Ludwig, *Mémoir on the East African slave-trade: ein unveröffentlichtes Dokument aus dem Jahr 1853*, Afro-Pub. 2002 [Editor: Clemens Gütl, 127 pages, Internet].

Krapf, Johann Ludwig, *Reisen in Ostafrika 1837-1855*, 2 Teile, Korntal 1858 (reprint 1964). Teil I: pp. 195-465, 484, 485, 501; Teil II: pp. 1-135, 499-521.

Krapf, Johann Ludwig, *Travels, Researches and Missionary Labours during an eighteen years' residence in Eastern Africa*, Abingdon: Frank Cass, 1860 [2nd ed. 1968 with an introduction by R.C. Bridges; 2006 digitised version on the internet].

Krapf, Johann Ludwig, 'Preface', in: Rebmann's *Dictionary of the Kiniassa Language*, 1877.

Krapf, Johann Ludwig, *A Dictionary of the Suahili Language: Containing an Outline of a Suahili Grammar* [with Introduction], London: Trübner, 1882 [also: Edinburg/London: Ballantyne/Hanson].

Petermann, August, 'Mittheilungen über wichtige neue Erforschungen auf dem Gesamtgebiete der Geographie', 1856, pp. 19-32, 41 and map by Erhardt and Rebmann.

Rebmann, Emma (née Kent) 'Journal 1852-1857', Basler Mission Archive [A typed manuscript, consisting of 23 pages, A4, of summarised reports dated 1852 (p. 1), 1853 (p. 2), 1854 (pp. 3-4), 1855 (pp. 4-8), 1856 (pp. 9-20), 1857 (pp. 20-23), including on the first page the following hand-written note: 'Tagebuch von Frau Missionar Rebmann, geborene Kent verwitw. Tyler (I Frau v. Rebmann). Auszug für Oelschner, IV 1948. Eine von Pfarrer Jehle in Aussicht gestellten Schluss des Tagebuches nicht erhalten. Vgl. IV 1935 durch Pfarrer Jehle, der das Tagebuch abschreiben ließ, das bei der Landesbibliothek Stuttgart aufbewahrt ist'. In a letter of 21-1-1935, Jehle informs BM-B (secretary Leuschner) about a journal in English by Mrs Rebmann, consisting of 119 small pages, at the City Archive of Stuttgart. I have been unable to find this document. However, the Kirchenarchiv in Nürnberg has a document portions of Emma Rebmann's Diary, in a German translation by a missionary of the Leipziger Mission, Bruno Gutmann (1876-1966), a typed manuscript of 41 pages, entitled 'Fragmente eines Tagebuches der Frau des Missionars Johannes Rebman 1952-1957', with a hand-written correction: '1852-1857'[The Rebmann Foundation in Gerlingen intends to digitalize the manuscript and publish it on their website: http://www.johannes-rebmann-stiftung.de/cms/missionare-aus-gerlingen/johannes-rebmann/].

Tozer, William George, 'Letters of Bishop Tozer and His Sister together with some other records of the Universities' Mission from 1863-1873', edited by Gertrude Ward, London: Office of the Universities' Mission to Central Africa, 1902 [Internet].

Zahn, J.M., 'Die neueste Missionsunternehmungen in Ostafrika', in: *AMZ*, 1881, pp. 241-264.

Secondary Sources

Anonymous [P. St.], 'Deutsche Missionspioniere in Afrika: Krapf, Rebmann, Erhardt', Evangelischer Missions Kalender, Basler Mission 1918.

Anonymous, 'Gerlingen ehrt seinen Größten Sohn: Enthüllung des Denkmals für den Missionar und Afrikaforscher Johannes Rebmann', Gerlinger Anzeiger 13/1957.

Anonymous, *Die Anfänge der M.Hahn'schen Gemeinschaft*, Böblingen: M.Hahn'sche Gemeinschaft, 2001.

Baur, John, 2000 Years of Christianity in Africa: An African History 62-1992, Nairobi: Paulines Publications, pp. 224, 225.

Carlé, Walter, 'Der Kilimanjaro', in: *Jh. Ges. Naturkde Württemberg*, 132. Jahrgang, Stuttgart, 15 Dec, 1977, pp. 56ff [Archive Ev. Brüdergemeinde Korntal].

Beidelman, Thomas O., *Colonial Evangelism: A Socio-Historical Study of an East African Mission at the Grassroots*, Indiana University Press, 1982.

Binder, Johannes, *Heimatbuch für den Bezirk Leonberg*, Leonberg: Reichert, 1924, 'Johannes Rebmann'.

Breugel, J.W.M. van, *Chewa Traditional Religion*, Zomba: Kachere, 2001.

Breuer, Judith, 'Das Rebmann Haus in Gerlingen: Sein Denkmalwert verlangt Erhaltung', Denkmalpflege Baden-Württemberg 4/1998, Landesdenkmalamt, 244-246.

Bridges, R.C., 'A Manuscript Kinika Vocabulary and a letter of J.L. Krapf', in: *Bulletin of the Society for African Church History*, vol. 2, No. 4, 1968.

Bursik, Heinrich, *'Wissenschaft u. Mission soll sich aufs innigste miteinander befreunden': Geographie und Sprachwissenschaft als Instrumente der Mission – der Afrikareisende Johann Ludwig Krapf*, Universität Wien, 2008.

Crummey, D., *Priest and Politician*, London, 1972.

Dammann, Ernst Karl Alwin Hans, 'Rebmann Johannes', in: *Die Religion in Geschichte und Gegenwart. Handwörterbuch für Theologie und Religionswissenschaft*. 3rd ed., vol. 5. Tübingen 1961, p. 815.

Daur, Johannes (ed.), Korntals Vergangenheit, 16, 'Missionar Johannes Rebmann von Gerlingen', Korntal: Evangelische Brüdergemeinde, 1925.

Dicks, Ian D., An African Worldview: The Muslim Amacinga Yawo of Southern Malawi, Zomba: Kachere, 2012.

dtv-Lexikon, vol. 15, Deutscher Taschenbuch Verlag, München, 1968.

Eber, Jochen, *Johann Ludwig Krapf: Ein schwäbischer Pionier in Ostafrika*, Riehen: Arte Media/Lahr: Johannis, 2006.

Eisler, Ejal Jakob, *Peter Martin Metzler (1824-1907): Ein christlicher Missionar im Heiligen Land*, Haifa: Gottlieb-Schumacher-Institut, 1999. ISBN: 965-7109-03-5

Embacher, Friedrich, *Lexikon der Reisen und Entdeckungen*, Leipzig 1882/ Amsterdam 1988, p. 244.

Evangelisches Kirchenlexikon, vol. 2, 'Ostafrika', Göttingen, 1956, col. 1767.5.

Fiedler, Klaus, *The Story of Faith Missions: From Hudson Taylor to Present Day Africa*, Oxford: Regnum International, 2nd ed. 1998.

Fiedler, Klaus, *Christianity and Culture: Conservative German Protestant Missionaries in Tanzania 1900-1940*, Blantyre: Kachere/Claim, 1999 [first published by Brill, Leiden, 1996].

Gerlingen Stadt, 'Johannes Rebmann (1820-1876)', in: *Festschrift zur Stadterhebung*, pp. 38-40, 1958.
Gerlingen Stadt, 'Johannes Rebmann: Missionar in Ostafrika und Entdecker des Kilimandscharo', in: *Gerlingen: von Dorf zur Stadt*, pp. 107 ff., 1983.
Groves, C.P., *The Planting of Christianity in Africa*, volume 2, London, 1954.
Grünzweig, Fritz, 'Johannes Rebmann, Entdecker des Kilimadscharo', Vortrag, Evangelische Brüdergemeinde Korntal, 20 September 1970.
Grünzweig, Fritz, 'Ein Leben für Afrika: Zum 100. Todestag von Johannes Rebmann, Entdecker des Kilimandscharo', in: *Stuttgarter Zeitung*, 2-10-1976.
Gundert, Hermann, *Biography of the Rev. Charles Isenberg, Missionary of the Church Missionary Society to Abysinia and western India from 1832 to 1864* [translated into English by C. and M. Isenberg], London: CMS, 1885.
Gütl, Clemens, 'Do' Missionary vo' Deradenga: zwischen pietistischem Ideal und afrikanischer Realität', in: *Beitrage zur Missionswissenschaft und interkulturellen Theologie,17*, Hamburg/Berlin/London: Lit. Verlag. pp. 45-48 etc. ISBN: 3-8258-5525-2 [Internet].
Gutmann, Bruno, siehe: Rebmann, Emma.
Gutmann, Bruno, 'Entwurf einer Biografie über Rebmann', in: Kirchenarchiv in Nürnberg [The Rebmann Foundation intends to have this document digitlized and published on its website [www.johannes-rebmann-stiftung.de].
Hastings, Adrian, The Church in Africa 1450-1950, Oxford: Clarendon, 1996 (first 1994).
Henze, Dietmar, in: *Enzyklopädie der Entdecker und Erforscher der Erde*, vol. 4, Graz 2000, pp. 557-560.
http://anglicanhistory.org/africa/krapf_career1882.html
http://othes.univie.ac.at/404/1/02-13-2008_9125172.pdf
Iliffe, John, *A Modern History of Tanzania*, Cambridge/New York/Melbourne, 1994 (first 1979).
Isichei, Elizabeth, A History of Christianity in Africa: From Antiquity to the Present, London: SPCK, 1995.
Jehle, Gustav Arthur, 'Johannes Rebmann: eine Erinnerung an die Zeit der Pioniermissionare', in: *Evangelisches Missionsmagazin*, 1935, issue 6, pp. 189-198.
Jehle, Gustav Arthur, *Der Entdecker des Kilimandscharo: aus dem Leben des Missionars Johannes Rebmann*, Stuttgart/Basel: Evangelisches Missionsverlag, n.d.

Khamisi, Joe, The Wretched Africans: A Tribute to Slaves and Descendants of the 19th-century Slave Trade in Eastern Africa, Plano, Texas: Jodey Book Publishers, 2016.
Knauß, Karl, 'Johann Ludwig Krapf', in: Bautz vol. 4, 1992, pp. 606-608, http://www.bautz.de/bbkl/k/Krapf.shtml
Kretzmann, Paul E., *John Ludwig Krapf: The Explorer-Missionary of Northeastern Africa*, Columbus (Ohio): The Book Concern, n.d.
Kustermann, Peter, 'Johannes Rebmann 1820-1876: Entdecker des Kilimandscharo'. In: *Gerlinger Heimatblätter: Gerlinger Missionare*, Verein für Heimatpflege Gerlingen, n.d. pp. 12-18.
Kustermann, Peter, 'Johannes Rebmann, Missionar und Entdecker', in: *1200 Jahre Gerlingen, 797-1997*, pp. 202-204, 491.
Ledderhose, Karl Friedrich, 'Johann Ludwig Krapf', in: *Allgemeine Deutsche Biographie*, vol. 17 (1883), pp. 49-55 [Onlinefassung: http://www.deutsche-biographie.de/artikelADB_pnd118715496.html].
Ledderhose, Karl Friedrich, 'Johann Rebmann'. in: *Allgemeine Deutsche Biographie*, vol. 27 (1888), pp. 485-489 [Onlinefassung: http://de.wikisource.org/wiki/ADB:Rebmann,_Johann].
Lehmann, Arno, 'Missionspioniere am Kilimandscharo', in: *Gottes Volk aus vielen Ländern*, (Ost-) Berlin: Evangelische Verlagsanstalt, 1955.
Lewis, I.M., *Islam in Tropical Africa*, London: Oxford University Press, 1966.
Link, Stephanie, 'Humaner Einsatz in Ostafrika: Briefe des Missionars Johannes Rebmann – Entwicklungshilfe im 19. Jahrhundert', *Leonberger Kreiszeitung*, 12 March 1998.
Lipschutz, Mark and R. Kent Rasmussen, *Dictionary of African Historical Biography*, University of California, 1989, p. 115.
Luckert, Helmut, 'Er entdeckte den Kilimandscharo: In Ostafrika unvergessen Johannes Rebmann aus Gerlingen', in: *Ev. Gemeindeblatt*, 12-12-1993.
Mayer, Ernst, 'Missionar Johann Jakob Erhardt aus Bönnigheim 1825-1901: Einem vergessenen Afrika-Pionier zum Gedächtnis', in: *Zeitschrift des Zabergäuvereins*, Güglingen, 1960, no 3.
McIntosh, Hamish, *Robert Laws: Servant of Africa*, Carberry: Handsel/Blantyre: Central Africana, 1993.
Meyer, Hans, Die Erstbesteigung des Kilimandscharo, Heinrich Pleticha/Edition Erdmann, 2001 [first 1889].
Meyers kleines Konversationslexikon, vol. 9, Leipzig, 1895, col. 1655.
Müller, G., *Christian Gottlob Pregizer (1751-1824): Sein Leben und seine Schriften*, Stuttgart 1961.
Mwachira, Kevin, 'Remembering East African slave raids' [Internet].

Nwulia, Moses D.E., *Britain, and Slavery in East Africa*, Washington DC: Three Continents Press, 1975.
Oeler, Wilhelm, *Geschichte der Deutschen Evangelischen Mission*, Baden-Baden, 1949/5.
Oliver, Roland, *The Missionary Factor in East Africa*, London: Longmans, 1965 (first 1952).
Paas, Steven, 'Priester Martin Boos: Prediker der Gerechtigheid', in: *Protestants Nederland*, April 1986 Nr. 4.
Paas, Steven, *Beliefs and Practices of Muslims: The Religion of our neighbours*, Good Messenger Publications, Zomba: 2006, p. 125-133 ('History of Islam in Malawi').
Paas, Steven, Christianity in Eurafrica: A History of the Church in Europe and Africa [554 pages, illustrated] CLF: Wellington (SA), 2016; NAP: Washington DC (USA), 2017.
Pirouet, Louise, 'The Legacy of Johann Ludwig Krapf' [Internet].
Rebmann Stiftung, 'Summary of Rebmann's Life and Work', www.johannes-rebmann-stiftung.de/en/start.html
Rebmann, Oskar, 'Missionar Johannes Rebmann' ['Manuskript eines Grossneffen des Missionars Johannes Rebmann': unpublished document, n.d., about 1935, transcript of 154 pages is kept by City Archive Gerlingen, KAT 5/17.1/23a No 876]. The content copied by Maria Müller 1958, consists of an almost literal representation of Johannes Rebmann's *Briefe* and *Tagebuch*.
Rebmann, Oskar, manuscript of appr. 360 pages, consisting of e.g. a journal of Rebmann's travels, which are also included in Krapf's *Travels, Researches and Missionary Labours*, and of extracts from Rebmann's Letters [The Rebmann Foundation intends to digitalize and publish portions of the manuscript on their website: www.johannes-rebmann-stifting.de].
Rebmann, Oskar, Menschenweise, Leipzig: Hillmann, 1937.
Reed, Colin, *Pastors, Partners and Paternalists: African Church Leaders and Western Missionaries in the Anglican Church in Kenya 1850-1890*, Leiden: Brill 1997.
Richards, C.G., *Ludwig Krapf: Missionary and Explorer*, Nairobi: East African Literature Bureau, n.d.
Ringwald, Walter, 'Johannes Rebmann 1820-1876: Missionar, Entdecker, Sprachforscher', in: *Ludwigsburger Geschichtsblätter*, Nr, 29, pp. 78-109, 1977.
Roessle, J., *Von Bengel bis Blumhardt*, Metzingen: Fransverlag, 1966
Rösler, Markus, 'Woher stammen die Vorfahren Johannes Rebmanns?', in: *1200 Jahre Gerlingen, 797-1997*, 1997, pp. 202-204, 491.

Rösler, Markus, 'Familie des Gerlinger Missionars und Geographen Johannes Rebmann (1820-1876)', 2005 [started in 1994]

Rösler, Markus, 'Johannes Rebmann – Kompakt', Stand: 24.07.2007 [Zusammenfassung].

Rössle, Julius, *Zeugen und Zeugnisse: Die Väter des rheinisch-westfälischen Pietismus*, Konstanz: Christliche Verlagsanstalt, 1968,

Schäfer, Gerhard (ed.), *Michael Hahn: Gotteserkenntnis und Heiligung* [Aus seinen Betrachtungen, Briefen und Liedern], Metzingen: Ernst Franz Verlag, 1994.

Schaffert, Friedrich, 'Johannes Rebmann aus Gerlingen: Missionar in Ostafrika und Entdecker des Kilimandscharo', in: *Hie gut Württemberg*, Beilage der Ludwigsburger Kreiszeitung, 9 April 1977.

Schaffert, Friedrich, 'Johannes Rebmann: Missionar in Ostafrika und Entdecker des Kilimandscharo', in: *Gerlingen: Von Dorf zur Stadt*, 1983, pp. 107, 379.

Scheffbuch, Rolf, *Ludwig Hofacker – Vor allem: Jesu*, Stuttgart: Hänssler, 1898

Scheffbuch, Rolf, *Aus den Anfängen Korntals*, vol. 1, 'Das Gute behaltet'; vol. 2, 'Nicht aus eigener Kraft', Korntal: Ludwig-Hofacker-Vereinigung/Evangelische Brüdergemeinde, 2001 and 2003.

Scheffbuch, Rolf, *Große Entdecker und schwäbische Apostel: Von Korntal bis ans Ende der Welt*, Holzgerlingen: SCM Hänssler, 2010.

Schlatter, W., *Geschichte der Basler Mission 1815-1875*, vol. 1, Basle, 1916.

Schöpfer, Otto, 'Ein Gerlinger der Weltberühmtheit erlangte', *Gerlinger Anzeiger* 39/1955.

Schöpfer, Otto, 'Notizen über Erwähnungen Rebmanns', in: *Der Große Brockhaus* IX 1956, p. 579.

Schöpfer, Otto, 'Neues über die Johannes-Rebmann-Forschung', *Gerlinger Anzeiger* 25/1958.

Schöpfer, Otto, 'Johannes Rebmann (1820-1876)', in: *Festschrift zur Stadterhebung*, 1958, Stadt Gerlingen, pp. 37-39.

Schöpfer, Otto, 'Vor ihm, so weit er sehen konnte, so weit wie die ganze Welt, groß, hoch und unvorstellbar weiß in der Sonne lag der flache Gipfel des Kilimandscharo', *Gerlinger Anzeiger* 7 February 1964.

Schöpfer, Otto, 'Ein Gerlinger entdeckte den Kilimandscharo: Ein Denkmal im Hafen von Mombasa erinnert an Johannes Rebmann und Dr. Krapf', *Gerlinger Anzeiger*, 21 February 1965.

Schöpfer, Otto, 'Johannes Rebmann und die Erforschung der Nilquellen', *Gerlinger Anzeiger*, 29 January 1965.

Schöpfer, Otto, 'Der Gerlinger Johannes Rebmann war wegweisend: Speke und Burton wollten den Missionar aus Gerlingen für Nilquellenforschung gewinnen', *Gerlinger Anzeiger*, 13 March 1965.

Shaw, Mark, *The Kingdom of God in Africa: A Short History of African Christianity*, Grand Rapids: Baker Books, 1996, pp. 187-191.
Shillington, Kevin, *History of Africa*, London: Macmillan, 1989.
Sievers, Wilhelm and Friedrich Hahn, Afrika, Leipzig 1901, 'Rebmann' pp. 24, 262, 263.
Smith, Warren S. and Kennedy Ofundi, *A Colony of Heaven: Bishop Hannington and Freretown – Early Christian Mission in East Africa*, Outskirts Press 2016.
Stadtarchiv (City Archive) Gerlingen. All its Archivleiters have contributed to the Rebmann collection: Otto Schöpfer (1958-1968), Friedrich Schaffert (1968-1981), Agnes Maisch (1981-1997), Klaus Herrmann (since 1997). Apart from the above mentioned primary sources the City Archive keeps a lot of secondary Rebmann material, letters, pictures, articles, documents, filed under the following codes: KAT 10/17.1/01 (Ordner und Kiste with variety of correspondence and articles from 1934-1999), KAT 5/17.1/07, No 858 (correspondence of Luise Friederike Däuble), KAT 5/17.1/19, No 871 (general Rebmann material), KAT 5/17.1/20, No 872 (his geographical discoveries), KAT 5/17.1/22, No 874 (1976 in remembrance of his death after 100 years), KAT 5/17.1/23a, No 876 (biographies), KAT 5/17.1/24, No 877 (100 years Church in Tanzania, Rebmann House 1996), KAT 5/17.1/25, No 878 (correspondence by Kiesel 1982-1997, on CMS Archive by Schaffert, on Rebmann Library in Majame, on church in Kalali).
Staiger, Gerhard, 'Gerlingen und die Mission', in: *Gerlinger Heimatblätter: Gerlinger Missionare*, Gerlingen: Verein für Heimatpflege, n.d.
Steng, Wolfgang, and Christian Haag, Ulrich Schäfer, Imanuel Stutzmann, *Das Rebmannhaus und seine Geschichte* (Broschüre zur Eröffnung des Rebmann-Hauses 12.Juli 2002), Johannes Rebmann Stiftung, Gerlingen, 11. Mai 2003 [u.a. Zusammenfassung des Vortrages von Imanuel Stutzmann].
Stock, E., *The History of the Church Missionary Society: Its Environment, its Men, its Work*, London, 1899.
Stutzmann, Imanuel, 'Vor 150 Jahren sieht Missionar Rebmann den schneebedeckten Kilimandscharo', in: *Schwäbische Heimat*, pp. 53-55, Januar-März, 1998.
Stutzmann, Imanuel, 'Johannes Rebmann im Spiegel seiner Briefe: Auszüge aus den Briefen von Johannes Rebmann', in: *Gerlinger Anzeiger*, Februar-Mai, 1998.

Stutzmann, Imanuel, 'Johannes Rebmann: Leben und Werk des Missionars', Vortrag gehalten am 11. Mai 2003 im Sitzungssaal des Gerlinger Rathauses.

Sundkler, Bengt and Christopher Steed, *A History of the Church in Africa*, Cambridge University Press, 2000.

Tiesmeyer, L., *Die Erweckungsbewegung in Deutschland während des XIX. Jahrhunderts*, issue 7 (vol. 2, issue 3) Württemberg, Kassel: Ernst Röttger, 1906.

Trautwein, Joachim, *Die Theosophie Michael Hahns und ihre Quellen*, Stuttgart: Calwer Verlag, 1969.

Turaki, Yusufu, *Foundations of African Traditional Religion and Worldview*, Nairobi: Wordalive, 2006.

Vortisch, Hermann, *Ein Marschall Vorwärts in der Mission: Dr. L. Krapf*, Stuttgart: Evangelischer Missionsverlag/Basel: Basler Missionsbuchhandlung, 1927. In 1954 the second edition was published, under a different title, *Bahnbrecher in Afrika: Das Leben vor Dr. Johann Ludwig Krapf*, Witten: Bundes-Verlag.

Warneck, Gustav, *Abriß einer Geschichte der protestantischen Missionen von der Reformation auf die Gegenwart*, Berlin: Martin Warneck, 7th ed. 1901, pp. 248, 249.

Weidmann, Conrad, *Deutsche Männer in Afrika: Lexicon der hervorragendsten deutschen Afrika-Forscher, Missionare etc.*, Lübeck: Bernard Nöhring, 1894 [190 'famous Germans, including 15 Basler Brüder, Krapf pp. 70, 71, and Rebmann pp. 144, 145].

Weishaupt, Martin, *Rebmanns Reisen im Dschaggaland – Mit 7 Abbildungen*, Leipzig: Verlag der Evangelisch-Lutherischen Mission, 1926 [40 pages].

Contemporary Mission Magazines

German

Magazin für die neueste Geschichte der evangelischen Missions- und Bibelgesellschaften, Basel: Im Verlag des Missions-Institutes: 1844 (13/6), III, 190, IV, S. 201. 1846 (21/1), II, S. 126, IV, 9. 1847 (25/8), II, S. 184, IV, S. 16-18. 1848. IV, S. 17. 1849, III, S. 11, 12. 1856, IV, S. 76-110, 111-183. 1858, S. 93-102. 1861, S. 22-56. 1862, S. 53, 54. 1866, S. 278. 1867, S. 429, 430. 1873, S. 95, 96. 1876, S. 152-176.

Allgemeine Missions Zeitschrift: Monatshefte für geschichtliche und theoretische Missionskunde, Gütersloh: Bertelsmann, 1874, S. 249; 1875,

S. 428; 1876, S. 383-393; 1877, S. 95f, Beiblatt, S. 24; 1878, S. 570; 1849, S. 143-160; 1881, S. 241-264; 1882, S. 192-201, 117-129, 164-175, 234-240, 241-247, 289-302, 296, 356-365, 360/361, 414-423, 414-416; 1885, S. 3, Beiblatt S. 1-6; 1886, S. 227, 229, B 49 (fehlt); 1887, S. 185-191; 1888, S. 386-388; 1889, S. 140ff, 368 (fehlt); 1893, S. 84, 364 (fehlt); 1894,?; 1895, S. 375; 1897, S. 497-528; 1899, S. 25, 26, 179-189; 1900, S. 339-348.

Der Evangelische Heidenbote, Basel: Der Direktion der evangelischen Missionsgesellschaft, 1844, July (no 7), S. 65; 1847, July (no 7), S. 55, 56, 60; 1847, September (no 9), S. 73-75; 1848, June (no 6), S. 42-48; 1848, October (no 10), S. 76-78; 1849, September (no 9), S. 72; 1851, September (no 9), S. 75, 76.

English

Church Missionary Society, *Intelligencer* and *Gleaner*, yearbooks of 1844-1875.

Church Missionary Society, *Proceedings*, London, 1846-1847, pp. 47-51; 1847-1848, pp. lxxiii-lxxviii; 1842-1843, p. 48; 1844-1855, pp. 49-51; 1848-1849, pp. lxxxiii-xciii; 1849-1850, pp. xcv-cvii; 1850-1851, pp. xcvii-cxxvi; 1851-1852, pp. 59-73; 1852-1853, pp. 52-60; 1853-1854, pp. 52-54; 1854-1855, pp. 57-59; 1855-1856, pp. 53-54, 64; 1856-1857, pp. 50-51,59; 1857-1858, p. 65; 1858-1859, pp. 56-57; 1859-1860, p. 60; 1860-1861, pp. xii, 55-59; 1861-1862, pp. 55-57; 1862-1863, pp. xii, 51-53; 1863-1864, pp. xii, 75, 76; 1864-1865, pp. xiv, 173, 178-180; 1865-1866, pp. 166ff; 1866-1867, pp. 164, 178; 1867-1868, pp. 134, 139-140; 1868-1869, p. 173; 1869-1870, pp. 206, 210; 1870-1871, pp. 197, 206; 1871-1872, p. 187, 191; 1873-1874, pp. 32-33; 1874-1875, pp. 37-40; 1875-1876, pp. 49-55; 1876-1877, pp. 37-44; 1877-1878, pp. 47-53.

Appendix I: Salimini's Chichewa

Andrew Goodson

Salimini's Home

The ex-Malawian slave Salimini seems to have been the only informant used by Johannes Rebmann in writing his *Dictionary of the Kiniassa Language*. Evidently he did look for other informants, but apparently without much success, as we read in chapter 9 above: 'Even in 1858, when in exile in Zanzibar and working on the Dictionary, he asked for Salimini to be sent to him, because he "could find no man here, who spoke that language as well as he did".' At any rate, in the dictionary itself there is no indication of any other contributor.[849] Rebmann refers to Salimini as 'my informant' five times in the introduction, and the name of Salimini's home village of Mpande (*Mphande*) or Kumpande or of Salimini himself is also mentioned or implied in no fewer than 35 entries in the dictionary.[850]

It is therefore interesting to ask what region Salimini came from, and whether his village of Mphande can be located from the information given. In the introduction we are told that it was two days' journey west of the Lake. The nearest place for crossing the Lake was apparently Senga (see the entry Dsenga), where the Lake is relatively narrow; but, Rebmann says:

> From that part of the lake's banks he used to come to from his home, the opposite side cannot be seen, but a boat starting at day-break will reach it at sunset.

We are also told that Mphande was at a location where ice was sometimes found:

---

[849] The dictionary also appears to be not quite finished, since on every page there are four or five entries which have no definition, or only an equivalent in Kiswahili or an untranslated example in Chichewa. It appears that Salimini explained the words to Rebmann in Swahili, which he then translated into English.

[850] See the entries Bua, Chada, Charera, Demera, Denge, Dsekuere, Dsenga, Dsimbiri, Fuma, Iai, Iwo, Karumbe, Kidsa, Kirobue, Kisambo, Kisumpi, Koma, Lingadsi, M, Mabuyu, Mankamba, Masie, Mbodo, Mgama/Mkama, Midawa, Mideme, Miriri, Misu, Mpande, Msauka, Msincha, Paso, Pogera, Tumbo.

When my informant spoke of the cold in his country, he described the water as getting a hard crust during the night, which of course can be nothing else but ice, called 'kungu' in their language.

Another clue is that the river Bua was 1½ days' journey to the West of Mphande:

Bua, (n.prop.)[851] of a river or perhaps a large swamp, a mile in breadth and overgrown with a kind of reed, the ashes of which are used as salt, one and half day's journey to the west of Kumpande.

These indications place Mphande definitely in the Central Region of Malawi, south of the Bua. One might at first suppose from the mention of ice that it was one of the higher villages, such as those near Ntchisi Mountain.[852] However, certain entries where the names of villages can be identified make it clear that the site was not near Ntchisi but in the Lilongwe region:

Mabuyu (*Mapuyu*), a territory one and half days' distance to the west of Kumpande. Its inhabitants belong to the Wakamdunda (*Ŵakamtunda*). – Mabuyu, Demera, and Misu; these countries are said to be much frequented by the Portuguese for trade, bartering slaves and cattle for guns and gunpowder.

Demera (*Demera*), name of a territory one day's journey W.N.W. from ku Mpande. The inhabitants belong to the Wakamdunda.

Kirobue (*Chilobwe*), name of a country 2 days N.W. from M-pande.

Lingadsi (*Lingadzi*), name of a river, a contributory of the Lintibe (*Linthipe*); going from Pande (*Mphande*) westward, it is forded after half a day's journey.

Mankamba (*Mankhamba*), a country, one day's journey to the west of M-pande (at noon they ford the Lingadsi).

---

[851] n.prop = *nomen proprium*, i.e. proper name.
[852] Ice is rarely if ever found today, but R.G. Willan in 'Some notes on the cold spell in August 1955', *The Nyasaland Journal*, vol 10, no. 1 (January 1957) records that 'frost occurs …in most years at Lilongwe'. It appears that in 1937 and in 1955 there was a very severe frost over a wide area. (For another mention of ice see the entry Guira.)

The villages of Mapuyu, Demera, Chilobwe, and the river Lingadzi can be easily identified. Mapuyu is near Namitete, about 27 miles to the west of Lilongwe; Demera is 13 miles N or NNE of Mapuyu; and Chilobwe, not far from the Bua, is 7 miles NW of Demera. The Lingadzi river joins the Lilongwe river at Lilongwe.[853] Assuming that a young man could walk about 25 or 30 miles in a day, all these entries would place Mpande a few miles to the east of Lilongwe, perhaps (but not necessarily) at the village of Kamphande, 12 miles NE of Lilongwe (between the Salima road and the railway line).[854]

The entry below might also fit this location, if we assume that 'S.W.' is an error for 'S.E.':

> **Midawa** (*Mitawa*): name of a country 1½ days' journey S.W. The inhabitants are Wamuale and are subject to King Undi who resides at Mano.

For there is indeed a village called Mitawa, near Linthipe trading centre, about 25 miles S.E. of Lilongwe; and 7 miles south of it is a village called Undi, which might reflect the name of the king. Mano itself is near the Kapoche river in eastern Mozambique, and Undi is the name of a well-known dynasty of Chewâ kings.[855]

Further evidence that Salimini came from near Lilongwe can be found in the names of rivers mentioned in the dictionary entries, which are mostly concentrated in this area: the Bua (with tributaries Kakuyu,

---

[853] As Rebmann points out (in the entry Rironkue) the Lilongwe river is itself a tributary of the Linthipe; so indirectly the Lingadzi is a tributary of the Linthipe. There is another Lingadzi north of Dowa, but it flows directly into the Lake. – Misu (*Mizu*) is not on Malawian maps; Rebmann says it is two days' distance S.W. of Mphande, which might put it just over the border in Mozambique.

[854] If this was Salimini's home village, when visiting the Lake he would presumably have reached the shore at Maganga, near the mouth of the Lilongwe/Linthipe rivers. The Lake is extremely wide here, but much narrower just a few miles further north at Senga.

[855] See Marwick: 'History and tradition in East Central Africa through the eyes of the Northern Rhodesian Chewâ', *Journal of African History*, IV, 3, (1963), p. 375-390. The present Kalonga Gawo Undi, now residing in Zambia, is regarded as the Paramount Chief of the Chewâ. It seems that Kumphande was not subject to Undi. Salimini says that the hereditary chiefs of Kumphande were called Chalera (see entry Charera).

Mdede (*Namitete*),[856] Liuye), the Lilongwe (with tributaries Mtedza, Nankaka, Lumbadzi, Lingadzi), and the Linthipe.[857]

Five mountains are mentioned, Tuma, Tumbo ('one day's journey N.W. of Mpande'), Kirenge[858], Msondore[859], and Kapfuramani. Of these at least one, Tuma or Thuma, can easily be identified. It is situated between the Lilongwe and Linthipe rivers, and Salimini would have passed it on his way to the Lake. This mountain is mentioned again in the entry Mbando as a dangerous place to cross:

> **Mbāndo**,[860] s. coll.[861] (wa) a robbing attack ... ana-di-chidira mbando (*anati-chitira mbanda*), they waylaid us for an attack, or they made an attack of robbery on us. Such attacks take place on the Tuma-mountains, over which the way leads through a narrow pass, where the robbers lie in ambush.[862]

Kapfuramani might also perhaps be possible to identify:

> **Kapfuramáni**, s. name of a mountain on the frontier between Binga and Chada.
>
> **Chada** (n.prop.) name of a territory E. of Mpande (about one day's journey).

An informant who was brought up near Ntchisi remembers hearing of two villages Benga and Tchada about 12 miles south of Ntchisi, with a hill Kapulamani close to them. However, recent enquiries in the area failed to find anyone who knew these names.[863]

---

[856] The Mdede and the Kakuyu are said to run N.W. into the Bua (see entry Msincha), although the Kakuyu is also said to be a contributory of the 'Mdidi' (see entry Kakuyu).

[857] He also mentions a certain Ugonde river (with tributaries Kabeni, Kamansi), and in the introduction he refers to the Temba, 'a large river to the south of his country', which people used to visit to obtain iron tools.

[858] Chilenje is a well-known mountain south of Nkhoma. Kirenge is said to be south of Dsimbiri, which we are told is about 3 days' journey to the south.

[859] A website, known as 'Cheeseburger', which conveniently lists the names and heights of 1054 Malawian mountains shows an Msondole on the other side of the Lake, roughly where Salimini crossed.

[860] The modern Chichewa for 'ambush' is *mbanda*; this spelling is found in the entry Gua.

[861] s. = substantive, i.e. noun; coll. = collective..

[862] This would presumably refer to the track through the Tuma Forest Reserve leading from the Lilongwe valley to Nkhoma.

[863] Benga is, however, marked on the National Atlas of Malawi.

The Name of the Language

Rebmann refers to Salimini's language as 'Kiniassa', which is a Swahili word (the equivalent of Chinyanja 'the Lake language'). We do not know what Salimini called it in his own language; it could well have been 'Kinyanja' or 'Chinyanja', since Salimini apparently regarded his own people, the Ŵakamtunda ('highlanders') as a branch of the Waniassa.[864] In one entry (M'ombo), Salimini distinguishes his own dialect, which he calls Kikamtunda, from Kimaravi, spoken further south, noting that the brachystegia tree which he called *kamphoni* in his own dialect was known as *mombo* in the Kimaravi dialect spoken in Mitawa.

The word Mcheŵa comes in only one entry in the dictionary, where it is said to mean 'innocent man' or 'kind man':

> **Mchewa**, s. (wa) wachewa; ndife wa chewa, si ife dinachida ipso (*ndife ŵacheŵa, si ife tinachita ibzo/izo*), we are innocent, it is not we who have done that; muntu uyu ni mchewa na-mu-onera kifundo (*munthu uyu ndi mcheŵa, ndamuonera chifundo*).[865]

The name 'Cheŵa' was certainly in use at this time, however, although perhaps not yet for this region; in 1831 the Portuguese traveller Gamitto recorded the 'Chévas' as living in a large part of eastern Zambia;[866] and in 1863 Dr Livingstone reported that the 'Machewa' or 'Macheba' were a section of the Manganja living between Kasungu and the Bua.[867]

The Spelling

The entries in the dictionary are amazingly precise about the meanings of the words,[868] seemingly with very few errors,[869] but the spelling is diffi-

---

[864] See the entry Mdunda, in which Rebmann says that the Wakamdunda are 'one of the tribes generally comprised under the name Waniassa'.
[865] 'This man is an Mcheŵa, I have seen his kindness'.
[866] See the map in Marwick (op.cit.). Apparently Gamitto was the first to record the name.
[867] *A Popular Account of Dr. Livingstone's expedition to the Zambesi and its Tributaries and the Discovery of Lakes Shirwa and Nyassa 1858-1864*, chapter 14.
[868] For example, Dsuruguda (*tsulukuta*) 'to rub (only said of the body in washing or oiling)'.
[869] One such error is Ino 'that (at a distance)'; (the correct meaning, 'this', is given in some other entries, such as Chaka). He also mistakes the names for some animals, such as Niumbu (*nyumbu*), which he thinks is a giraffe (in fact it is probably a gnu or wildebeest).

cult for modern readers, since several letters (namely b, d, g, k, s, w, ch, ds, gn, pf, ps) are used for more than one sound. We do not know how much of this confusion is due to Ludwig Krapf's editing, and how much to Rebmann's difficulty in distinguishing the unfamiliar sounds.[870] Some examples are given below. The spellings in bold are those found in the dictionary, those in italic the modern equivalent.

b = *b/p*: bara (*bala*) 'wound', bamenebo (*pamenepo*) 'there'.

ch = *ch/tch*: chaga/chaka (*chaka*) 'year', chenche/tshentshe (*ntchentche*) 'fly'.

d = *d/t*: dia (*dya*) 'to eat', dadu (*tatu*) 'three'. In some words a dot is written over the d.[871]

dh = *d*: ndodho (*ndodo*) 'stick', diso/dhiso (*diso*) 'eye'.[872]

ds = *dz/ts*: dsancha (*dzanja*) 'hand', chodsa (*chotsa*) 'to remove'.

g = *g/k*: gona (*gona*) 'to sleep'; mgadi (*mkati*) 'in the middle'.

gn = *ng'/ny*: gnombe (*ng'ombe*) 'cow', gnienga (*nyenga*) 'to cheat', nieregnesa (*nyerenyesa*) 'to tickle'.

i (after a consonant) = *y*: niama (*nyama*) 'animal'.

j = *j*, but is rarely found, being usually replaced by y: chaje/chaye (*chaje*) 'empty'.

k = *k/kh*: karúru (*kalulu*) 'hare', kasu (*khasu*) 'hoe'.

l = *l/r*: lila/lira/rira (*lira*) 'to cry'. As with d, in some cases a dot is written over the l.[873]

---

[870] Krapf put a note in the dictionary to say that in editing it he had altered the orthography from Lepsius's system to that of Dr. Steere. Among other changes he made was to replace d with a dot under it by ch. The use of 's' for both s and z is particularly puzzling, since both Lepsius and Steere make a clear distinction.

[871] E.g. Dambe '[baobab fruit]', Dambo, Demba, Dodoma, Dogo, Dogoda. Possibly it represents a sound between l and d.

[872] See for example entries Diso, Funda, Ndodani/Nlodani, Nkuiro, Psidirira. D is however much more common than dh.

[873] E.g. Laula/raura 'to be obscene', Lakua, Laga/raga, Lalada..

nch = *ntch/nj*: nchido/chido (*ntchito*) 'work', nchopfu (*njobvu*) 'elephant', mdsinche/mdsinge (*mtsinje*) 'river'.

o, u (after a consonant) = *w*: indsoa/insoa (*inswa*) 'termites', chingue (*chingwe*) 'string or small rope'.

p = *ph*: para (*phala*) 'food made from flour and water'.

pf = *pf/bv*: pfuba (*pfupa*) 'bone', pfara (*bvala*) 'to put on, wear'.

ps = *ps/bz*: psa (*psa*) 'to be burnt', psala/psara (*bzala*) 'to plant'.

r = *l/r*: Rironkue (*Lilongwe*) 'name of a river', rero (*lero*) 'today'.

s = *s/z*: sinta (*sintha*) 'to exchange', sanga (*zanga*) 'my (pl.)'.

t = *th*: tandisa (*thandiza*) 'to help'.

tsh = *tch*: tshera (*tchera*) 'to set (a trap) for'.

v = *v/ŵ*: vipsera (*vipsera*) 'scars', riviro/liviro (*liŵiro*) 'speed'; but v is usually replaced by *bv* (spelled **pf**).

w = *w/ŵ*, watu (*wathu*) 'our', wantu (*ŵanthu*) 'people'.[874]

y = *y*: yake 'his'.

z (rarely written) = *z*: muesi/muezi (*mwezi*) 'moon'.

Occasionally Rebmann writes accents over the vowels, e.g. ō, ū etc for long o, u, e.g. bōra/boora (*boola*) 'to bore', ĭ, ŭ for short i, u, e.g. dĭa (*dya*) 'to eat', é, ú etc. for an accented vowel, e.g. edsémŭra (*yetsemula*) 'to sneeze'. But the accents are not consistently used, and do not seem to correspond to the tonal accents of Chichewa; e.g. Rumbádsi (modern Lúmbadzi) 'name of a river'.[875]

---

[874] The continuant sound ŵ is generally pronounced (and written) the same as w in modern Chichewa.

[875] See the entry kibára (*chipala*) 'a smithery', in which he claims that the accent changes to m'kíbăla when m' is added; although *chipala*, being toneless, has no accent.

Grammatical Features

Salimini's Chichewa differed in several ways from modern Chichewa. Here are some of those differences:

1) The prefix chi- is generally, but not always, written ki- in the dictionary: chiko/kiko (*chiko*) 'calabash', kibande (*chipande*) 'a ladle', kidsa (*chitsa*) 'the stump of a tree', chida (*chida*) 'a weapon', chaka kino (*chaka chino*) 'this year'. (In the entry Kigamu we find: 'see *chigamu*, of which is is only a different pronunciation.') According to Rebmann's translations, ki-/chi- nouns were often diminutive, e.g. kignoma (*ching'oma*) 'a small drum', chigo (*chigo*) 'a small log', which is not always the case today.[876]
2) The plural of chi-/ki- nouns can be bzi- (spelled psi-), bvi- (spelled pfi-) or vi-, not zi- as in modern Chichewa; e.g. pfiko/viko/psiko (*bviko/viko/bziko*) 'calabashes', pfintu pfidadu (*bvinthu bvitatu*) 'three things', vipsera (*vipsera*) 'scars', psida (*bzida*) 'weapons', psaga psiwiri (*bzaka bziŵiri*) 'two years'.
3) Nouns of type *munthu* 'man' and *galu* 'dog' (classes 1 and 1a) have plural ŵa- (spelled wa-) instead of a-, for both polysyllabic and monosyllabic roots: wantu wawiri (*ŵanthu ŵaŵiri*) 'two men', wagaru (*ŵagalu*) 'dogs'.
4) Ka- class nouns have plural tu- (spelled du-) instead of ti-: kambéni aka (*kampeni aka*) 'this small knife', pl. dumibeni udu (*tumipeni utu*) 'these small knives', dumibeni duanga (*tumipeni twanga*) 'my small knives'.
5) Bu- class concords (now obsolete) were still in use: buado buanga (*bwato bwanga*) 'my boat', ubuána ubu (*ubwana ubu*) 'this childishness', ufa buanga/ufa wanga 'my flour', udsi bonse (*utsi bonse*) 'all the smoke'.
6) Ma- class nouns usually had the concord ya- (as in Swahili) instead of a-: masiku yonse 'all days, always', maroyanga (*malo yanga*) 'my sleeping place', maere yake ya-ni-sungusa (*maere yake yandizunguza*) 'his tricks bewilder me'; but with the Present or Past tense the concord is a-, as in modern Chichewa: madsi alimo anata? (*madzi alimo anatha?*) 'is there still water (or) is it finished?'. With numbers it seems that this class could have any of the concords ma-, a- or ya-: masira masano (*mazira asanu*) 'five eggs', mapada airi/mairi (*mapata aŵiri*) 'two roots', yawili (*yaŵiri*) 'two'.[877]

---

[876] Other examples: kidsuba (*chinsupa*) 'a small gourd-bottle', kigunda (*chigunda*) 'small garden', kigudhu (*chigudu*) 'small piece of cloth', kidambo (*chitambo*) 'small cloud', kibuma (*chibuma*) 'small lump of earth or clay', kibukudu (*chipukutu*) 'small bundle of anything'. In modern Chichewa *chigunda*, *chigudu*, *chibuma* and *chipukutu* are diminutive, but not *chitambo* or *chinsupa*.

[877] See the entries Alimo, Mabasa, Mabira, Madhenda, Maere, Mamina, Mankaka, Mamba, Mano, Maro, Maronda, Marungo, Masiku, Nunka, Pada, Yaba, Yabo, Yawili.

Appendix I: Salimini's Chichewa

7) The Future tense (both remote and near) was -ta- (spelled da) as in Swahili, not the modern Chichewa -dza-: adakudsa mawa (*atakudza mawâ*)[878] 'he will come tomorrow', muomba ada-i-ta dsaruyanga lero (*muomba ataitha nsalu yanga lero*) 'the weaver will finish my cloth today', chaka cha mawa ndabanga ulendo (*chaka cha mawâ n'tapanga ulendo*) 'next year I shall make a journey'.[879]

8) In the Past Simple tense, for which -na- and -da- are used more or less interchangeably in modern Chichewa, there is a clear distinction: -na- generally refers to today or a very recent time, e.g. ina pfumbidsa mpfura rero (*inabvumbitsa mvula lero*) 'it rained heavily today', madsi ana dera (*madzi anatera*) 'the water has subsided', kúdia dinádia (*kudya tinádya*) 'as to eating, we have eaten'. The -na- tense often seems to be equivalent to a Perfect tense, but there is a slight difference: niama i yapvunda (*nyami iyi yabvunda*) 'this meat smells' but: niama i inapvunda (*nyama iyi inabvunda*) 'it smells (said when actually decomposed)'.[880]

9) -da- (spelled da or dha) on the other hand refers to the remote past (yesterday or earlier): dsuro didabagana (*dzulo tidapangana*) 'we agreed yesterday'; nchira uda-i-bida kamodsi muona udhodhoma dhodhoma? (*njira udaipita kamodzi muona udodomadodoma*) 'have you passed this way (only) once, as you keep hesitating so much?', Chiuda adha-m-lenga nkuiro kode kode anadsera mu buáro (*Chiuta adamlenga ngwiro, khotekhote anadzera mu bwalo*) 'God created him entire, the crooked came from without (by an injury)'.[881]

10) Other tenses found in the dictionary, but less commonly, are the Imperfect with -ma-: nimadenga nkawa (*ndimatenga nkhawâ*) 'I was afraid';[882] 'would have' with -kada-: saka dadere aba ku lákua kua dsiku limodsi (*sakadatere apa kulakwa kwa tsiku limodzi*) 'he would not have behaved thus to one who was faulty just once';[883] 'if/when' with -ka-: ukabuera (*ukabwera*) 'when you return';[884] and -ki- to mean 'if I had': ine ni-

---

[878] It seems that -ku- is sometimes added if the verb is monosyllabic: a-ta-ku-dza.
[879] See the entries Amba, Banga, Dandara, Dsa, Eda, Kinchenche, Ni, Rera, Ta, Ulendo or further examples.
[880] See the entries Amba, Bo gona, Burumuka, Dera III, Dsansa, Dsirisa, Mansa mansa, Mbango, Pfumbidsa, Pfunda, Psa etc. In modern Chichewa, the Recent Past tense with -na- implies that a subsequent action occurred: *nyama inavúnda* = 'the meat got rotten (so I threw it out)'. It is not clear if this is also true of Salimini's Chichewa.
[881] See the entries Amba, Du, Fungo, Kamodsi, M'lomoe, Mlongo, M'mangidue, Muona, Nkuiro, Pfundo I, Ukuadi.
[882] See entries Denga, Pŏa.
[883] See entries Kale, Gururu.
[884] Entry Uina.

kidsiwa, sikapfomerera (modern Chichewa: *ine ndikadadziwa, sikadavomerera*) 'if I had known it, I should not have assented'.[885]

11) The sounds pf- and bv- generally still kept their p and v: pfungo (*fungo*) 'a smell', nchopfu (*njovu*) 'elephant'. We also have (n)ts- in n'dsomba (*nsomba*) 'fish', dsúngui (*nsungwi*) 'bamboo' etc.

12) Verbs which begin with y- in modern Chichewa generally have no y- except at the beginning of a sentence, e.g. amba (*yamba*) 'to begin', ankula (*yankhula*) 'to speak', edsémŭra (*yetsemula*) 'to sneeze', enda/yenda (*yenda*) 'to go (walk)'. In a couple, w- can be dropped: erama/werama (*werama*) 'to stoop', erenga/werenga (*werenga*) 'to count'. Similarly aba (*apa*) 'here' alternates with yaba (*yapa*).

13) 'Is' and 'I' are ni rather than ndi in Salimini's Chichewa: e.g. ni mbale wanga (*ndi mbale wanga*), 'he is my brother'; nchoka ana-ni-ruma (*njoka inandiluma*) 'a snake bit me'; but ndiye, ndine etc. retain their d.

14) 'And/with' is usually na, not ndí as in modern Chichewa, e.g. isano na idadu (*isanu ndi itatu*) 'five and three'; although Rebmann points out that 'ni' was sometimes used for 'na'.[886]

15) Words which end in -be/-je/-ja in modern Chichewa such as *chabe/chaje* 'empty', *palibe* 'there is not', *ndilibe* 'I do not have', *paja* 'there', *uja* 'that man', *uje* 'so-and-so' in the dictionary become chaye/chaje, paliye, ndiliye, paya, uya/uja, uye/uje etc.; that is, they are usually written with y (sometimes j). Possibly this is merely a feature of Rebmann or Krapf's spelling rather than the actual pronunciation.[887]

16) Words for certain animals of the I-Zi- class could optionally take the concords of class 1 in the singular (as in Swahili), e.g. gnombe wa mkasi (*ng'ombe wamkazi*) 'a (female) cow', mbusi wanga (*mbuzi wanga*) 'my goat', kosa mmodsi (*nkhosa mmodzi*) 'one sheep'. In modern Chichewa only concords of the I-Zi- class can be used (i.e. *yaikazi, yanga, imodzi*).

17) The prefix bvo- (written pfo-) was used to make adverbs where modern Chichewa generally uses mo-: pfodele (*bvotere*) 'thus', pfokoma (*bvokoma*) 'well, orderly'.[888]

18) There are some irregular plurals which are not in use today, e.g. mako (*maiko*) 'countries', madu (*matu*, i.e. *makutu*) 'ears', marambo (*madambo*) 'meadowy grounds', (mi)gniendo (*miyendo*) 'feet'.

---

[885] See the entry Pfomera. Modern Chichewa sometimes uses -chi- in this meaning: *pachipanda ine* 'had it not been for me'.
[886] See the entry Ni.
[887] The sound 'j', unaccompanied by n, is rare even in modern Chichewa, except in the final syllable of words.
[888] One such adverb used today is *dzolimba* 'hard', using the Southern Region dzo- for bvo-.

19) kuna is used for modern kuli 'there is/are': kuna miombo ya nkani ku Midawa (*kuna miombo yankhani ku Mitawa*) 'there are numerous brachystegia trees in Mitawa'.[889]

20) ana (kina etc.) are used for modern *ali ndi* (*chili ndi*): kiko kina chea (*chikho china cheya*) 'the gourd has hair'.[890]

Vocabulary

With some 30 or so words on each page, Rebmann's dictionary contains over 5000 entries, and it is a treasure house of words which are now becoming rare or obsolete. Very few of the words appear to be borrowed from other languages. The following, however, seem to come from Portuguese:

Barasugu or **mbarasugu**, s. (wa) (pl. wabarasugu) A bottle; barasugu uyu, this bottle; wabarasugu awa, these bottles; kisiwo cha m-barasugu, the stopper of a bottle.[891]

Fódia,[892] s. (wa) Tobacco, but which never smoked, but only taken as snuff. The expression for both smoking and taking snuff is however one and the same, viz. ku góga (*kukoka*),[893] because each is a kind of drawing; ku goga fodia (*kukoka fodya*), to take snuff, but ku goga chamba is "to smoke hemp"; Fódia wa muisi (*fodya wamwisi*), green or unripe tobacco; pande za fodia (*mphande za fodya*), the small round leaves of tobacco, just shooting forth (from their resemblance to a kind of thin, round shells worn as ornaments by the natives.)

Kama,[894] s. (wa) (no pl.) A native sleeping place made of sticks, which rest on little forked posts, fixed into the ground. The sticks are made of a tree called dsoyo (*tsoyo*) (Kis. kilalo cha mtu). kama wa dsinta dsinta (*kama wa tsinthatsintha*).[895]

---

[889] See entries M'ombo, Mdsisi, Msasa, etc.
[890] See entries Chea, Kabeifa, Mimbu, M'pada, Usiwa, Wanche etc.
[891] Modern Chichewa *balasuku* 'fragment of broken glass'. Scott & Hetherwick record the word as *palasuku*, meaning 'bottle'. Presumably ultimately from Portuguese *frasco* 'bottle, flask'.
[892] From Portuguese *folha* 'leaf'.
[893] *kukoka* 'to draw'; *fodya wamuwisi* 'green tobacco'; Scott-Hetherwick define *mphande* as 'a species of shell of a round disc shape, attached to a necklace and worn as an ornament'.
[894] Portuguese *cama* 'bed'.
[895] *Tsoyo* is *Vernonia amygdalina* 'tree vernonia' . In the entry (N')dsinta n'dsinta, Rebmann explains *tsinthatsintha* as meaning 'unequal (one stick longer than another)'.

Kàba, s. (wa) (pl. wakàba) a scarlet cloth (worn by royalty only).[896]

Mbadada,[897] s. (ya) (pl. id., with sa). The sweet potato (Kis. kiasi pl. viasi). Prov. muana wa m-pfuru ni mbadada, ukongóra (contr. from uka ongora), watshora (*mwana wa mfulu ndi mbatata, ukaongola wathyola*), meaning: the son of a free man does not (easily) allow himself to be corrected or blamed.

The inclusion of the word dogo (*doko*) 'a landing place' proves that this word does not come from the English 'dock' as is sometimes assumed.[898] Another interesting word is the word for 'maize' (or 'Indian corn', as Rebmann calls it), which is *pamanga* rather than *chimanga*. Surprisingly, despite starting with pa-, it takes the concord cha-:[899]

Bamanga (s. pl. id.) Indian corn (Kis. mahindi); bamanga changa (*pamanga changa*)[900] 'my Indian corn'. One would expect banga (*panga*). Bamanga cha kucha (*pamanga cha kucha*), Indian corn of to ripe, i.e. Indian corn which is ripe.

Cultural Information

Rebmann's dictionary is not only of interest for those studying the Chichewa language as it was spoken in the 1840s, but also is a mine of fascinating information about life in Malawi at that time. Here are some examples:

Asamidsa (*yasamitsa*) (v.int.) to open (the mouth) very wide (as for instance is required for widening the space between the two front-teeth, which is their custom).

Chanzi, n. (cha) (pl. psansi (*bzanzi*)). The name of a small tree, with which they brush the walls and roofs of their cottages, the scent keeping off mosquitoes.[901]

---

[896] Portuguese *capa* 'a cape'.
[897] Portuguese *batata* 'potato'. The proverb means literally, 'The son of a free man is a sweet potato, if you straighten him, you have broken him.'
[898] E.g. the dictionary *Mtanthauziramawu wa Chinyanja* s.v. doko.
[899] President Kamuzu Banda, whose Kasungu dialect was recorded in Chicago by Mark Hannah Watkins in the 1930s, also used *pamanga*, but with the concord vya-. See Watkins, M. H. (1937). 'A grammar of Chichewa: a Bantu language of British Central Africa', *Language*, vol. 13, No. 2; pages 74, 92, 134.
[900] By a misprint, 'danga' is written for 'changa', but see the entries Kafumbu, (M-)pada, Ramba, where the phrase is repeated.
[901] Chanzi is *Lippia Javanica* or *Clematis uhehensis*.

Edsémŭra (*yetsemula*) (v.n.) to sneeze. kuatu muntu aka edsemura-sudi atshure pfugorake dikose ku-m-dsiwa (*kwathu munthu akayetsemula kuti atchule pfuko lake tikhoze kumdziŵa*), with us, when one sneezes, he must name his tribe, that we know him. The reason for this custom is their aversion to a man being married to a woman of his own tribe. **Kadse** or **nkădse** (*nkhadze*), s. (ya, pl. id.) a kind of tree, used for planting live-hedges round their villages (Kis. utúba); – there are different kinds, such as may be transplanted with the roots, and more commonly such as are planted by slips.[902]

Kakisi (*kachisi*), s. (wa) (pl. wakakisi), a very diminutive temple (too small for a man to enter) at which they pray to the Chiuda (*Chiuta*) and Wazimu, to perform their superstitious practices. It is erected at the entrances of their towns and villages.

Kisambo, name of a country 1½ days' journey to the S. of Mpande. The people of Kisambo have a peculiar art in shooting arrows which consists in an arrow repeatedly touching the ground and leaping further (see tadsa). They are therefore frequently hired by different chiefs in war. (Wakisambo wadsiwa ku bonia mipfiyao ku omba n-tadsa (*Ŵachisambo ŵadziŵa kuponya mibvi yawo kuomba nthadza*)).[903]

Mānda, s. (ya) pl. (contract. from maanda); 1) tokens of mourning for a deceased relative, exhibited by not shaving the head, or bathing the body, nor wearing any ornaments; the wife also separates from her husband. This is continued till the deceased has been paid for, from the belief, that all who die in the prime of life, have been bewitched It is in childhood only and age that death is considered natural, and in such cases the show of mourning is only of short duration. – 2) ku manda, to the grave (= Kis. ku simu) usaone lidsiro, kuna manda kuao (*usaone litsiro, kuna manda kwawo*), do not see dirt (do not say, they are dirty or uncleanly) there is mourning with them (they are in mourning).

Mbedede (*mbetete*), s. (ya, pl. with sa), a sort of trumpet (made of the tree called mbuabua (*mbwabwa*)).[904]

---

[902] *Euphorbia tirucalli*. Livingstone explains: 'the village of Chitimba ... like all other Manganja villages, is surrounded by an impenetrable hedge of poisonous euphorbia. This tree casts a deep shade, which would render it difficult for bowmen to take aim at the villagers inside. The grass does not grow beneath it, and this may be the reason why it is so universally used, for when dry the grass would readily convey fire to the huts inside; moreover, the hedge acts as a fender to all flying sparks (*Expedition to the Zambesi*, ch. 3). – The tree is unusual in having green twigs instead of leaves. It is not much found in Malawi these days.
[903] 'the people of Chisambo know how to shoot their arrows so that they bounce'.
[904] The *mbwabwa* is the octopus cabbage tree, *Cussonia arborea*.

Meidaniro (*meitaniro*) (contract. from maidaniro, and derived from "ku idana (*kuitana*)[905]"), s. (ya) the expressed but only pretended reason for calling anyone; e.g. the woman in calling for her husband will say: madsi yafunda (*madzi yafunda*), the water is warm (come and bathe), while the true reason may be any thing else (see at marunga).

M'lega (or **mrega**) (*mdeka, mleka*), (wa) (pl. mi-), lit. a yielding, a leaving; 1) The track made by rats and other animals in the thatching of a cottage and in the standing grass or reeds; – 2) a small furrow cut with a hoe; ku lima mileka or mileka mileka, is to cut small furrows in a piece of ground to be cultivated, which run parallel to each other and divide the place into narrow strips, each of which is taken up by a different person to finish it. This way of agriculture seems to be peculiar to the Waniassa.

Mpiga (*mphika*), s. (wa) (pl. mi-), a small pot (for cooking meat only). The kali (*nkhali*) is used for the Dsima (*nsima*), and is therefore larger.

Mbódo (*mpoto*) s. (wa) the north; ku mbódo, at or towards the North. The ku with the m is pronounced as one syllable, kumbodo (Kis. kibuda); mpfura ya mbodo inapfundira (*mvula ya mpoto inabvundira*), a rain from the north is warm. Pakumbodo, the of the north, the northern people. Of the Wakamdunda N. of Mpande, Salimini said that they never fight, going without bows and arrows, while their spears are only the ornamental ones of women, called msama. Their country being lower and warmer, they raise much cotton (for which it is too cold with the Wakamdunda); they also weave their own clothes, and are in the habit of washing them. Usa-kugnienge mbodo kuliye mpfura ya mpfumbi (*usakunyenge mpoto kulibe mvula ya mvumbi*), let the north not deceive you, there will be no heavy rain (because in this country rain from the north is soon over and never cold).

M'maravi (*Mmaraŵi*), s. (pl. wa-), the name given by the tribes E. of the Niassa to those in the west, including not only the Wamaravi proper but also the Wakamdunda (*Ŵakamtunda*).

Msámiro (*mtsamiro*), s (wa) (pl. mi-), a wooden pillow (similar to those used in Egypt); msámiro ni mdengo wa-u-sema, wa ku samirira (*mtsamiro ndi mtengo ŵausema, wa kusamirira*), lit. the msamiro is a tree which they hew (for) of to recline on.

Msasa, s. (wa) (pl. mi-), a booth hastily put up of branches and grass. This is peculiar to the Wavisa (*Ŵaŵisa*), who, when coming for trade in large num-

---

[905] *Kuitana* 'to summon, or call'.

bers, are said never to sleep in other people's houses. kuna miganda yoo churuka ku msasa (*kuna mikanda yochuluka ku msasa*).⁹⁰⁶

Ngésa, s. (ya) (pl. sa), small round cakes, procured by the Waniassa from the Portuguese and valued for the stimulant properties ascribed to them.

Niada (*nyata*), s. a clammy place, i.e. a place where the earth is clammy. Bamanga cha niada (*pamanga cha nyata*), Indian corn of a clammy soil (i.e. grown in a clammy soil; also: bamanga cha mniada of in); yaba ni baniada, dichide n-tuntu, dikogere chamba. Wabusa wakoga chamba ku niada (*apa ndi panyata, tichite nthunthu, tikokere chamba; ŵabusa ŵakoka chamba ku nyata*).⁹⁰⁷ Boys who tend cattle make a hole in the mud to smoke hemp, because they are not allowed a proper pipe.

Niara (*nyala*) (v.n.) to exercise shame (by keeping out of sight) i.e. sons and daughters in law will strictly avoid being seen by their fathers and mothers in law and vice versa.

Nsembe, s. (pl. id) (ya, sa) offerings, but only consisting in flour mixed with water (Kis. ku gonia koma, sadaka), put on the ground near the "gagisi" (*kachisi*) for the "wazimu",⁹⁰⁸ in order to procure their favour and assisance. This is done before they go into battle or set out on a journey, and on behalf of sick relatives. The workman also in ivory brings this offering that he may be successful in cutting his arm-rings (makosa (*makoza*)).

Psidi psidi (*psitipsiti*), s. (uyu) (pl. wa-), an apparition, a ghost, being different from the kiwanda, kidsodókua and kisúkŭa (*chiŵanda, chidzodokwa,*

---

⁹⁰⁶ 'there are numerous beads in the hut'. – Dr Livingstone met the Babisa at various points in his travels: 'We meet with these keen traders everywhere. They are easily known by a line of horizontal cicatrices, each half an inch long, down the middle of the forehead and chin. They often wear the hair collected in a mass on the upper and back part of the head, while it is all shaven off the forehead and temples. The Babisa and Waiau or Ajawa heads have more of the round bullet-shape than those of the Manganja, indicating a marked difference in character; the former people being great traders and travellers, the latter being attached to home and agriculture. The Manganja usually intrust their ivory to the Babisa to be sold at the Coast, and complain that the returns made never come up to the high prices which they hear so much about before it is sent. In fact, by the time the Babisa return, the expenses of the journey, in which they often spend a month or two at a place where food abounds, usually eat up all the profits.' (*A Popular Account of Dr. Livingstone's Expedition to the Zambesi and its Tributaries and the Discovery of Lakes Shirwa and Nyassa 1858-1864*, chapter 14.)

⁹⁰⁷ 'maize of (in) clammy soil; here is a damp place, let's gather things together, and smoke chamba; the herd-boys smoke chamba in a damp place'.

⁹⁰⁸ *kachisi* 'hut for offerings', *ŵazimu* (*azimu*) 'spirits'.

chisukwa), which are only seen at a distance, while the psidipsidi pays visits in their houses, and looking like a common man, is only known to be a ghost by his not speaking nor accepting of any food. They also believe, that in one town he appears as a man, and in the next as woman. He is prognostic of epidemics.

Sámbisa (*sambiza*) (v.a.) to let or make swim (Kis. ogolésa, osha), to take across by swimming. When the rivers are swollen and boats become useless from the force of the current, small huts are constructed at fording places by men expert in swimming, where they station themselves to help over those who cannot swim; mda-m-ta ku-mu-sámbisa? (*mutamtha kumusambiza?*) can you 'swim' him over?

One surprising omission from the dictionary is that although there are words describing warfare, weapons, food, agriculture, trade, travel, relationship terms, domestic utensils, cooking, burial practices, religion, trees, animals, social customs, superstitions, musical instruments, and numerous other features of African life, there is no reference at all to the Cheŵa's famous masked dancers (*gulewamkulu*), apart from the following solitary entry:

Gúre (*gule*), s. name of a kind of play.

The most likely explanation for this is that Salimini was himself an initiate, and because of the traditional vow of silence he completely omitted to tell Rebmann about this important aspect of Cheŵa culture.

Appendix I: Salimini's Chichewa

A slave caravan in East Africa, on its way to the coast and the slave markets (S. Paas).

Title page of Rebmann's Kiniassa Dictionary, St. Chrischona print, 1877.

Appendix II:
A history of Chichewa lexicography[909]

Steven Paas

Two names, one language

The English language has acquired an important position in Central African societies. Nevertheless, vernacular languages have remained indispensable vehicles of communication. This is also true for Chichewa/Chinyanja. The combination of the words Chichewa and Chinyanja indicates that I look upon the two as basically the same language, although I do not underestimate differences and preferences. The designation refers to a family of very related language groups or dialects, of which Malawi is the most important location. Chichewa/Chinyanja is also spoken in Mozambique, especially in the provinces of Tete and Niassa, in Zambia, especially in the Eastern Province[910], as well as in Zimbabwe where, according to some estimates, it ranks as the third most widely used local language, after Shona and Ndebele.[911] The language is also used in countries like South Africa and Botswana that have received many immigrants who speak one or more of its strands.

There is an ongoing debate on the question whether the name of the language should be Chinyanja or Chichewa. Sometimes the discussion becomes bitter, especially among those who have condemned the decision of the Malawi Congress Party under Kamuzu Banda of 1968 to replace the name Chinyanja by Chichewa. Which one, Chichewa or Chinyanja, is the main language, and which one is the minor dialect? I have tried to dodge the question by using the double-name Chichewa/Chinyanja.

---

[909] This is a revision of the article appended to the first and second editions of the Chichewa/Chinyanja-English and English-Chichewa/Chinyanja Dictionary, published in 2009 and 2010.

[910] M.G. Marwick, 'History and Tradition in East Central Africa through the Eyes of the Northern Rhodesian Cewa', in: *Journal of African History*, IV, 3, 1963, p. 375, distinguishes in Zambia's Eastern Province three groups of Chewa, including Chipeta and Zimba, (a) the Southern Chewa, (b) the Northern Chewa, (c) the Chewa in Lundazi. They are all in various degrees loyal to paramount Chief Undi, who resides in Mozambique.

[911] Sam Mchombo, 'Chichewa: Backgound and History', http://www.humnet.ucla.edu/humnet/aflang/chichewa/background.html

Those who defend the ascendancy of the name Chinyanja over Chichewa say that as Chinyanja the language had been known in all its territories long before the arrival of the missionaries and of colonial power. They claim that the Chewa, when the Portuguese first encountered them in Mozambique, had adopted the label of Nyanja and that for a related group they used the label Mang'anja, which basically has the same meaning, people of the Lake. Most adherents of this thought say that Chinyanja and Chimang'anja together with Chichewa are the same language. Their view is that Chinyanja is the main language and that those who retained the names Chichewa represented a dialectical variant of the Chinyanja. They like to refer to David Livingstone, who on his journey of 1863 passed through the area of 'the Machewa or Macheba'. In Livingstone's observation the Chewa were a small subtribe inhabiting a district starting south of Kasungu and extending as far as the river Bua.[912] This was also Watkins' observation, the Chewa 'are a division of the Nyanja group', Chichewa is 'only a variant' of Chinyanja. Watkins in his Chichewa Grammar described it as a minority language, 'representative of that spoken at Kasungu (postoffice)'. All information for his grammar Watkins 'obtained from Kamuzu Banda, a native Chewa, while he was in attendance at the University of Chicago from 1930 to 1932'.[913] Much later, as Malawi's first President, Banda would make Chichewa the national language of Malawi. In the colonial era the official name for the language was Chinyanja, and today many non-Chewa have continued to prefer or demand it. Mchombo shows that the primary position of Chinyanja in comparison to Chichewa derives support from scholars who classified the Bantu languages. They classify Chinyanja as the main language, whereas they do not mention Chichewa or just define it as one of its dialects.[914]

---

[912] 'We spent the first night, after leaving the slave route, at the village of Nkoma, among a section of Mang'anja, called Machewa, or Macheba, whose district extends to the Bua' ('A Popular Account of Dr Livingstone's Expedition to the Zambesi and its Tributaries', 1865, ch. 14).

[913] Mark Hanna Watkins, *A Grammar of Chichewa: A Bantu Language of British Central Africa*, University of Pennsylvania, Philadelphia: Linguistic Society of America, 1937, p. 5, 7.

[914] Mchombo, 'Chichewa: Background and History', mentions Greenberg (1966) who is silent on Chichewa, and Guthrie (1948), who identifies it as 'the second dialect of the main language'. Watkins, *A Grammar of Chichewa*, p. 5, refers to the conclusion of J Torrend, *A comparative Grammar of the South African Bantu languages*, London, 1891, p. xix, who says that Chichewa is a variant of Chinyanja, found especially in 'Kasungu, Dowa and Lilongwe Districts'.

Appendix II: A history of Chichewa lexicography

The defenders of the primacy of the name Chichewa claim that the name Chewa was already in use before the Portuguese explorers and travellers first touched Malawi. Marwick (in 1963) says that the Portuguese army officer Gamitto in 1832 was the first to record the name.[915] He realises that that the name Chinyanja also existed. It was in use by the people who lived close to the Lake, whereas the name Chichewa belonged to those who lived at a considerable distance from the Lake. He thinks that before 1832 Chinyanja speaking peoples start to call themselves Chewa.[916] In Marwick's observation the name Chinyanja represented a minority group. Yet it became the most important designation for the language after the arrival of the missionaries in 1875. The Chichewa is 'the majority dialect or group of dialects, spoken by about ... two-thirds of the so-called Nyanja speakers'.[917] He says that if the Chinyanja or Lake variant not were first recorded and standardised by the missionaries, the names Chichewa or Chimalawi might have been a more appropriate designation for the language as a whole.[918] In this line of thinking, the decision by the MCP Convention in 1968 to change the official name of the language was in agreement to the nation's independence. Malawi's most important vernacular language became the national language, and it was renamed Chichewa, thus dethroning the name given by missionaries and colonizers. The year 1994 marked the down-fall of the Banda regime, and the beginning of democratic rule in Malawi. This also meant the end of the monopoly position for Chichewa as the only national language. The name Chichewa remained, but it has to share its status with the other vernacular languages of Malawi.

For me the problem of names became urgent in the course of my lexicographical activity directed at the compilation of a dictionary. Is it possible to find a decisive answer to the question which name should be in a

---

[915] Marwick, 1963, p. 378 says, 'the name Chewa (in the form Chévas) does not appear in the records until 1831-1832', and on p. 383, he says that Gamitto in 1831-1832 applied the name Maraves (Malawi) to the people south of the Chambwe stream, and those north of that stream he called Chévas (Chewa), 'this being the earliest recorded reference to this name'. M.G. Marwick, 'An Ethnographic Classic brought to light', in: *African Journal of the International African Institute*, vol. 34, No. 1 (January 1964), p. 49, said the Zimba and Chipeta were branches of the Chewa.

[916] Marwick, 1963, p. 375.

[917] Marwick, 1963, p. 375, The Achewa, to who he also counts the Zimba and the Chipeta, 'are found not only in the Eastern Province of Northern Rhodesia [14%], but also in the Central Province of Nyasaland [77%], and the northern part of the indendencia of Tete in the district of Manica and Sofala of Mozambique [9%]'.

[918] Marwick, 1963, p. 377. Marwick, 1964, p. 50.

primary position on the title page of the dictionary of Malawi's most widely spoken language, Chichewa or Chinyanja? According to Pascal Kishindo it is impossible. The debate 'is interesting but also unresolvable. People have their own entrenched positions. No amount of linguistic evidence can shift people's position'. Apart from the discussion on the history of the two names, Kishindo has noticed that 'Chichewa is the more internationally recognized name'. As to the title of the dictionary, he thinks it is prudent to call it 'Chichewa/Chinyanja Dictionary', especially to accommodate users outside Malawi who know their language only by the name Chinyanja.[919] There are alternatives, e.g. changing the order to Chinyanja/Chichewa, or replacing both names by the designation Chimalawi. The first alternative satisfies those who want to see the rooting out of all remnants of Banda's legacy, but does not offer a fully satisfying scholarly solution. The second alternative was supported by Marwick in the 1960s and is advocated by D.D. Phiri these days.[920] Phiri realises the undeniable fact that Chichewa/Chinyanja practically has become the main vehicle of internal communication in almost every corner of Malawi. The name Chimalawi may sound nice, and could serve a number of positive ends, not in the least national coherence and identity. However, it weakens the unity with Nyanja speakers outside Malawi, and it rouses the anger of Tumbuka, Lhomwe and Yao protagonists who feel their linguistic position in Malawi is offended by it.

My choice for the combined designation Chichewa/Chinyanja, in that order, is purely practical or pragmatic. Whether we like it or not, since the 1970s the world has come to know the language in the first place by the name Chichewa. On the internet 'Chichewa' appears more often than 'Chinyanja'. The order of the two words does not express my personal preference, but is simply inspired by convenience and the reality of the political situation. Let us look at the Chichewa/Chinyanja language as a family of dialectical variants. These variants make a language stronger, if their contribution to the richness of the language is recognised.

---

[919] Pascal Kishindo, Director of the Centre for Language Studies of the University of Malawi, 16 February 2011.
[920] On the competition between the names Chinyanja and Chichewa, D.D. Phiri, in a discussion about the *Constitution* in 2006, suggested that both should be abolished and replaced by the name Chimalawi. Cf.: <www.lawcom.mw/docs/ddphiricomnts.pdf>.

Lingua franca

The family of dialects being the one language of Chichewa/Chinyanja has been dominant in a wide region around the Lake for a long time. Chichewa/Chinyanja has gained importance and strength by developments in its written and oral use, and because an increasing number of its speakers have come to discover and emphasize their common linguistic heritage and practice. Chichewa/Chinyanja has become an intermediary language, a *lingua franca*, for all the ethnic groups in Malawi.[921] Probably about 90% of the Tonga, Tumbuka, Lhomwe, and Yao people in the urban settings in Southern Malawi speak Chichewa/Chinyanja 'most of the time'.[922] Even in the remote regions of Malawi, where Chichewa/Chinyanja is not the traditional language, it gradually has become more popular and more generally used. Moreover, Chichewa/Chinyanja is an important means of communication between people outside Malawi. Millions of inhabitants of Zambia, Zimbabwe, Mozambique, Botswana, and South Africa use it as their first or second language in daily life. At least 15 million people use the language in the family, at school, in church, at work, in relationship with governments, with NGO's, and with the mass media. Probably it has become the most important language of Central Africa, at least if we go by the words of 19th-century missionary Robert Laws, who defined the Chinyanja language as 'one of the most useful and, when its dialects are included, one of the most widely-spoken of African languages'.[923]

Another proof of the vitality of Chichewa/Chinyanja is the apparent process of adopting words from other languages, either African or Western. Modern speakers of Chichewa/Chinyanja are not trying to invent the wheel again. More than ever they feel free to select words from Tumbuka, Lhomwe, Yao, Ngoni, Sena, Swahili, English, Portuguese, Afrikaans and other languages that seem fit to be used in fields where Chiche-

---

[921] Robert Laws had this position for the Chinyanja in mind, in his *Reminiscences of Livingstonia*, Edinburgh, 1934, p. 127: 'he thought that Nyanja would be the best *lingua franca* for the wole Lake District' (Hamish McIntosh, *Robert Laws: Servant of Africa*, Carberry: Handsel/Blantyre: Central Africana, 1993, p. 81).

[922] P.J. Kishindo, 'Language and Miscegenation', in: *The Lamp,* March-April 2003, p. 24-25.

[923] Robert Laws, *An English-Nyanja Dictionary: Of The Nyanja Language Spoken In British Central Africa*, Published for the Livingstonia Mission of the Free Church of Scotland, in Edinburgh, by James Thin, Publisher to the University of Edinburgh, 1894, p. vi. The book has 242 pages (xi, 231). In June 2008 Kessinger published a facsimile reprint, ISBN-10: 1436770513, ISBN-13: 978-1436770514 [facsimile reprint in 2009 by BiblioLife, Charleston: <www.bibliogrande.com>].

wa/Chinyanja still has not coined its own vocabulary. This phenomenon of the absorption of loan-words shows a remarkable ability to adapt to new situations. Parallel to this and mixed with it we see how the Chichewa/Chinyanja invents its own terms and definitions in its encounter with modernity. These are signs of adulthood. The Chichewa/Chinyanja language is on its way to overcoming the limitations of ruralism, tribalism, racism and nationalism. It has grown up to play its role in the modern world.

Crisis of communication

In all aspects of life, users of Chichewa/Chinyanja experience a process of change and learning. There is a hunger for information. However, information is often only available in foreign languages, especially English. Yet one should realise that the knowledge of English has remained restricted to a certain level and to a part of the population. These facts have caused a crisis of communication. Speakers of vernacular languages, who do not know English or are not good enough at it, fail to grasp or misunderstand the particularities of modern developments that are not presented to them in their own language. Real understanding of the important things of life requires translating the information into a tongue that is familiar to one's own culture and psychology. In general, that is one's own mother tongue.

In their inevitable encounter with the English language, native users of Chichewa/Chinyanja are being challenged to re-word and re-define English vocabulary in their own language. Malawians need language tools to assist them in this continual meeting between the two cultures and languages. Language tools are also helpful to expatriates. In their contacts with African people, they are frustrated by the same language barriers. In all categories of knowledge and for all kinds of people, there is a necessity of translating information into and from the vernacular languages. This has created a demand for dictionaries, Chichewa/Chinyanja into English (CE) and the other way round (EC).[924]

---

[924] This article deals with the lexicography of Chichewa/Chinyanja and English, which does not deny that there is also a history of Chichewa/Chinyanja dictionaries into and from other languages, e.g.: Missionarios da Companhia de Jesus, *Dicionário cinyanja-português*, Lisboa: Junta de Investigações do Ultramar, 1963 (i-xxv, 1-291 pages),1966 (266 pages); M. Ferreira-Zondagh, *Cinyanja Hulpboekie*, Mkhoma [sic]: Sendingsdrukkery, 1937 [115 pages including a list of vocabulary Nyanja-Afrikaans].

CE Dictionaries

When I first tried to find the roots of Chichewa/Chinyanja lexicography I was helped by Martin Pauw[925] and Jouni Maho.[926] References to the earliest roots, however, I found with Marwick, who points to expeditions from early 17th century by Portuguese explorers into the territory that now is called Malawi. Probably no Chichewa/Chinyanja vocabulary was recorded before the 19th century.[927]

A Portuguese army officer from Tete in Mozambique is probably the first compiler of a Chichewa vocabulary. His name is Antonio Candido Pedroso Gamitto (1806-1866). In the years 1831 and 1832 he made an expedition in Chichewa/Chinyanja speaking Africa. Commander of the expedition was Major J.M.C. Monteiro, Captain Gamitto was the second in command and the chronicler. They set out from Tete and crossed through Malawi to enter Chipata and Bisa country. On their westward march they visited Kazembe's Capital. Gamitto recorded many ethographical, biological and anthropological details and recorded the language of the people. Gamitto used the Chichewa/Chinyanja vernacular freely in the text and appended two vocabularies to the two volumes of his Diary. The words are recognisable for readers of contemporary Chinyanja/Chichewa.[928] In 1960 an English translation by Ian Cunnison,

---

[925] C.M. Pauw, *Mission and Church in Malawi: The History of the Nkhoma Synod of the Church of Central Africa Presbyterian 1889-1962*, PhD, University of Stellenbosch, 1980. In this study he examined the first stages of developing Chichewa literature of 19th-century and early 20th-century Malawian Church History.

[926] Jouni Filip Maho, 'Bantu Online Bibliography: Electronic Bibliography for African Languages and Linguistics', version of August 8th 2008, http://goto.glocalnet.net/jfmaho/bob.pdf>.

[927] Marwick, 1963, p. 382. In 1616 Gaspar Bocarro passed the Nyasa-Shire basin when he went from Tete to Kilwa on the Indian Ocean coast. If he made a collection of vocabulary, it probably has not survived. Marwick, 1963, p. 382. There is a diary by Manoel Barretto who 'spent many years in the Zambezi basin', and travelled to Malawi in about 1656. Unfortunately it does not contain a vocabulary. Marwick, 1964, p. 47, De Lacerda e Almeida, *The Lands of Cazembe*, London: John Murray for the Royal Geographical Society, 1873. This is a translation of the journal of the expedition by De Lacerda e Almeida in 1798, which after his death was continued by F.J. Pinto [Translated by Richard F. Burton].

[928] Gamitto, Antonio Candido Pedroso, *O Muata Cazembe e os Povos Maraves, Chevas, Muizas, Muembas, Lindas e outros da Africa Austral: Diario da Expedição Portugueza, commandada pelo Major Monteiro e dirigida Aquelle Imperador nos Annos de 1831 e 1832*, redigido pelo Major A.C.P. Gamitto, segundo Commandante da Expedição, com um mapa do Paiz Observado entre Tete e Lunda, Lisboa: Impresa Nacional, 1854 [572 pages]; reprinted in 1937 in two volumes by the Divisão de Publicações e Bi-

was published.[929] Unfortunately the translator omitted the list of vocabulary, 'though in some measure replaced by a glossary'. Marwick added to his article on Gamitto's diary 'a selection of [26] words taken from the first vocabulary'.[930]

Apart from Gamitto's Portuguese-Chichewa list of 1832, and the Chichewa-English vocabulary of Johannes Rebmann in the 1850s, which was printed, probably for the first time in 1877, as the *Dictionary of the Kiniassa Language*,[931] the history of lexicographical collection of Chichewa or Chinyanja vocabulary goes back to at least the period somewhat before 1880. In that year Alexander Riddel, a Presbyterian missionary at Cape Maclear, published his grammar and limited word list.[932] Riddel, who accompanied Robert Laws and his party in 1875, used a hand-written copy of Rebmann's work, and rightly recognised it as a dictionary of Chinyanja. Rebmann's manuscript may have circulated in hand-written versions from about 1855.

For a long time the work of David Clement Ruffelle Scott and Alexander Hetherwick dominated the history of Chinyanja/Chichewa dictionaries. They were both Presbyterian ministers from the Church of Scotland, working for the Blantyre Mission (later to become CCAP Blantyre Synod). Their lexicographical work significantly contributed to the moulding of the Chichewa/Chinyanja language, especially in its written form. Scott started by compiling his *Dictionary of the Mang'anja Language*, representing the variant of Chinyanja that is spoken in South Malawi (parallel to the Chichewa variant that dominates Central Malawi). In 1892 it was published.[933]

---

blioteca, Agència Geral das Colónias [399 and 200 pages]. Gamitto uses the vernacular Chévas or Chewa freely in the text and appends two vocabulary lists.

[929] Antonio Candido Pedroso Gamitto, *King Kazembe and the Marave, Cheva, Bisa, Bemba, Lunda and Other Peoples of Southern Africa: Being a Diary of the Portuguese Expedition to that Potentate in the Years 1831 and 1832*, 2 vols, Lisboa: Junta de Investigação do Ultramar, Estudos de Ciências Politicas e Sociais, nos 42 and 43, 1960 [translation by Ian Cunnison]. Cf. Marwick, 1964, p. 46.

[930] Marwick, 1964, p. 50.

[931] See: chapter 9.

[932] Alexander Riddel, *A Grammar of Chinyanja as Spoken at Lake Nyasa, with Chinyanja-English Vocabulary*, 1880. Cf. McIntosh, *Robert Laws*, p. 36, where we are informed that of the 1880 edition 500 copies were published. Riddel's work was followed, in 1891, by George Henry, *A Grammar of Chinyanja: a Language Spoken in British Central Africa on and near the Shores of Lake Nyasa*, which probably also had a list of vocabulary.

[933] David Clement Ruffelle Scott: *A Cyclopaedic Dictionary of the Mang'anja Language spoken in British Central Africa*, Printed in Edinburgh for the Foreign Mission

Appendix II: A history of Chichewa lexicography 317

In the same year, Margaret Woodward published her book of CE and EC vocabulary from Likoma Island.[934] In 1902 and 1929, UMCA missionaries Barnes and Bulley published revised versions of Woodward's work, under the title *Chinyanja-English Dictionary*. These publications were much smaller than Scott's work. They were different in another aspect as well. They focused on the 'middle lake' Chinyanja, and consequently had a wider variety, not in the least because of the Swahili influence.[935]

Hetherwick updated and extended Scott's work. However, he followed Barnes' approach by adding vocabulary from dialects other than Mang'anja. He first compiled his *Manual of the Nyanja Language*, which mainly dealt with 'grammatical details necessary for a working knowledge of the language', but also included lists of vocabulary.[936] His main work was the *Dictionary of the Nyanja Language*, first published in London in 1929 (620 pages, A5). Reprints followed by Lutterworth Press in 1951 and 1957,[937] and by the National Educational Company of Zambia in 1970 and 1974.[938]

Committee of the Church of Scotland. Edinburgh MDCCCXCII (1892). The Dictionary has a 'Preface' on the Mang'anja language (v-vi) and also a 'Guide to the Dictionary, Phonological and Grammatical' (p. vii-xxii), followed by a folded page on language structure (xxiii). Part I of the dictionary (pp 1-682) is for Mang'anja-English. Part II (p. 685-737: Index and Vocabulary) is for English-Mang'anja. Later reprinted by Gregg International (ISBN-10 0-576-11620-3).

[934] Margaret E. Woodward, *Vocabulary of English-Chinyanja and Chinyanja-English as spoken at Likoma, Lake Nyasa*, London: Society for Promoting Christian Knowledge (SPCK), 1892 (pages 67), reprint 1895 (pages 88).

[935] B. Herbert Barnes revised, extended, and republished Woodward's book in 1902: London: Society for Promoting Christian Knowledge (SPCK). Pages viii, 183. Fr. Barnes was an Anglican missionary in British Central Africa Protectorate (from 1907: Nyasaland) from 1899 to 1904. According to Price, *Vocabulary* (see footnote, op.cit.), Barnes focused especially on 'middle Lake Nyasa dialects'. Other editions of probably the same list by Woodward followed in 1925 by M.W. Bulley, London: SPCK (pages viii, 76), and in 1929, also by M.W. Bulley, London: The Sheldon Press (pages x, 164), printed by: Richard Clay & Sons, Bungay, Suffolk. Format 12,3 mm x 18,3 mm.

[936] Alexander Hetherwick, *A Practical Manual of the Nyanja Language*, 1st ed. 1904 (?); other editions/prints that are mentioned: 1907, 1922, 1927 (7th),1932 (8th). Published by: African Lakes Corporation, Ltd., printed by Oliver and Boyd in Edinburgh. The *Manual* has Chinyanja-English vocabulary (p. 247-273) and English-Chinyanja vocabulary (p. 274-299).

[937] Alexander Hetherwick, *Dictionary of the Nyanja Language: Being the Encyclopaedic Dictionary of the Mang'anja language by the late David Clement Scott, edited and enlarged by Rev. Alexander Hetherwick*. London & Manchester: Lutterworth Press for the United Society for Christian Literature (USCL), 1929 . In his Preface on page v

These dictionaries encouraged writing and reading in the vernacular language. Gradually a literature in Chichewa/Chinyanja emerged, for instance the translation of the Bible, published first in 1922, as *Buku Lopatulika*.[939] Smaller lists of English-Chichewa vocabulary have circulated, e.g. the ones of the *U.S. Peace Corps*,[940] and the *Word List* by J.K. Louw, a South African Reformed missionary in the Central Region of Malawi (Nkhoma Mission/CCAP) and later Professor of Chichewa at UNISA.[941] There is also a Chichewa-English wordlist of about 2700 words compiled in 1979 by Fr Jan Vermeullen of the White Fathers.[942] Botne and Kulemeka compiled a small dictionary, especially for foreign students in a Malawian or Zambian university environment.[943] Special in their respective species are Ntara's little book on Nyanja words with abstract meanings,[944] and the dictionary on the names of plants by Binns and Logah.[945] There is also a

---

Hetherwick acknowledges Scott's work. He deleted some anthropological sections from Scott's original work. The book was reprinted 1951 and 1957 by Lutterworth Press in London in association with the Northern Rhodesia & Nyasaland Publ. Bureau (pages viii, 612).

[938] Idem, London: National Educational Company of Zambia (NECZAM), 1970, 1974. pp vii, 612.

[939] *Buku Lopatulika, Ndilo Mau a Mulungu,* first edition 1922, orthography revision 1936, revised edition 1966, enlarged edition 1922, reprint 2001, published by the Bible Societies of Malawi, Zambia and Zimbabwe. Ernst R. Wendland, 'In the Beginning: A Brief History of the Word of God in Chichewa', in: *Buku Loyera: An Introduction to the New Chichewa Bible Translation*, Zomba: Kachere, 1998.

[940] The *Peace Corps* Publication has two volumes and a Teacher's Manual, <http://africa.msu.edu/>; see: S.M. Samu, *Chichewa language manual*, Washington DC: Peace Corps, 1985 (141 pages incl. word list).

[941] J.K. Louw, *Chichewa, A Practical Course, Part 3: Word lists,* Pretoria: UNISA, 1987. The *Word List* has Chichewa-English vocabulary (pp 17-80) and English-Chichewa vocabulary (pp 81-123), 225 mm x 150 mm. It includes the words found in: J.K. Louw, *Little and often fills the purse: Learning a language in the context of relationship* (197 pages, 205 mm x 145mm), Pretoria: UNISA, 1983 (also published in Chichewa: *Pang'ono pang'ono ndi kumanga mtolo*).

[942] http://www.fenza.org/files/documents/Vermeullen_Chewa_Dictionary.pdf>.

[943] Robert Botne and Andrew Tilimbe Kulemeka, *A Learner's Chichewa and English Dictionary*, Series: Afrikawissenschaftliche Lehrbücher Volume 9, Ruediger Köppe Verlag, 1995 (pages xxviii, 90). The main section consists of a Chichewa-English and English-Chichewa word list. Tones of the words are included. Reprinted 2004.

[944] S.J. Ntara, *Nyanja words with abstract meanings*, Lusaka: Zambia Publ., 1967 (89 pages).

[945] Blodwen Binns, *Dictionary of Plant Names in Malawi*, Language Editor J.P. Logah, Zomba: Government Printer, 1972. It is both CE and EC, and apart from Chichewa, it includes other Malawian languages as well, and also the Latin equivalents.

small dictionary of 111 (A5) pages, compiled by J.M. Massana, a Franciscan priest.[946]

EC Dictionaries

Between 1861 and 1863 Horace Waller compiled a list of English-Chichewa vocabulary.[947] He was probably first in a succession of EC compilers. Waller belonged to a group of missionaries headed by Bishop Mackenzie, who tried to start mission work for the Anglican Universities' Mission in Southern Malawi. In 1894, *An English-Nyanja Dictionary* appeared, compiled by Robert Laws of the Presbyterian *Livingstonia Mission* in the north of Malawi.[948] During his long career in Malawi, Laws was not always exposed to Chichewa/Chinyanja. He lived in a Chewa-speaking region for only five years (Cape Maclear, 1875-1881). In Bandawe, his next station, until 1891, Chewa played a role also, but in Livingstonia where he went in 1894, the main languages were Tonga, Tumbuka and Ngoni. Nevertheless, Laws filled a gap as his dictionary for a long time was the largest collection of EC vocabulary. With its 232 pages (A5) it was more in quantity than Woodward's list, even after the latter was extended by Barnes, and more than the modest 25 pages in Hetherwick's abovementioned *Manual*, which saw light for the first time probably in 1904.

Next in the sequel of EC dictionaries, there are various editions of the dictionary of the *Zambezi Industrial Mission*, under the title *English-Chinyanja Dictionary*. Its compiler or editor is not mentioned. The first edition was published in 1914.[949] Probably the publication of 1915 is a revision of the 1914 one.[950] It was reprinted in 1940 and 1964.[951] Since

---

[946] J.M. Massana, *Chichewa-English Dictionary*, The Franciscans, P.O. Box 27, Dowa.
[947] Horace Waller, Vocabulary list English-Chichewa transcribed by Elias Mandala], Archive Rhodes House, Oxford, 'Horace Waller's Papers', Mss. Afr s.16, 10 vols; Horace Waller diaries, 11 vols (1860-1864).
[948] Laws, *An English-Nyanja Dictionary*, 1894 (for details, see above). After 5 years in Cape Maclear (1875-1881), Laws moved to Bandawe (near Nkhata Bay), and in 1894 to Livingstonia. Cf. McIntosh, *Robert Laws*, p. 237: 'Laws ... was also responsible for having more than one African language reduced to writing, and produced school Primers in both Chinyanja and Chitonga, as well as a grammar ... in Chinyanja.' He also translated the New Testament into Chinyanja and wrote books on Chingoni history and grammar.
[949] Anonymous, *English-Chinyanja*. Mitsidi & Blantyre: Zambesi Mission Press, 1914. The title is mentioned by: Simooya Jerome Hachipola, *A Survey of the Minority Languages of Zimbabwe*, Harare: University of Zimbabwe, 1998, p. 113.
[950] Anonymous, *English-Chinyanja dictionary*. Blantyre: United Society for Christian Literature (USCL) for the Zambesi Industrial Mission, 1915, xv, 381 pages.

1972, the Zambezi Mission book has been re-published by the Christian Literature Association of Malawi (CLAIM).[952] A revision was published in 1980 and there are two reprints of 1986,[953] entitled *The Student's English-Chichewa Dictionary*. This dictionary of 173 pages A5, has functioned as an important tool for learners of Chichewa and for Malawians wrestling with English texts. It has been the only dictionary of its kind for decades, and as such it has done a useful job. The Zambezi Mission/CLAIM dictionary by an anonymous writer offered much more than the lists of vocabulary by Thomson (22 pages, appr. 1955),[954] and by Salaün (31 pages, first published in 1969).[955] It was also more helpful than Louw's *Word List* of 42 pages of English-Chichewa of 1987.[956] Nearest to it was *A Short English-Nyanja Vocabulary* (127 pages), published in 1957 by Tom Price, a Blantyre missionary who later worked for the Department of African Studies in Glasgow.[957] However, modern users of the *Student's Dictionary*, and of Price's work too often miss important words and expressions.

Another small EC collection is offered in the above mentioned list by Botne and Kulemeka of 1995. It contains not only CE but also a section of

---

[951] Anonymous, *English-Chinyanja dictionary*. Blantyre: Zambesi Mission Press for the Zambesi Industrial Mission, prints of 1940 and 1964, xv, 381 pages.

[952] Anonymous, *English-Nyanja dictionary*. Blantyre: Christian Literature Association in Malawi, 1972, ii, 173 pages

[953] Zambezi Mission, *The Student's English-Chichewa Dictionary*, Blantyre: CLAIM, 1980, printed by Nkhoma Press. CLAIM, *The student's English-Chichewa dictionary*, Blantyre: Christian Literature Association in Malawi, 1986, 173 pages (A5). There are two versions. The brown cover one was printed by Malamulo Publishing House in Makwasa. The blue cover one was printed by Mercia Industries, Blantyre.

[954] T.D. Thomson, *A Practical Approach to Chinyanja*, Zomba: Government Printer, n.d. 63 pages (EC vocabulary on pp 41-63). A short note prefacing 'the present edition' is dated May 1955. Thomson claims he was helped by one 'Mr J.S. Sheriff of the Nyasaland Administration'.

[955] N. Salaün *Chichewa Intensive Course*, reprint 1978 (1st ed. 1969 in Lilongwe by Likuni). Reprinted 1979 by Mission Press Ndola, Zambia. Distributed by Mission Language Centre, Lusaka (146 pages, 215mm x 155mm). English-Chichewa vocabulary p. 112-144. Reprinted in 1993 by Teresianum Press in Lusaka. Reprinted by Montfort Media in Balaka nd. and also available (anonymously) on the internet.

[956] Louw, *Word Lists*, op.cit.

[957] Tom Price, *A Short English-Nyanja Vocabulary* (127 pages), Lusaka: National Educational Company of Zambia/Blantyre: The Publications Bureau, 1957. In and after 1970 it was reprinted several times by the National Educational Company of Zambia After 1970 it was reprinted by Robert Maclehoe & Co, Great Britain and The University Press, Glasgow.

Appendix II: A history of Chichewa lexicography 321

EC. These days there are various lists of EC and CE vocabulary online on the internet, most of them limited to comparatively few pages.⁹⁵⁸

Finally, from 2000, there has been the Chinyanja/Chichewa monolingual dictionary, *Mtanthauziramawu wa Chinyanja* (abbr.: MWC), composed by the Centre for Language Studies (CLS) of the University of Malawi.⁹⁵⁹ For those who want to find the right explanation of Chichewa terms in Chichewa words, this volume of 366 pages has proved a helpful tool. Apart from its own research, mainly in the Central Region,⁹⁶⁰ CLS in principle became the possessor of the material of its predecessors. After independence, President Hastings Kamuzu Banda promoted lexicographical activity e.g. by establishing in 1970 the Chichewa Research Committee with J.K. Louw and E.J. Chadza as its leaders. The Committee existed until 1977 when it was succeeded by the Chichewa Board. In 1995, the new democratically elected government disbanded the Board. In April 1996, CLS started its work. It became the heir of the material collected by the Committee and the Board. Unfortunately not all of it was used. Kamwendo claims that part of the collected material was deleted from the computer of the disbanded Board by some of its outraged members.⁹⁶¹ In addition to the available collections, various preceding dictionaries served CLS as sources for the new one, of which the works of Hetherwick and of Guerins are mentioned by name.⁹⁶² Although Guerin's work was said to belong to the collections that were made or possessed by the Chichewa

---

⁹⁵⁸ E.g. the vocabulary lists of A.I. Mtenje and of P. Parker <www.websters-online-dictionary.org>, Webster's Online Dictionary: <http://www.websters-online-dictionary. org/translation/Chichewa/>.

⁹⁵⁹ Centre for Language Studies, *Mtanthauziramawu wa Chinyanja*, Blantyre: Dzuka (Private Bag 39), 2000. Further referred to as *MWC*. See: <http://unima-cls.org/printLexicon/>.

⁹⁶⁰ *MWC*, page v, 'Mawu omwe ali mu mtanthauziramawu uyu adatoledwa m'madera osiyanasiyana a dziko la Malawi komwe anthu amayankhula Chinyanja/Chichewa makamaka maboma a ku Chigawo Chapakati'.

⁹⁶¹ Gregory Hankoni Kamwendo, *Language Policy in Health Services: A Sociolinguistic Study of a Malawian Referral Hospital*, Helsinki 2004, p. 52, says the dissolution of the Chichewa Board was resented by its members. 'The anti-dissolution feelings were so high among the Chichewa Board's staff that some of them deleted from the computer a part of the Chewa dictionary that the Chichewa Board had been working on for many years. One story has it that the deletion was ordered by the head of the Chichewa Board.'

⁹⁶² *MWC*, idem, 'Mawu ena adatengedwa ku mabuku osiyanasiyana, monga mtanthauziramawu awa: *English-Chichewa Dictionary* (J Guerins), *Dictionary of the Nyanja Language* (Hetherwick) ndi ena otero.'

Board, I only found some references to its existence, probably in two volumes, EC and CE,[963] but not to its being published.

The dictionary that was published by CLS is different from all preceding dictionaries in that (a) it has Chichewa throughout, (b) it did not originate from missionaries or church institutions, (c) it was produced by and under the supervision of Malawians only.[964] This entirely new Malawian approach does not mean that the tradition of making dictionaries in Malawi has dramatically changed, but it adds to its variation.

New Dictionaries

The initiative to compile new and more extended dictionaries was born in 1997 when I started to be a learner of Chichewa/Chinyanja. Only the above-mentioned *Student's Dictionary* was available to me at that time, and a rare copy of Hetherwick/Scott's work. Soon I felt the urge to make my own collection of vocabulary. Subsequently in 1998, while teaching at *Zomba Theological College* (ZTC), the idea emerged of involving others, and of making the work available to the general public. The community of students and fellow-lecturers of ZTC provided an ideal environment for a language project like this. Until 2007 a selected number of them, together with others, all native Chichewa/Chinyanja speakers, were active in collecting vocabulary and in checking and improving the lists that in the process led to various editions of dictionaries. From 2007, when we left Malawi, I have continued the work with a smaller team, now communicating mainly through email.

In early 2002, the first edition of the *English-Chichewa/Chinyanja Dictionary* was published. It was followed by three improved and enlarged editions, the last one in 2008.[965] In the meantime, a parallel process took

---

[963] *International Journal of Pest Management*, vol. 48, issue 4-10-2002 , in the bibliography to an article by A. Orr, B. Mwale, D. Saiti, p. 265-278, the work is referred to as follows: Guerin, J., 1985. A Concise English-Chichewa Dictionary, 2 vols (Blantyre). Probably it is the same work once seen by Kishindo, i.e. a double-volumed hardbound dictionary, stencilled, and claimed to be compiled by a Roman Catholic priest.

[964] MWC, p. iii. Final responsibility for the work was in the hands of the Head of the Centre for Language Studies, A.I.D. Mtenje, and his deputy Gregory Kamwendo. Collectors of vocabulary were: Alick Bwanali, Shem Nyirenda, Martha Kamwana, Stella Kachiwanda, Frank Nantongwe, Linda Gondwe. The committee deciding on the meaning of words consisted of: R.E.M. Kathewera, N.J. Chimbalangondo, S.J.L. Ngoma, A. Chauma, P.J. Kishindo, F. Moto.

[965] Steven Paas, *English-Chichewa/Chinyanja Dictionary*, Zomba/Blantyre: Kachere/Claim, 2002, 2003, 2005 2008. 2008.

place, converting the EC list to a CE list and adding other CE vocabulary. That work resulted into a dictionary too. In 2004, the first edition was published, and in 2005 the second edition.[966]

In 2009 the CE Dictionary and the EC Dictionary were combined to one volume. A CE-EC Dictionary was published. Publication of the second edition followed in 2010. The third edition was published in 2012 and the fourth edition in 2013.[967] By its size and contents of more than 40,000 entries it shows the continuing process of extension and improvement. Most copies of these editions found their way to schools in Malawi and Zambia. In 2016 the fifth edition (45,000 entries) was published, by *Oxford University Press*, to be distributed not only in the countries of Chichewa speaking Africa but also worldwide.[968] Since May 2010 the CE-EC Dictionary has been accessible online.[969]

---

[966] Idem, *Chichewa/Chinyanja-English Dictionary*, Zomba/Blantyre: Kachere/Claim, 2004, 2005.

[967] Idem, *Chichewa/Chinyanja-English and English-Chichewa/Chinyanja Dictionary/ Mtanthauziramawu*, Zomba: Kachere, 2009; Heart for Malawi, 2010; Nuremberg: VTR, 2012, CLAIM, 2013.

[968] Idem, *Oxford Chichewa Dictionary*, fifth edition, Cape Town: Oxford University Press Southern Africa – ORBIS, September 2016 [1158 pages].

[969] http://translate.chichewadictionary.org

The title page of the original 1854 edition of Gamitto's Diary of his 1831-1832 expedition, with an appended list of the Chichewa/Chinyanja vocabulary he collected.

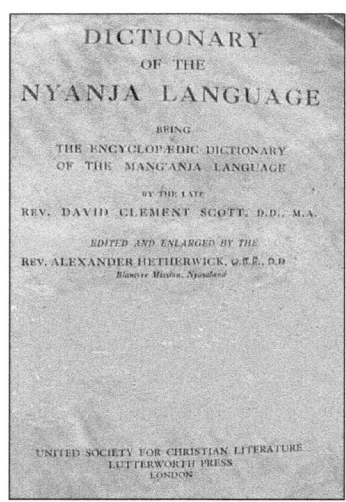

Title page of the 1957 print of Alexander Hetherwick's Chinyanja English Dictionary, published in 1929, basically a re-edited version of Scott's book of 1892

Appendix II: A history of Chichewa lexicography 325

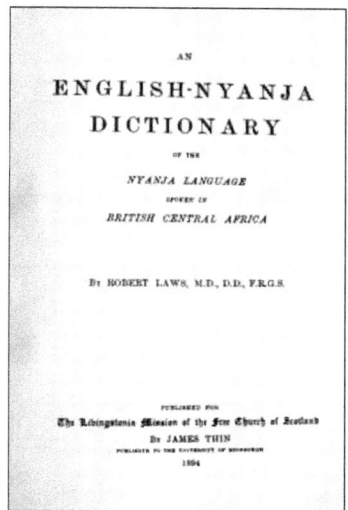

Title page of Robert Laws' English-Nyanja Dictionary of 1894 reprinted in 2008.

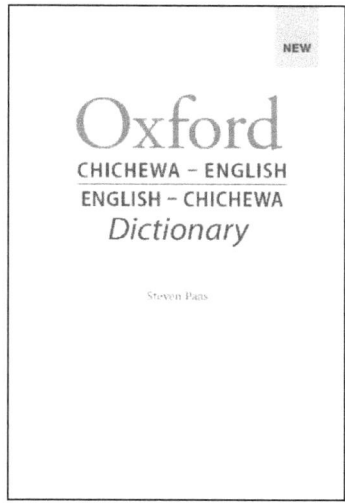

Title page of Steven Paas' Oxford Chichewa Dictionary of 2016.

Index

Abyssinia 56, 74, 237
Acheson, Alexander 48
Africa Inland Mission (A.I.M.) 267
African Traditional Religion 155, 205, 224, 245
Albert von Sachsen-Coburg-Gotha 68
Alexandria 74, 172
Altlutheraner 27
Altpietisten 28, 33
Antinomianism 28
apokatastasis panton 30
Apostelstraße / apostles' street 60, 75, 76
Augsburg Confession 31
Bagamoyo 120, 126, 141, 148, 150, 266
Banda, Hastings Kamuzu (President) 205, 309, 310-312, 321
Barghash (Sultan) 210
Barnes, R. Herbert 317, 319
Barth, Karl 83, 85, 86, 93, 185
Barton 142, 143
Basler Mission 11, 13, 16, 18, 41, 44, 46-48, 60, 68, 74, 84, 96, 126, 163, 171, 172, 173, 178, 183, 194, 204, 227, 251, 277, 281, 286
Bengel, Johann Albrecht 26, 29, 30-33, 35, 285
Berlin, Rudolf (oculist) 167, 168
Berlin Conference (1884/1885) 260
Berlin Mission 266
Bethel Mission 266
Bialloblotzky, Christoph Heinrich Friedrich, 120
Binns, Blodwen 318
Bismarck, Otto von 265
Blumhardt, Christian Gottlieb 30, 31, 45, 46, 56, 285
Blumhardt, Karl Heinrich 56, 57
Bogatzky, Karl Heinrich von, 32, 48, 248
Böhme 29, 35
Bombay 71, 101, 102, 106, 116, 117, 123-128, 130, 142, 143, 146-150, 154-158, 163, 164, 187, 192, 210, 262, 278
Bönnigheim 65, 284
Boos, Martin 27
Botne, Robert 318, 320
Braun [teacher in Gerlingen] 43, 100
Brüdergemeinde, see Evangelische Brüdergemeinde 32-34, 229
Buganda (in Uganda) 261
Bulley, M.W. 317
Bunyan, John 96
Burton, Richard Francis 18, 59, 66, 97, 104, 120, 211, 221, 230, 315
Butterworth, Edmund 123
Cairo 71-75, 93-95, 99-101, 134, 202
Calvin, John 25, 27, 29, 249
Calw 93, 123, 172, 248
Cameron, Verney Lovett 121
Cameron, Scott 267
Cameroon 59
Candace 81, 119
Candy, George 126
Chagga, see: Jagga chain of mission 59-61, 67-70, 72-77, 83, 157, 232, 237, 263, 264
Chain of mission 59
Chancellor, William B. 128, 149, 155, 156, 158, 160
Chichewa / Chinyanja 9, 10, 199, 200, 203-206, 220, 224, 264, 309-322
Chrischona 46, 60, 69, 73-76, 93, 103, 104, 122, 123, 133, 171, 177, 188-191, 200, 203-205, 263
Christoph, Duke of Württemberg 26
Church Missionary Society, see: CMS
Church of Scotland 265
Churchill, Henry Adrian (Consul) 210, 211
Classical Missions 266
CMS (Church Missionary Society) 11, 17, 18, 20, 35, 36, 45-48, 56-59, 64-87, 93-133, 139-179, 183-204, 214, 216, 219, 227, 230, 231, 233, 235, 238-240, 243, 251, 253, 254, 261-268, 277, 279,

280, 283, 287, 289
Coates, Dandeson 47, 48
colonialism 217, 236, 239
Consolata Fathers 265
Cooley, William Desborough 18, 62, 103, 121
Cust, Robert 178, 190, 198, 199
Dann, Christian Adam 245
Dar es Salaam 150
Däuble, Family 17, 21, 171-173, 183, 199, 277
David, George 124, 127-130, 154-156, 167, 235
Decken, Baron Karl Klaus von der 17, 63, 103, 120, 121, 243
Deimler, Johann Gottfried 17, 73, 102, 105, 122, 126-128, 130, 142, 143, 149, 156, 163, 164, 176, 186, 192, 196, 197, 267
Deimler, James 130
Diehlmann (Dihlmann), Conrad 69
Dietrich (Krapf), Rosine 57
Doddridge, Philip 244
Dürr, Wilhelm 36, 44
Dürr, Marie 67
Enlightenment 25, 26, 31, 42, 155, 164
Erhardt, Jakob Johannes 17, 64-70, 72, 73, 76, 78-80, 83, 85, 86, 96, 99, 100, 102, 107, 113, 120, 176, 185, 196, 197, 216, 230, 238, 262, 267, 278, 284
Ethiopia 35, 36, 56, 60, 74-75, 120, 126, 185, 237, 260, 261
Evangelical Awakening 25-27, 31, 41, 125, 158, 209
Evangelische Brüdergemeinde 179
Faith Missions (Post Classical Missions) 74, 157, 267
Fearne, Thomas Gleadow 93, 94
Fenn, Christopher Cyprian 82, 124, 129, 144, 176, 197
Finckh, August Hermann 17, 172
First World War 266
Fjellstedt, Peter 35
Flad, Johannes Martin 36, 74, 75
France, French 35, 42, 62, 81, 120, 212, 215, 230, 237, 260
Francke, August Hermann 25, 26

Freetown 126
Frere, Henry Bartle (Sir) 106, 130, 150, 151-160, 177, 183, 211, 218, 235, 261, 262
Frere Town 158, 159, 261, 263
Friedrich Wilhelm IV (King) 68
Fuga 73
Further Reformation 25, 27, 31
Gabriel (Upanga man) 116, 118
Galla /Oromo 56-61, 72, 74, 75, 81, 119, 123, 126, 127, 139, 146, 185, 237
Gamitto, Antonio Candido Pedroso, 200, 311, 315, 316
Gerhardt, Paul 244, 269
Gerlingen 10, 15, 16, 18, 20, 26, 29, 32, 36, 41-48, 63, 93, 99, 104, 121, 133, 163, 167, 168, 170, 173, 183, 227, 229, 231, 241, 248, 256, 260, 269-272, 278, 283-287
German /Germany 9, 14-21, 25, 26, 35, 41, 45, 58, 62, 63, 70, 79, 81, 83, 84, 94, 118-123, 133, 141, 152, 153, 163, 164, 167, 171, 172, 176, 184-189, 194, 228, 235-238, 244, 247, 259, 261, 264-266, 271, 277-279
Geyser, Paul 27
Giriama (people) 107, 115, 117, 118, 146, 161, 198, 261
Gobat, Samuel (Bishop) 56, 74
Göring, Christian E. 245
Graevenitz, Fritz von 269
Grant, James Augustus 120, 211
Guerin, J. 321
Guinness, Fanny 267
Gundert, Hermann 20, 56, 103, 104, 123, 283
Gunja (Abe / Abraham) 73, 99, 107, 115, 131, 202, 249, 252
Gutmann, Bruno 266
Guyon, Madame de 35
Hagenmann 69, 73, 104
Hahn, (Johann) Michael 28-30, 34, 35, 68, 253, 254
Hamedi 222, 223
Hamerton, Atkin (Consul) 80, 81, 126, 210
Hannington, James (Bishop) 263, 266

Index

Harms, Ludwig and Theodor 16, 27, 81
Hasani 252
Heidelberg Catechism 115, 183, 187, 252, 278
Henderson, Henry 202, 263
Henhöfer, Aloys 27, 28
Hetherwick, Alexander 205, 316, 317, 319, 321, 322
Hofacker, Ludwig 28, 31, 42, 48, 96, 248, 249, 255, 286
Hoffmann Family 19, 20, 33, 44-47, 183, 251, 255, 280
Holliday (Lieder), Alice 94, 95, 183
Holy Ghost Fathers (Congregation of the Holy Ghost) 265, 266
Humboldt, Friedrich Wilhelm Heinrich Alexander von 60, 62, 68
Hutchinson, Edward 82, 106, 130, 149, 153, 155, 168, 169, 175, 195, 235
Ibo 212, 222
imperialism 131, 237, 260, 261
Isenberg, Karl Wilhelm 56, 126, 283
Islam 55, 56, 66, 103, 113, 140, 155, 161, 205, 215-217, 236-240, 247
Islington 19, 41, 47, 48, 68, 69, 248
Ittameier, Max 266
Jagga (people) 61-64, 76, 139, 156, 158, 184, 240, 244, 266
Jehle, Gustav Arthur 18, 21, 45, 47, 59, 63, 81, 134, 199, 227, 261, 268, 269, 281, 283
Johnston, Harry (Governor) 268
Johnston, Henry Hamilton 63
Jonas 168, 169, 172, 175
Jones, William Henry 117, 127, 129, 130, 143, 144, 156, 157
Josenhans, Joseph Friedrich 46, 68, 69, 77, 83-87
Joseph (Masai man) 116
Josiak (Daniel) 118
Jumbe (of Nkhotakota) 216, 217
justification 25, 28, 42, 249, 251, 254
Kabbala 35
Kaiser (farmer) 69, 93, 104
Kalali 269
Kamba (people) 59, 61, 64, 72, 79, 96, 104, 105, 139, 146, 156, 185, 187, 198, 214, 215, 217
Kammerer, G. 171
Kappus, Georg 100
Karonga 217
Kazembe 215, 315, 316
Kent (Tyler/Rebmann), Emma 18, 20, 81, 93, 94-102, 104-106, 183, 200, 201, 214, 219, 222-224, 228-230, 238, 281, 284
Kenya 9, 18, 46, 60, 63, 72, 120, 130, 157, 184, 198, 213, 215, 223, 236, 262, 265, 267, 269, 271, 277, 285
Kersten, Otto 121
Kheri (bwana) 240
Kibo 62
Kigofi (Nathanael) 118
Kikuyu (people) 61, 215
Kilimanjaro 17, 61-63, 66, 72, 103, 119-121, 162, 184, 230, 266, 268, 269
Kilwa (Isle) 65, 212, 213, 215, 218, 315
Kiniassa Dictionary 106, 119, 175, 186, 191, 199, 201, 204, 206, 209, 219, 221, 261, 263, 264, 279
Kinika Dictionary 178, 185, 198
Kirk, John (Consul) 210
Kisuludini / Kisulutini / Kizurini 58-69, 73-83, 93, 96-108, 113-118, 120, 122-124, 126, 127, 130, 133, 139-141, 143-145, 147, 151, 152, 155-158, 160, 161, 163, 164, 183, 196, 200, 202, 219, 238-240, 244, 262, 278
Kivoi (Chief) 72
Kmeri (King) 73
Knack, Gustav 27
Kohlbrugge, Hermann Friedrich 27
Köhler, Horst and Eva Luise (President) 271
Koi, David 157
Kolb, Immanuel Gottlieb 31, 36, 68
Kölle, Sigismund Wilhelm 193, 194
Korntal / Kornthal 20, 32, 33, 36, 45, 63, 71, 73, 76, 83, 86, 168-179, 183-190, 194, 195, 197, 199-201, 203, 204, 229, 250, 269, 271, 280
Kottwitz, Baron von 27
Krapf, Johann Ludwig 11, 17-20, 25, 28, 35, 36, 46, 48, 55-79, 81, 83-87, 93, 94,

96, 99, 102, 104, 107, 113, 115, 118, 120, 122, 124, 126, 131, 142, 143, 145, 157, 160, 168-179, 183-198, 200, 201, 203, 204, 213, 219, 228-230, 232, 234-237, 248, 249, 251-255, 259, 260, 262-264, 266-269, 272, 277-280, 282, 284, 285, 288
Krummacher, Karl Emil et al. 27
Kuba, Arnsha 67
Kugler, Christian 56
Kulemeka, Andrew Tilimbe 318
Lamb, James Abner 159
Lamu (Isle) 82, 101, 123, 213
Lancaster, Joseph 95
Last, Joseph T. 156
Lavigerie, Charles Martial Allemand (Kardinal) 266
Laws, Robert 205, 264, 313, 316, 319
Ledderhose, Karl Friedrich 17, 19, 21, 44, 46, 61, 63, 94, 105, 120, 134, 173, 229, 284
Ledeboer, B. 47
Leipzig Mission 266
Leonberg 178
Lepsius, Karl Richard 68, 176, 188, 264
Liberia 260
Lieder, Johann Rudolf 43, 94, 95, 99, 101, 183
Likoma Island 263, 317
Livingstone, David 57, 121, 127, 145, 156-158, 162, 200, 203, 211, 214, 218, 230, 263, 264, 267, 268, 310
Löhe, Wilhelm 27
Loikop (people) 66, 67
Louw, Johann K. 318, 320, 321
Lugo (Jonathan) 115, 116, 131
Lukas (Isaac Nyondo's brother) 118
Luther, Martin 25, 26, 33, 47, 240, 249
MacDonald, Duff 202
Mackay, John 263
Mackenzie, Charles Frederick (Bishop) 263
Maisch Family 41, 45, 93, 232, 270
Majid (Sultan) 75, 105, 108, 210
Malawi 9, 217, 261, 309-325
Malenga (Chief) 217
Mamkinga (King) 62, 240, 250

Mang'anja (people) 317
Männer, August 171
Masai (people) 67, 96, 100, 101, 104, 105, 107, 113, 116, 122, 146, 215
Masaki (Chief) 62
Massana, J.M. 319
Mauritius (island) 105, 126, 147, 212, 215, 261
Mawenzi 62
Mee, J. 82, 129
Methodist Mission 18, 27, 47, 75, 120, 122-124, 133, 156, 263
Metzler, Peter Martin 69, 93, 104, 252, 282
Meyer, Hans 63
Mgindo (people) 127, 128
Mijikenda (people) 198
Mill Hill Fathers 265
Mlozi 217
Modernism 31, 32
Moffat, Robert 76
Mombasa 48, 55, 57-61, 64, 67, 69, 71, 72, 74-76, 78, 80-82, 96, 100-103, 105-108, 113-119, 122, 124, 126-132, 139-141, 143-147, 149-151, 154-163, 167, 169, 184, 185, 192, 198, 203, 212, 215, 216, 222, 223, 229, 240, 250, 253, 260-262, 266, 267
Money, Robert 126, 127
Monteiro, J.M.C. 315, 316
Moravian Mission 266
Moresby Treaty 80, 139, 209
Mozambique 206, 213, 215, 217, 222, 293, 309-315
Mrari 161
Mringe 59, 115, 131, 252
Mtesa (King) 177
Mua Muamba 107, 108, 115, 116, 131
Mua Zua (David) 115, 116, 131
Muigni Wasiri 240
Munandoru (Chief) 240
Muscat 58, 80, 108, 209, 212, 213, see: Oman
Muslims 9, 58, 67, 73, 76-81, 83, 84, 87, 97, 98, 105, 106, 113, 115, 117, 118, 126, 139, 140, 141, 151, 158, 159, 192, 209, 211, 213, 222, 224, 231, 238-240,

247, 261
Mwanga II, Kabaka (King) of Buganda 263
Mzomba, Andreas 118
Napier, Robert (General) 75
Napoleon 32
Nasik 127, 140-143, 151, 154, 155
Natal 81, 94, 119, 233
Nathanael (Nika man) 116
New, Charles 63, 122, 123, 156
Ng'owa (Abe) 117, 131, 147
Nika (people) 20, 57-59, 71, 72, 74, 79, 99, 101, 103-108, 115-118, 123, 127, 129, 134, 139, 141, 144, 146, 149, 153, 156, 183, 185, 187, 188, 191-193, 195, 198, 199, 213, 228, 233, 241, 252, 279
Nkhonde (people) 217
Nkhotakota 216
Nofa 209, 223
Ntara, S.J. 318
Nyasa (country, people, language) 65-67, 86, 99, 102, 106, 118, 121, 124, 130, 162, 185, 192, 200, 201, 204, 205, 211, 212, 216, 218, 219, 233, 263, 264, 315-317
Nyondo (Isaac) 115, 123, 128, 130, 131, 160, 167-170, 172, 177, 178, 249, 252
Oetinger, Friedrich Christoph 29, 35, 253
Oman 58, 80, 108, 139, 209, 210, 212, 213, see: Muscat
Oromo (people), see: Galla
Pakaya 223
Palmerston (Prime Minister) 68
Parnell, E. 143
paternalism 252
Pearson, John G. 156
Pelargus (Krapf), Charlotte 75
Pfefferle, Charles 69, 267
Philipps, Mary Ann 132
Pietism / Pietismus 11, 21, 26-28, 31, 32, 36, 41, 42, 46, 48, 249, 251, 272
Playfair (Consul) 132, 210, 259
Polly (Nyondo's wife) 128
Portuguese 79, 121, 199, 209, 211, 212-215, 222, 223, 260, 310, 311, 313, 315, 316

Post-Classical Missions (Faith Missions) 267
Prazeros 214, 215
Pregizer, Christian Gottlieb 28
Preiswerk, Samuel 245
Price, William Salter 127, 142, 155, 156-159, 167, 186, 261, 320;
Price, Tom 317, 320
Puritanism 25, 31
Purtscheller, Ludwig 63
Rabai 58-73, 77, 83, 94-96, 100, 101, 103, 107, 108, 113, 114, 116-118, 122, 124, 127, 130, 139, 144, 145, 147, 150, 151, 198, 227, 230, 232, 240, 248, 249, 262, 270
Rebmann Family 16, 41, 48, 95, 99, 100, 168, 268, 285
Remington, David S. 156, 160
Rhodes, Cecil 261
Ribe 122, 123, 133, 156, 186, 198
Riddel, Alexander 203, 263, 264, 316
Rigby, Christopher P. (Consul) 106, 114, 210
Roscher, Albrecht 118, 119
Rothe, Johannes Andreas 121, 244
Russell, William F.A.H. 159
Sachsen-Coburg-Gotha 68
Sahila Selassie (King) 56
Salaün 320
Salim bin Abdallah (Jumbe) 216
Salimini 9, 99, 106, 199, 200, 209, 216, 218-224, 240
sanctification 28, 249, 251, 254
Sayyid Majid 75, 105, 108
Sayyid Said 58, 80, 104, 209, 212
Schmid (Krapf), Nanette 76
Schwabenkaserne 45
Scotland 27, 202, 263, 313, 316, 317
Scott, David Clement Ruffelle 264, 316, 317, 322
Scott, Peter Cameron 267
Scramble for Africa 260
Second World War 18
Semler, Ishmael 117, 127, 130, 156
Seychelles (island) 126, 146, 147, 151, 156
Sharanpur 127, 130, 155

Shire (river) 214, 215, 218, 263, 264, 315
Shoa (province) 56, 57, 74, 237
Sidi (Abe) 117, 131, 161, 261
slave-trade 66, 76, 78, 80, 82, 85, 113, 114, 121, 122, 140, 141, 150, 155, 157, 209-211, 213, 218, 219, 238, 264
Somalia 260
Sparshott, Thomas E. and Margaret 117, 129, 132, 133, 139, 141, 144, 146-150, 155, 159-164, 186, 188, 198, 199, 238, 279
Speke, John Hanning 18, 59, 66, 97, 104, 120, 211, 221, 230
Spener, Philip Jakob 25, 26
Spittler, Christian Friedrich 45, 46, 59, 74, 251
Stange, Karl Friedrich 20, 36, 42-44, 100, 168, 183, 229, 239, 251, 256
Stanley, Henry Morton 121, 156, 158, 263
Steere, Edward (Bishop) 86, 147, 177, 188-190, 195
Steinkopf, Karl Friedrich Adolf 44, 45, 280
Steward, James 202
Strauß, David Friedrich 42
Stundenleute 26, 44, 241
Stutzmann, Imanuel 16, 19, 21, 26, 42, 43, 45, 46, 100, 160, 178, 227, 228, 234, 251, 259, 270, 271, 287, 288
Sudan 260
Suez 55, 101, 172
Sumner, John (Archbishop) 68
Swahili 55, 57-60, 119, 129, 176-177, 183-203, 214, 216, 217
Tanga 67, 76, 196, 216
Tanganyika (Tanzania) 19, 20, 120, 215, 216, 261, 263, 265, 266, 269
Taylor, James 132, 133, 143, 160, 267
Taylor, Hudson 282
Teita (people) 61, 62, 69, 101
Tewodros (King) 74, 75
Thomson, T.D. 320
Tozer, William George 124, 129, 147, 148, 204, 263, 281

Tübingen 16, 17, 35, 46, 57, 67, 68, 185, 187, 282
Tulu Nadu 171
Tüsmann / Tiismann 123, 133, 139
Tyler, Emma, see: Kent, Emma
Tyler, William F. 93
Ubie (Prince) 56
Uganda 120, 261-265, 268
Ugandan Martyrs 263
Ukambani 64, 69, 72, 78, 83, 86, 145, 215, 222
Universities' Mission in Central Africa (U.M.C.A.) 118, 124, 129, 130, 162, 177, 203, 263, 317
Usambara 64, 66, 67, 69, 72, 76, 77, 79, 86, 216
Venn, Henry 36, 48, 68, 69, 70, 77-82, 84, 86, 99, 100, 143, 148, 158, 184, 186, 197, 200, 231
Vermeullen, Jan 318
Victoria Lake 120, 215, 216, 261
Victoria (Queen) 68, 238
Waalim (sg. mwalimu) 215, 217
Wagner, Johannes 64, 160, 168, 267, 268, 271
Wainwright, Jacob 156
Wakefield, Thomas 75, 122, 123, 186
Waller, Horace 203, 319
Wanje 161
Watkins, Mark Hanna 205, 310
Weitbrecht, Johann Jakob 48, 96
Wesley, John and Charles 27
White Fathers 263, 266
Whitefield, George 27, 251
Wiederbringung aller Dinge 30, 34, 35
Wilberforce, William 125
Wilhelmsdorf 32
Williams, John 156
Woodward, Margaret E. 264, 317, 319
Wright, Henry 86, 160, 167-177, 185, 186, 188, 189, 200, 201, 204
Yao (people) 66, 118, 119, 121, 127, 185, 212, 214, 215-217, 223, 263, 312, 313
Young, Edward D. 203
Zambezi (river) 121, 214, 218, 263, 264, 315, 319, 320
Zambia 261

Zanzibar 55-65, 75, 80-83, 86, 87, 101, 102, 105-108, 113, 114, 116, 118-120, 122, 124, 126-129, 132, 139-141, 144-148, 150, 151, 153, 157, 158, 162, 177, 186, 188, 192, 193, 200, 209-218, 222, 223, 240, 247, 253, 260, 263, 265, 266

Zimbabwe 261, 309, 313, 318, 319
Zinzendorf, Nikolaus Ludwig von 25, 27, 28, 33, 42
Zuia (Johannes) 116

www.ingramcontent.com/pod-product-compliance
Lightning Source LLC
Chambersburg PA
CBHW061427300426
44114CB00014B/1572